On Meaning-Making

FOUNDATIONS & FACETS
Editorial Board

Adela Yarbro Collins
University of Notre Dame

John Dominic Crossan
DePaul University

John H. Elliott
University of San Francisco

Robert W. Funk, editor
Polebridge Press

John S. Kloppenborg
*St. Michael's College,
University of Toronto*

Lane C. McGaughy
Willamette University

Carolyn Osiek
Catholic Theological Union

John L. White
Loyola University of Chicago

PUBLISHED VOLUMES
Robert W. Funk, *The Poetics of Biblical Narrative*
Burton L. Mack and Vernon K. Robbins, *Patterns of Persuasion in the Gospels*
Mieke Bal, *On Story-Telling: Essays in Narratology*
Mieke Bal, *On Meaning-Making: Essays in Semiotics*

On Meaning-Making

Essays in Semiotics

Mieke Bal

POLEBRIDGE PRESS
Salem, Oregon

Copyright © 1994 by Polebridge Press.

All rights reserved. Printed in the United States of America. No part of this book may be used or reproduced in any manner whatsoever without written permission except in the case of brief quotations embodied in critical articles and reviews.

Library of Congress Cataloging-in-Publication Data

Bal, Mieke, 1946–
    On meaning-making : essays in semiotics / Mieke Bal.
      p.   cm.—(Foundations & facets. Literary facets)
    Includes bibliographical references.
    ISBN 978-0-94434-439-2 : $29.95
    1. Semiotics. I. Title. II. Series.
P99.B25 1994
302.2—dc20   93–49544
                                                                                                                             CIP

Printed in the United States of America

10   9   8   7   6   5   4   3   2   1

Contents

		Acknowledgments	vii
		Introduction	1
PART I		**Narratology as a Semiotic Theory**	21
	1	Interdisciplinary Narratology	23
	2	Reflection on Reflection: Mise en abyme	45
	3	Murder Story	59
PART II		**Reading the Subject**	77
	4	Psychopoetics	79
	5	Why I?	99
	6	Force and Meaning	109
PART III		**Semiotics and Art History (co-author Norman Bryson)**	137
	7	Visual Communication?	139
	8	Peirce, Saussure, and Visual Art	165
	9	Art And . . .	179
PART IV		**Discourse and Image**	205
	10	Visual Poetics	209
	11	Love-Story	243

12	Body Politic	263
13	Lots of Writing	281
	Bibliography	305

Acknowledgments

The material in this book has been previously published as follows:
Chapter 1 as "The Point of Narratology." *Poetics Today*, 11, 4, 1991, 727–753.

A different version of Chapter 2 as Mise en abyme et iconicité. *Litérature* 29, 1978, 116–128.

Chapter 3 as "Experiencing Murder: Ritualistic Interpretation of Ancient Texts," in Kathleen M. Ashley (ed.), *Victor Turner and the Construction of Cultural Criticism: Between Literature and Anthropology*. Bloomington, Indiana University Press, 1990 3–20. Elements of this chapter are also in *Murder and Difference. Gender, Genre and Scholarship on Sisera's Death*. Bloomington, Indiana University Press, 1988; 2d edition, 1992.

Chapter 4 as "Introduction," *Poetics*, Special Issue: *Psychopoetics: Theory*, 13, 4/5, 1984, 279–298, and *Style*, Special Issue: *Psychopoetics*.

Chapter 5 as "Why I? Discussing the Subject in/of Semiotics. *Poetics Today* 5, 4, 857–965.

Chapter 6 as "Force and Meaning: Rembrandt and the Interdisciplinary Struggle of Pyschoanalysis, Semiotics and Esthetics," *Semiotica* 63-3/4, 1987, 317–244. Some elements of this chapter also appeared in *Reading Rembrandt: Beyond the Word-Image Opposition*. New York and Cambridge: Cambridge University Press, 1991.

A shorter and different version of chapters 7, 8, 9 as "Semiotics and Art History," *The Art Bulletin* LXXIII, 2, 1991, 174–208 (co-author: Norman Bryson).

A different version of Chapter 10 as "On Reading and Viewing. Word and Image, Visual Poetics, and Comparative Arts." *Semiotica*, 76-3/4, 1989, 283–320, and in *Reading Rembrand: Beyond the Word-Image Opposition*. New York and Cambridge: Cambridge University Press, 1991.

Chapter 11 as "Narrativité et manipulation." *Degrés* 8, 24–25, 1980–1981, c-1–c-24 (numéro spécial *Texte et idéologie*).

Chapter 12 as "A Body of Writing," *Crossroad/Continuum* 1, 2, 1991, 110–126.

Chapter 13 as "Lots of Writing," *Semeia* 54, 1991, 77–102.

Introduction

This book is a companion-piece to *On Story-Telling*, published two years earlier. Both volumes together represent the intellectual itinerary of a person who has been moving for about ten years between countries, theories, fields, and disciplines. They contain a variety of essays published here and there in three different languages and in periodicals belonging to different disciplines. The wish of Polebridge Press to collect this dispersed material and make it more accessible reflects and responds to an increasing interest in the intersections of narrative theory, semiotics, and a socially oriented critique informed by interdisciplinary reflection. While the first volume remains largely within the domain of written texts, albeit that the texts discussed stem from a wide variety of contexts, the present volume is more radically interdisciplinary.

The essays collected here represent a phase in my work which has developed partly parallel to my work in narratology, with an increasing emphasis on semiotics during the last five or six years. Not that narrative has disappeared from my mind; I don't think it ever will. But I have been interested more and more in exploring those questions that an intradisciplinary field such as literary studies takes for granted or ignores. Inclined to interpretation and speculation, and fascinated by the little details left aside, I have become what can be called somewhat pompously a practicing semiotician. This volume demonstrates that itinerary.

There are many ways to bring order into diverse material such as this. One obvious order would be chronological. Such an order would have given an idea of the intellectual itinerary I went through in terms of theoretical obsessions. It would show a decrease in theoretical austerity: in my earlier work I as a sign. That is, the specific form suggested to him a relation to something else. A form brings forth a sign when the sign-user sees that it stands for something else, something absent. The sign is useful precisely because of that absence: had the other person been there, his footprints would not have had any meaning for Robinson.

Signs allow us to communicate about something which is absent. As soon as a sign-event occurs, the question of that absent item arises: what is it that the sign stands for? What does it mean? For Robinson the footprint meant that there was a human being on the island. Let us say that this is the first meaning. Few people will want to deny that meaning. Yet this agreement does not imply that the first meaning is fixed. For those who have never seen a footprint before, or who know nothing about scouting, even this interpretation will not present itself. Such a person will perhaps only think, "What a strange form," or, "This is an irregularity in the sand." In other words: even this first interpretation is "only" an interpretation, not an objective fact. It occurs only in the mind of the interpreter, and of all those who share his knowledge and assumptions, his habits of looking.

Robinson pursues his quest for meaning further than this. He derives from the trace a second meaning: this is the end of my loneliness. How does this second meaning come about, and what is its relation to the first? The sign (footprint) and the first meaning (human being around) together bring forth a new meaning. Sign and first meaning become a new sign. The new sign can be described as, "footprint as trace of nearby person." For Robinson, this sign means: no more loneliness. This second meaning is not some vague secondary meaning. Nor is it arbitrary or less important than the first. On the contrary, in this case the second meaning is more important for Robinson than the first. It is the second which will change his life. Only because he is capable of seeing in the trace a sign of the end of his loneliness is the sign, the print and hence, the proximity of the other person, a crucial event in his life. If the idea of "second meaning" does not imply vagueness, arbitrariness or lesser importance, what does it imply? The word "second" refers to a temporal succession and a logical implication. In the order of succession, the first sign necessarily precedes the second: without interpreting the first sign, the receiver cannot reach the second interpretation. Logically, the first sign implies the second: the second sign consists of the first sign *and* its interpretation.

It is precisely because second (and further) meanings are developed out of first, previous meanings, that they are neither vague nor arbitrary. They are not vague but, on the contrary, more specific than the first meanings. Of all possible second meanings he could have attached to the interpreted sign "footprint as trace of nearby human being," Robinson chose one, specific second meaning. His choice was determined by his own situation, loneliness, and his interest, to end that loneliness. His ability to steer the interpretation in the direction of his interest allows Robinson to promote the quality of his life.

Robinson is the model of the semiotic human being, the species which is able, thanks to its semiotic competence, to build up a society and to develop it to an extremely high level.

The second interpretation is not arbitrary either. Had Robinson attached that second meaning to the interpreted sign without any ground, then the interpretation would have been arbitrary. Too bad for him, then; he would not have made any progress: no end to his loneliness. Such a sorry mistake could have happened in both phases of the interpretation, and even before. He could have mistaken the footprint of a monkey for a human one. That would have been a mistake of perception. Then, he could have interpreted the human trace as, "This is the print of a human foot" without attaching to it the interpretation, "Hence, there is a human being nearby." That would have been a mistake of first interpretation. What he would have missed, then, would be the ground on which the sign-event occurred: the rule which establishes that something can stand for something in its proximity. Thirdly, he could have ignored the second meaning, or he could have made a different second interpretation. For example, he could have interpreted "Trace of nearby human being means danger" and have killed his future friend. In all these cases the relation between signs and interpretation would have been more arbitrary than in the case of our story.

Does this mean that Robinson did it "right"? He did, but only in his case. Interpretation is a subject-bound activity. Even the first interpretation needs the specific person Robinson, or another member of the same group–people who know about traces–to occur. The first meaning is not more "right" than the second, nor more exhaustive, more certain or more "objective." It is, however, more *general*. That is to say that it holds for more people than the second, in more situations, in more cases.

The Robinson story confirms what we knew already: that signs-events occur only when signs are interpreted and that interpretation occurs in an interaction between sign and sign-user. It teaches us a little more about the process of semiosis and especially of the activity of the receiver or addressee in it, about interpretation that is. In teaches us in the first place that semiosis is a process, which involves agents, events, things and time. Specifically, we have seen that meaning, the result of interpretation, is no more than the sign itself, not a fixed, objectified thing, but a complex process.

The following features of this process can be retained:

- a second interpretation is the interpretation of a combination of sign and interpretation;
- second interpretations are more specific than the first; first are more general;
- second interpretations represent a further stage in the development of the sign-event;
- second interpretations are not vague, not arbitrary and not less important than first interpretations;

12 ■ ON MEANING-MAKING

- no interpretation can be "right," "exhaustive," "certain" or "objective";
- but interpretations can be "wrong," that is, inadequate, when the relation which the sign-user establishes between sign and interpretation does not exist, is different, or insufficiently grounded;
- mistaken interpretations will show by the lack of follow-up; they stop the interpretation, remain isolated, or bring no new insights;
- first interpretations are sometimes called denotations; second and further interpretations, connotations.

Allow me to review now a few cases of problematic interpretations, of messages which are in one way or another "hidden": difficult to get, contradictory, subliminal. In the footsteps of Robinson, I will make a case for the importance of maximal interpretation for social life.

Our first example is a set of traffic signs, slightly more complex than the green light. In the city of Rochester, New York, everyone who drives out of campus to the nearby airport meets with the following, confusing signpost at a crucial intersection in the road [figure 1]. If you are going to the airport, it is important to interpret the signs adequately, and if you want to avoid a car-crash, you had better do it quickly. From top to bottom, you see 1. an image of a plane, pointing to the right, 2. an arrow pointing to the left, and 3. a word, and 4. a number. For simplicity's sake we will ignore the second arrow, which compounds yet another message. You can immediately construct the following message: 1. the way to the airport 2. is to the left 3. via route number 22 south.

That is, you can construct that message on the condition that you are trained to pick up automatically a number of aspects of the sign. First of all, you are only capable of doing this interpretation if you are trained in American traffic signs with their combination of images and conventional signs. For one thing, as a European I was myself just well enough trained to get the message, because much of European and American cultures overlap; but not entirely so; but it took me a little while to decide that the direction the image 1 was pointing in was *not* a sign, while its object, a plane, was. The image 1 and arrow 2 are equally clear, but not on the same grounds. You have to *recognize* the plane as referring to the real planes one of which you wish to catch, and to *connect* arrow 2 to the direction it points in and, in fact, is already itself part of. Less crucial is the interpretation of the word and the route number, signs 3 and 4, but it could be crucial in case, for example, you knew that one route to the airport is blocked and route 22 is a detour you must follow. You then have to *know* that numbers stand for certain roads.

What could make this compound sign confusing, is the variety of grounds on which the interpretation of each element is based: recognition, connection and previous knowledge, all three embedded in the more general previous knowledge about American traffic signs. You have to know, first, that images of this kind can represent the things you are looking for, and are not ad-

Figure 1: Signpost in Rochester, New York.

vertisements for toys, jokes, or works of art. In other words, you need to be able to activate various rules, embedded and overlapping, by which the members of the culture you live in have agreed to provide signs with meanings and to set up signs in order to convey meanings—in brief, to communicate.

The rules we have thus to know how to activate correlate signs and meanings, one by one. But they are not enough. Signs seldom operate alone. There are also rules according to which signs are combined in order to produce complex messages. In order to read your way to the airport, for example, you also have to be accustomed to the composition of the set of signs itself. Had the order of the sequence been different, all those accustomed to the top-bottom order as the "logical" one would have been confused. The same happens if the words in a sentence or the shots in a film are presented in reverse order. The order of the elements of a compound sign participates in the semiotic process. Had sign 3, the road number, been the first one we see, it would make no sense. The road number is irrelevant as long as we don't know where the road leads to.

Less conspicuously, but based on the same cultural training, is the composition of a complex visual image. In cultures where writing and reading proceed from left to right, as in most Western countries, photographs of landscapes tend to focus on a point slightly above and right of the middle. Trained to look from left to right, we tend to sweep our eyes in the same direction, and the photograph being supposed to hang slightly above eye-level, the eyes are drawn toward the central interest of the image. This can be easily seen when we compare the visual effect of photographs from a culture where reading and writing go from right to left, like Japan. Japanese photographs, even when subject, style and colors are not recognizably different from Western landscape pictures, are often "composed" from right to left and are less immediately appealing to those trained in the other tradition–and, of course, the other way around. The position of the central point of the image determines the interest of the whole, even if we hardly realize it. This is a subliminal, minimal sign that still has a crucial influence on the interpretation of the photograph as a whole.

The combination of strictly conventional rules and rules which combine a cultural convention with other relations makes the set of rules on which basis most sign-events can take place—that is, if the sign-user has the competence, learned throughout his or her life, to work with them. One more example will demonstrate how complex the combination of rules at work can be and why acquiring maximal competence in interpreting the signs built on that combination is worthwhile. What does a tour guide mean who tells tourists in front of a beautiful temple belonging to the Jain religion in India: "The Hindus worship the three main gods, but the Jains don't believe in those idols"? The sentence is not extraordinarily complex or difficult to understand. The tourists who listen to this guide and are eager to visit the temple are likely to be content with a global interpretation: the Hindus have three main gods which the Jains don't recognize. Maybe they will conclude from the statement that this difference between the two religions was the initial cause of the split between them. Making such an interpretation is sufficient and easy, and no major interest is done any harm if we stop the process there.

Yet a trained semiotician or someone who simply likes getting more out of signs will soon be baffled if s/he tries to understand the sentence beyond the level of tourism. There are two elements that show that the statement is not a neutral description: "the main gods" on the one hand, "those idols" on the other. The respect toward the gods expressed in the hierarchical "main" is undermined by the contempt expressed by "those idols." The difference indicates a contradiction to which we are led when we try to figure out where the speaker himself stands. One cannot hold both beliefs at the same time. Yet both views are presented partially, neither of the two parts of the sentence, hence neither of the two views, is presented from an outside perspective. There are signs in the sentence which make the acute listener feel that there is a continuity between the speaker and the statements, in each of the two conflicting parts of the sentence. This continuity is expressed by signs which, like the arrow in Rochester, "point" from the speaker to the view, connect them together so strongly that the one almost stands for the other. We first get a sense that the guide *is* a Hindu, then that he *is* a Jain. This continuity is not so much expressed in the words "main" versus "idols. The signs that produce the contradiction are, rather, the small, seemingly unimportant details. A person who speaks of *the* main gods does hold them to *be* the main gods, or otherwise there would be no definite article; the person who speaks of *those* idols expresses contempt. A more neutral rendering would have been, say, "The Hindus worship three main gods, but the Jains consider those to be idols." Hence, the small, unimportant words "the" and "those" become major signs that produce a problem of interpretation.

We must conclude that the sentence, descriptive at first sight, is deeply illogical because contradictory, unless we return the charge and explain the contradiction as the effect of yet another sign. That sign is the structure of the sentence itself, including the ill-matching signs. While we listen to the first part, we identify, or are asked to identify, with the Hindus and take the major status of Brahma, Shiva and Vishnu for granted. The speaker speaks in their name, expresses their views. The opposition introduced by "but" changes the perspective. It introduces, not a factual opposition but an opposite view, and we go along with the Jains. The speaker has turned around 180 degrees, and we no more identify with the Hindus. In both parts, we are in fact not addressed by one speaker, but by a speaker who presents someone else's view. In comparison to the more neutral rendering, we could say that the speaker presents an inside perspective, makes us sympathize with both parties, and thus makes us aware of the deep and painful conflict they each experience in a society where some feel offended by the other's use of "idol" for what they cherish. Thus conceived, the sentence is not confused or unclear, but deeply effective. It not only tells us something, but, by making us participate in both views *and* in the implied experience of conflict, it impresses upon the listener a different kind of knowledge than sheer touristic, superficial, global knowledge.

We can do several things with the tour guide's sentence. We can ignore the contradiction, ignore the little signs. We can acknowledge the little signs, hence, the contradiction, but be simply baffled by it. This attitude comes to a refusal to pick up the message that doubtlessly counts more for the guide, a member of the torn society he talks about, than the factual message. Or, worse, we can take it as a sign of the speaker's defective competence, as his inadequate mastery of "our" language and logic. But we can also work with the assumption that even difficult or strange signs could very well have meanings that we can usefully take in. In the former cases we respond non-communicatively to the speaker's otherness, in the latter positively, thus reducing the difference between him and the tourists. This latter process can be pursued further, for example, by seeing a similarity between the Hindu-Jain conflict and the Catholic-Protestant one. The Indian situation then stands in for, becomes a sign of, the European one.

The semiotic situation in this sentence is much more complex than in the Robinson story. We can, however, simplify it and distinguish three steps. First, we only interpret the sentence as one sign and get the factual, superficial message. Then we notice the contradiction, brought about by "the main gods" versus "those idols." Then we realize that what seemed a contradiction is a highly sophisticated narrative-empathic form, constructed by "the" and "those" and based on ambiguity as a logical possibility. Each step implies a more analytic treatment of the sentence, for the signs become smaller and smaller. At the same time, the message becomes more interesting, reaching more levels of communication and meaning production. The semiotic effort pays off.

In the case of the Indian tour guide, the problem of interpretation was solved once we accepted that ambiguity is not a mistake but a sign in itself. Narrative devices like the empathic form–variously called Free Indirect Discourse, Free Indirect Style, or Embedded Focalization in literary theory–have been used by the guide in order to express what he could not express by sheer informational language. Technically, he conveyed the ambiguity in the relationship between Hindus and Jains in India by using the subliminal meanings of respect and contempt embedded in "the" and "those" and establishing a connection between himself and those meanings. But his technique only works if we recognize it, or if we are at least open to take it in subliminally. If we eagerly denounce contradiction before we try to understand the message, than the effort is lost on us. And we can only recognize the signs if we have previous knowledge or experience of the conventions of narrative that allow such connections to be established.

Like in the Robinson story, we need to make second and third interpretations of the same signs in order to get at the message about the Hindu-Jain conflict. For the Rochester signpost as for the tourguide, we needed to activate various rules which correlate signs with meanings, and signs with other signs. The interpretation of signs requires the activation of various rules of correlation between signs and meanings. One such rule is the recognition of the image as a representation of an object (the plane, the conflicting sentence of the tour guide as an image of the Hindu-Jain conflict, and eventually the Hindu-Jain conflict as an image of the Catholic-Protestant conflict). This rule is also called iconicity, producing iconic signs or icons. Another such rule is the connection of a sign to something with which it exists in continuity (the arrow and the direction of the airport; the "the"-"those" views and the speaker who pretends to hold them). This is the indexical rule, producing indexical signs or indices. Another such rule is the conventional agreement that certain signs mean certain things (the road-number for a certain route, the words of the tour guide). That is the rule of symbolicity, producing symbolic signs or symbols. These rules are also called codes.

The difficulties of getting messages are related to the number and variety of codes to be activated, the obliteration of the message under the more obvious message, and the combination of signs relating to different subjects which can produce a sense of contradiction. In addition, compound messages consist of concatenations of signs and a nebula of meaning elements which form a complex, but not necessarily coherent whole.

One final example. Imagine overhearing the following dialogue in a hospital's consultation room:

"Ever had scarlet fever as a child?" "No, doctor." "German measles?" "No, doctor." "Ra. . . Ricketts?" "Eh. . . no, doctor." "Do you know what ricketts is?" "Well, no, doctor." "Why do you say 'no' then?" "I was afraid that you would ask further questions if I said 'yes.'" "But you can also say 'I don't know,' can't you?" "Is that allowed, doctor?" "How many times have you been pregnant before?" "I don't know, doctor." "You don't know?!!" "Yes I do, doctor. Eight times." "Eight?" "No no, doctor, eleven." "Are you absolutely sure?" "To tell you the truth, no . . .eh . . . doctor." "But you must be able to tell me how many children you have exactly?" "Oh dear, professor, you look so intimidating." "I am not a professor. I am a training resident." "Really. . . my friend was also delivered by a training resident. She had some very good laughs with him." "No wonder. I bet your friend knew exactly how often she had been pregnant." "Or, that the resident was not as intimidating and less precise. . . Good, now you are laughing. What a relief. You were just glaring at that paper from behind those glasses. To be exact, I have seven children, and I've had two miscarriages and one was still-born. Is that clear enough for you to do the counting?" "And, eh. . . your last period, could you guess, approximately, no need to be precise, about which month, which week it was perhaps? Before the vacation or after?" "The 28th of June." "The 28th of June?!!" "Absolutely, the 28th of June. A woman does know those things, you know."

The exchange of signs between the two people pursuing the same goal, adequate medical treatment, is very unsuccessful in the beginning. The resident uses normal English words, and if the woman patient is reasonably educated and English-speaking, there should be no problem. Yet, there is. The accompanying signs preclude communication at the expense of both parties. The doctor gives signs of various kinds which the woman interprets as intimidating: his impatience when she hesitates, and the rebuff when she gives an inadequate answer, and his looking at the papers instead of at his partner; his firing off question after question, leaving no room for hesitation, the whole setting in his office, and the social context of power that pertains to it. These signs, subliminal in various degrees, are not intended by the speaker, but are nevertheless decisive. No more than the sun, the sign-post and the tree does this speaker want to produce the sign-events that have this negative event. No more than they could he help their occurrence.

What is meant as a question, an open request for information, becomes, in the eyes of the intimidated woman, an order. This confuses her, and prevents her from responding adequately. The result is the total incapacitation of the woman: she cannot answer any question any more. To see this woman as stupid, uneducated or unable to cope is one way of interpreting her behavior. But that would be a pretty rude, unsophisticated response, unworthy of the competent sign-user. To think with the doctor that it is utterly stupid not to know how many times you have been pregnant is missing the various possibilities in the question. Did he mean the number of medically acknowledged pregnancies, the number of deliveries, or the number or actual living children? For a woman for whom each of these possible questions yield a different answer, the question is hard enough and some time to think should be granted her; but the situation of intimidation does not let her. This exchange in fact shows that in some ways, the doctor who does not realize this is no more competent at communication than the woman. His question is unwittingly ambiguous.

The kinds of signs the doctor intends to send out—questions clear enough to yield clear answers—do not match the interpretations the addressee makes of them—seeing them as orders or as unanswerable. This situation could go on forever, and the interview would turn out to be useless. The woman manages to reverse the situation, however, by breaking through the false relation of authority, and restores communication. Exchange of information becomes possible. Now that the sign [question] is no more interfered with by the subliminal sign [order] and by the other contextual signs, it can be answered. No trace remains of the impression of incompetence.

The dialogue was, in fact, a short story, entitled "Anamnesis" and published in 1984 by Hanna Verweg, in a Dutch newspaper. The title is relevant: it is a word that not all readers know; for one, I did not. It is certainly not a word expected in a small newspaper column. As a consequence, the word is intimidating. It makes the reader insecure. Just like the image of the plane in Rochester and the empathic style of the Indian guide, it is an image of what is going to be the story's point: an icon. Unlike the fellow-patient overhearing that dialogue who may respond by identifying with the patient—if she is next—or by proudly taking her distance and looking down on her—if she has been more successful—the reader intimidated by a difficult word is likely to sympathize with the woman immediately, warmed up as s/he is by the title at the doctor's expense. There is, then, a continuity between the writer who is also the first speaker of the story, the woman-speaker in the story and the reader at the other end.

As in the other examples, the interpretation of signs is dependent upon the subjects who use them. The writer of the piece could write in this way because s/he had, for whatever reasons, sympathy for the intimidated woman. The reader is strongly suggested to do the same, but a training resident who reads the story before setting off to his first practice may very well put his sympathy elsewhere. The women readers will better understand the final exchange, and probably be more strongly gratified by the role-reversal at the end than most men readers will, but this division according to gender lines does not necessarily hold for every single person. Each person brings to the signs her or his own baggage. The story itself shows that roles are not fixed. It displays how the initial incapacity to get the message is changed into a perfectly adequate semiotic behavior which includes, aside from the information requested, a surplus to it, a subtle humorous message, a view on gender-boundaries and a sign of restored self-confidence; in the original Dutch text, the resident is clearly male; in English, it is not the language that shows he is male, but the traditionally male role s/he takes on suggests as much. And the author, writing under a woman's name, turns out to be a man.

Signs and meaning are not only determined by the individual sign-users, but are at the same time contingent on the alliance to a social group. It is clear that the positions in "Anamnesis" are determined, not so much by individual character, but by gender and class. Gender and class are, in turn, not isolated divisions in a society, but are produced by the history of the culture. Thus there is virtually no end to the relations which determine the nature, occurrence and success of sign-events.

If all sign-events happen according to systematic rules, how can innovative semiosis take place? Firstly, the rules which govern the interpretation of signs are fixed in some systems, more flexible in others. But the number of possible rules is limited by the capacity for the people sharing in the communication to grasp and to memorize them. Although there is an enormous difference between the sign-system of Morse-code, with one rule of correlation, and that of cinema, which uses language, images, light, movement and much more, most signs and combinations of signs operate according to rules of correlation, of choice, of combination, and of use. Innovation, the production of as yet unknown signs and meanings is possible and takes place constantly within the systems consisting of those rules.

Yet, some degree of innovation, not within the rules but of the rules themselves, is possible. The difficulty of many to feel comfortable with avant-garde film has to do with the relatively high input of new possibilities for meaning, not yet known. The same holds for other avant-garde art, for cultural productions the sign-receiver is not familiar with. Two processes begin then: on the one hand, the viewer tends to look for meaning, and if s/he cannot interpret the signs, s/he will bring in his or her own ideas and *suppose* some basis for meaning to be active. This can be a new basis, unknown to the cultural community at large, maybe even to the film-maker who had not foreseen the viewer's interpretation. On the other hand, those new ways of making meaning which are recognized will soon become more familiar and lose both their unsettling and their creative power. They become part of the system.

But let me stop this introduction to semiotics here. The preceding remarks should suffice for anyone who so far has not been acquainted with semiotics to follow the arguments in the various essays collected here, as well as any number of semiotic publications. Semiotics, then, enables humanists in any field not only to address the traditional questions of their discipline in new ways, to raise new questions, and to re-examine their assumptions in terms of a social perspective. It also encourages connections between the disciplines. My own experience with this kind of crossing-over has been exhilarating, and I am pleased to share some of it through this volume.

I began *On Story-Telling* with a discussion of the main strands of criticism my work on narratology has encountered. Much of what was said in the introduction to that volume could be kept in mind for this one, too. But I wish to mention something else as well. When I decided—by a number of historical accidents as well as by motivations of which I was not aware at the time—to change fields and explore such diverse bodies of texts as biblical narrative, seventeenth-century painting, and twentieth-century cultural images, I did not expect to be recieved so hospitably by the fields I invaded. I am deeply grateful for the keen interest in my work within the fields of biblical scholarship and art history. That interest betokens a real change in the academy towards dialogue and interdisciplinary reflection. Together with *On Story-Telling* this volume traces an intellectual voyage that many of my colleagues have also taken, albeit with different routes, detours, and destinations. Semiotics is a collective endeavor in more senses than one. I am extremely grateful to all those, students, colleagues, and friends, who have been so important to me in the years during which these essays were written, and whom I can, alas, not begin to enumerate.

PART I

Narratology as a Semiotic Theory

Throughout my work on narrative I have insisted on the need to account for the semiotic status of narrative. Not that anyone would deny that status; but the theories and models of narrative developed in narratology more often than not fail to account for that status. Indeed, even an explicitly semiotic narratology like Greimas' does not theorize the consequences of the fact that narrative itself, as a mode of communication, has specific semiotic features. Nor does any other narrative theory that I know, other than by simply posing the text as a whole to be a message in a situation of communication. Sure, but so is any other text. Narrative is specific in its structuring, through the staging of a variety of subjects, of a multiple, heterogeneous bundle of semiotic acts. Hence the insistence on agency in my own narrative theory—the subject-oriented structure, the principle of embedding, the inscription of narratee and other addressees within the narrative text.

The chapters in this section each address aspects of this problematic. In "Interdisciplinary Narratology" I explore a number of ways in which the semiotic status of narrative allows the use of narrative theory for texts that complicate the very notion of narrative: visual, scientific, anthropological discourses. This paper was written in commemoration of a conference on narratology which took place in Israel, ten years earlier, and which occasioned two special issues of *Poetics Today*. I have decided to keep the somewhat personal tone of the paper, because it implies an assessment of the state of the art in the poststructuralist present. "Reflections on Reflection" is a much older essay, written more than ten years ago in response to Lucien Dällenbach's book on mise en abyme—a book which, as it happens, has just been translated into English. This essay belongs to a series of attempts to reformulate current, attractive concepts and ideas within a more rigorous semiotic framework. "Murder Story" is a case of "application": it proposes an interpretation of an ancient text based on an interdisciplinary mustering of narratology in conjunction with anthropology. The reading is a symptomatic one, taking up tiny details that seem unfitting and assigning meaning to them. This essay integrates elements of my book *Murder and Difference* with a genre-specific analysis of "spoken" discourse.

▪ 1 ▪

Interdisciplinary Narratology

INTRODUCTION

By the accidents of life, I started out in the literary profession as a narratologist, having French as my foreign language and structuralism as my training. By another accident, I started in Israel. As one of the young, unknown invitees of the Synopsis 2 conference where an unusual number of established stars were mixed with a good number of beginners like myself with the most fortunate result, I optimistically brought a formalist, quite technical paper written in French to a conference where people tended to speak English and some to suspect formalism. Feeling awkwardly out of place: such was the experience to be combatted by actively participating in the debates. That this was possible, that within half a day I felt excited and encouraged while having completely revised my views of narratology, was due to the exceptional intellectual and humane qualities of this conference. I have been to a large number of conferences since, but just as childhood bliss is irretrievably lost in later life, so never did I feel the same deep satisfaction again.

What was so special about this conference that it deserves memorialization? First of all, it was intellectually open and yet focused enough: a wide variety of topics and of attitudes toward narratology and its assumptions made for lively and serious debates. In retrospect, it really gave an overview of narratology as a field, neither taking it for granted nor rejecting it a priori. It also marked a turning-point in the discipline. Looking at what the field is today, it seems hard to tell if the conference was at the vanguard or at the core of the development, if it announced what was going to happen or demonstrated what was already happening. It thus exactly fulfilled the promise of the Synopsis series as announced in the program: "to clarify the state of the art in one specific area of poetics or the semiotics of culture, both through synoptic reassesment of existing theory and through presentation of new departures or seminal work in progress."

In those days, the construction of a narrative grammar was still being pursued and less formalist structural models partly inherited of pre-structuralism were being improved. The rigorously structuralist, programmatic papers by the late Marc Adriaens and Gerald Prince alternated with more specific topics and "gentler" approaches. In that category, Free Indirect Discourse was a central subject (Ron, Banfield, Perry), in addition to character (Tamir-Ghez), space (Frank), repetition (Rimmon-Kenan) and redundancy (Suleiman), to name only a few of the rich scale of topics, all clearly narratological. At the same time, deconstruction was beginning to flourish widely, and Jonathan Culler's opening paper effectively undermined one of the basic tenets of structuralist narratology, the distinction between story and plot, while Rolf Kloepfer pleaded for a non-hierarchical structuralist model of Bakhtinian inspiration. Empirical psychology (Kreitler) and anthropology (Ben-Amos, Winner) also posed a challenge to narratological model-building, while semiotics (Eco, Doležel) proposed a wider framework for it. Finally, excellent samples of narratology-in-use were given by Kittay (Renaissance), Lodge (realism), McHale (postmodernism), demonstrating that the often alleged opposition between historical and systematic analysis is a false one.[1]

Ten years later: Superficially, it may seem that today narratology has gone out of fashion. We have moved on to other things. Thus one of the participants of Synopsis 2, Susan Suleiman, composed a double issue of *Poetics Today* on the female body, and although this volume is definitely not void of narratological concerns, these certainly do not predominate. Text grammars have ceased to appear, formalist models are deemed irrelevant (Brooks), and while some hold on to early structuralist distinctions, many of those who discussed the criteria by which to spot Free Indirect Discourse in 1979 moved on and practice analysis rather than worrying about how to do it. The options, today, seem to be regression to earlier positions (Genette), primary focus on application, or rejection of narratology. All three positions are problematic. Regression demonstrates a powerlessness to move on, application may imply an unwarranted acceptation of imperfect theories, and rejection is motivated by a shift in priorities, but it is also a denial of the importance of the *questions*—rather than the answers—of narratology, sometimes even a lack of understanding.[2]

---

1. Most of these papers have been published in *Poetics Today* in 1980—1981. Quite a few have led to books (a.g. Prince, Kittay & Godzich, McHale, Bal, Banfield), which is another way of measuring the conference's fertility.

2. See my review article of Brooks, Stanzel, and Gennette in *Poetics Today*, 1986. I claim, there, that Stanzel never took up the challenge of structuralism, that Genette did but then gave up, and that Brooks by-passed it. All three, then, failed to address the issues structuralism has raised, to the detriment of their own theories.

In general, more important issues, mainly historical and ideological, have taken priority. In my own case, concerns of feminism have taken the lead but not, I wish to argue, at the cost of more formal narratological issues. Rather, the concern for a reliable model for narrative analysis has more and more been put in the service of other concerns, considered more vital for cultural studies.

In this situation, for those of us, like myself, whose reputation is based on the kind of narratological work central at Synopsis 2, the title of narratologist seems to call for an apology, a denial, or a justification. The apology consists in maintaining that so much of literature is, after all, narrative in kind. It misses the point of the challenge, for not the existence of narrative texts but the relevance of narrative structure for their meaning is the issue. The denial consists in claiming that one does other things now. It is throwing away the child with the bathwater, for those "other things" like ideological criticism cannot but be based on insights one has developed earlier, or else one considers one's earlier work really futile, an attitude which is in itself a token of futility. Given the dialectic, yet reasonably stable continuity in scholarly work, the justification may be the more realistic response, even if one *also* does other things. In my own variant, it consists of demonstrating the use of narratology for those other things which are being done today. In other words, the most responsible attitude I imagine consists in answering the question what's the point? while taking that question seriously. And that question was already posed in 1979. It is the question that all academic work should constantly be asked to answer.[3] It is for posing that question seriously, dialogically, and with historical consciousness, that I feel the conference deserves to be memorialized today.

In this paper, I will try out one possible answer to this question, which happens to be my own personal answer. The point of narratology, defined as reflection on the generically specific, narrative determinants of the production of meaning in semiotic interaction, is not in the construction of a perfectly reliable model which "fits" the texts. In addition to unwarranted claims on the generalizability of structure and on the relevance of general structures for the meaning and effect of texts, such a construction presupposes the object of narratology to be a "pure" narrative. Instead, narrative must be considered as a discursive mode which affects semiotic objects in variable degrees. Once the relation of entailment between narrativity and narrative objects is abandoned, there is no reason any more to privilege narratology as an approach to texts traditionally classified as narrative. Instead, other approaches may be better

---

3. The fashion of the "empirical" study of literature—in quotation marks, because I do not believe it is empirical in any scientific sense—markedly fails to address the question of its own point. (e.g. Fokkema 1988). For example, the "documentary" search for authorial intention—less empirical and more traditional than the author seems to be aware of—seems to me entirely beside the point of the search for insight into literary processes. This falling back into regressive positions could be countered by the kind of permanent self-criticism the question "what's the point" summarizes.

equipped to account for those aspects of narrative texts that have traditionally been under-illuminated, partly because of the predominance of a text-immanent, structuralist approach.[4]

Narratology, here, is considered guilty of repressing other concerns, and discarding it may be a healthy move. Nor, for that matter, does this giving up of the method-object bond give us reason to limit the use of narratology to narrative texts. One may then want to replace the approach with a different one, be it ideological, psychoanalytic, or rhetoric, but one may also want to mobilize narratological insights for other objects. Here, in contrast, narratology can help supply insights that the field wherein different objects are studied has traditionally not itself developed. Paradoxically, the very discipline that tends to rigidify its traditional object is able to de-rigidify other objects. One example among many is Leroux' narratological analysis of philosophical texts. I will present three cases based on my own work of the past ten years to see if this use of narratology is indeed sensible. My contention in this paper— or my desire, one could argue—then, is that narratology, ten years after Synopsis 2, is flourishing, but less within the study of narrative texts than in other disciplines. And that so it must be, as far as I am concerned.

CASE 1: ANTHROPOLOGY AND THE SUBJECT

In the decade between Synopsis 2 and this special issue, an increasing interest in narrative theories from anthropologists, and in anthropology from (often dissatisfied) narratologists has emerged. One recent token of the relevance of narratology for anthropology and vice versa is the volume that Indiana University Press brought it out in 1990 in homage of the late Victor Turner, a key figure in contemporary anthropology, and which is called *Between Literature and Anthropology: Victor Turner and the Construction of Cultural Criticism*. Several contributions to this volume come from narratologists or use narratology, e.g. Thomas Pavel's "Narratives of Ritual and Desire."

The interdisciplinary interaction between narratology and anthropology is more profound, however, than the two-way borrowing that seems to be going on. No symmetry can be assumed in this interaction. Anthropology helps address the issue of the grounding of literature in reality without regressing to a reflection theory, and provides, in its key-themes like ritual and kinship theory, background information that helps filling in that grounding. More

---

4. I do not really think that the corpus of predominantly narrative texts has been sufficiently explored with the help of narratology. On the contrary, most studies of those texts are weak precisely in that there authors fail to use adequate descriptive tools. But the point I am making is that even if one assumes there have been enough narratological analyses of narrative texts, it is obvious that there have hardly been any narratological analyses of non-narrative texts, which undermines the very generic distinction the idea of "narrative texts" is based on.

closely and specifically, anthropology's interest in orality provides insights into the *Sitz-im-Leben* of a whole body of narratives that can help relativize the generalizations about narrative structure we have been building up on the basis of written texts (Lemaire 1987).

In an altogether different manner, narratology is grafted upon anthropology: anthropology's self-definition and self-critique are grounded in problems of narrative, for narrative is the stuff of anthropological knowledge. As is only too well known, the major problem of the discipline of anthropology has traditionally been its contagion by the colonialism out of which it emerged. Although from very early on, ethnographers have been aware of the problems inherent in their work, they have not been able to avoid a cultural imperialism that obscured the sight of the objects of their descriptions: foreign cultures. Difference seems to be hard to understand and otherness hard to accept.[5] A flow of critical analyses of anthropology as a discipline has accompanied the growing awareness of the problematic attitudes toward otherness in contemporary society.[6] In fact, few disciplines practice self-criticism so consistently as anthropology does.

Yet little attention has been paid to the relationship between the generic conventions of ethnography and the failures of these texts to do justice to their object: the other. But it is to the extent that these texts are narrative, that they have a structure—traditionally called "third-person narrative"—which entails distortion, that the problem can be analyzed. As narratologists know, objective narration is impossible by definition because the linguistic constraints imposed on narratorial voice and the subjective focalization any speaker cannot but adopt, shape the fabula or content of the narrative decisively. Of course, ethnographers know this, too, but narratologists can provide the means to theorize this problem as a textual one. In this section I will explore some ways in which this problem can be addressed, albeit not solved.

At the same time, this discussion addresses a problem of interdisciplinary methodology. The specific relations between two disciplines involved in interdisciplinary exchange are never adequately perceived if they are one-sided and hierarchical: a master-code prescribing a target discipline how to behave. Instead, a variable interaction occurs, whose tenets can be usefully assessed. Let me give one small but significant example. The title of Clifford Geertz's seminal paper, "'From the Native's Point of View': On the Nature of Anthropological Understanding" is programmatic enough. Geertz presents a few case

---

5. For a sustained critique of anthropological field-work and the resulting ethnographies, see Fabian; from a gender perspective, Coward. Literary critics who wrote major works on these issues of difference and otherness are Said (*Orientalism*) and Todorov (*La découverte de l'Amérique; Nous et les autres*).

6. An awareness that, unfortunately, is not accompanied by real acceptance and respect, as we see daily in many domains, such as the growth of sexual violence, the growth of racism in multiethnic communities, and continuing political and military oppression of the "others," as in South Africa and Israel, to name only the most blatant examples.

studies meant to provide insight into the fundamental problem of anthropology. He picked his cases extremely astutely. The issue Geertz chose to discuss this problem is precisely the concept that lies at the heart of the relations between ethnographer and autochthonic subject as well as at the heart of narratology: the concept of subject, person, individual, as a node in a network of social and textual relations. As such, it is a problem equally difficult for both disciplines. As Geertz demonstrates, both the content of the concept of subject—what defines an individual in a given society—and the structural properties of the system of interpersonal reference vary greatly according to different cultures. Hence, the very notion of subjectivity, so central in narratological considerations of, for example, description, cannot be given a fixed, universal meaning, lest we imperialistically build a theory valid for a limited section of Western literature only while claiming general value for it. So far, then, anthropological analysis helps narratology refine its categories and circumscribe their validity.

But the different concepts of the subject Geertz describes are more clearly demonstrated in the person-to-person interaction in which he perceived them, in drama if you wish, than in the ethnographic narrative itself. For there, while exposing the different conceptions of the subject, Geertz constantly doubles up the Balinese, Javanese, and Moroccan voice with his own perspective, which he leaves for the purpose of the demonstration blatantly ethnocentric. Thus he explains how the Balinese widower represses his grief and derives his subjecthood from the denial of mourning, and how the Moroccan person is indicated through a network of features of kinship, profession, and location, but he does so in a structure built on the Western concepts of person, the ethnographic third-person narrative. On the one hand, narratology can formulate this. Simplifying, in terms of my own narratological categories, "we" speak, and focalize, the focalization of "them," but "they" do not speak, and "their" focalization only comes to us filtered by "ours." As a result, Geertz' explicit lesson concerning the difference between the two conceptions of the subject, magnificently taught, obscures itself the very core of anthropology's problem, the imperialist contamination inherent in narrative "about" another.

To a certain extent—and such is Geertz's conclusion—this is the inevitable limit of understanding, and the acceptable form of anthropological knowledge. We now know what a subject is (in the Moroccan village) and how a subject fulfills its being (in the Balinese village) but not *how* this concept makes the narratives produced in such a culture *mean*. Hence, we cannot adequately interpret the culture's own narratives. This conclusion is a bit too aporetic. I doubt we must accept a form of understanding that reduces the understood to a filtered object. Nor does it seem we need to. For a subtle narratological analysis of anthropological material can go a bit further, precisely because such an analysis temporarily brackets both ends of the embedding reality, the reality of the events "out there" and the reality of the colonizing reporter; for the duration of a prior analysis, the narratologist presupposes that the narrative is structurally self-sufficient, hence, fictional.

I have experienced the usefulness of such an integration of anthropological eagerness for understanding real otherness and a narratological discipline of structural textual analysis in my studies of the Hebrew Bible, particularly the Book of Judges[7] which poses a number of acute problems of alterity. Studying Judges closely, I was particularly struck by the fact that three concepts referring to women seemed inadequately rendered in translations and commentaries by modern Western concepts: virgin, concubine, prostitute. At first sight, the problem with virgin was that the occurrences' immediate contexts systematically overdetermine the concept, adding phrases like "who have not known a man" (e.g. Judges 11); with concubine, that no primary wife is mentioned (e.g. Judges 19); with prostitute, that the certainty of paternity seems to contradict the very idea of prostitution (again Judges 11 and 19).

My first response to these problems was, let's say, "anthropological." For just as Geertz became particularly suspicious in the face of a concept that is so central in Western culture, the individual subject, and rightly set out to challenge its universal validity, just so I became suspicious before the concurrence of these three concepts indicating female status in a culture we have reasons to assume to be thoroughly patriarchal, but translated into modern patriarchal terms. In other words, these translations seemed too smoothly to endorse the notion that patriarchy is a monolithic, transhistorical social form. As a consequence, they suggest patriarchy is unavoidable; they blame ancient Judaism for our being saddled with it; they obscure the ancients' otherness; they even obscure the "otherness within," the pluralities of modern society in relation, precisely, to patriarchy.

Quite specifically, the modern translations of the ancient text are comparable with the Western narratives about Eastern behavior of which Geertz' account is an example. In both cases, our source of knowledge is a narrative, by definition imperialistically filtering the utterances of the other.

But my second response was narratological: checking immediate contexts, speakers, focalizers, and combinations of the problematic terms, I was soon led to reorganize the material. Instead of lumping together the three terms that at first had drawn my attention,[8] a careful narratological analysis suggested a different structural context for virgin on the one hand, for concubine and prostitute on the other. Accordingly, I aligned "virgin" with two other terms referring to young women—according to age/life phase, the series then became *na'arah, bethulah, 'almah*—while concubine and prostitute became

---

7. See my "trilogy," 1987, 1988a, 1988b. The following remarks on the status of young women are elaborated in 1988b, chapters 2 and 3, esp. page 48.

8. Needless to say, this focus was as much informed by my own modern feminist interests as by the texts' incongruities. In this respect the literary analyst has no choice but to endorse Geertz' pessimism.

synonyms, of which the projected features of "secondariness" and "harlotry" could be suspended.

These decisions were motivated by structural properties of the text. For example, the noun *bethulah*, traditionally universalistically rendered as virgin, is in Judges either hilariously overdetermined and then spoken by a male voice, or not explicitly connected to virginity at all and then spoken by a female voice. Compare, for example, Judges 21:12: "found. . . four hundred young girls, 'virgins,' that had not known man by lying with him," where the overall narrator speaks and the women do not focalize their own fate, to 11:37: "leave me alone two months, that I may depart and wander upon [towards] the mountains, and lament [until] my *bethulah*," where the "virgin" herself expresses her view of self.[9]

In no case in Judges is *bethulah*, virginity, in any way connected with *zonah*, prostitution, which suggests I examine them separately. In contrast, the one juxtaposition of *bethulah* and *pilegesh*, concubine, in 19:24 ("Behold, my daughter the 'virgin' and his 'concubine'"; quotation marks added) is revealing, but in favor of the earlier separation as well as of the interpretation of *bethulah* as referring to a life phase—sexually ripe, but not yet married girls—rather than to a state—bodily integrity. The speaker here is the father of the one woman and host of the other. He transfers his focalization of the two women to the rapists ("behold"), filtering for them. The issue is to protect the male guest from gang rape by offering a more attractive alternative. Now, if being a virgin in the common sense is a recommendation to the rapists, then being a concubine in the common sense is not. The host would have been well advised to leave the women's status unspecified. Unless the terms refer to age: two mature women, sexually useable, hence, rapeable, but still pretty "fresh."

Without going into the details of the two other concepts, may it suffice to point out that those, too, change their meaning according to narrative structure. This time, it is not the shift in voice and focalization that decides, for these two terms are only used in narratorial commentary and narration. The issue is situation on the level of the fabula. Here the usefulness of the provisional suspension of both contemporary and modern reality becomes visible. Suspending moral views of sexual lasciviousness as well as assumptions about ancient Hebrew life often based on projection, looking at the fabulae for which these terms are used reveals a structurally recurrent combination, in which the terms referring to female status are linked up with the father's house, inheritance, and displacement (mostly literally, travel). The key is the location of marital life. In all cases where these terms occur in Judges, including the verb *zanah*, the status of the female spouse is at stake, and that status is related to

---

9. My translation. In square brackets are elements that I argue to be appropriate in *Death and Dissymmetry*, chapter 2. I will not repeat the arguments here.

her not living or not staying in the house of the husband, but staying in or going back to the house of her father.

The terms, then, must not be related to a moralistically loaded concept like prostitution or a class-bound condescendent concept like concubine—the apparent display of the father's wealth, in Judges 19, hardly imposes the view that this woman has been sold by her poor relatives to serve as secondary wife. Instead, they must be related to the issue of marriage forms. Judges displays other symptoms of a violent transition from patrilocal (wrongly called matriarchal) marriage to virilocal marriage (e.g. Judges 15), and the hypothesis that this tension underlies the narratives as well as the uses of the problematic terms, helps explain the most obscure passages, in particular of the book's final section.

What is the interdisciplinary interaction going on here? Let us assume that I learned from Geertz to suspend the content of category of the subject. For he suggested we take apparent incongruities as evidence of otherness, not of stupidity. Thus, anthropology "came first." As a result, I refrained from wondering what Jephthah's daughter may have thought of her imminent death, as a modern realist psychologism would entice one to do, and instead took her words as indicators of some sort of ritual behavior.[10]

Incidentally, ritual is an anthropological favorite, and much of Turner's work is devoted to it (e.g. *Structure and Anti-Structure*, on precisely the kind of rite of passage at stake here, but also the second chapter of *A Forest of Symbols* with useful methodological considerations supplementing the other book). The meaning of the term could then be related to phase rather than state. But I could only do this because in a second move I had related the detached term to narrative structure. This second move is the one Geertz does not make; instead, he narrates in the double voice I have pointed out.

In the second case—re concubine and prostitution—the transaction between the two disciplines is different. Narratological analysis of the fabula "came first." The structural property found—systematic connection between female status and marriage location, inheritance, and property—again covers an anthropological favorite. It suggests an anthropological background. But that background is a matter of established knowledge, not of method. The methodological issue is in the suspension of reality that narratological structural analysis entails. That suspension, paradoxically, is necessary in order for the less ethnocentric view of reality—of otherness—to emerge. In other words, narratology and anthropology, here, are constantly and polemically intertwined. By virtue of the refusal to establish direct relations between text and society, as do those who construct an anthropological view of ancient Hebrew society in their own image and likeness (e.g. McKenzie), Geertz'

---

10. Seidenberg (1966) blames Jephthah's daughter for too eagerly accepting her sacrifice. This is precisely the sort of anachronistic ethnocentrism Geertz' paper argues against.

lesson could be endorsed in spite of the fact that anthropologists emphatically deal with reality.

This kind of interaction between narratology and anthropology is the more relevant as it addresses implicitly the major challenge posed to narratology: that of, precisely, the social embedding of narrative, in other words, its relationship to reality. As we have seen, privileging structural analysis over a reflection theory of language has in fact helped to reach reality, by a detour that made it more rather than less accessible. What is at stake is the intertwinement of three ideologies and their influence on real lives: the ancient male ideology according to which women's value is derived from bodily integrity, the ancient female ideology according to which shifts in life-phases are crucially important moments, and the modern ideology which projects sexual exclusivity as the major issue of an ancient narrative. Narratological analysis helped disentangle these. Thus it helped do justice to otherness. It also, albeit implicitly, makes it easy to see the nature of the otherness in sameness: that is, to what extent these modern translations are informed by an ideology that is male, and thus represses female concerns.

CASE 2: SCIENCE AND THE NARRATIVITY OF RHETORIC

This question of gender is also acutely relevant in my second case. Another domain where narratology can be helpful is the growing field of "literature and science."[11] Among the many questions involved in the cross-examination of two domains traditionally so distinct, philosopher of science Evelyn Fox-Keller addresses in her work that of the language of science and the ideological aspects of that language. Starting from the premise that distinctions between realms or levels of discourse, the distinction between technical and ordinary idiom, is relative rather than binary, and differential rather than polar, she wonders if discourse displays the symptoms of the limits of the human ability to be logical in language, or the limits of logic (a "language") itself. In other words, how does the language of science relate to the results of the inquiry it represents? Is discourse a disturbance or a part of science? Should we aim at minimizing the input of discourse, or aim at listening to it, learning from it?[12]

Keller's view that the language of science is profoundly rhetorical and that its rhetoric is motivated by specific, ideological views of gender led me to

---

11. The following remarks grew out of two recent events. In May 1988, the departments of Science Dynamics and of Comparative Literature of the University of Amsterdam organized a three-day workshop on "(Meta-)Theory and Practice in Literature and the Sciences" where the question of narrative was acutely present in the discussions. Later in the same month, the Stichting Praemium Erasmianum organized a symposium on "Three Cultures," one day of which was entirely devoted to the question of the language of science. Key-speaker Evelyn Fox-Keller raised questions which called for narratological reflection.

12. I am freely interpreting here the enterprise of Keller's three papers in the book published by the Stichting Praemium Erasmianum (1989) as I see it.

examine more in detail the narrativity of rhetoric itself, and of this specific gender-related rhetoric in scientific discourse in particular. This inquiry was in turn based on the premise that narrative is a kind of language; hence that it is, like language, different from actual narrative speech or discourse, but not separated from it —and that narrative is a system, but not ahistorical; collective, but not unchangeable; regulated by abstract rules, but not uninformed by concrete uses and adaptations of those rules; in short, on the premise that I had also endorsed in the work on Judges. The premise which had earlier induced me to endorse a subject-oriented narratology.[13]

My hypothesis is that narrative entertains—displays and hides—a special relationship between people—individuals socially embedded and working collectively—and their language: a relation of representation. In other words, the scientist is present in his or her language to the extent that s/he narrativizes his or her discourse. The endeavor, then, is to place narrativity within rhetoric, and thereby to explain the dynamics of the vital influence of this narrativized rhetoric on the actual accomplishments of scientific theories which Keller has in effect demonstrated.

Again, one tiny example will have to suffice to make my point clear. Keller's argument for the intrinsic relationship between the scientific impulse to know the secret of life—and of death (not only DNA but also the nuclear bomb are characters in the story of Keller's cases)—and male attitudes toward gender, is illustrated with, among other quotes, a saying by Richard Feynman, speaking about his urge to discover the secret of life: "anything that is secret, I try to undo."[14] The relevance of a subject-oriented narratology begins with the undecidability of the verb "to undo": is the object "secret" or "the thing that is secret"? This ambiguity establishes a metaphorical identification between the secret—the unknown, the unknowable—and the object of that knowledge: nature. This metaphor is the more powerful as it passes unnoticed; it is one of those "metaphors we live by" (Lakoff & Johnson 1980). Thus nature, although itself without the will that makes a subject, is made the guilty enemy who deserves to be undone. This shift generates the notion, as yet entirely metaphorical, that nature requires and deserves to be "undone," to be violated. The question is, then, if this metaphorical notion remains metaphorical, and if that metaphorical status makes it innocent of real violence. Teresa De Lauretis, basing herself on Eco's analysis of Peirce's account of the place of reality in

---

13. See my *Femmes imaginaires* for a justification of this conception of narrative. There I tried to refine the model put forward earlier (*Narratology*) by distinguishing three different aspects of subjectivity which cut across the three narrative agencies of narrator, focalizer, and actor: the subject as source (of meaning), as theme, and as agent (of any of the three narrative activities). This renewed model allowed me, for example, to maintain the focalizer position of Jephthah's daughter even though a different agent determines the subject—theme of the tale. It also allows me to both acknowledge the collective and "dead" status of the metaphors in the discourse of biology and maintain the ideological agency at work therein.

14. See for this and other examples Keller's first paper in the publication mentioned in the previous note.

semiosis, would call this an instance of the connectedness of the rhetoric of violence and the violence of rhetoric.[15]

It is certainly no coincidence that Keller's story of the motivation for the scientific impulse as displayed by this kind of metaphorical expression, is modeled upon a double generic intertext. The urge to discover has a psychoanalytic antecedent in the child's impulse to discover its own origins, and a literary one in the structure of the mystery novel, that narrative genre *par excellence* in which a secret to be found out constitutes the fabula, and desire for the discovery and punishment of the guilty party the motivation to engage in reading. The former intertext accounts for the gender-specific nature of the urge, the latter for its hierarchical underpinning.

Narrativity comes in as soon as we realize two things. Firstly, we know that a metaphor represents a view, and that this view has its source in a subject, the speaker/focalizer. Secondly, we know that the very idea of secrecy presupposes an acting subject. To begin with the latter implication: according to the semantics of secrecy this subject is guilty of excluding some members of a community from what some others apparently know. This implied subject produces a split in the focalization of the object. It is obvious that nature is no such subject; nor is "life." This is why Feynman's phrase had to be ambiguous. The secret to be undone must be known by somebody; how else could it be undone?

This narrative aspect of the rhetoric cannot be detached from historical considerations; the rhetoric obviously has a history. In a previous phase of that history, the subject of secrecy was God, the creator of life. The closest signifier for that creative power is the subject of life in the sense of pro-creation. Hence, the ambiguity of "secret" produces a metaphor that identifies women with nature. Keller quotes an impressive number of phrases in which this metaphorical identification is indeed produced, repeated, taken for granted. That narrativity motivates, indeed necessitates the gap opened by the discarding of the Supreme Subject to be filled by woman implicates narratology in this critical examination of scientific discourse.

This brings us to the first narrative aspect of rhetoric: the focalization implied. This aspect in turn has two sides to it: the systematic character of the metaphor, primary symptom of focalization; and the semantics of the focalizer it entails. Firstly, the symptomatic detail of Feynman's saying is only interesting to the extent that it does not stand alone. Keller's analysis demonstrates

---

15. See De Lauretis, 1987:31—50. Her example is the strategies used by social scientists to cover up the sexual violence taking place within the family. Eco's paper appeared in *The Role of the Reader* (1979), a book that came out literally during Synopsis 2. The debate, in semiotics, on the status of the referent, is endlessly complex; it is more than just a reflection of the realism-nominalism debate in philosophy of science. Like there, it affects the theory itself, but also, the status of the referent affects the very content of the other, related terms of object, interpretant, and hence, also, of sign. Eco's primary source is Peirce, esp. the following items of the *Collected Papers*: 1.372 (1885), 1.422,477 (1896), 2.310 (1902), 2.441 (1893), 2.275 (1902).

that the metaphor of secrecy for the scientific impulse is embedded in a whole series of metaphors, a metaphorical system of the kind analyzed by Lakoff & Johnson. This series is constructed upon the principle of binary opposition, which it needs for its effectiveness. In a set of scientific papers Keller analyzes, the following pairing of terms come up: secrecy—knowledge; women—men; fertility—virility; nature—culture; dark—light; life—death. In its apparent inevitability, "naturalness" or "logicality," this binary ordering of terms is itself ideological; it precludes other modes of thinking and ordering. As the smallest underlying ideological unit, binarism itself is an ideologeme (Jameson 1981).[16]

It is immediately obvious that these pairs do not constitute logical opposites of a single type. The opposition holds within the entire series, and this seriality entails the implied opposition between the terms of each pair. The thought on which this systemic effect is based, the mode of focalization that is to say, is metonymic association and conflation. The terms on each side of the opposition are considered to stand to each other in a relation of entailment, causality, or implication. Metonymy accounts for the series' self-evidence.

When we take the discursive samples Keller analyzes at their word, the pairs can be ordered in the following way:

1. secret   knowledge
2. women   man
3. fertility virility
4. nature   culture
5. dark   light
6. life   [death]

Such a set implies a hierarchy between the two series, where the left column is the primary one, a chain of associations generated by the ideologeme, the implicit but continued opposition to the right column's terms. Typical of ideological systems is a specific "logic," hovering between a rhetorical ambiguity and associative mechanisms. The rhetorical system can be seen as a kind of zigzagging sewing machine: moving from left to right, yet primarily preoccupied with the left seam, it links together all terms in ways that are hard to disentangle.

One example is the association between "men" and "virility," simply tautological at first sight. But as it is produced by the association, on the other, primary side of the opposition, of women and fertility. Virility becomes, not the negative of fertility but an answer, polemical or even aggressive, to it. But if

16. This has serious consequences for narratological theories based on binary opposition, such as Greimas (1965; 1970; esp. 1976). Not that such theories are useless; they do help map ideological structures in narrative, but they must be stripped of the positivistic truth claims often attached to them. For example, the so-called semiotic square displays ideological thinking and can help us see that; if alleged to account for fundamental structures of meaning, it is itself participating in what it should rather denounce.

we take these associations at the letter we may wonder why it takes all of men's self-image, virility, to counter what is after all just one aspect of feminity.[17]

The systematic character of the series, on which more shortly, produces the semantic image of the focalizer, whose contours become more visible as we enter into the detail of the rhetoric. Of the aspects of metaphor traditionally distinguished, vehicle (the metaphoric expression), tenor (the idea omitted but implied on the basis of assumed similarity) are most often discussed.[18] since similarity is not only *assumed*, not real, but also *partial*, not total, the motivation is the more crucial aspect—the which implies narrativity.

The motivation of the metaphoric associations between the pairs listed above can briefly be sketched as follows. Between 1. and 2.: synechdochical or *pars pro toto*. Secrets being the property of women, they represent women as a detail or feature represents the whole. Between 2. and 3.: *totum pro parte*. Women possess, among other things, fertility, which is therefore taken to characterize them. Between 3. and 4.: *pars pro toto* again, but with a difference. Nature is, among other things, a locus of fertility. Between 4. and 5.: metonymy. What is dark about fertility is precisely its secrecy. This is the logic of tautology. Between 5. and 6.: this association is hardly simple. The connection from darkness to life is itself, as an association, the representation of the secret *including* its unbearability. It is only plausible if passing through that motivation, or else it would be totally absurd. As a consequence, the negativity of darkness has to be both activated and suspended, according to contexts, but always be kept available.

The rhetorical subject of motivation is not just the speaker who comes up with the metaphor, for it takes a context, a group identity, to make such metaphors understandable at all. Hence the relevance of a narratological perspective, which accomodates in the concept of focalization both the individual subject of vision and that subject's embedding in the historically and socially specific situation of language, exemplified by group talk. In the founding metaphor of secrecy, the tenor is "secrets of nature." The untenability of the opposition between figurative and literal (van Alphen 1987) is immediately

17. This is one place where the Judges analysis joins this analysis of scientific discourse.
18. I use the terminology derived from Beardsley, 1968, because it is more current than Black's focus and frame, which in addition might be confusing in combination with my narratological terminology. The literature on metaphor is rich and confusing. For a critique of the traditional view of metaphor, see Ricoeur; also Mark Turner, who rightly endorses Lakoff & Johnson's basic or systematic metaphor theory, and especially argues for the centrality of kinship metaphor; also Goodman, who speaks of networks of metaphors. And Cooper, who (178) provides arguments for the relevance of the ideological critique I am practicing here without falling into the trap of a massive condemnation of metaphor as such, based on the illusion of "pure" language. Hrushovski usefully elaborates on Black's frame, and emphasizes the decisive influence of the frame of reference. Van Alphen (1987) rightly stresses the undecidability of these frames of reference, due to the reader-text interaction, and completes the circle which undermines the very distinction between literal and figurative language, hence, by implication also that between dead and live metaphors. The untenability of these distinctions supports the relevance of Keller's work from a literary perspective.

obvious, for it already enforces a *certain kind* of metaphor: one which fills in the missing subject of witholding. The vehicle or substituted term is "women," not all of women but their sexual difference from men. This factor is not "just" a vehicle either, since the aspect of women especially focused on in the metaphor is their difference from men, presented as opposition. The motivation, that is, the aspect which makes the metaphor plausible, is the logic of opposition.

The logic of opposition allows us to associate women with secrecy *because* the men who feel excluded by this (self-constructed) narrative of secrecy have privileged access to language and story-telling. This opposition, in turn, is plausible as the underlying motivation, because it is already *in* language, as a dominant strategy of meaning production. Hence, this metaphor does not need an explicit linguistic modalizer; the ideologeme makes the linguistic word superfluous.[19]

Note that the self-evidence of opposition as a meaning-maker allows semantic specifications of opposition itself to pass unnoticed in turn: opposition becomes polemical opposition, which leads to hierarchization, so that the "other side" becomes both enemy and lower half.

Keller's analysis demonstrates an extended network of metaphors grounded in this rhetorical story of secrecy. The above analysis of the narrativity in the metaphor of secrecy makes it easy to see the links between the various terms. If the starting point is a secret, then the goal is to *unveil* or *penetrate* it —another one of those words whose metaphorical nature is metonymically motivated, a motivation already shared by the group whose talk has gained the status of "normal" language. Note, for example, that the innocent word "discovery" precisely means "unveiling." In addition, the secret calls for a strategy, the method, and if the secret is already tainted with darkness, then the method will be visually oriented: "seeing" becomes the aim. The next section of the present paper will show that from "seeing" to "forcing entrance" there is only a small step, as another of Keller's quotes suggests (Watson and Crick: "a calculated assault on the secret of life"). The military language ("assault") must of course be read in terms of war, but as the rest of the context shows, it is a war of the sexes.

It would take me too long, here, to go into the pertinent and difficult question, raised by De Lauretis, about the relation between the representation—metaphor as an innocent figure of style—and the justification, hence, the ongoing production of sexual violence; nor can I do more than simply refer to Elaine Scarry's pertinent analysis of the relation between language and pain in the practice of torture. These two studies strongly suggest that the very

---

19. This is a case among many others which demonstrates the need for the concept of gap, indispensible in spite of its theoretical problems. See Perry (1979) for a demonstration, Hamon (1983) for a critique. Also chapter 1 of my *Femmes Imaginaires*.

attempt to argue that discourse has no real bearing on reality, partakes of the ideology of oppositional separation, e.g. of mind and body, of science and political reality, or of realism and nominalism, which allows violence and torture to take place and be either justified or obliterated.

The gain of a narratological perspective in this joint venture is to reach a clearer view of the semantic and pragmatic dimensions of the ideological language at stake. The insight that the semantic place left by the evacuation of religion from science, had to be filled by the "other" of science, and that the "self" of science thus further specifies his gender-specificity is certainly not new; Keller's work alone already amply demonstrated this. But the narrative impulse inherent in discourse does further support these insights while providing them with an explanation that can be added to the psychoanalytically oriented one Keller proposes herself. That this additional explanation is linguistically oriented, more specifically based on the two most common linguistic systems, rhetoric and narrative, helps in turn to account for the paradox that this kind of impulses, urges, and motivations are both utterly individual and utterly social.

CASE 3: VISUAL NARRATIVES AND THE FIST OF DOMINATION

A third domain where narratology has quite a bit to contribute is visual analysis. During the last few years, the steady current of studies of the relations between texts and images has dramatically grown.[20] In addition to studies of the interaction between literary and visual art, there is also an increasing interest in the literary aspects of visual art itself, and narrativity has pride of place in that inquiry. Again, the relation is two-sided and a-symmetrical: the analysis cannot be limited to the application of narratological concepts to visual representations ("how do images tell?"); rather, the confrontation between the narratological apparatus and the visual image inevitably changes or even subverts the categories. Thus the notion of fabula can benefit from this interdisciplinary work, but only if one leaves the question behind how an image tells a pre-determined story, in favor of the question what story the visual representation produces, thus thoroughly modifying its pre-textual "source."

The relevance of visual analysis for feminism does not need to be argued anymore. The most pertinent publications for a feminist theory of culture over

20. Wendy Steiner and W. J. T. Mitchell are famous examples of literary scholars examining visual art; Michael Fried is an art historian preoccupied with literature; all three are interested in the relations between the two arts. Journals like *Representations* and *October* are significant contributions to this field. See also the special issue of *Style* on *Visual Poetics*. See also Ernst van Alphen's contribution to this issue, where the question of narrativity is not only applied to a body of visual art, but to the problem of visual representation as such. Norman Bryson has demonstrated spectacularly how enriching a literary perspective is for visual analysis per se.

the past ten years come from film studies, with narratology being a minor but relevant element. Again the major foundation of this interdisciplinary venture is psychoanalysis, with special emphasis on the questions of voyeurism and the oedipal structure which, according to some film theorists, is inherent in narrative.[21] Thus a complicity between narrativity, gender politics and the visual regime is suggested whose range extends beyond cinema into the plastic arts on the one hand, television on the other, and which needs in my view a more specifically narratological analysis.[22]

Of the many aspects of visual art which has connections with narratological concerns, it is again focalization that seemed particularly relevant for a feminist perspective. Precisely because the narratological concept of focalization does not overlap with the concept of spectatorship in visual analysis, does the relationship between the two contribute to insight into the mechanisms of cultural manipulation. And again, the tiniest of details can help demonstrate my point.

In the painting *Susannah Surprised by the Elders* allegedly painted by Rembrandt in 1645, now in the Gemäldegalerie in Berlin-Dahlem [figure 1], the conventional representation of the semi-nude exposed to the voyeurism of both characters and viewers, is complicated by a few changes in the traditional iconographic scheme.[23] These changes, of which the representation of hands is the most striking one, affect the position of the internal focalizer and, as I will argue later, the possible viewing attitudes opened up to the external spectator. How exactly the image-internal, formalist-narratological analysis can provide arguments for ideological critique, is my concern here.[24]

Garrard has argued that many of the representations of the story of Susannah give the victim of the assault the pose of the Medici Venus, thus suggesting erotic appeal and availability. This tradition thus contributes to the "naturalization" of rape, suggesting that the victim herself provokes the rape by displaying her attractions. This Venus pose is iconographically marked by the figure's left hand, extended forward so as to display her breast and the elegance of her body. If this scheme is fixed by the pictorial tradition in which

---

21. See De Lauretis, 1983; 1987. Seminal publications on voyeurism in film are Mulvey's classic (1975) and Kuhn (1985) and Kaplan (1983), and the brilliant study by Silverman (1988). Narratological considerations of film are markedly present in Silverman (1983; 1988) and implicitly in Penley (1989). For a feminist attempt to define narrative structure outside of the oedipal model, Smelik 1989.

22. I have devoted some work to this aspect of the feminist debate by analyzing the relation between spectatorship and internal focalization in drawings and paintings by Rembrandt. By another accident of life, I was led to explore visual art for an occasion that, again, occurred in Israel, a conference organized in 1985 at the Hebrew University in Jerusalem. The conference was devoted to "Discourse in Psychoanalysis, Literature and the Arts," and was organized by Shlomith Rimmon-Kenan and Sandford Budick, July 1985.

23. See Mary Garrard's seminal article "Artemesia and Susanna," in which she mentions this painting briefly in connection with the voyeuristic tradition.

24. This section develops an argument I have made in my book *Reading "Rembrandt": Beyond the Word-Image Opposition*, New York and Cambridge, U.K.: Cambridge University Press 1991.

Rembrandt also inserted himself, then it is striking that the woman's hand in this painting is slightly displaced toward the back. As a result, her breast is covered rather than displayed, while her hand is actively involved in fabula agency: it suggests resistance against the assailant. However slight this suggestion of movement may be, it does contribute to the narrativization of the work.

Now, it has been noticed that hands in Rembrandt often accompany acts of seeing.[25] This is less clearly the case for the Susannah figure in this painting than for the hands of the two men, spectators by definition, whose acts of seeing actually lead to the use of their hands. I wish to draw attention to one of the three emphatically significant hands: the hand of the Elder in the background, holding firmly onto his seat of power, the hand of the other man, already acting out the transition from seeing to touching, and this man's other hand.[26] The latter hand is frankly bizarre. So is, I wish to contend, the man's gaze.

The represented ways of looking, or diegetic focalization, constitute the "line of sight" which is offered for identification to the external spectator. In this work, the Elder in the background, the representative of social power, is looking at the other man, who is looking at Susannah, who is looking at the spectator. I will not go into the question if Susannah is appealing to, or enticing, the spectator; since the representation is strongly narrativized, that question, precisely, cannot be answered without a prior narratological analysis. My focus is on the Elder who is acting out the threat of rape; it is he who presents a figuration of the connection between looking and touching. Hence, the question of his way of looking is acutely relevant.

True, at first sight the situation looks pretty bad. Susannah is caught between the men and the water, and has no place to go. The fabula thus constructed repeats the textual version in the apocryphal section of the Book of Daniel: Susannah is threatened with rape, but, we know, resists successfully; and reassured by the known uplifting denouement, the spectator can enjoy the rape scene. The attractiveness and the vulnerability of the young female might be appealing to sadistic voyeurism. Such a viewing attitude is indeed possible. But I am interested in how, precisely, the work at the same time counters such a response; how it draws attention away from plain eroticism, complicating,

---

25. This is Svetlana Alpers' view. See her *Rembrandt's Enterprise*. There, Alpers specifies this view by relating it to role playing, which she considers typical of Rembrandt's works. Hands, then, dramatize, and thus foreground, seeing.

26. The transition from seeing to touching is, of course, the hot issue in the debate on pornography. See Kappeler's *The Pornography of Representation*. The simplistic assumption of an immediate link makes the more sophisticated feminist analysts of culture uneasy, as it tends to make feminism complicit with prudish fundamentalism. Andrea Dworkin's recent *Intercourse* is a disquieting example. Dworkin in fact comes dangerously close to the biological argument for inequality, joining, then, the most reactionary sexist arguments. On the other hand, an equally simplistic denial of such a link is untenable and damaging as well. My analysis of the Susannah case can be seen as an attempt to avoid either extreme of these positions.

indeed, critiquing it. How, in other words, it does not represent a single, monolithic ideological position but promotes a self-conscious reflection *about* such a position.

For two details continue to bother me: the look and the fist of the represented rapist. It is strange that the man does not follow up on the voyeurism; he does not look at Susannah's body. And although his one hand is undressing her, his other hand does not do anything to her; it is closer to his face than to her body. The diegetic status of his behavior changes the fabula, or rather, precludes the traditional fabula's construction. If we try to trace the object of his gaze, we must conclude that he is staring over Susannah's head; at the most, he is looking at the top of it. To be more precise, he is looking at the pearls braided into Susannah's quite sophisticated hairdo. Why?

This raises the question of the nature of visual narratives. Traditionally, we interpret this kind of image in the light of the prior text, its "source," of which the image is supposed to be an illustration. A visual narrative, however, partakes of the semiotic means of narrativization on the basis of its own medium's specific sign system. The Susannah painting, for example, not only represents a fabula constructed in a play of focalization, but also the fiburation of figures on a surface. The man's fist is thus on one side of an empty space, delineated on the other side by the top of Susannah's head. This empty space is filled by paint, applied in the "rough" mode which, in Rembrandt, contrasts with the technique of "fine" painting. Now, the pearls braided into the hair, also adorned by a scarf, are so to speak the climax of the "fine" in this painting. And this finery is what the man is gazing at. His gaze narrativizes this division of the canvas in significant areas of "rough" and "fine": it connects it to the fabula in which the man figures.

What about the fist, in this connection? That this fist is meaningful is not only arguable by its very deviance; it is also a presence in a few studies whose relevance for this particular painting is obvious, although it is denied by Benesch.[27] In one, a sketch dated about 1637 (Benesch 155; private collection, Berlin), the combination of a strongly concentrated gaze and the clutched fist is already present. The gaze is, however, not malign, while the fist does not have the raised thumb as in the painting. It does, however, express a keen interest, which we tend to relate to the gaze (whose object, of course, we cannot see). Compared to this sketch, another one, a drawing also dated 1637 (Benesch 157: Melbourne, National Gallery of Victoria) has the same combination of gaze and fist but comes much closer to the Berlin painting. In addition to the recognizable turban which makes the man in the painting so utterly ridiculous—another, more obvious aspect of the critical undermining

---

27. Benesch's catalogue of Rembrandt's drawings mentions for Benesch 155 that a suggested connection with the Berlin painting cannot be maintained, for stylistic reasons leading to an earlier date (45). For Benesch 157 the connection is not denied.

Figure 1: Rembrandt, *Susanna Surprised by the Elders*. Berlin-Dahlem, Gemäldegallerie

of the ideology of the scene—and the other hand, indicated in its grapling, the gaze is clearly malicious and directed a little bit lower.

The keen concentration and excitement which the fist seems to suggest in Benesch 155 is replaced in Benesch 157, as I see it, by a more technical concentration. This man, malicious as he is, is also an expert in looking. The thumb becomes part of his technological apparatus of looking, and the act of looking gains a technical dimension. But if this technology of looking comes with an increase of malice, then the meaning of the combination is that the two themes are closely related. It is in this direction, I contend, that we must look for the critical dimension of the painting; the gaze-and-fist, there, can be read as a mise en abyme of the visual narrative.

In order to see the "fine" quality of the work on Susannah's hairdo, the shine on the pearls, the braid, one needs a magnifying glass. We might even go as far as projecting such an additional technological tool for looking in the empty fist: empty yet tensely clutched, it lends itself for such a projection to the extent that the meaning of the fist in Benesch 155 is lost, without being replaced by any "logical," that is, narrative, alternative meaning. The gaze, the closed and tense mouth, it all suggests that this man is *not only* a criminal rapist but *also* an expert in visuality. The sign of the gaze-and-fist, then, is not only the token of a criminal connection between looking and touching, but also a token of pictorial representation, raising questions about the complicity of the pictorial tradition and the misuse of the female body.

Such an interpretation of the gaze-and-fist must not be taken to imply the accusation that Rembrandt not only partakes of the voyeuristic tradition but, by implicating his art, promotes it. On the contrary, drawing attention to the work of visual representation *within* the representation of its abuse, confronts the spectator with the troubling interrelation between the visual culture in the West and gender politics. Thus, a new narrative is produced, one in which self-reflection plays its unsettling part, cutting through the realist illusion that promotes the enjoyment of the represented body without further ado. The real spectator is free, of course, to ignore this self-reflective detail, this mise en abyme of visual representation as embedded in power. It is possible to ignore the fist, to displace the look, to further undress Susannah. A simplistic view of visuality according to which the spectator only takes in what is visually there, can only work if one denies the deviant details as well as the narrativization of the work. In other words, a narratological perspective helps to complicate the visual model as well as the eternalizing view of women as pure victims. If this woman is the victim in this painting, it is because the visual culture in which this work is inserted is impregnated with gender politics; but by addressing that issue, the work undermines the "naturalness" of that situation.

CONCLUSION

I have tried to make several general points about the current state of narratology with the help of this patchwork of my research of the past ten years. The first point concerns the range of narratology. These three brief samples of narratology at work within other fields, although, of course, too fragmentary to propose full analyses, have hopefully suggested that if one does not confine narratology to "narrative texts," the discipline's range of relevance is extended without losing the specificity of its perspective. While narrative texts may profit from an in-depth narratological analysis, other dimensions of such texts do also need clarification; but objects which do not traditionally fall under the rubric of narrative may even more strongly benefit from such an approach.

The second point concerns ideology. The connections I have tried to establish between a narratological perspective and ideological concerns, moreover, counter the view that narratology's formalism entails its futility in the face of social concerns. Rather than opposing structural analysis, then, feminism can use such an approach in order to counter simplistic arguments based on an untenable binary opposition; one should not be "for" or "against" erotic art, but one needs, first, to understand it, and second, to differentiate between such works, so as to avoid a new censorship while still being combative where needed.

The third point, less developed but implicitly argued, concerns history. I disagree with those who claim that narratology, being a systematic theory, is by definition ahistorical, that is, another of those unwarranted dichotomies. On the contrary, to the extent that a careful analysis of narrative structure counters interpretation on the basis of prejudice, convention, or ideology, the more precise such an analysis is, the better it helps position the object within history. Thus, in the Judges work, the standard view of the status of women in the Book of Judges is arguably anachronistic; the narratological analysis, in contrast, helped to make other possible meanings visible, more plausible in light of ancient history. The gendered quality of the rhetoric of science, made apparent through narratological analysis of the expressions, became understandable in light of the gap left by prior historical developments. And Rembrandt's painting was not detached from its iconographic background, from the history of the Susannah tradition that is, but, on the contrary, received its critical dimension in relation to that background.

▪ 2 ▪

Reflections on Reflection: The Mise en Abyme

INTRODUCTION

In an analysis of the sequence of Genesis 37 through 39 (Bal 1987), I have proposed to consider a sidewards deviation from linear chronology or paralepsis a potentially subversive figure, interruptive of chronological coherence as well as of the illusion of gratuitousness of rhetoric itself. In the pursuit of subversion which is the fate of the feminine position in the biblical narratives which have worked their way so deeply, but aslant, our culture sets us on the trail of another antichronological figure. Disguised as some other figure of the aesthetic system of narrative rhetoric, this figure distinguishes itself by an aspect emblematic of the feminine situation: the mirror. That figure, whose definition is the subject of the present remarks, is called *mise en abyme*.[1]

Among the concepts of classical narratology, the mise en abyme is doubly off-center. In the first place, it is often evoked but at the same time has hardly found a place within the overall theories elaborated for the analysis of narrative texts. Greimas, for example, does not make use of it; Genette evokes it every now and then but does not integrate it into his "discourse of narrative." Secondly, and the second eccentricity easily explains the first, it is a phenomenon profoundly anti-narrative, if one considers, as one continues to do, the narrative as a chronological development, as linear. This subversive aspect is inviting, as much for the experimental novelists who freely declare themselves subversive in their turn, as for a critical theory of narrative.

The concept is typically French. It is metaphorical, borrowed from the visual field of heraldry. Up to the present, the monograph which Dällenbach

---

1. These remarks have initially been inspired by a remarkable book by Lucien Dällenbach, published in French in 1978, called *Le récit spéculaire*, and which only recently appeared in English as *The Mirror in the Text*.

(1978; English 1989) devoted to it remains the sole serious theoretical study on the subject. Dällenbach examined patiently the occurrences of the term and its equivalents, its sources and its usage in literary criticism; he constructed a classification and went so far as to sketch out a diachronic perspective. The typology is based on the Jakobsonian model of communication.

Dällenbach's book suffers from a surprising disregard of semiotic considerations. The author does not examine the status of the phenomenon as a sign, and he does not establish in general any relationship between it and other aspects of semiosis. Therefore, its place in narrative communication as precisely the potential subversion and disturbance of communication will remain unexplored. For that reason the author will not be able to extricate it from the vagueness whereto it would appear to be confined from the outset.

The first concern of the present chapter will be, then, to reintegrate the concept of mise en abyme within its semiotic context. To this end, it will be set alongside concepts closely related but distinct: iconicity, indexicality, synecdochality. Immediately after this first move, however, this framework itself will be called into question. Descriptive semiotics, after all, explains little.

This is only a starting point for an explanation, necessarily tentative, of the phenomenon of mise en abyme, so that it will be possible to formulate suppositions concerning its effect, and to search out a point of entry for critique. Its reflexive character, in the multiple senses of the term, will serve as a plumb line. In opposition to the infinite regression so admired by Leiris and others stands the frontier, the limit imposed on every phenomenon which one means to interpret. The limits of the mise en abyme are at the same time what defines the mise en abyme as a limit. Paradoxically, the "infinite regression" depends on these limits. And it is on this that the narrativization of the mise en abyme depends. Having thus made both ends meet, I have been able elsewhere (1987) to grapple with the innocent corpus of the Book of Ruth, innocent because ignorant of the theories formulated from Gide onwards as well as of the experimental novels of our day. And it is there that I could construct the mise en abyme par excellence: that which refers, and in referring recounts, in infinite regression, all that has already been recounted, to the future.

Many of the essays collected here reflect on reflection as a critical strategy apt to understand our own entanglement within the ideological positions we like, in this ideology-aware era, to denounce. This essay remains theoretical in a more formal way. Discussing the mise en abyme as a sign, it will only suggest, not elaborate, what such a subversive figure can do for a reflective critical attitude.

MISE EN ABYME AGAINST CHRONOLOGY

A theory of mise en abyme

Starting from the genesis of the concept since Gide, Lucien Dällenbach first retraces its adventures. He compares with care the different uses which have been made of it in criticism, and he defines, then eliminates occasionally, the different distinctive traits which have been attributed to it. In the second part, a typology of mise en abyme is elaborated. The typology is based on the model of linguistic communication, the *elementary mises en abyme* identified as presenting an analogy with the whole text on the level of content, form, or enunciation. In the third part are collected a considerable number of analyses, first of the Nouveau Roman of the '50s, then of the Nouveau Nouveau Roman of the '70s. The point of this assemblage is, on the one hand, verification of the proposed typology, on the other, a new location in diachronic perspective, not of the concept itself, but of its functioning. These analyses disengage an important difference between the novels of the two periods, a formal difference which points up a change in the relationship between literary texts and literary function.

Taking as a starting point the first reference to the mise en abyme (the well-known text in which Gide explains why he has a predilection for the form in question), Dällenbach defines mise en abyme thus:

> a mise en abyme is a whole *enclave maintaining* a relationship of likeness with the work which contains it (18).

This provisional definition is based on Gide's remark:

> I rather like it when in a work of art one rediscovers transposed in this way, to the scale of the characters, the very subject of the work (Gide 1948:41).

Gide's text is thereafter analyzed in its details. This explanation reveals the Gidian ambiguity of the word *subject*, which permits itself to be interpreted as either the thematic content or the narrating subject. Now Gide was interested above all in the power of the narrating subject, a power which appears to increase when the subject is divided. For something to be a mise en abyme, in this conception, a homology is necessary between the relationship of the narrator with his narrative, on the one hand, and of the character with the narrative which she or he is recounting in the role of character-narrator in the second degree, on the other. This precision should eliminate some cases which have long been interpreted as mises en abyme (the reader may recall Ricardou's analysis of *The Fall of the House of Usher*), in which the reflection of the narrative—complete or partial, true or false—has as its object only the story, and not the reciprocal construction of a story and of a narrator. However, the comparison, ingeniously conducted, between *Paludes* and *Les Faux Monnayeurs*, reveals that Gide was only partially faithful to his own preference, an observation which leads Dällenbach to accept despite all the broad definition of the concept:

> A mise en abyme is every internal mirror reflecting the ensemble of the narrative by simple reduplication, repeated or specific.

(By the last category he designates "a fragment deemed to include the work which includes it." [51]). Thus the differing conceptions are set in order, and the terrain is cleared for the principal segment of the study: the construction of the typology. Unfortunately, the author does not avoid falling into the trap of hasty typology.

The extension of a term often needs specification if the risk of indeterminacy is to be avoided. The author has not failed this principle. He considers, in the definition, the word *narrative* as analyzable in its different aspects. Thus he proposes a first differentiation of possible reflections according to whether they bear on the *utterance*, the *enunciation*, or the *code* of the narrative.

Not everything is Jakobsonian which is meant to be: if the choice of three aspects of the six which Jakobson distinguishes is justified for practical reasons, the confusion between context and enunciation, and the confusion (even provisional) between sender and receiver are even more dubious, while the extension of the species to the "transcendental" (131) mise en abyme, there where the typology is said to be based on Jakobsonian functions, sticks out from the frame depicted here.

The reflexive utterance (the mise en abyme) will identify itself often by the presence of an index assuring its decoding: homonymy, repetition, or another symptom indispensable because the utterance is reflexive only in front of the spectator, that is to say, if it is perceived as such (61). The author of a literary text makes use of a "code"—let us accept for the moment this metaphorical use of the term, which has come to mean *style* in the broad sense—which she has only partly in common with the reader. To the extent that he is himself the inventor of the code which he uses, the author should work toward the signifying efficacity of his message. To do this, she will insert her "directions for use" indices, but these in their turn make reference to the code partially unknown to or unconscious in the reader. The problem is not easily resolved. Dällenbach proposes a common-sense solution, certainly, but it is nothing other than a return, albeit camouflaged, to an intentionalist geneticism: for him an utterance permits itself to be decoded as reflexive only if it is *destined* (by itself, in Dällenbach's terminology; by the author, evidently) to be. In other words, the *intention* of the author—of "the encoder"—decides. By associating the mise en abyme with Jakobsonian poetics, Dällenbach critiques interpretive overloading, the danger of a reading too systematically retrospective:

> Legitimate in principle, the latter ceases to be just that, in our view when the decoding is entirely disconnected from the encoding and when one applies it, for example, to texts *which do not subscribe* to it, the principle according to which fiction is only an allegory of the functions which install it (68). (I underline the words which reveal a genetic conception.)

He reserves the ascription of reflexivity only to those texts which in their entirety can make the emphasis on auto-reflexivity carry at the expense of their external referentiality. However, it is not enough to personify the text in attributing to it the intention of getting rid of the author.

But if one sets aside *intention* it is difficult to delimit the domain of the mise en abyme, as the author rightly wishes to do. Dällenbach opts for an intuitive approach which restrains less the range of the concept of mise en abyme than its field of application. And for good reason: he assigns first place, in the diachronic part of his study, to the New Novel. Another solution, as pragmatic as this one, could be the following: a mise en abyme is every utterance in the second degree in which the interpreter can point out convincingly one or more symptoms of reflexivity.

Alongside a reflexivity which should be *readable*, a second criterion has been founded on the words of Gide's text: the mise en abyme will be "on the scale of the characters." These words do not signify anything other than the attribution of the reflexive utterance to the universe of the diegesis. Thus are excluded, for example, interventions of the author(s), invocations of the Muse, etc. The mise en abyme therefore will always be *interruption*, of the narration relayed to the character, often also relaying focalization, and/or interruption of the diegesis. The mise en abyme is reflexive and diegetic, object of the narration at the second degree.

The author discusses in detail the status, definition, and functioning of three elementary mises en abyme: the mise en abyme of the *utterance*, or *fictional*; the mise en abyme of the *enunciation*, or *narrative*; and the mise en abyme of the *code*, or *transcendental*. The first is defined as a "citation of the contents" (76). Augmenting, by its repetitive character, the redundancy of the narrative, it reduces the content of information in the narrative:

> from the sole fact that it permits the maximal closure and codification of the narration, it diminishes in the same proportions its polysemic virtualities (78).

Two types of text, opposed one to the other, are capable of making this sacrifice: those which mean their message to be unequivocal, and those which mean to attract attention to the status of the text. The *mise en abyme of the utterance*, or the *fictional mise en abyme*, will also be able to illuminate what the diegetic content can obscure, restricting or enlarging its signification.

The semantic functioning of the mise en abyme is in strict connection with another important element of variation: its distribution in the text. The placement of the mise en abyme, whether it presents itself "en bloc" or in pieces, whether it is unique or repeated, is a problem of narrative temporality.

Condensation and interruption of the narrative, the mise en abyme of fiction destroys its chronology; it would be anachronic by definition. In this view, it can be *prospective, retrospective, retroprospective*. The tripartition receives in the domain of the mise en abyme a very particular importance. Dällenbach drew from it everything possible and composed around it one of the richest parts of his study. The author links the distribution of the mise en abyme to its value as information: the prospective mise en abyme risks revealing in advance and with too much clarity the denouement of the story; to avoid this untimely revelation it will only unveil one aspect or it will produce "noise" to mask what it reveals. Retrospection, on the other hand, does not risk depriving the diegesis of its interest, but of losing its own. Also it will often have recourse to an extension of the signification, which, through it, acquires a general value. The "pivot," the retrospective mise en abyme, which occupies an intermediate position between that which is known and that which remains to be uncovered, is proportionally and qualitatively privileged. It allows "the reader to *presume* starting from that which summarizes" (90). It is the structural center of the narrative, even if it is, for compositional reasons, displaced toward the beginning or toward the end.

The second elementary species, the *mise en abyme of the enunciation*, reflects the process of narrative production: its producer, its receiver, the context which conditions the phatic communication. One might add the domain of the contact, the phatic function. These mises en abyme "all aim, by contrivance, to render the invisible visible" (100). If the author assigns a common denominator to this species, he analyzes nothing less than the consequences of the different postures of the protagonist, according to whether he is the fictive sender or receiver. The producer of the narrative mise en abyme will in general have something to say, intending to fictionalize the relationship between life and art. Most often, however, the protagonist will have the role of receiver. Witness to his own actions, he will profit or not profit, as is the case of K. in *The Trial*—from the teaching that the *exemplum* offers him, and this self-examination imposed on the character reflects that which the narrative imposes on the reader.

This mise en abyme will always be a fictional mise en abyme with an enunciative aspect: it is first of all the action of a character which is summarized, and, if he is witness-receiver of the message, he is from the first an actor by default.

What Dällenbach named from the start the *mise en abyme of the code* is that which reflects the *style*, the *form*, the *commentary* of the text. It is basically a *textual mise en abyme*, in opposition to the fictional mise en abyme as the mise en abyme of the sign is opposed to that of the referent. The discourse of the text (D) can be reflected in the discourse of the reflexive utterance (D'), or in the referent of the latter (R'). Among the privileged topoi in the narrative, textiles, works of art, and machines occupy the privileged position according to the emphasis having been put on the structure, the play of correspondences, and the functioning. Imitating, and thereby commenting on, the functioning of the narrative, this textual mise en abyme is at the same time *metatextual*.

The textual mise en abyme however can reflect more than its own discourse. If the reflection of the text crosses over its own boundaries, in reflecting its beginnings and its ends, it becomes a new elementary species: the *transcendental mise en abyme*. Thus the mise en abyme of the *code*, successively renamed textual, metatextual, and transcendental by virtue of a line of reasoning which mythifies a little the essence of language, becomes a contradiction. Its object, the beginning and end of the text and its writing being located outside the text (before and after the text), this object can only be fictionalized, that is to say, replaced by a diegesis which symbolizes it. And fictionalized in this manner, does it not rejoin, by a movement significantly circular, the object of the *fictional* mise en abyme—the fictive diegesis? One finds oneself confronting three species of mise en abyme which in the end join themselves into one unified species.

MISE EN ABYME AGAINST TYPOLOGY OR THE APORIA OF THE MIRROR

Is the circle vicious? I fear it is. The distinction between elementary mises en abyme, fruitful in that it has revealed some important nuances, has shown at the same time the species' tendency to be confounded. The problem is a question of displacements of emphasis rather than of fundamental differences. Dällenbach asserts that all the *types* (simple reduplication; repeated and specific) can be constituted beginning from each *species*, a condition of being relinked to the central species, the *fictional* mise en abyme. A mise en abyme, therefore, will always be fictional, or it won't be.

The species, dubbed *elementary*, which create the illusion that they are corollaries of a distinction no less elementary, concern, as I have said, the *object* of the reflection. I take into account that, in employing the word *species* as a synonym for *elementary mise en abyme* I seem to attribute to the author a pretension to typology which he might not endorse. However, this term (which I employ because it is shorter and therefore less clumsy) does not contradict at all the spirit of the typology; on the contrary, I contend that it reveals that spirit. It is significant in this regard that the initial table, empty, never comes round filled up. This table visibly has typological pretensions which justify the use of the word species. But these pretensions are only partially realized.

The *types* concern the very nature of reflection: does this reflection reflect one time or several times, truly or only in appearance?

This typology has something disconcerting about it. After 60-odd pages devoted to the distinction of species, the structure seems to give way, and the hasty shoring up of the last chapter of this central section ("the emergence of the types") serves only to emphasize the abysmal clivage (pun intended) which separates species and types. However, the numerous analyses of very diverse examples, taken from world literature, do not confirm this pessimistic impression. They are examined with a subtlety which permits us to grasp in what regard they are similar, and in what regard they are different. The differences reveal some effects which up to this point have gone unnoticed.

The problem then is of a theoretical order. It hinges on the fact that

Dällenbach sought to "wrest the concept from its indeterminacy" without striving to the same degree to tear it from its isolation.

MISE EN ABYME AND ICONICITY
OR THE PLEASURE OF SPECULATION

The relative independence of the mise en abyme—one has seen that it constitutes, in one way or another, an interruption—and, on the other hand, its strong signifying value—it is capable on its own of disturbing, of upsetting from top to bottom the signification of a narrative—would be enough to confer on it the status of *sign*. The description of the phenomenon should thus be inserted, in my opinion, into the semiotic frame. From this perspective, I am going to attempt to rewrite Dällenbach's definition cited earlier. I first transcribe Dällenbach's version underlining the ambiguous or metaphorical words, for which I will substitute in turn terms which in my opinion provide more clarity.

> A mise en abyme is every internal *mirror* reflecting the *ensemble* of the *narrative* by simple *reduplication*, repeated or *specious*.

Mirror, *reduplication*, and *specious* belong to the same semantic field. The three words contain the element "resemblance." *Ensemble* can denote the whole, the total, but also "the main lines," the structure, the composition. In fact, the word has to be interpreted that way, or else we are stuck with total repetition. (Rimmon-Kenan 1980) The word *narrative* is ambiguous. It denotes the narrative text as well as the story and the narrative.

Here is the revised version (provisional):

> A mise en abyme is every *sign* having for its *meaning* a relevant and continuous aspect of the text, the story, or the fabula which it *signifies* by means of a resemblance, one time or several times.

The distinction between *species* (mise en abyme of the utterance and of the code) and *types* (simple, repeated, or specific mise en abyme) becomes that between the meaning (the author calls it referent) and the mode of signification. The sign itself (the mirror) has been scarcely studied by Dällenbach. It is necessary to point out first of all the status of the sign of the "mirror," then to home in on its features: form, method of signification, meaning.

The selection of signs in general poses the same problem as the selection of mises en abyme. It is crucial, first of all, that the sign can be perceived as such, or else it does not signify. The pernicious question of knowing if the sender has from all evidence intended that a textual phenomenon function as a sign can be set aside. It is enough that the receiver is capable of being convinced (and of convincing other receivers) that the fragment in question *signifies*. She can base her conviction on symptoms, on indications in the fragment which make explicit its signifying function; for example, in the case of a *sign*/mise en abyme: resemblance. An obvious example is the verb *to resemble* and its (para-) synonyms, or a key-word which functions also in the whole text: Everything sent back by a mirror as the image is not *identical* to the object reflected, just as by the same token the mise en abyme can only present an appearance, a partial resemblance. The same applies obviously to the icon (see Eco, 1976). The perfect mise en abyme (that of the box of Dutch cocoa) is an illusion in literature.

To know there is in effect resemblance, the relationship between sign and meaning—conceived as the concept evoked by the referent—should be moreover describable in metadiscursive language. The verbal description which the investigator can make of the sign and the referent ought therefore to have an important element in common. As far as the nature of this sign is concerned, comparison with one category of signs which signify in the same way as the mise en abyme can be instructive: A mirror sends back the image of the reflected object. The replica resembles the object reflected. This notion of resemblance is found likewise in the notion of *icon*.

If the mise en abyme has in common with the icon its status as a *sign which signifies by resemblance*, it differs perhaps in its form. The mise en abyme should form an isolable whole, constituting an interruption, or, at the very least, a temporary alteration of the narrative.

Van Zoest (1977) distinguishes two groups, icons which occur at the level of phrase, micro-structural, and macro-structural icons. In the first case, it is easy to delimit the fragment in question, to isolate it, and to investigate whether it responds to the other criteria which constitute a mise en abyme. If Sartre calls his grandparents *Karlémami*, to denote the irritating character of their claustrophobic union, one can isolate the sign *Karlémami* which has visibly a meaning equally isolable; if the latter coincides with "the narrative as a whole" (to be specified further later on), which is not the case, the sign would be a mise en abyme; if not, it remains an icon. In the case of a macro-structural icon, the matter is less easily resolved. Two examples given by Van Zoest permit us to circle in on the problem.

The "disordered narration" in a fragment of Donald Barthelme's novel *Unspeakable Practices, Unnatural Acts* signifies the disorder in the life of the characters. (This example has been borrowed from Browne.) If this sign were a mise en abyme, it would be, according to Dällenbach, textual, with reflection by D' (the literal discourse in the reflection) of R (the referent of the entire text) (124–125). In Zola's *Le ventre de Paris*, the "narrative desolidarization" (a displacement of focalization which "withdraws" from the character), toward the end of the novel, is iconic, according to Van Zoest, for a "desolidarization on the plane of the fictional characters" (the protagonist is abandoned by his entourage at the moment of his arrest). Disregarding, for the moment, the difference between the referents of the two signs, one can claim that they could be mises en abyme if the textual unity constituting them were isolable. According to Dällenbach, this can only be the case if it is (hypo-)diegetic. This criterion is not always observed by Dällenbach himself, who accepts examples in which the focalization alone changes (see, for example, the texts from Beckett, 134; de Maupassant, 86; Zola, 64). Enlarging the criterion in this regard one would be able to accept the example drawn from *Le ventre de Paris* while rejecting the one drawn from Barthelme, which is not isolable from the whole text. Why not adopt here the same criterion as for the perception of signification: as long as one can *isolate* a fragment—eventually with the help of frontier-symptoms, at the level of the sign—this fragment can be a mise en abyme. Here, then, is a first distinction between the two notions based on the *form* of the sign.

As regards the sign itself, one can then attend to the example from Zola and see afterwards if the nature of the referent justifies the designation mise en abyme for the sign in question. According to Dällenbach, the referent of the mise en abyme is "the narrative as a whole." I have replaced these ambiguous terms with *a continuous aspect relevant and continuous to the text, to the story, or to the fabula.* The specification text-story-fabula is indispensable for distinguishing the different levels of signification, each of which can, even by Dällenbach's account, be mise en abyme. By "an aspect relevant and continuous" I mean to indicate that the meaning or the concept of the referent should concern the whole narrative, but it always will represent only one aspect of the whole: structure, the principal thread of the fabula, the dominant mode of narration, the vision (mistaken or correct) of some protagonist, etc. If however I add "relevant," it is because this aspect will not be perceived, hence, cannot be interpreted as mise en abyme, if it has a minor interest in the totality of the narrative. Obviously, to determine the relative interest of an aspect, one cannot but appeal to the receiver-reader. The reader will always be bound to be able to discern in the aspect in question an element which influences the total signification of the narrative in a decisive manner, in that it depends on the action of the characters or on their features, on the narration or on the focalization, even on the choice of words or on the figures of rhetoric.

This poses a problem for the hierarchization of signifying elements within the narrative text. The problem has been formulated by Philippe Hamon (1982) in a domain which appears to be the most restricted but is in fact quite difficult to grasp, that of character. The system of analysis which this author proposes, with the goal of giving solid semiological grounding to the distinction between heroes and secondary characters, demonstrates rather how complex such a hierarchization is.

Often also, the perspective is subverted by symptoms which attract the attention of the reader to the signifying function of a mise en abyme of the code, for example, where, without them, such a sign would pass unnoticed

These are notably the cases in which the mise en abyme functions as an operating manual, as a recipe for a satisfactory reading. It is, then, a sign which is *hypo-discursive* to the *meta-discursive* function: *from inside* the fabula, the sign addresses itself directly to the reader, *outside* the fabula, and gives bits of information *about* it. This is the case, often, of intercalated songs, such as in *Le voyeur*, or in the *L'après-midi de Monsieur Andesmas* by Duras. It is, then, the author who in the text valorizes the "code" which she employs and the attentive assenting reader will heed her instructions. Most often, signs of this category are, in my opinion, reducible to metaphorical icons: we will deal with this later.

To know if the example of *Le ventre de Paris* can function as a mise en abyme would require asking if the desolidarization manifested at the end of the text and in the denouement of the story is a crucial aspect of the signification of the novel as a whole. The temporal coincidence of the sign and the meaning (the desolidarization does not intervene until the end), which prevents the requisite condensation, is opposed to it (a "little" sign should signify a big text, hence the *summing up*). Not only the form of the sign but also the *status of the referent* differentiates thus the mise en abyme as a specific class of icons.

Finally, how does the sign signify? In other words, what is this "reduplication" which, in the literal sense, should consist of copying the book and which should therefore have a figurative sense? A return to iconicity obtrudes here since the icon, like the mise en abyme, signifies by resemblance.

Van Zoest notes that there are three types of relationship between the iconic sign and its meaning. If the relationship is spatial (figurative, pictural), one speaks of the *topological icon*. A well-known example is the blank page of *Le Voyeur*, a mise en abyme of the blank in the conscience of Matthias. A less familiar and less spectacular example of the same order is the blank page in *L'après-midi de Monsieur Andesmas*, whose meaning, also an omission, a blank in the conscience of a character due to a brief sleep hollows out a dramatic abyss between the phase of hope and the phase of despair. This last icon, however, is not a mise en abyme. If the repression by Matthias constitutes a pertinent and sustained aspect of the entire novel, the sleep of Monsieur Andesmas coincides with a precise moment of the fabula. In *Le Voyeur*, then, a topological mise en abyme, in *L'après-midi*, a topological icon.

The second category is that of diagrammatic icons in which the resemblance rests on the relationship between elements of the sign and on the relationship between elements of the meaning. Most of Dällenbach's examples which refer to "conspicuous text and code" (123 ff.) where D' (the form of the mise en abyme) reflects D (the form of the entire text) belong to this category.

Once again (124), the criterion will be the verbal description which the critic can make of the sign and its referent. If one analyzes in detail the description of Rouen in *Madame Bovary*, one comes to the conclusion that the elements of that description maintain among them a relationship of opposition between the positive and the negative, an opposition which manifests a structure fluctuating up to the point of resolving itself in an absolute negative.[2]

One can describe in the similar terms the relationship between the different elements (stages) in the life of Emma. If one agrees that this life, with these stages, constitutes a pertinent and continuous aspect of the novel (and it would be difficult to deny it), the description is a diagrammatic icon—mise en abyme.

The third category is that of the metaphorical icon, the most difficult to grasp. The sign likely to be called a metaphorical icon is characterized by the fact that it denotes two referents at the same time, one first, the other second. The connection with resemblance is, in this case, situated at the level of the relationship between the two referents. The criterion which permits the selection of such icons is the following: one can speak of a metaphorical icon if in the verbal description of the sign and the referent one employs a metaphor. The metaphor by itself alone is not an icon. But one is dealing with a metaphorical icon when a sign, in its function as well as in the description which one can make of it, involves metaphorical imagery.

In order to see the difference between the two last icons, the example of *The Trial*, invoked by Dällenbach as well as by Van Zoest, can be enlightening. Dällenbach considers as mise en abyme of the enunciation the parable which the priest recounts to K. In contrast to the protagonist of *The Fall of the House of Usher*, K. misapprehends the lesson which is propounded to him: he does not grasp the resemblance. Thus K resembles the receiver of the message in the parable which is recounted to him, in his relationship to the events which happen to him. This mise en abyme is a diagrammatic icon. *At the same time* the hypodiegetic character of the parable and K both resemble man in general, and the relationship between the character and that which happens to him resembles as well the relationship between K. and the events toward which he is hurtling, as well as the relationship between the reader and his life. This last relationship, mediated, can be connected to the narrative of *The Trial* only if the reader means to attribute to it this metaphorical signification. In this case, the signification becomes obviously a pertinent and continuous aspect of the novel: this metaphorical icon will be mise en abyme or it won't be.

Dällenbach's *mise en abyme of the code or textual mise en abyme* is most often a metaphorical icon without being a mise en abyme for all that. If, for example, the image of tissue (cloth) signifies the structure of the text, this "fictionalization" (131 ff.) by-passes the metaphor by the "parallelism in something else" of Peirce, since tissue does not present any primary resemblance to the text. It has a partial resemblance mediated by virtue of the metaphor:

---

2. This case is the subject of an extensive analysis in *On Story-Telling* (Bal 1991).

tissue-structure. But the structure and functioning of the text cannot, by definition, serve as meanings of mises en abyme, according to Dällenbach's criteria, since they do not take part in the fabula. Dällenbach in this respect contradicts his founding principles, derived from Gide's text: the mise en abyme should function in the diegetic universe, "on the scale of the characters." Moreover, it would be difficult to pretend that the fact of being structured (cf. tissue) or of functioning (cf. machine) constitutes a pertinent aspect of one novel rather than of another. Here it is simply a a trait considered characteristic of writing in general. There are, consequently, two reasons for denying to such an icon the status of mise en abyme: the absence of diegetic pertinence, and, in short, the absence of pertinence at all, in regard to a particular text.

In the final analysis, the radicalization of the mise en abyme in the Nouveau Nouveau Roman postulated by Dällenbach is, perhaps, at least in part, an abandonment of the mise en abyme itself, which, then, would be replaced by the metaphorical icon, less "fictional," less diegetic, which is in harmony with the decrease—almost to the point of destruction—in diegesis in the novels of this anti-mimetic trend.

Summarizing what precedes, one can say that every mise en abyme is an icon, topological, diagrammatic, or metaphorical, but that every icon is not a mise en abyme. What we have here is a sub-class of iconic signs. An icon can have any possible form; any phenomenon whether it is isolable or not from the entire text can function as an icon. The icon can be a mise en abyme if it constitutes an isolable textual unity, delimited by an interruption at some level whatever that is.

An icon can also have any possible meaning, pointing to any referent; but the meaning of an icon—mise en abyme will be an aspect pertinent and continuous to the entire novel. The meaning of a mise en abyme will thus be more *expansive* than that of the icon; it will stretch out on a grand scale while the sign itself will be in principle more *limited*.

Within the framework of this essay I will not explore the critical value of this concept, as I have done elsewhere (1987). Nor can I stop to explore the consequences of the ambiguity in the concept of reflection itself. In this essay, reflection refers to mirroring, reduplication, resemblance. But the difficulty to pinpoint resemblance already suggests that there is more at stake. As it happens, self-reflection, the key-word in contemporary critical discourse, is also central to mise en abyme. What is at stake, then, is the precise relationship between two forms of reflection: specular and discursive, which, as I argue in "Lots of Writing," seem to be in opposition. Indeed, specular reflection suggests a powerlessness, a submission to the directions given by the text. Such a passive reflection works against the critical project. That is why I resist the appeal to authorial intention. On the other hand, the very opposition between specular and discursive reflection obscures the role of the former within the latter. As many of the essays in this volume, and especially the essay on Esther suggest, as long as the concept of self-reflection is not theorized more consistently, critique, be it feminist, post-colonial, or marxist will miss its goal.

The purpose of this revisionist theory of mise en abyme is to free the concept from its idiosyncratic position, its confinement to French theory of a specifically aestheticizing kind. By inserting it within a semiotic typology of signs I hope to relieve it from its free-floating status, so that it can be of use in a critical project which musters semiotics to further our insight into ideological pressures of which each critic partakes.

3

Murder Story

In this chapter, which provides elements of my interpretation of Judges 4 and 5 as laid out in my book *Murder and Difference*, I will explore the possibilities for use of the concept of *ritual* for the interpretation of ancient texts. The concept is examined solely in its problem-solving capacities for the specific purpose of interpretation, and secondarily for the explanation of problems of interpretation. In order to be as specific as possible, and as the transposition of a concept from one discipline into another requires, I will discuss in some depth a single case of a text that scholars have found difficult to interpret, the account, in the biblical book of Judges, of Sisera's murder by Yael. I will try to argue that the concept of ritual, used as an "experience-distant" (Geertz) concept that allows the interpreter to bridge the gap between his or her framework and the context of the text, is indispensable (1) to avoid ethnocentric and sexist interpretation and (2) to interpret the text as a semiotic object at all. Hence, it serves the purpose of a critical analysis (in the Habermasian sense) as well as a subtle literary one, while it can be fruitfully integrated in the toolbox of women's studies. I will mainly draw from one paper by Turner (1967), not only because it provides a carefully formulated definition of ritual which defies too-easy transfer into a different discipline, but also because it discusses explicitly the relations between symbolic anthropology and other, related fields. Although the issue of ideology is not raised, I will argue that it is precisely the explicit discussion of interdisciplinary relations that allows us to integrate Turner's ideas, and the concept of ritual in particular, into ideological criticism.

THE CASE

The murder of Sisera by Yael has been found, in the history of exegesis, a most disturbing case. In the book of Judges, murder occurs quite frequently, sometimes within military action, sometimes in combination with rape, and sometimes within personal relations. Among all these violent events, there are three cases of the murder of a man by a woman. It is indirect in the case of Samson and Delilah, which appealed so strongly to the imagination that it has become one of the best-known stories of the Bible, although systematically distorted. The murder is changed at the very last moment into suicide when the tyrant Abimelech, who has his brain crushed by an anonymous woman, keeps just enough of it to ask his servant to kill him quickly in order to avoid the shame of being killed by a woman. The case is alluded to in II Samuel 11:21 in a most disturbing—reversed, that is—manner (Bal 1987); there are also three murders of women by men: Jephthah's daughter in Judges 11, Samson's first wife in Judges 14, and the Levite's wife in Judges 19. (These murders are discussed in Bal 1988, *Death and Dissymetry*.) Our case under consideration here is the third of this series. It is narrated in detail, and as a result the story is almost as tough as the rape and murder of a woman by men in chapter 19, which is definitely less often discussed. Yael's act is disturbing: on the one hand, the victim is an enemy of the people, so the woman is doing well; but on the other hand, she is a woman and kills a man, and this is just not done. Obviously the case raises the problem of conflicting loyalties for the massively male readers who have commented on the text (for an extensive account of commentaries, see *Murder and Difference*). Second, the case is disturbing because the cruel details are expanded in the text, as are the horrible and taboo-transgressing procedures and the explicitly mentioned shame befalling not only the victim but also, in one of the versions of this story, the failing executioner, the leader Barak who shares his enemy's shame.

The third reason why the case is problematic is the most interesting one, and makes it available for my purpose in this chapter. It consists of the doubling of the account. Indeed, the story is narrated twice, in chapter 4 and in chapter 5 of the book. Moreover, the first version is part of the epic tradition and is generally attributed to a male poet; the second version is part of the famous Song of Deborah and is generally attributed to a female voice (although the latter attribution is less general than the former). The epic version is considered the more recent one; the lyric version is seen as one of the oldest texts of the Hebrew Bible (not necessarily in its present form; see van Dijk-Hemmes 1988). Hence, questions of date, of genre, and of gender seem to be related.

The interpretation of ancient texts requires that historical considerations are integrated; furthermore, the history of their reception cannot be ignored, since it is *with* their subsequent reading traditions that they have reached us; moreover, the key moments of that tradition have to be explained. These extra considerations are needed because of the otherwise unbridgeable gap between the context and function of the texts in their past and the present use made of them. The case of Yael, then, poses the following problems of interpretation:

(1) What are the differences between the two accounts?
(2) Why are there two accounts at all, and why have both been integrated into the canon?
(3) Why is it that critics react so emotionally to this murder, much more so than in other, similar cases?
(4) Why are critics inclined to ignore or explain away the differences between the two accounts, conflating them in their emotional reaction to the event?
(5) Why is the question of gender of the respective poets so rarely seriously discussed?
(6) What is the relation between ethnocentrism and sexism in these reactions, and in what way does the text provoke them?

These problems can be solved with the substantial help offered by Turner's discussion of ritual. But why and how is that concept applicable at all?

RITUAL AND TEXT

"By 'ritual' I mean prescribed formal behavior for occasions not given over to technological routine, having reference to beliefs in mystical beings or powers," writes Turner (1967: 19) in his theoretical paper that serves here as a basic methodological subtext. At first sight, this definition makes the application to written texts, whose contexts have necessarily been lost, highly problematic. One side issue, however, the relation between ritual symbols and social values, helps us solve this problem: "dominant symbols are regarded not merely as means to the fulfillment of the avowed purposes of a given ritual, but also and more importantly refer to values that are regarded as ends in themselves" (20). This enlarged view of the basic units of ritual allowed Turner to develop his ideas of the place, function, and importance of ritual in society, which constitutes in my view one of his major contributions. It allows textual critics to start at the other end, at the symbol, that is, and reverse the argument that then comes to lead to the assumption that a given unit, once conceived of as a symbol, can be understood much better if considered part of a ritual, with the social implication that entails.

The book of Judges contains stories where the element of ritual is explicitly mentioned (the weeping over Jephthah's daughter) or which are not understandable without the assumption that there is a ritual involved (the dance before the bride-capture scene in the last chapter), or which are utterly unacceptable, hence their incorporation into the canon, incomprehensible without a ritual context (the cutting into twelve pieces of the dead body of the murdered woman in chapter 19). The assumption that this body of texts has partly originated from ritual traditions is therefore plausible beforehand. Second, in the case of Yael, one element of the story is generally acknowledged as ritualistic: the invitation of Yael addressed to the weary Sisera on his flight from the battlefield, which is assumed to be part of the hospitality ritual so sacred in the ancient Mediterranean area. Third, the hospitality ritual can be pointed at because of the fixed, stereotyped language used. *Verbal* elements of rituals share with nonverbal symbols the qualities of condensation, unification of disparate signification, polarization of meanings, and the implication of several distinct levels of the social order (Turner 1967: 28). I will argue that it is only through the assumption that this is the case that the invitation scene (Judges 4:18) can be interpreted at all.

A fourth argument in favor of a ritualistic interpretation can be laid out only in the course of analysis. A great number of details that are generally acknowledged as striking or problematic receive an integrated meaning when conceived of as ritual symbols. This concordance argument shall come to stand in the place of the informants that we will by necessity do without, supported in this function by the reception of the texts. A fifth argument can be used as a background for the enterprise. Literature has, by its linguistic and cultural nature, a mediating function between the individual and the social motivations. This mediating function, according to Turner (37), characterizes the ritual symbol as well. The integration of social norms and individual desires can be acted out, ideally, through language, since the expression of fantasies in language is culturally validated and allows for otherwise unacceptable thoughts to escape from repression. Language itself shares this conjunction of the utterly individual and the utterly social in its functions as a tool that bridges the gap between the two as far as it is possible at all.

The implications of this commonplace idea have been seen as far-reaching: literature, or art in general for that matter, has been considered a form of ritual. Hardin rightly argues against such a generalization, that, first, it deprives the concept of the limitation indispensable for any concept to be of use, and, second, it ignores the basic difference between ritual and representation, as that between a happening and the representation of a happening. Nevertheless, the mediating function of representation allows for two ways of conceiving of art, not as identical but as related to ritual to a certain extent. On the one hand, ritual can be represented, as is the case within the dialogue between Sisera and Yael in Judges 4. On the other hand, the participation in a representational practice can be, under specified circumstances, such as oral, communal performance, a ritual practice. The common aspects between ritual and a literary event, such as the use of condensed symbols, repetition, community, make for a relation that allows us not to equate the two but to understand the one better through insight into the other.

This, however, entails a paradox. The very loss of the context which, as I have argued, necessitates the use of ritual for interpretation makes it extremely difficult to provide evidence for it. As a result, a ritualistic interpretation can never be tested. In order to make up for this, I will try to show that some textual problems and elements make a better case than others, while those are at the same time the cases that needed the concept most badly. If literature as a process can be considered ritual, there is no point in such a general claim. Therefore, I will not develop it in general but rather will try to distinguish different levels of meaning where the concept of ritual is helpful, and delimit where it ceases to be specific enough.

Earlier I termed the concept "experience-distant." In this sense, it helps to make Turner's distinction in levels of meaning operational. Where the latter argues (1967: 48–58) that exegetical or indigenous interpretation sometimes closes off the interpretative process itself, Geertz would formulate the same problem differently: the closure is brought about by our incapacity to understand experience-near concepts. This distinction not only is a welcome justification for me for dealing with biblical material as a relative outsider, but also will help delimit the field of application of the concepts. Turner's second level, the operational, indicates what the symbol does within a given ritual. This level can be conceived of as the bridge between the two sets of concepts. The positional meaning specifies what a symbol means within its semantic field in the given case; this will allow me to differentiate, within the text, the presence of different semantic fields, which entails the misunderstanding between the two characters that brings the event about.

These preliminary remarks are meant to both justify and present the use of the concept of ritual in a differential interpretation of the two accounts of Sisera's murder. In order to gain space, I will not go into the details of the history of the reception of these texts, which I have done elsewhere *(Murder and Difference)*. I will start with a first analysis that should enhance the difference and the need for the anthropological concept.

DIFFERENCE

The two fragments of the murder scene both occur toward the end of the respective chapters; both are followed by one closing episode. The murder scenes are as follows:

Judges 5:24–27
24. Blessed above [the] women be Yael the wife of Cheber the Kenite above [the] women in the tent blessed.
25. He asked for water milk she gave in a lordly bowl she handed him cream.
26. Her hand she stretched out to the tent peg her right hand to the worker's hammer and she hammered Sisera, she smashed his head and she shattered and pierced his temple.
27. Between her feet he collapsed, fell down, he lay still between her feet he collapsed, he fell down there where he had sunk, he fell down, destroyed/mastered.

64 ■ ON MEANING-MAKING

Judges 4:17-21
17. And Sisera fled on his feet to the tent of Yael, the wife of Cheber the Kenite, for peace between Jabin King of Hazor and the house of Cheber the Kenite.
18. And Yael went out to meet Sisera and said unto him: Turn in my lord, turn in to me, fear not. And he turned in to her, to the tent and she covered him with a covering.
19. And he said unto her: Let me, pray, drink a little water for I am thirsty. And she opened the milkbag and she gave him to drink and she covered him.
20. And he said unto her: Stand in the opening of the tent and it shall be when a man comes and he asks you and says: is here a man, you shall say: none.
21. And Yael the wife of Cheber took the peg and she took the hammer in her hand and she came softly unto him and she smote the peg into his temple and it penetrated the ground and he was in a deep sleep and he was weary and he died.

Since the lyric version is often taken to be historically the first, I have put it first here, too; I assume the order of the sequence does have some impact on the reading of the two passages. The canonical order is not impossible, but it seems useful to estrange the texts from their traditional readings.

The lyric version (5) devotes four verses to the murder. One is praise of Yael, one describes the ceremony that precedes the murder, one the act itself, and one the agony. The epic version (4) has three verses which describe the ceremony of the encounter, one has a dialogue on Sisera's initiative, and one describes both the act of the murder and the victim's death.

A first comparison shows that the lyric is more extensive on the killing and the agony, while the epic is more elaborate on the encounter, and shortens the description of the murder and death. This distribution of topics points at a significant difference on focus, and forms the starting point for the analysis. Let me first draw a guideline from the direct context, which is revealing here. In the epic version, considered younger, Deborah is "quoted" by the poet as threatening her partner Barak when the latter dares not undertake the battle without Deborah's help. The threat consists of the prophecy of this murder: if Barak needs Deborah's help, then the enemy will fall by the hand of a woman. This attribution to Deborah of an "ideologeme" (ideological unit, see Jameson) that relates the opposition honor/shame to that between the sexes, *is entirely absent from the lyric version* and can be considered therefore a contribution of the male subject. Being specific to the version uttered by the male voice, it is a neat example of *projection:* the woman who represents shame is supposed to utter its conditions. It can be represented as in figure 1.

The murder scene is the imaginary realization of this fantasy. In the epic version, the issue of honor and shame is stressed throughout the whole story. Commentaries have indicated Barak, the leader of the Israelite army, as its real victim. He consumes his shame as a *focalizer* (for this concept, see Bal 1986); he *hears* Deborah utter the threat, and he *sees* the result when confronted with Sisera's body in Yael's tent. Sisera's annihilation is in fact Barak's. This narratological structure reflects the projection hypothesis: the *focalizer*, he who *has* the fantasy, makes the woman who is the major character in his fantasy be its actor, carry it out.

This necessitates a subtle, analytical treatment of the category of the *subject*. The primary subject, the male voice, delegates the task of utterance of the ideologeme to a female voice, but the latter exists only as embedded in the male voice; the subject of action, the active murderess as well as the active prophetess and second military leader, is doing only what the male fantasy supposes her to do. It is the *subject of focalization,* although, or perhaps because, utterly passive, who is the most characteristic subject of this fiction.

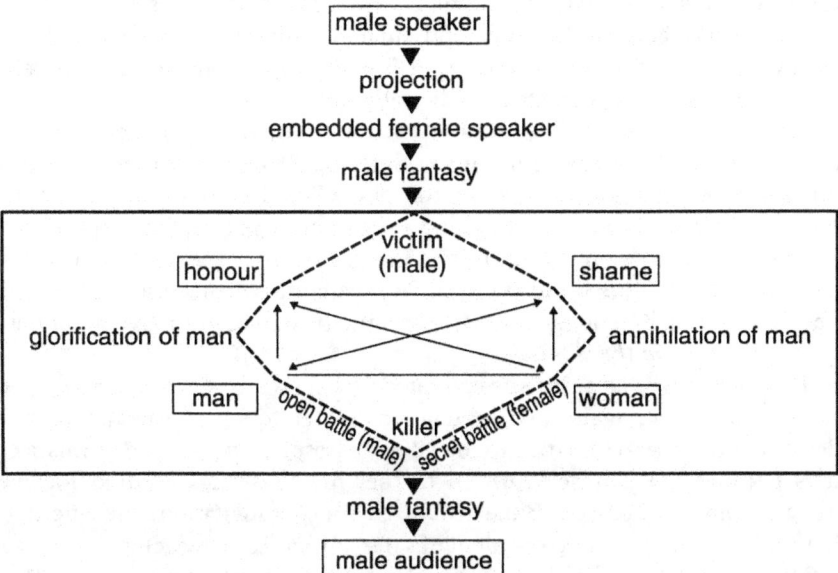

These narratological categories will not be elaborated here, but one point has to be enhanced. The question who, in a given text, can be considered the subject of a given narrative act, pertains not only to narrative analysis in itself. It will be shown shortly that those questions have their bearing on the decision whether, and to what extent, the concept of ritual applies. What functions as a ritual symbol for one subject may be devoid of such a function for another. The difference between the ritual and the directly pragmatic function of language makes for the misunderstanding between Yael and Sisera in the epic version, and for the profound difference between the two versions as a whole.

RITUAL LANGUAGE

The question that arises from this is: why is this honor/shame opposition so important, and why should it be related to the opposition between the sexes?

In other words: how arose this particular "ideologeme" that differentiates the epic version from the lyric? It is here, I would venture, that the concept of ritual can be of help, in several respects. It will help to understand the text, but through that understanding, it will help undercut the essentialist view of gender that makes sex-specific views seem universal, and historically specific views seem eternal. In other words, it will serve the purpose of both literary analysis and feminist critique.

The leader Sisera, whose superiority was defined by the iron chars he had and the Israelites did not have, ceases to exist as a powerful social subject when he leaves his char while quitting his army. Between the moment of abdication of his social position and the moment when Barak focalizes his dead body, Sisera's world becomes smaller and smaller. Arriving at Yael's tent, he is trapped between the two armies, in a friendly camp, but one which is only recently and ambivalently so; he is literally lost.

We can formulate this in a more experience-distant language. Sisera has been separated from his community. Entering a domain where loyalties are unclear, where his position is marginal, and where he can be only in a state of transition, he seems to be undergoing a rite of passage (van Gennep). If that is the case, the next step should be the integration into the adult world. I will argue shortly that this is indeed what Sisera attempts to accomplish but which he fails to succeed in doing, precisely because he fails to grasp the *ritual nature of the "passage," of the transition.*

How can this claim be substantiated? First, we have to examine Yael's words—projected, again, by the male voice that "quotes," invents them. Indeed, if critics are so sensitive to the taboo of hospitality involved in this scene, it is because the phrase "turn in to me, my lord" has a ritual meaning. Throughout the Hebrew Bible it is used for the invitation, the offering of hospitality, which is the equivalent of safety. It has the character of a formula, a fixed phrase that will always have the same form whenever used within a similar context. It is this context that gives it the connotation of safety. For the weary traveler, especially when the latter is fleeing from a major danger, the phrase is welcomed as an absolute guarantee. So much so that the next phrase, "fear not," which seems part of it, is disturbingly superfluous. The insistence on safety, in a negatively formulated second phrase, introduces the possibility of misunderstanding and abuse.

In fact, "fear not" *is* equally a ritually symbolic expression, but not within the same ritual. Quite to the contrary, it is part of the exhortation to battle. It is within this context that it is used throughout the war reports of the Bible. For an experienced military man, the phrase should have rung a bell; for the initiate in the state of transition that Sisera has become in the meantime, it is evidence only of his radical dispossession that he fails to grasp the contradictory character of the statement as a whole. What Yael is proposing, then, is an invitation to battle within the usually safe harbor of her home. The opposition between these two meanings is mediated by a third possible ritual meaning: sexual initiative. It is only when we assume that the scene is a mixture of the two well-known rituals that we are able to notice that both are repeated within the tent, where the woman covers and feeds the man, and next, kills him. When we provisionally maximize the ritualistic assumption, we will be sensitive to this repetitive structure.

How, then, can the sexual domain be integrated at this point? We know that there is another ritual known from biblical sources, and that is the election of the sexual partner. The strongest evidence is given in Genesis 24, where the whole procedure is narrated *four* times. It consists of asking for water and then getting more; the surplus given by the woman indicates her as the chosen. Yael is thus proposed as a sexual partner (Zakovitch). At the same time, the surplus she offers differentiates water, as the minimal condition of life, from food, as the beginning of restoration, of new life, in this case *milk*, the beginning of life.

If this ritual is implied here, it becomes inevitable to integrate the set of rituals as played out within the *rite of passage*, as van Gennep has examined and Turner further analyzed them (van Gennep, Turner 1969). In this ritual, social roles are reversed; here, the former leader is represented in a state of absolute dependency, isolation from the world, regressing to the very beginning of life. The ritual provokes strong anxiety, and in fact, the capacity of living through this anxiety is the primal test the initiate undergoes. Sisera fatally fails to recognize the ritual, hence the temporal character of the situation as well as the conventional need to respect and accept it. He displays his lack of insight when trying to escape the position that has befallen him by giving an order for which he does not qualify.

That is indeed his fatal mistake: Sisera tries to reestablish the contact with the outside world which would undo the ritual situation. He significantly attempts to secure the border between inside and outside, while he gives an order to her who has over him the absolute power of a mother over her baby. Ironically, he does so by inadvertently confirming that he does not qualify: making use of the possibility of ambiguous use of fixed expressions in Hebrew, the poet makes him say "none" as the required answer to the possible question, "Is there a man in here?"

The scene within the tent, indeed, is a repetition of the invitation scene. Again, Yael has the initiative; again, care and war are mixed. And again, the two characters speak a different language, Yael speaking that of the rite of passage, Sisera only acknowledging the hospitality ritual. The dialogues between the two characters represent but one level of meaning. At the level of the diegesis, of what happens, the other factors play their part. The tent itself, as the location of the (ritual) death, represents the site of the rite of passage. Within that space, there is again a mirroring unit that reflects the separation brought about, respectively, by Sisera's flight from his army, his arrival at the intermediate space of the friendly camp within the enemy's territory, his enclosure within the tent. There is a word used here which scholars have taken great pains to translate: the word indicating the object used by Yael to cover Sisera. The word is a "hapax," and one can only guess what it means. Some (Boling) say blanket or fly-net, the one being related to the act of covering, the other to the ethnographic context (the climate). *Curtain* is another possibility. Zakovitch insists that the object does function as a blanket, and derives from that function the sexual connotation of the event. The meaning *curtain* connoting also the bed scene, since beds in hot climates can have curtains, seems to me the most stimulating translation because it connotes equally well *separation:* the curtain around the bed makes for the function of the doorway, so crucial in ancient literature, as the border, the very site of transition from one state to another. What the doorway, and the neutral domain of the camp, refer to in the first part of the episode, the curtain then comes to indicate in the mirroring indoor scene.

I can hardly blame the reader who would feel that there is some excess in this ritualistic view. Indeed, there is a dizzying number of rituals involved, and the repetition of the whole set makes for another ritual aspect. I will try to justify the apparently loose use of the concept later; here, it is relevant to notice that Sisera himself has been entangled in this complex whole of ritualistic language and behavior. And that is precisely the idea. As Boling put it, Sisera is duped and doped by the same move. Doped: the goat milk offered to him when he asked for water is said to have been slightly somniferic; some argue (Zakovitch) that milk here is a euphemism for wine, and that before the murder, the couple had a merry party. The doping adds to the duping, by the false offer of hospitality and safety, of food, rest, and loving care. Critics have been particularly keen to stress these aspects of the story. Their sensitivity to them suggests that we should take this pragmatic dimension into account. How can it be explained?

The most striking features of this epic version of the murder scene should be considered apologetic. The episode is made up of explanations of or, I would say, excuses for, Sisera's death. This links the ritualistic analysis to the honor/shame problem. Even an enemy of the people needs excuses for getting killed by a woman, and the excuses consist exactly of those factors that relate honor and gender: the ritual of social relations (hospitality) and of military bravery (exhortation to battle) are related to the election of the sexual partner, the motherly care, and are all integrated in the rite of passage that suspends Sisera's manhood until he shows, by his attempt at escape, that he cannot face the anxiety it represents. Choosing to be "no man," then, he cannot survive the ritual. As a non-man, he will *undergo* the penetration, in his soft flesh, of the hard object, that men are supposed to *perform*. What I am interested in, so far, is the *representation* of danger for the male sex by the rite of passage and more specifically by the tent of the woman, in other words, the female domain, in this semi-nomadic culture where the rite is accomplished, combined with the stress on apologizing explanation. It is obviously from the point of view of the honor/shame opposition that Sisera's fate has to be *excused*.

All this is in the epic, not in the lyric, text. If the epic version is indeed younger, we can consider these specific additions; in any case, I submit that these relations between honor/shame and gender are specific for the male voice. It is easy to understand why, on the other hand, details have been *suppressed*—again, if we can take this epic to be a response to the lyric. The most striking difference here is the shortness of the account of Sisera's death. Instead of the extensive description of his agony, we find only the verb "died" preceded by, again, an explanation. Modern translations, which replace the general Hebrew conjunction by conjunctions of causal relations, have: he was in a deep sleep, because weary, *so* he died. He died because he was sleeping, and he slept because he was weary. The fantasy is full of *causal logic*, and that is perhaps its most characteristic feature. (This may be relevant also within the problematic of orality-literacy, since one feature of orality is the style of juxtaposition; see Ong; Lemaire.)

YAEL AT WORK

In order to understand *what* exactly has been suppressed in this remarkable shortness of the representation of death, we have to take a closer look at the representation, by the female voice of Deborah, of the "same" event. The first striking difference is, of course, the phrase that introduces the murder: "blessed above the women be Yael," repeated with the addition "above the women *in the tent."* (Fokkelien van Dijk-Hemmes wrote an extensive study of this phrase in her assessment of the relations between Judges 4 and 5, in which she assumes the lyric to be a Midrash on the epic.) The change in what is considered "blessed" for a woman is an obviously relevant issue. Let me just point out that the praise of Yael by Deborah, suppressed from the epic version, disturbs many commentators who use it as evidence of the "primitive" and even "savage" spirit of this very early text. It seems obvious that such a judgment is based on implicit sexism, combined with ethnocentrism and the straightforward evolutionism that usually supports it. Moreover, such hasty and unwarranted—and irrelevant—evaluations ignore generic difference. The Song of Deborah has many of these enthusiastic appraisals, none of which are called "primitive" by the critics, and which are a feature of the lyric as a genre. The problem here is clearly the conflict of loyalties pointed at earlier. Yael is blamed not so much for killing but for killing a man while being a woman, thus bringing shame upon her victim. Her praise by Deborah is therefore not acceptable for whoever identifies with the victim of shame.

A second "detail" that has disappeared in the later version is the cream handed to him in a lordly bowl. The lordly bowl contrasts with the worker's hammer, while the cream is the third element of an instance of the device, common in lyrical poetry, of a gradation in three phases. Finally, the repetition in the description of Sisera's agony and death has been described by many commentators as set in a tone of "savage delight" and as "the gloating preservation of the gruesome details," and has been blamed systematically.

The epic version presents, in a circular structure, a series of male characters—the king Jabin, the leader Barak, the enemy leader Sisera, then back to Barak, and ending with Jabin—and in the epic Sisera is the center of that structure and the mediator between the parties involved, as well as the principal character. The episode in the Song of Deborah represents only one character that acts as a subject: the woman Yael. In the introduction of this character, her sex and her *place* are specified. The phrase "the women in the tent" reminds us of Sara, whose only subversive action—standing in her tent, she *laughed*—disturbed fellow characters (the messengers of the lord) and critics, and reminds us of the division of labor and space in the semi-nomadic society of the days. This "detail" has an important structural function to which we shall return. Yael is the main character. Her name is mentioned, while the name of Sisera is replaced by a pronoun. Grammatically, Yael is the subject of all verbs save the verb "asked," which implies dependency on the addressee, and the verbs of verse 27 which express Sisera's suffering. Sisera becomes the subject of active verbs, becomes a character only at the moment of his destruction.

Verse 25 has a parallel construction in three phases, a classical tricolon. In the epic, the gradation *water-milk-cream* has been replaced by a simple binary opposition between the minimal water and the nourishing milk. Moreover, the framework of the ritual of hospitality is absent from the lyric version. If we take the "lordly bowl" also into consideration, we have a gradation going from the water as minimal supply for survival, through milk as nourishment, to a sumptuous treat. As such, the gradation points at the honorable reception that befalls Sisera. The lordly bowl signifies the honor that becomes a man who is allowed to enter into the female domain. But this gesture has a ritual aspect as well, as the honor that accompanies the sentenced-to-death. Most striking, the *honor* is represented here outside the opposition honor/shame which gave it its meaning in the epic version. The honorable reception of Sisera is simply due to the *other* who visits Yael in her domain.

The lordly bowl stands also in sharp contrast to the laborer's hammer. The honored guest is treated not only as honorable but, by the same token, also as a non-laborer, as a useless member of society. The worker's hammer, by contrast, is the instrument of work, of daily life, of activity, and in the case of nomadic tribes where the task of dressing the tents was the women's part, it is the instrument of female activity. Taking the worker's hammer, Yael is treating the intruder as a *stranger* who came to transgress the limits between the world of work and the world of social hierarchy on the one hand, and the world of women and the world of men on the other.

It is not surprising, then, that the following verse presents Yael *at work*. Indeed, manipulating the instruments of the world of labor that her society has assigned to her as a woman, she accomplishes the gestures that represent her work. At the same time, she acts as a member of the larger group wherein the group of women is integrated by destroying the enemy of the people to which she decided to belong. The verse requires the combination of two codes to be understandable: a political code, which would stress the integration of what happens in the life of the semi-nomadic tribe, and a sex-specific code that would stress the relation of what happens to gender. The theme that is thus enhanced can then be described as the ritual suspension of the transgression of limits between different worlds.

REALISM VERSUS REPRESENTATION

Consequently critics address one question here. How is it possible that Yael could kill Sisera who, in this version, is supposed to be standing or sitting, and not asleep? The question is related to a realistic view of representation which is not necessarily relevant in the case of mythical expression of fantasies. If we compare the two versions, we can assume that the author of the epic version was worried by the same question, and answered it, as we have seen, by alleging apologetic explanations. Some critics, including talmudic commentators (quoted by Zakovitch), go even further. If the epic author specifies that Sisera was killed *because* he was asleep, and asleep *because* he was weary, they follow this track and assume that he was weary *because* he was drunk, doped, or/and exhausted by sexual efforts; drunk *because* the goat milk was somniferic, and according to some, Yael gave him wine instead of milk. In short: he could be killed because Yael has duped him, and the circle is complete. Realism, then, is related to sexism: in order to be *true*, logically motivated, that is, the account must blame the woman.

Realistically speaking, the gesture *is* indeed, hardly likely. The tent peg was of wood, we may assume, since the military inferiority of the Israelites was due to the fact that they did not have iron. Yael beats the enemy with her own weapons, in her own domain. Imagining the gesture as accomplished on the temple of an awake man, and according to the poetic rhythm of the verse, we cannot but wonder: was he "really" standing? The penetration of the hard object into the soft flesh, in the hammering rhythm, is doubtless one of the "details" that have suggested the so-often-proposed sexual interpretation of this scene. Within such an interpretation, Yael is courting Sisera with the honorable reception that she gives him, and she qualifies, according to the ritual selection of the sexual partner, as his future wife. Her generosity becomes slightly ironical then: the ritual prescribes that she give *more* than the water that was asked for; by giving still more, she is pushing it. But her hammering points to a reversal of sexual roles.

The problem at stake involves the status of literature in relation to representation, and entails its distinction from ritual. It has been advanced (Hardin) that literature and ritual are incompatible at precisely this point. Since ritual involves the participation of the community in and for which it functions, the idea of representation would undermine its very effect. The question is pernicious, because representation is an ambiguous concept in itself, but it has to be answered in order for the place of the concept of ritual in literary studies to be specified. I will return to it shortly; in order to make a convincing case, I will first have to go further into the problem of this case. The question was: was he really standing? To put it differently: is the question of his position simply not taken into account, considered irrelevant? That cannot be. For in the next verse, it is specified that he fell.

My answer to the realistic question will have to be, then, that, ignoring the standard of realism, the poetess presents him as standing *because he had to fall*. To fall is not only the passage from the standing position to lying down; it is also the transition from the position of the respectable leader to that of annihilation, from life to death; and, according to those who read the text within the isotopy of sexuality, the transition from sexual tension to post-orgasmic relaxation. The verb is repeated three times, and at the end of the gradation, the result is given: destroyed, which is, significantly, the same verb as "mastered." The question of realistic plausibility, then, is relevant only from the point of view of the later epic version; as it stands, the lyric version has a strong internal logic, where the position of the victim is motivated from the point of view of the major event to which all the other events lead.

So, he had to fall, for yet another reason. He had to fall in order to activate the thematic line that was latent in the milk motif, and which receives a place, here, in a quite different structure. According to Yair Zakovitch, who summarizes rabbinic commentaries in his plea for a sexual reading of both versions, the phrase "between her feet" is the strongest evidence for such a reading. The phrase is striking indeed, for its concretely bodily aspect, and its repetition stresses it. But I doubt whether the sexual imagery is so clear *here*, for I consider this conflation of the body with sexuality a simplistic fallacy, informed by a simplified view of psychoanalysis. As recent feminist studies have pointed out, the relationship between mother and child is also a bodily one (e.g., Gallop; Hirsch). Interestingly, "between her feet he sank" echoes directly Deuteronomy, and there, in 28:57, it describes *afterbirth*. The logic of Zakovitch's argument is not quite clear: he finds in the idea of the placenta evidence for the theme of sexual pleasure! If we take a closer look at the passage in Deuteronomy, we find that the phrase represents the utmost *misery;* the afterbirth, there, is eaten by the woman who produces it, and the image does depict the misery that will befall the disobedient people. *If* the image of mothering is inherent to the milk motif, it must be in order to oppose it ironically to this negative, absolute representation of regression in relation to the mother. The nursed baby becomes a failed baby, and even that only token of beginning existence regresses back, eaten by where it came from.

The image *is* disturbing. How can we interpret it? Sisera's destruction is not represented here in the fantasy of shame as opposed to social honor, opposing man to non-man. It is represented in three phases which appeal to the resources of fantasy at the disposal of women in a social context where their place is so constricted. He falls, he stops living, he returns to the phase of the beginning of life in order to make a false start as afterbirth, as aborted. In other words, language, here, tries to express that he *has never existed*. The opposition man/non-man, which is predicated upon the derogation of women in the epic, turns out to be a resentful perversion of the opposition human/non-human, predicated upon the power of women to give or to withhold life as potential mothers.

Using the verb "to express" here is to opt for representation as opposed—if it is indeed to be considered as its antonym—to ritual. Two levels have to be distinguished. On the level of the text as it stands, we cannot but conclude that the language of the Song is basically different from the formulaic phrases in the epic version. If the latter are fragments of a body of ritualistic language at the disposal of those who participated in the performance of these texts as oral poems, the evocation of Sisera's death in the Song is not, as far as we can ever know, related to such stereotyped language. This is not to say that the Song lacks ritual aspects. It has the status of a ritual as a whole, as far as it has been sung, probably at a festival commemorating the battle. The force of Deborah as leader, poetess, and prophet makes her an ideal ritual performer (Bal, *Murder and Difference*). But the fragment of her Song under consideration here is precisely that narrative part of it that has no ritual function separately. If the introductory phrase "Blessed be Yael . . ." certainly suggests audience participation, there is no event other than the cathartic emotions that is the purpose of it; hence, calling this narrative a ritual as narrative would be pointless.

It is the cathartic effect in its specifically female character here, as distinct from the specifically male apologetic flavor of the epic version, that has been misunderstood later or, perhaps, too well understood by those who reacted so violently to it. The effect has to be seen as historically specific, and ethnographic circumstances cannot be ignored. In a society where women are "in the tent," where their position is restricted by a strong division of labor, the moments when they have power over a man are likely to be limited and specific to gender roles. The confrontation of a woman with the enemy of her people liberates the imagination of the reversal of power positions. How is it when a woman has power over a man? The images that come, liberated as they are from the constraints of the epic tradition that is not involved in the Song, are metonymically inspired by the experiences of power this woman can imagine: to kill, to cohabit, to give birth. To kill takes the form of a reversal of sexual intercourse, of a reversal of birth-giving. The woman penetrates the man, the mother eats the child. The pleasure of this power is the pleasure of the subversion of roles, as a carnival (Bakhtin; Morson and Emerson), within the very limited space assigned to women: the tent. To be, as a character, the representation of this pleasure makes Yael "blessed above the women in the tent."

Is this to suggest that, as soon as women are free to fantasize, they become cruel monsters, abusing their power over life? In other words, should the fantasizing man of the epic version feel he is right to fear women and to feel ashamed of being involved with them? It is here that the concept of ritual as I have used it can help to avoid both ethnocentrism and gynephobia.

THE FOREST OF RITUALS

"I came to see performances of ritual as distinct phases in the social processes whereby groups became adjusted to internal changes and adapted to their external environment. From this standpoint the ritual symbol becomes a factor in social action, a positive force in an activity field." This is how Turner (1967: 20) substantiates his claim that ritual is basically a social process, and yet relates to the mental life of individuals. The methodological consequences of this conjunction are numerous, and include the necessity to differentiate the meaning of symbols in each context. This is crucial in the interpretation of the Sisera murder. Although the "event" is most surely the same, there is no similarity whatsoever between the meaning of this event in the two accounts. This seemingly obvious conclusion has, to my knowledge, never been reached. At the level of the cathartic effect of each account for the participating audience—say, the least "ritual" of all ritual aspects involved, and in any case the least specific—the meanings are in no way related. The most striking feature here is not so much the shift in the stress laid on the agony versus on the circumstances surrounding it, but the importance of the opposed character. Where Sisera is utterly futile for the evocation of female power in the hallucinatory representation of such a situation, Yael is extremely important, more so than Sisera himself, in the epic representation of female danger and the shame it entails. This has to be so because the function assigned to the woman here is that of the scapegoat (Girard) who is by definition the most relevant character where the scapegoat is the issue.

In this reconstruction, the literary process has the exorcizing effect that rituals can have also. This is not to say that a text *is* a ritual; in certain ways, it *functions as* one. This is a first level where ritualistic interpretation can have something to say. The context, not the text, or rather, as Culler argued, the pressure of the framing on the text; the audience, not the author; emotions, not cognition, determine in what way the two processes are related. The epic text functions, by its effect of relief when the scapegoat is expelled, to strengthen the community. This is how the temporarily revolutionary effect of ritual is ultimately conservative: the evocation of Sisera's liminal position releases the acceptance of a social order where a leader such as he has the power that structures the group. Rephrased in experience-near language, this amounts to the following caricatural idea: let the woman have power for a moment, feel the anxiety that situation triggers, and you will never let her have it again.

A second level of ritualistic interpretation is at stake when one claims that a given text is *about* a ritual, that there is ritual in a text. This is not the case in the Song of Deborah, while it may be the case in the epic version. If critics react emotionally to the violation of the hospitality rite, it is because they have been made aware that such a rite is "told." The belief in rules as powers whose transgression/offense will necessarily endanger the social order, as distinct from the view of rules as patterns of behavior willingly submitted to for the sake of the community, makes for the feeling that the promise of hospitality *entails* safety, makes one *feel* safe. Sisera's behavior in the tent, his mistaken reappropriation of the commander's position, represents, hence is about, the strong feeling that ritual brings forth: the certainty of magic.

The third level, which is also absent—or not traceable—in the Song and strongly present in the epic, is the synecdochical adoption of ritual. The insertion in the dialogue of portions of ritual language is not a representation in the thematic sense. The text, here, is not "about" ritual, but inserts it, integrates it. Fragments of the text can receive a context that is ritual, while at the same time they keep their semantic function in the text. The relations are graphically represented in figure 2, where the square (the magic box) is part of the text and part of the ritual, each only partially. The double co-text thus provided makes such a fragment particularly "symbolic" in Turner's sense: condensed, contradictory, multileveled. Since different rituals are involved at this level, formulas receive a different meaning for each antagonist. "Fear not" means "safety" for Sisera; "you are at war" for Yael; and the answer dictated "no man" means, within the one context "hiding," hence "safe," and within the other "nonexistent," hence "dead." The two characters appeal, then, to a different exegetic meaning, and therefore, their semantic fields are incompatible.

If interpreted in this way, the text does not need to appeal to common sense or moral standards, nor does it need to be "excused" for its cruelty by ethnocentric contempt. There is, moreover, not so much a matter of opposition between the two accounts, but a deep, irreducible difference. The experiences involved are ultimately gender-specific. The language used is generically specific, and one can venture that the two are related. What is "primitive," ancient, that is, becomes a matter of the entire process. Perhaps the allegedly older text is so striking—or even considered older—because it is concerned so exclusively with the female fantasy, and so insultingly little with the male anxiety. The concept of ritual, even though it has been shown to apply at so many levels and in so many ways, is discriminatory enough. The incantatory version is clearly less directly ritual than the exorcizing version. And although less "realistic," it is more representational.

Against the opposition worded by Hardin, who feels that the concept of ritual is in danger of becoming too general, I would argue that it can be fruitfully used in many different ways which all enrich literary criticism considerably, as long as one distinguishes the different meanings it generates: the semantic level ("about"), the structural level (how it is inserted), and the pragmatic level (its emotional impact). Each helps us to understand why ancient texts continue to fascinate and continue to make people angry, according to the group to which they belong.

PART II

Reading the Subject

With my abiding interest in the subject, it was inevitable that I would sooner or later have to come to terms with psychoanalysis. I had some reluctance to do so, as I had been trained to consider psychoanalysis an often misused, difficult, quite specialized discipline. In spite of its wide-spread use, psychoanalysis is not just another framework within which to interpret texts; with its axioms about the existence and the nature of the unconscious, this discipline is at first sight hardly apt to accommodate the highly conscious, elaborate artifacts that humanists analyze. I still believe there is something deeply problematic in psychoanalytic interpretation of literature and visual art. But instead of maintaining my resistance against it, at a crucial moment I took it on to scrutinize the why and how of that difficulty, and the why and how of the ways in which various humanists have tried to overcome it. My own beginning toward a solution was a sustained semiotic reflection on psychoanalysis.

This section brings together three different projects to bring psychoanalysis to bear on a specifically semiotic discussion. These essays were written about six years ago in specific contexts, allusions to which I decided to keep here. "Psychopoetics" was written as an introduction to two special issues on psychoanalysis and literature, appearing simultaneously in two different journals. The initial call had been for one journal only, *Poetics*, a journal with a strong methodological bend, and I had asked for papers which would address methodological issues in conjunction with concrete textual analyses. The number as well as the variety of papers I was lucky enough to receive made it not only necessary to spread them out over two journals, but, more to the point here, to write an introduction that would make sense of the variety.

"Why I?" steps back to question the assumptions regarding the status of the individual subject which psychoanalysis, in spite of its Lacanian poststructuralist bend, takes for granted to be the agency of utterances, including texts. These reflections were occasioned by the simultaneous appearance of two studies of structuralism from a post-structuralist perspective. As it happened, I liked the one very much and the other much less so. This made me ponder about the need, for post-structuralist thinking, to endorse, albeit critically, its structuralist roots, and it seems worthwhile to keep that need current as a token of my own allegiance to such an endorsement.

"Force and Meaning" constitutes the transition from my narratology-only phase to my keen interest in visuality. This was one of the first essays I wrote on Rembrandt, and I did so while I had still ahead of me the obligation and the opportunity to write what became *Death and Dissymmetry*. At the time, this toying with art seemed to me a symptom of escapism, the wish not to have to do another book on the bible. But it turned out this preface was crucial; later on, when literally stuck before the most tricky problems of the Book of Judges, attention to visuality helped me greatly. After finishing that study I was able to develop the paper presented here into a book, *Reading Rembrandt*. This article is still very much embedded in my methodological concerns, which makes it suitable for this section.

■ 4 ■

Psychopoetics

DELIMITING PSYCHOPOETICS

In her opening to the 1977 issue of *Yale French Studies* devoted to "Literature and Psychoanalysis," Shoshana Felman challenges the common view according to which literature, a body of language to be interpreted, is submitted to psychoanalysis, a body of knowledge whose competence is used to interpret. One of the alleged motives for this questioning of the common view of the relation between "discipline" and "object," is the feeling many critics have that literature is not recognized as such by psychoanalysis; that, therefore, it is misused, misread, unrecognized in its specificity. And why should psychoanalysis display such arrogance, being itself, among other things, a body of language, while literature is a body of knowledge in its own way? Felman pursues the argument stressing the mutual inclusion of the two fields: "in much the same way as literature falls within the realm of psychoanalysis (within its competence and its knowledge), psychoanalysis itself falls within the realm of literature, and its specific logic and rhetoric" (7). The mutuality between the two takes the form of a paradoxical subject-object relation: the work of literature resembles the work of the psychoanalyst, while the status of the object, the text, is not that of a patient but that of a master. Conversely, the literary critic resembles the analyst in his work of interpreting the text, and the patient in the relation of transference. (Note that this confusing implication of both still does not fall under the taboo of an analogic argument. The relation may be complicated; it is not inextricable.)

Compared to these concepts, the scope of the issues in which this chapter was initially published as an introduction, was, however, more limited. If Felman's scornful metaphor applies, those issues do promote psychoanalysis, but at the same time relativize the metaphor. Although the mutuality between the two fields cannot be denied, and may indeed be one of the hidden motives for the taboo on the approach in some circles, the papers presented in the "Psychopoetics" issues are meant to examine the cognitive relation, not as absolutely one-sided, but yet as one in which the starting point is the question of how psychoanalysis can inform poetics, rather than the other way around. Indeed, the search for a "psychopoetics" is broad enough in itself and can only be touched upon here. It is not for a determined epistemological presupposition that the concept of the issue is narrowed down to the relevance of psychoanalysis to poetics. Rather, the sloppiness of the relation, as it is more often than not displayed in literary studies, had not been retained in these special issues; the question *what a psychopoetics is/can be* the crucial one in the discussions that composed the issues of *Poetics* and *Style*.

The relation between psychoanalysis and literature presupposed by the term "psychopoetics" is the following. Psychoanalysis is considered as an unstable, questionable, but as yet undeniably functioning body of language used as knowledge about the human mind and behavior, specifically its unconscious parts, related to the conscious ones. It is used as a "medium range theory" embedded in a more complex procedure (Wolff 1981). As such, it can both be challenged by and related to literature in general and various literary phenomena in particular. It informs poetics from its own angle of vision. Psychopoetics is, then, a poetics, that is, a body of language about literature, used as knowledge, characterized by a relation of information with psychoanalysis. That relation is not one of master and slave, as Felman (6) warns us, for the information is not *a priori* acceptable nor is it a direct subject-object relation. Indeed, it is not literature itself but poetics—that is the body of statements about literature—that is informed by psychoanalysis. Accordingly, poetics is not defenseless against the information which it can reject, adjust, or selectively use. Nor is psychoanalysis its only informant. Psychopoetics is one part of general poetics that will always interact with others. It is partial in its concern with traces of unconscious processes and the way these traces interact with other textual elements. It is hermeneutically oriented in its search for meaningful interpretations for which it tries to construct appropriate conditions, and it is critical in its striving for explanation within socio-historical contexts. It is not monolithic, but it consists of very divergent statements on various phenomena, from the literary process in general to the conditions of writing and reading, to specific genres, figures and structures, works of authors, singular texts. All those statements coherently hold together by their reducibility to statements drawn from psychoanalytic theory and practice. It is not as yet a full, coherent theory but it consists of elements of a possible theory, from which a method, a taxonomy, an axiology, a hermeneutics and, indeed, a critical method can be drawn.

In a first attempt to delimit the specificity of psychopoetics as a field of study, Gallop presents, in the first paper of the *Poetics* section entitled "The

Field," the problematic status of the age-old division between "humanities" and "science" from an original, that is, a "local" point of view. If the scission in the academic fields is that between humanities and sciences in some countries, in others there is another split between "letters" and what should be called to avoid misunderstanding, "the other humanities." The labels are, of course, far from innocent, displaying each a thorough insight into their own fields, if not a presupposition of what they are really concerned with. The change, within psychoanalysis, from humanistic inferences to scientific linguistics is in that sense a significant one. Gallop analyzes the reading process as the most basic part of psychopoetics, since it has a specific relation to interpretation as an exercise of power. The key concept of transference is perhaps the marked point where psychopoetics can be constructed as informed by psychoanalysis. The process of transference being the structuration of the interpretative authority, the analysis of it in the reading process has a critical dimension from the start.

Rogers seeks to inform a process model of a scientific hermeneutics which would conceive of understanding as the awareness of the organization of patterns of information. His is an informational model which would be holistic in purpose, hence, less exclusively focused on language. Analyzing the main assumptions of discourse analysis and post structuralism, both linguistically oriented, Rogers is able to formulate preconditions for such a model. Drawing upon both Habermas' concept of self-reflection, which includes not only the interpretation of the meaning of distorted texts but also of distortion itself, and upon Rabbinic thinking with its openness and dialectically critical attitude, combined with commitment to method, the author can integrate the contribution of psychoanalysis in the model. He does so only after, first, criticizing its limitations in relation to thematics and to a focus of inquiry. The holistic perspective does not necessarily include, however, the need for concrete completeness, totality, but rather, the assumption that one should not lose sight of the whole. If psychopoetics is, as a matter of course, narrowed down to its specific concerns, the holistic perspective will not exclude the approach but include it, while safeguarding the integration with other forms of poetics. Rogers' theoretic epistemology, indeed, promotes such attitudes.

In an overview of the development theory as held in psychoanalytic theory, compared to Piaget's theory, Grimaud broadens the scope of psychopoetics even more. He favors an extension of the approach to all psychologic theories which can in any way inform poetics. True, the closure of the concept to psychoanalysis may only wrongly suggest that there is no way to integrate other psychologies. His interesting attempt to open up, rather than delimit the field, has the advantage to link this issue with other special issues of *Poetics*, especially the one on cognitive psychology and literature. If his view of poetics as multidisciplinary and multi-methodical may seem to become unmanagable, it rightly necessitates a rethinking of the relations to other disciplines and the choices we make, most of which have an arbitrary aspect. Only on that basis can one hope that a multidisciplinary approach will evolve toward genuine interdisciplinarity.

Van Heusden, from outside the discipline, places the papers of this section in the framework of one semiotic theory, the one which is mainly related to Hayden White's metahistory. Van Heusden studies the different dimensions of poetics, which enables him to consider the field of psychopoetics in a similar fashion. Thus, he anticipates already the next section, where Orlando will consider the different approaches in Freud's writings as variously acceptable because their scopes differ, their procedures and aims vary, and their place in the different dimensions of poetics is divergent.

PSYCHOPOETICS AND METHOD

The relationship between psychoanalysis and literary texts, between readings and writings, has taken different routes, most of them not or hardly accompanied by their own proponents' critique. I will first delineate a few models as they have been practiced by psychopoeticians, then sketch the awkward position the discipline has often taken—and been forced to take—in the methodology debate; the papers of the second section will come to stand in the light of the need for rational justification and recognition, a concern most familiar to the readers of *Poetics*.

One widely practiced and questionable model is the *analogical model* of psychopoetics, mostly taking the form of psychocriticism. In her introduction to the *Yale French Studies* issue, Felman explains why literature and psychoanalysis have more in common than not. Even if, as she rightly shows, the relation is not purely analogical, since the different positions of analyst and patient are unevenly distributed among text and reader or critic, the basic assumption is clearly the strong analogy not only between the products of each practice, but also between the processes themselves. In the early days of what was later called psychocriticism, the analogy was based on one of two comparisons. A first, most common one studies texts insofar as they display the "story" of the psychoanalytic development theory. Numerous "cases" of oedipal desires, incest taboos, and their transgressions were collected, and interpretations of classical masterpieces as oedipally motivated appeared. Jones's interpretation of Hamlet's hesitations is perhaps the most famous example. A methodological discussion of this type of criticism is hardly called for at this point. I wish to stress, however, risking to take an unfashionable position, that many objections against it simply do not hold. The argument that Jones did not take the structural composition of the play into account, for example, can easily be countered by the remarks he makes on the function of the play-in-the-play. On the other hand, it is a fact that the very question—why does Hamlet not kill his uncle right away?—falls under the "how many children had Lady Macbeth?" type of question. Reformulated as a typically readerly question—that is, taking as a starting point not the text but the response it provokes, using empirical methods for the collection of data concerning response (Groeben; Holland)—it is not *a priori* an unacceptable question, and Jones's answer to it can be differently situated as well. Nevertheless, the great majority of analyses of this type are not considered as "literary" enough, while their underlying assumptions are not accepted any longer.

The second comparison is the one between text and psychoanalytic theory itself. Although it presents the same problems, this comparison can be illuminating in several aspects. First, it illustrates psychoanalytic theory; hence, it can be used as a didactic tool. In fact, that is how Freud used it. From a critical point of view, those comparisons are even alleged as evidence that the whole theory is mythically based. This is, however, an unjust critique. It misunderstands both myth and its relation to science, while it also misses the difference between the context of discovery and the context of justification. It is the same type of argument as the one alleged by the school of Greimas, whose analyses of scientific texts demonstrate narrative aspects in those texts, implying, then, that this undermines the scientific status of the texts. The relationship between narrativity and discoursivity is not thoroughly argued to start with, while the model itself on which the analysis is based is not in itself examined and could very well presuppose the necessity of narrativity in any text.

The problem with the second comparison drawn from the analogical model is a different one. It considers texts as stated theories, thus neglecting the different status of theories and their object. To demonstrate that a literary text displays features of the psychoanalytic process—that is, that it holds instances of condensation, transference or repression—is not a revealing conclusion as such. The relation must, in spite of Felman's preference for a more democratic mutuality, be reversed. The psychoanalytic process of condensation, transference, and repression should not be seen as staged in the text, but as concepts which allow analysis of literary phenomena which manifest those features. But, then, the analogical model is not applied any longer; it is replaced by what I will call the "specification model."

The example of the creation story in *Genesis* 2–3 may illustrate this. Using the first comparison of the analogical model, one could say that the creatures "man" and "woman" who, at the end of chapter 2, are "naked but not ashamed," resemble the child who has not yet gained awareness of his/her body. When they discover their nakedness later, and, indeed, become ashamed, they can be considered to have grown up. The comparison is more detailed. The shame is not caused by their sheer nakedness, but by the appearance of YHWH, the third person who institutes difference, hence, law. Retrospectively, then, the undifferentiated earth-creature which was first formed, and which is not a man but a non-sexual being, represents the infant who cannot yet differentiate itself and the other, taking the parts of the mother's body as parts of its own. The whole story becomes, then, an illustration, not only of the *story* of the development theory, with its specific characters—the infant and its motherly total environment, here the earth; the child who discovers difference when s/he becomes aware of the body at the appearance of the third person, the father; and the grown children who test reality by transgressing the interdiction of the father, in order to become adults in their own right. It also dramatizes the theory itself: it shows how the desire to become like the father necessitates repression of older desires whose archaeology has been buried with the death/sleep of the pre-oedipal child who is reborn as sexually differentiated. (For an extensive analysis of this text, see Bal, 1987.)

At its best, such an interpretation sheds a specific light on a story, which can be interpreted in many other ways. The case is interesting, because it has, indeed, been used, not only by psychoanalysis, but by other disciplines as well. Different currents in evolutionary anthropology each interpret the story differently (see Reed). The use of the two comparisons, however, does not protect the text against any arbitrary interpretation, nor have they given any insight in the text drawn from the theory. In fact, the theory and its interpretative schemes have been taken as a whole, as a story in itself, which is superposed on the other story. Such doubling is a much practiced procedure which presents the inconvenience not only of being basically non-falsifiable, but worse of allowing no surplus knowledge to be gained.

The analogical model in itself cannot, therefore, be considered as a method. It is not, however, completely pointless. The import of the analogic mode of thinking is, as both Rogers and Van Heusden argue, basic to our ways of dealing with the world as it is accessible in discursive practice. The procedure presented here should be seen as one instance of that mode. It helps in different ways to gain access to discursive items which do not by themselves deliver their meanings, that is, offer precisely the analogies we need to make meaning. Hence, those interpretations have didactic, semiotic, and communicative value; object rather than method, they offer interesting material for the study of the place and function of psychoanalytic concepts in everyday life.

A variant of this model is what may be called the *specification model*. It uses psychoanalysis as a searchlight theory, allowing specific features of texts or readings to be illuminated, sometimes explained, by means of psychoanalytic concepts. The goal of such interpretations is not to confirm the psychoanalytic content of the material, but to make explicit in what ways the presumed subject exposes itself as existing through various psychoanalytically theorized problems. For instance, Verhoeff's analysis of Constant's *Adolphe* is not conceived to demonstrate that the title-character has symptoms of a pre-oedipal *complexe d'abandon* which pushes him to leave women in order not to be left by them. Quite to the contrary, specific textual elements like the famous phrase, "je veux être aimé, me dis-je, et je regardais autour de moi" (I want to be loved, I said to myself, and I looked about me), where the conjunction *et* has puzzled many critics, are interpreted in the light of the pre-oedipal trouble in order to analyze their interrelations which form a network of highly symptomatic, but at the same time literary, instances. The novel does not display *the* psychoanalytic concept, then, but a unique version of it, which turns the book into what it is: a great novel which irritated many of its readers. Hence, the text forms not the only object of the analysis, but the interaction between author and readers as well. True, thus analyzed the novel becomes in its turn an informant of psychoanalysis. It makes an interesting case, stimulating the use of literature as document for the social sciences. But such is not the goal of the semiotic project.

The study of *Adolphe* analyzes and interprets features recognized as literary devices: metaphors and their distribution in the novel, in relation to the diegetic moment; the split of the narrative voice, and its unequal distribution, which enhances specific effects; the problem of identification; the status of diegetic truth and the protagonists' attitude towards it. The psychoanalytic theory informs that analysis, but it does not reduce it. There lies the difference between the two models discussed until now. The specification model protects semiosis against reduction, while, as we have seen, the analogical model rather encourages the latter. Analogy is a summarizing procedure, while specification is an extending one. (For a detailed discussion, see Skura 1981.)

The two models are, however, not contradictory, and indeed, combinations of them are many. In case of combination, the second procedure protects the text against the reduction risked by the analogical model. For it allows specification of the features which may anchor the analogy but still remain textual phenomena which require explanation. The case of *Genesis* 2-3 may again illustrate this. The literary problem the text presents is that of the unity of the character. Indeed, most theories of character presuppose the stability of characters in the course of the text. They do admit evolution, change, reversal of being and appearance, elimination of characters, but the very possibility of change depends on the assumption of some sort of semiotic "existence" which remains unaltered. (See Rimmon-Kenan 1983; Hamon 1983.) One can change only what is constantly present. If, on the other hand, one assumes the applicability of the analogical model, one of the consequences it implies is the disruption of the character. For in that case, the creature formed in verse 2:7, and which remains the same until 2:20 only, is basically a different "character," an ontologically separate one, from the new set of characters formed after the "profound sleep" of the first character. Similarly, the woman and the man before the so-called transgression are basically different beings, to be distinguished from the characters which present the rather realistic image of the human condition of the adult. The psychoanalytic theory of development informs the analogical interpretation, which cannot, however, validate itself as a procedure of literary analysis. But once the interpretation is established, it can draw further support from, and clarify at the same time, the literary problematics of the convention which presupposes the stability of character. Indeed, once the stages of the creation/development of the anthropomorphic characters are differentiated, it is easy to see the possibility of a general hypothesis about fictional characters. They can be assumed, then, to be "slices" of semiosis, where the relation between the different entities is at least as constitutive as the diachronic evolution of one entity and where no continuity can be presupposed. As a result, the concept of character becomes the means of its own deconstruction, and instead of serving the ideologically pernicious interpretations based on retrospective unification, like those which claim women inferior because "Eve was formed after Adam," it will serve as a critique of those influential readings.

The main point, here, is the possibility to use psychoanalytic theory to inform literary theory by means of hermeneutic specification. It is not so much the contribution of psychoanalysis to the interpretation itself, as the possibility it offers to gain access to literary features, hence to inform concepts of literary theory without losing sight of the literary object itself. It is the spanning of the gap between the two disciplines, then, which protects from arbitrary and uncontrollable interpretation. In the given example, the literary problem of character, one of the conspicuous examples of the difficulty of literary theory to reach knowledge beyond naïve realism, is also used as a protective concept in that it sets the limits to psychoanalytic speculation. Without the intermediate position of the concept, there would be no way to yield privilege to this particular interpretation, but the combination allows one to overcome the tautological aspects of the analogical model. In this particular case, supplementary check points can be built in: given the abundant material, evidence from anthropological sources (Oosten and Moyer 1982) and even from Talmudic practice (Lévinas 1973) confirms parts of the result, while this evidence in its turn is further informed by it. Hence, the combination of the searchlight theory with the one that needed information fulfills a new searchlight function in relation to other theories. This interaction between different disciplines certainly comes close to the interdisciplinarity required by Grimaud. Paradoxically, then, psychoanalysis does not close off or reduce, but on the contrary opens up and extends its scope to other disciplines.

In this context, another variant of the analogical model must be viewed less positively. I am referring to what may be called the *medical* model. It is the procedure that comes closest to the reversal of the information relation. Psychoanalysis is, then, not so much informant but the informed discipline. There is nothing inherently wrong with the use of literature as document for psychoanalysts, if they think they can overcome the problems of the difference between unconscious discourse and written, elaborated texts. But the medical model is also used by psychocritics whose aim, then, seems to be to demonstrate that a given author, character, or even text suffers certain troubles, has dreams which mean specific things and are symptomatic (Bellemin-Noël

1981). The result of the analysis, in those cases, is as clear as possible a picture of the disease. Of course, stated like this, no literary critic would openly adhere to such a position. The practice of this type of criticism is, however, far from extinguished. The problem is not so much that the text has no unconscious, or that the status of textual features is questionable in relation to symptomatics; rather, this is a psychoanalytic rather than a poetic problem. The main problem is, I think, one of information content. Indeed, such interpretations offer results that are coherent and complete in one sense, the medical one, but assemble disparate and detailed features of the literary corpus without justifying their relative importance within the overall object of study. Contrary to the specifying model, and even to the simple analogical model, there is no check on the type of information drawn from the object. It is theoretically possible to build up a coherent picture of a neurosis on the basis of loose ends and arbitrarily picked words. What is lacking is the double check the specifying model offers. The required coherence of the depiction of the trouble is not balanced by a similar requirement on the literary side. The random character of the material as part of a literary object makes the procedure pointless for poetics.

What I will indicate here as the *semiotic model* of psychopoetics is distinguishable from the previous exposed procedures in that it does not use the content of psychoanalysis to inform poetics, but, instead, draws on its basic assumptions and axioms, its theorizing of the unconscious, its ideas on language, the subject and the relations between both, as keys and as descriptive concepts for interpretation. This procedure is not so much interested in traces of the oedipal drama or the pre-oedipal confusions, but rather in traces of the unconscious and the forms it takes which disturbs coherency: signs of censorship like condensation and displacement; contradictions and incoherencies and their status in relation to the coherent, "conscious" statements of the text; and their ability to disturb the common interpretations which seek coherency. If carefully used, it can yield surplus information, it can relate to traditionally acknowledged literary problems, and it can contribute to the rethinking of the subject in the socio-cultural sciences.

Interpretation is now commonly recognized as both indispensable and inherent to any discursive practice, and methodologically problematic in that it cannot separate itself from its object/subject matter. The latter difficulty cannot be radically overcome; it does, however, allow relative differentiation. The use of the language of another hermeneutic theory can eventually create the indispensable if relative distance between the object-language and the semiotic meta-language, or, as it is more appropriately called, para-language. Without allowing the critic to step out of the discursive event, it does, then, allow him/her tot draw a new body of language into it, thus adding new elements which shed new light on it. The case of *Genesis* 37–39 can illustrate this possibility.

In traditional, philologically informed hermeneutics, *Genesis* 38 is considered problematic. It is the story of Judah who conceives twin sons/grandsons with his daughter-in-law Tamar, who tricked him into it because he had failed to keep his promise. The chapter poses the problem of continuity, a frequently thematized issue in biblical narrative. Indeed, in Chapters 37 and 39 we learn about the misadventures of Judah's younger brother Joseph, who is sold by his brothers as a slave in 37, and misused by his master's wife in 39. Between the three chapters, there is neither temporal nor thematic continuity, and many biblical scholars comment on this problem. One group (Speiser 1964) assumes that 38 has been displaced by subsequent editing. Another (Alter 1981) on the other hand defends thematic similarity among the three chapters. Alter cannot, however, analyze how the thematic structure would yield a certain *continuity,* nor can he explain why the rather loose thematic similarities between 37/39 and 38 can be assumed to have motivated the editorial policy. Indeed, both critics arrive at their conclusions without considering either the poetic or the possible psychoanalytic motivations, let alone the relations between the two. Therefore, their hermeneutic efforts cannot reach beyond reductive paraphrase.

Now, the sequence of the three chapters displays a tension between similarity and difference which does yield a certain type of continuity, while looking very much like the half-admitted, half-censored signification of some unconscious meaning. In the three, family relations are thematized. Each time, a subject is deceived with the help of an object. The object in question serves as evidence of the presence of a subject at the moment the crucial event took place. The object is metonymically related to the identity of the subject. The metonymic bond itself is questioned, or rather, differentiated from its variant: the object is part of the synecdochic subject's equipment, not independent by itself, thus leaving space for mistakes or falsification. The object is, however, a significant or central part of the equipment; hence it is used as evidence of the victim's identity; it is mistaken as synecdoche. Since the object is acknowledged at the end as absolute evidence, it becomes a metaphor of the subject which can, by means of that reification, recover its subjective status which was in danger.

Most of the thematic similarities are identified by the critics who defend continuity. They do not, however, interpret them further, so that the analysis remains paraphrastic: the text delivers these details, but they do not as such make sense within the biblical conception of continuity. If some editing policy would be inferable from these elements, it would be a rather sloppy, hasty action on the basis of thematic relations which are just obvious enough to assume that "the three chapters have something to do with each other." Psychoanalytic theory with its insistence on the "letter" (Lacan 1966), on one hand, on the textual detail that is, and with its stress on family and sexual relations on the other hand, can pursue the inquiry further. Indeed, the seducer in 37 is the misused victim's brothers. In 39, the seducer is a woman.

In the problematic chapter, the seducer is also a woman, but, contrary to 39, she is justified since she was trapped in the first place. Here the victim is the initial seducer. In 38, the trap concerns a woman and a set of brothers, and as such, the chapter is pivot between the two others. In 37, the brothers ill-use their innocent brother. In 39, the woman misuses the same young man. In 37, he suffers for his filial obedience. Separated from his father, facing woman in 39, he keeps his innocence, which now becomes sexual purity. In 37 and 38, the father is deceived. In 38, however, the father is also the deceiver. In both cases, the father overprotects his young son. In 39, the father is replaced by the social father-figure, the master. This father is deceived like the father in 37 and 38, but he participates in the misuse of the son by letting himself be deceived. He thus resembles both the father in 37 who cannot protect his son any further and the father in 38 who deceives in his turn, if, this time, unaware.

Two more displacements between the three tales censor the similarities. The object with the help of which the deception takes place consists of clothes in 37 and 39. Undressing the innocent victim obviously is the first step towards deception and ill-treatment. In 38, the object is threefold and consists of the signs of paternal dignity. The father being the deceived person, this symbolic undressing replaces the more concrete, which would be highly inappropriate. Secondly, the position of sexuality is different in each case. In 37, the whole topic seems irrelevant, except for three details: the undressing, the blood smeared onto the dress, and the separation from the family, which brings the young man into sexual danger. In 39, sexuality shifts from the side to the center. The undressing is here literally meant for sexual purposes. The dress is considered as evidence of sexual misbehavior, and rightly so: the young man is imprisoned for having undressed, officially for having committed, but in fact for having refused sex. The position of the brothers moves to the opposite direction. In 37, they are central and clearly guilty, as is the woman in 39. In 38 they are less central, not involved in the deception (except for the younger brother, who is indirectly involved) and their position in sexual matters is highly problematic. In 39, they have disappeared.

The position of the character Tamar, on the one hand, and that of the set of brothers, fathers, and sons in the whole sequence, on the other, becomes clear in verses 28:24–26. The issue is Judah's readiness to condemn to death the woman guilty of his own act. In other words, he is confusing subjects, problematizing the distinction between subject and object. What exactly is Tamar's role? She is a focalizer (see Bal 1986) in the first place. She sees what Judah does not see. In 14, she sees the injustice done to her. In 16–17, she sees that Judah is not to be trusted. Judah, in his turn, sees a whore *(zonah)* where the narrator points to a cultural servant (wrongly referred to in philology as "cult prostitute"), indicated by the word *gedeshah*, and where the character is a relative. In 25, she forces him to see the truth. In fact, her wit, used to restore what was wrong, serves to make Judah see his own neurotic errors. His error was the illusion that the course of history can continue while protecting his son from the imaginary danger: the woman. Instead, historical chronology had to be restored: first man has to do away with his fear of woman; *then* the new generation can be conceived. To show him this, Tamar had to veil herself, seeing without being seen. The double camouflage is needed: man is so afraid that the woman has to cover herself in order to trick him into having sex; and for the truth, his own fear, to be revealed, because it is so shameful, it can only be uncovered by a stratagem of covering. "Discern," says Tamar to Judah in 25, "whose these are." The children she bears are fathered by the owner of the patriarchal attributes she possesses. Discernment is what she teaches him. Her action does not provide her the husband which was her goal. It does provide Judah with the offspring he was longing for. The course of history, interrupted by this episode, can be resumed.

As an account of self-insight won by the help of the feared woman, the tale serves within the sequence as advice not to fear for Joseph excessively. The very dangers he is entangled in by his contact with the woman will be the source of his future power. In fact, that is what happens: from the prison, he is called to reign. The weak position of Judah's sons is reflected in his own weakness: the powerful father is helpless without the other. He is dependent on the place he occupies in the system, the Other. Narration is an expression of the system. The history of the formation of the subject is interrupted here only to show how unavoidable the course of chronology is. The paralepsis (Genette 1972: 195), the narrative figure which constitutes the problem in the sequence, is, then, in the first place a sign that refers to its own limited possibility. Dependent as it is on the subject in relation to which chronology and its disruptions are to be interpreted, it can only expand on the very topic that, by its sheer centrality, promotes the development of the narrative.

The apparent distortion in the sequence can be interpreted *with* its distorting aspects, and not in spite of them as in Alter's account. This is certainly not to say that philology is to be short-circuited. The text studied is the one that is, for some reason or another, canonized as it is. The object of study, then, is not some "original" version, but what is already a reading—the edition we have. Sensitivity to the unconscious problems as outlined above is assumed to have motivated the edition. Indeed, the assumption of text-corruption or displacement is another way of repressing the conflict, just as is the readiness to smooth the problem out by unproblematic thematics. Psychoanalysis serves as a heuristic tool, but unlike the specifying model, this procedure interprets problems rather than texts. The problem outlined here was a philological one, chosen purposely because the strongest resistances against psychopoetics come from the more traditional disciplines. At the same time, the problem was a reading difficulty, since, first, the edition can be considered as a reading, and, second, the subsequent readings by Speiser and Alter, each with their own specific solution to the problem, are taken as objects of explanation as well. Psychoanalysis supports the presented interpretation and provides the concept of displacement and its signifying capacities as well as the assumptions on the problematic formation of the subject and its relation to problems of family and sexuality. Neither philology nor literary criticism could accomplish this. The distortion was first to be assumed, as in philological questioning, then explained, but not explained away.

These four procedures, operating in isolation or in combination, are optimally verifiable when related to problems derived from alien disciplines. That is the motivation for my insistence on problems of linguistics, philology, or poetics. The contribution psychoanalysis can offer is always limited, and it should be delimited clearly. Only then can it be protected from, on the one hand, reductionism and at the same time imperialism, which combine to claim too little meaning with too much pretension; and protected on the other hand from misunderstandings, resistance, and refusal altogether.

The previous discussion leaves, however, the methodological status of psychoanalysis as such unargued. Although it seems to me that too much attention has been diverted from problems of poetics by the sheer unending methodological challenge put on the approach, it must be admitted that psychopoetics can only be acceptable if its basis can be considered reasonably sound. Like any approach to any object-domain which seeks rational acknowledgment, psychopoetics cannot withdraw from the methodology debate. This is, however, often the attitude of its proponents. On the other hand, its antagonists too easily project outdated requirements, which have not proven fruitful for a progressive theory of knowledge about this particular discipline which so outrageously defies the common rules of rationality. The following statement may illustrate the problematic point: "Far from being the avenue to truth, reason may serve as a powerful defense against the recognition of truth, masking anxiety by its quest for certainty, perpetuating illusion by elaborate rationalization" (Kaplan 1977: 77). The statement was meant to defend psychoanalysis, but at the same time it points exactly to the bias where proponents and antagonists of the approach cease to understand each other. Claiming, as Kaplan does here, that reason and rationalism are often used as defense against the recognition of unpleasant truths or, eventually, the unpleasant recognition of the impossibility to reach the truth, is the very argument that makes the opponent powerless. If its relative truth is undeniable, that makes it only the more irritating. The statement is significant, so much so that it can almost figure as a *mise en abyme* of the discipline it is meant to defend: it is adequate, and *therefore* unacceptable; it defies rules, and forces the other to revise standards, under the threat of becoming the object of the statement. Whoever refuses psychoanalysis represses it.

The statement should not, however, be taken as an "anything goes" device, nor is it necessarily an attack on rationality. First, it should be considered within the context of the already forgotten debates of the fifties, where even Hempel had to admit, and in fact did admit frankly, that "it is precisely the 'fictitious concepts rather than those fully definable by observables' that enabled science to proceed to explanation and prediction" (Frenkel-Brunswick 1977: 107). Horwitz formulates this even more polemically when he writes:

> Most philosophers now recogize that rigid operationalism leads to an undue narrowness and sterility in science and that only through the use of "fictitious concepts" or "hypothetical constructs" which may have a tenuous tie with the level of observation can the creative scientist construct the theories which will ultimately clarify the unknowns in nature. (1977: 124)

Scriven finds the operationalist-empiricist position untenable for that reason: "a term is fruitful only if it encourages changes in its own meaning; and, to some considerable extent, this is incompatible with operational definition" (1956: 113). In other words, Kaplan's statements, like other, similar ones, should not be considered out of context and interpreted as a refusal to accept rationality as a standard for the evaluation of psychoanalysis as a scientific discipline. On the contrary, it is meant to encourage reflection about those standards, not with the idea of adopting them for the sake of opportunism but for the purpose of gaining deeper insight into rationality itself.

According to Habermas' new book, rationality should not be measured in its cognitive dimension only. Behaving in a rational way means having good reasons for cognitive, moral, practical, evaluative, expressive, and hermeneutic decisions. His extensive account of the rules that within a given social environment can decide whether the said reasons are good is not relevant here, but the main point, the broader view of rationality, that is, may serve not to protect psychopoetics against rational critique but on the contrary to practice that critique in a reasonable, subtle way.

In different ways from different viewpoints and with different standards, three papers in the issue of *Poetics* consider the method of psychopoetics. Orlando examines the procedures Freud applied when he discussed literature. Distinguishing eleven different procedures, he demonstrates that already at its beginnings the approach was not unified, hence, should not be discussed as if it were. Orlando's attitude is, I would say, doubly semiotic in the first place. His concern is to interpret Freud's statements as procedures in order to display their eventual usefulness for a semiotic psychopoetics. Sullivan's is a different goal. She practices the reversible relationship between the two fields, as indicated by Felman, in such a way as to draw from one body of psychoanalytic language statements on what poetics can do with it. Westlund, who comments upon this section from his own point of view, finds the Lacanian poetics not entirely satisfying, mainly because of its one-sidedness. He develops another direction that psychopoetics can also take, thus enriching the scope of the section. Groeben, on the other hand, examines claims on which psychoanalysis bases its procedures, before entering into the specific problems of psychopoetics as dependent on the former. His standards differ from those implied by the empiricist background of the two other contributors to this section. He thus allows the reader to have a clearly recognizable sample of each of the two attitudes toward the discipline, between which it would be so interesting to find a rationally based common understanding. The juxtaposition of these papers in their pointed difference is one step toward that understanding.

Westlund places the discussion in its historical context, rightly arguing against the common strategy of sticking to Freud. Other work has been done, and more recent arguments have contributed to the debate which avoid Freud's sometimes naïve scientism while taking the problem of the discipline's scientific status seriously. Westlund points to the tendency, figuring in many works of psychopoetics, to remain faithful to a defensive attitude no longer called for in that situation. Stressing the importance of narcissism for the literary process, he attempts to extend the method toward a more socially oriented direction. Drawing upon work by Melanie Klein and Winnicott, he opens up the scope of psychopoetics to an approach informed by readerly questions which address problems of response rather than of production. He is critical of the overdemanding, hence, reductive attitude of one contributor, as well as of the lack of historical awareness of the two others. In combination with the three papers of this section, Westlund's comment gives an idea of the actual position of the approach in the methodology debate. He concludes by addressing the question which arises from Kaplan's quoted statement: that is, why psychopoetics has more difficulty in justifying itself, than, say, structural criticism. Taking the question seriously, he suggests that the problem can be overcome.

CRITICISM AND CRITIQUE

Psychopoetics is shown at work in the *Style* part of these twin issues. Although the concept of criticism has come to cover any approach to literature, be it a set of concepts (critical theory), a comment or even a paraphrase, psychopoetics has a critical vocation in the more specific, German sense. In the context of the debate between the proponents of the Frankfurt School and the positivist sociologists, a critical theory is not a theory of literary criticism but a theory which is itself critical in the pointed, programmatic sense. Without discussing literature at all, Habermas (1968) uses psychoanalysis as a paradigm of critical science because of its inherently self-critical structure. True, Habermas' model of the use of critical theory to bring about social changes has been shown to be idealistic and transcendental. The concept itself, however, allows us to grasp the basic properties of one side of psychopoetics which is today widely discussed outside the domain of literary studies: critique of ideology. Critical theory is based on the idea that the limits of reality—that which resists symbolization—are unstable. Therefore, a possible satisfaction of desires can change into an institutionally acknowledged gratification. Technical progress enlarges objective possibilities to reduce the needed social repression under institutionalized systems. Utopian components of former illusion can then be freed from their embedding in ideological and estranged elements of culture. Such liberation allows a critique of the power structure because the latter has become expendable.

A critical theory of culture is able to distinguish theoretical propositions which relate to invariable regularities from those which express ideologically fixed relations of dependence which could change. To the point at which ideas are used to justify actions, the rationalizations (on the individual level) or ideologies (on the collective level) obliterate the uncritical relation between the subject's consciousness and the hidden interests that orient it, thus enabling the subject to create the illusion of autonomous judgments. Any critique of ideology is based on the premise that information about the pseudo-invariant relations between idea and action may trigger within the subject who is subjected to those pseudo laws a critical process of self-reflection. To the point that the reader is subjected to the literary text which presents such pseudo laws as "natural," a critical interpretation of literature can contribute to that process. Psychoanalysis, as Habermas argues, is doubly appropriate for this critical work. Its theory has the process in question as its object-domain, and its procedure is based on the self-reflective activity of the analysand. In much the same way, the psychopoetic critic is involved in self-reflective work while criticizing the text and the reading process. Hence the increasing attention paid to the concept of transference, stressed by Gallop and by Culler: in a sense, self-reflection *is* transference.

The cognitive problems inherent in this view of self-reflection as a critical procedure are not easy to disentangle. The general interpretations which underlie the major part of psychopoetic criticism should be taken into consideration at this point. True, the well-known general interpretations like the Oedipus complex do allow conditioned predictions, but they do not do so on the basis of a methodologically neat separation between the object-domain and the theoretical propositions they hold. The general interpretations are themselves narrative in that they explain events narratively. They show how subjects are engaged in a fabula which needs representation. Such a representation implies the claim of the fabula's uniqueness. The function of the general interpretation is precisely to undermine that claim without transgressing the limits set by narrativity. As a systematically generalized narrative, it provides us with a schema of many possible fabulas which are each unique while following predictable lines. In that sense, the general interpretation functions as *type*. Analyst and analysand, literary text and critic, can orient themselves, not in relation to an example but to a schema.

General interpretations are models in the sense that they do not use names of individuals but instead use roles, be they indicated by proper names (Oedipus), classes of individuals (children, parents) or by theoretical terms (subject, desire, object). They do not represent contingent situations but recurrent figurations, represented graphically by triangles, hexagons, lines. They do not use typical processes but they describe, by means of key concepts, the synopsis of some action with its variants. Since the terms of the model contribute to the structuration of the narrative, their formalization is not possible and even not desirable. The semiotic interpretation as a specific performance is not an operational application which leaves the theoretical deductions as is; it *completes* the background the model constitutes. It defines one actualization of the general interpretation.

It is in this view that the papers by Verhoeff, Chaitin, Brooks and Frappier-Mazur should be considered. They each show in a different way the critical capacities of general interpretations as mediators between both subjects involved in a critical work. Verhoeff's oedipal reading of *Oedipus Rex* insists on variation between myth, text, and model, analyzing the various modes that the analogical model allows him to uncover. Sophocles' tragedy is not the source but the product of oedipal transformation. Psychoanalysis provides the key terms in which the tragedy can be reformulated. The relation between general interpretation and specific text is illustrated by a discussion of the tensions between the Oedipus complex and the literary text, a tension which evolves from the status of characters and dramatic situation, events and thematic structure. The conclusion, that Oedipus is surrounded by characters displaying oedipal complexes but does not have it himself, being engaged in pre-oedipal problems, is not only paradoxical; it is evidence against the charge of reductionism, and most convincingly so. The problems the character deals with in relation to the fatherly position, power, and the mother lead to an implicit critical dimension in that the latter's basically impossible position is the final word of this analysis.

Starting from Freud's often discussed theory of jokes, Chaitin constructs a taxonomy of subjective modes in the beginnings of French novels. His theory—the subject of desire, the object of love or aggression, and the addressee of the unconscious—to the three grammatical persons. The meeting ground of both systems allows the critic to elaborate three modes of narrative action as well as three types of narrative theories. He is thus able to interpret the concept of *aveu*, crucial to *La Princesse de Clèves* and typical of many subsequent novels, in its full disruptive force. Unlike Oedipus' case, the *aveu* is not meant to discover oneself but to disclose to others secrets, those of illegal desire. In his comment on both these essays, Sonne rightly raises the problem of knowledge in fiction, a question inherent in the texts of secrecy that the critics deal with. If knowledge is the issue of psychoanalysis itself, it is also an often evoked theme in fiction and specifically in the texts considered in this section. In Sonne's view, intertextuality is a key term which relates the problem of the unknown in fiction to the unconscious in psychoanalytic theory—informing, that is, the former by the latter.

The two remaining papers of this section attempt to define narrative categories by means of psychoanalytic concepts, desire in one case, initiation in the other. Pavel expands the issue to the general one of anthropological generalizations. Brooks, unsatisfied by formalist narratology, sees the ambitious hero of nineteenth-century novels as the paradigm of the motoric force of Eros, which propels the narrative toward its end. His is an energetic conception of narrative, to be understood as a force from within. This view is exemplified by an analysis of Balzac's *La Peau de chagrin,* a choice challenged by Pavel. Brooks draws largely upon *Beyond the Pleasure Principle* when he radicalizes the desire hypothesis and states that the ultimate goal of both meaning and narrative lies at the end, reaches for the end. In a related fashion, Frappier-Mazur starts her analysis of Georges Sand's *La Comtesse de Rudolstadt* with the identification of a *lack,* whose liquidation constitutes the narrative movement. The search for identity which is the force that lies behind initiation is related to the ideological problem of sexual identity. Drawing upon Kristeva's notion of abjection as a precondition of narcissism, in fact as its primary version, the blurring of distinctions which characterizes it is related to the young woman's pains to distinguish herself from the mother. Pavel is not convinced by Frappier-Mazur's attempt at a definition of the feminine based on the novel, and he uses anthropological sources to argue so. It will be left to the reader to decide; both authors use the psychoanalytic general interpretation in much the same way. If called for, this provides, again, evidence for the interpretative freedom the psychoanalytic framework leaves us.

Frappier-Mazur draws explicit conclusions whose critical import goes beyond criticism toward critique. The other papers suggest the potential for expansion in that direction without actually doing it themselves. In the field of sociology and media studies as it is practiced, among others, by the Birmingham group, psychoanalysis is much used for the construction of a theory of ideology (see Coward and Ellis 1977; Camargo Heck 1980; Hall 1980). In the line of Althusser and Lacan, these attempts struggle with the problem raised by the assumed analogy between the formation of the individual subject and the social processes which govern ideological influence—and literary communication. Jameson stays too close to Althusser to be able to overcome that problem, in spite of his fine work and subtle analysis; his is an overtly Marxist attempt to integrate Freudian concepts which too easily assumes the plurality of the subject as a solution. The formation of the subject is not necessarily defined in all its aspects by Lacan's somewhat fatalistic theory, as Silverman convincingly argues. But also, the social processes which constitute the object-domain of any critique of ideology cannot be accounted for without the key concept of the social in psychoanalysis: transference. Both final papers of the *Style* issue bring up these problems. Culler's and Abicht's reviews show what is currently being done in the United States in the field of psychopoetics. Should these two approaches be integrated in the empirical study of reading processes as practiced mainly in Germany, then there is a way to establish psychopoetics not only as a procedure for literary criticism and its theory, but also for a genuine *critique* of the social process of literary communication. That is why I present these two issues here, as exemplary tokens of a semiotically informed way of thinking about cultural issues, wider than literature, yet poetically informed.

▪ 5 ▪

Why I?

INTRODUCTION

The evolution from early structuralist to post-structuralist semiotics is generally thought of as the evolution from the repression of the phenomenological subject to the acknowledgment of its centrality in language, not as the transcendent subject which determines meaning, but as the determined one who suffers meaning. If considered from this latter angle, early structuralism has often been surprisingly misunderstood. In particular Benveniste, who published his *Essais* at the period marked by Barthes' early writings, may be easily updated in his definition of subjectivity in language.

Post-structuralist thought, specifically in the Lacanian version, denounces individualism as idealistic, and analyzes the factors which set limits to the possibilities assigned to the subject to go his/her own way. Linguistically, the pronoun *it*, indicating the subject, replaces *s/he*. The resulting reification of the subject, however, fixes the ideological aspects of this theory. Becoming a helpless *it*, the subject is paradoxically constrained within a pre-determined sexual difference, hence, *it* precludes he or she. In that context, Althusser's critique of Lacanian closure becomes acute.

Among the many books often used as textbooks on the status of the subject in contemporary semiotic theory, two draw attention to its relations to literature, that is, semiotic practice, in a particularly significant and instructive way. Both carry the term *subject* in their title, discuss the evolution I have mentioned, and aim at a critique of semiotics. One, *The Subject in Question,* is critical from the start, eager to point out contradictions and skeptical of the claims made—or assumed to be made—by semiotic theories. The other, *The Subject of Semiotics,* displays quite the opposite attitude: it uses whatever is considered useful, patiently and clearly explains before it applies theoretical points, and happily acknowledges their possibilities for a critique of culture.

Paradoxically, it is the latter book which accomplishes a pointed critique of semiotic theory in relation to sexual difference, while the former does not go beyond a mild critique of extreme and already out-dated formalism rising, that is, to the defense of meaning. Silverman manages to use semiotics, claiming that it contains the means of its own disruption, while Carroll does not overcome the form-meaning opposition, hence accepts its foundation in the very binary thought-structure that so powerfully and harmfully determines the meaning of difference. In discussing these two books, then, I want to discuss two attitudes common in the teaching of semiotics.

QUESTIONING QUESTIONING: QUESTIONING THE SUBJECT

Within the context of the resistance presumably still prevalent in some American universities against theoretical approaches to literature, Carroll's book offers an account of the dialectically justified position that there is not such opposition between theory and fiction. As the author states, his intention is to

> use fiction strategically to indicate the limitations of theory and theory to indicate the limitations of fiction—each revealing the premises, interests, and implications of the other (2).

This intention is carried out by the structure of the book. Each chapter consists of the critical analysis of a theoretical position and of a reading of a novel by Claude Simon, an author who is known for the theoretical import of his novels.

In the introductory chapter, the author gives an overview of the development from phenomenology to structuralism, from the assumption of a transcendent, signifying subject to that of the absence of the subject. Benveniste's distinction between subjective and subjectiveless discourse is seen not as an attempt to do away with subjectivity but as the resituating of the problematic within language. This the author does not find satisfying: "A truly radical questioning of the subject (. . .) can only be realized by a repeated working through and undermining of the premises on which the subject depends and which depend on it" (26). The structuralist attempt to undermine the phenomenology of the subject thus failed, according to Carroll.

Each of the chapters that follow deals with one theory, or, rather, one or more theoretical points of several theorists: Lacan, Henry James, Lukács, Foucalt, Lévi-Strauss, Ricardou. The discussion leads to the conclusion of the inherent and inevitable failure of the theory to support its own claim. As such, the opposition to deconstruction (6–8) seems hardly called for: the book practices deconstruction. The analysis of Simon's novel in light of the concept or theory discussed interestingly and convincingly shows the novelist's preoccupation with, and opposition to, the theory in question. The analyses, however, present two problems. They take the relation between theory and fiction as mainly thematic (e.g. 82), and hence they contradict the author's own opposition to naïve representation. Secondly, they implicitly argue the inherent superiority of the novelist over the theorist: the novelist always knows better.

These two problems become even more serious in the light of this particular novelist's relations with, and admiration for, theorists. By the questioned subject Carroll means in the first place the subject-matter of theory and fiction, less easily definable than is sometimes claimed, rather than the question eventually raised of the (textual) subject in the sense of the presumed origin, starting point, speaker. The two are interrelated however, if only because contemporary theory is preoccupied by the question of the subject in the latter sense—and questions it—and because fiction can never be without theory, as the author rightly argues, so that modern fiction cannot but deal with the same problems. The case of Simon, who has strong connections with theorists like Ricardou, connections which are sometimes (e.g. 176) even presented as an argument, is perhaps too appropriate a choice. The double sense of the term subject haunts the whole book, the larger part of which is devoted to the problem of history and formalism, while the introductory chapters deal mainly with the theoretical and fictional status of the subject in the second sense. The ambiguity can be argued, but this is never done. As a consequence, it is a bit difficult to discover the overall structure of the book.

The choice of theoretical texts is not limited to one author (consistency of subject does help, sometimes); hence, it must be justified by some other principle. Chronology can be such a principle, or the division of the field according to different disciplines or schools of thought. Here again, the author has not opted for one solution. Starting out with a chapter on phenomenology, structuralism and the New Novel, one could expect either of the three to be the guideline. The second chapter moves to psychoanalysis, while the third is concerned with Henry James' views on fiction as a center of consciousness. This is followed by three chapters on history, time, and the relation between diachrony and synchrony, and the excesses of formalism.

Obviously, I have no *a priori* problems with unordered collections of essays, but I would rather have the structure or lack of it clearly stated, and the different topics related to the overall "subject" of the book.

In the last chapter, the author denounces the binary opposition inherent in formalism, which presupposes that the more formal and technically complicated a novel is, the further it is removed from problems of meaning and representation. The argument advanced by critics like Ricardou holds good as long as the opposition is to preestablished meaning. But it soon forgets its own critical import when it gives in to reducing itself to the "pure formal play" of the signifier (173). The concept of *mise en abyme* and its aim of rendering the self-generating force of fiction, is analyzed as an example of Ricardou's formalistic fallacy. Indeed, confining fiction to its own self-enclosed space is no less of a preconceived project than any other critical strategy (178). Hence the well-known impossibility of opposing the *bricoleur*-critic and the *engineer*-writer, as Lévi-Strauss tried to do long ago.

The dismissal of formalism was already argued in the first chapter of Carroll's book; but there the argument concentrated upon the objective fallacy of early structuralism. The discussion is particularly hard on Genette's *Figures III*, whose modest afterword is mistaken for an epistemological statement. Genette's modesty there has apparently irritated the critic eager to lay his finger on traces of scientism. But scientific claims cannot be drawn from what is no more than a pursuit of knowledge, taken as historically and epistemologically relative from the start, as is Genette's outspoken position in the book. (It is true that in the later *Nouveau discours du récit* he changes his attitude, but that the author cannot have foreseen.) The opposition between *récit* and *histoire* in Genette's book is said to cover, "of course," the one formulated by Benveniste (20). Unfortunately, this is not the case. The author apparently bases his excessively bitter account of Genette's "typically formalist criticism" on the latter's review of Benveniste's article in *Figures II*, so that he must concede with some amazement that "here Genette calls *histoire récit*' (21). I do not think a productive critique of formalism can be carried out by authors who so obviously do not know the formalist thought from within, let alone by those who do not bother to read the texts they criticize with due care.

In general, it can only be regretted that the interesting project of this book has not been based upon a more precise analysis, a more consistent use of terms, a more extensive knowledge of the theories under consideration, especially as far as their status as theories, their epistemological claims and, even more importantly, their specific content is concerned. James' theory of the "eye," the center of consciousness, is hardly related to, let alone differentiated from, more recent theories of focalization. Ricardou's theory of *mise en abyme* is taken at its word, even if the word is lacking: neither in Ricardou's, nor in Carroll's book is the concept ever defined and analyzed. Booth's concept of the implied author is discussed on the basis of a quote (Booth 73–74) whose words *completed artistic world* and *total form* are underlined by the critic. Nevertheless in his following paraphrase he states: "the implied author is the true origin of form" (59). Does Carroll really not see the difference between the completed, that is, *resulting* form and its *origin?* Thus, the key-concepts of his own discussion are so loosely handled that no clear insight can possibly be arrived at.

The title of this book is very attractive. I regret that it keeps its promises poorly. Questioning is only possible if one knows what one is questioning. Otherwise, the answer is given in advance and the question not clearly asked. At the end of this book, the same question still comes to one's mind: what exactly is questioned?

DISPLACING DISPLACEMENTS: RETHINKING THE SUBJECT

Carroll's eagerness to show contradictory attitudes in theoretical texts differs spectacularly from Silverman's much more fruitful, and indeed opposite approach. Benveniste is not, in her book, the proponent of a desperate attempt to tame and repress the subject, but the theoretician par excellence who fully assumed its centrality in language.

Silverman outlines the evolution of semiotic theory from de Saussure's exclusive attention to a closed sign system, through the various stages of structuralist thinking, to Benveniste's most radical "subjective semiotics," which integrates Freudian and Lacanian psychoanalysis within a theory that remains inherently linguistic. She fortunately does not, as most overviews do, limit herself to the Fashionable French, but includes Penetrating Peirce. Indeed, the latter's almost exaggerated insistence on the subjectivity of the *interpretant*—the mentalistic connotations of the concept can be, and here are, suspended —links his theory more to post-structuralist thinking than has long been assumed. In her account of Barthes' theory of ideology as presented in *Mythologies,* Silverman rightly stresses the paradox of the latter's concept of connotation: it opens up denotation in order to close it off ideologically (41). The coincidence of ideological motivation in this theory and the Peircian view of the motivated—iconic or indexical—sign seems, however, oversimplified. Ideological motivation is a semiotic phenomenon—it uses semiotic means to act—but it is not semiotic *motivation:* the interest (in the Frankfurt sense) of the ideological agent as such has a priori nothing to do with the iconic or contiguous relations which motivate signification (contra 30).

Contrary to Carroll, Silverman extensively outlines the positions of the subject in semiotics in one, unambiguous sense. After the outline of semiotic theories in chapter 1, the subject as agent of speech, being represented and/or signified in the discourse, and/or spoken by it, is discussed, firstly in terms of Freud's theory of the primary and second processes, and secondly in Lacan's interpretation. With a clarity which makes this book a precious tool for teaching, the author confronts the three famous pairs of concepts so often analyzed yet so often confused, of condensation/displacement, metaphor/ metonymy and paradigm/syntagm, displaying, by her questioning of their assumed equivalence, on the theoretical level the disruption of the signifying system (binary thinking) which she analyzes elsewhere in cinematic and literary texts.

Her statements do not become confused, pretentious or uncritical. Clarity, here, is shown to be the royal road to insight. The clarity of her explanations can be demonstrated almost randomly, for instance in the following:

> Whereas condensation and displacement treat similarity and contiguity as the basis for absolute identification, and paradigm and syntagm establish an irreducible difference among similar and contiguous elements, metaphor and metonymy re-

spond to similarity and contiguity as the basis for the *temporary replacement* of one signifying element by another. In other words, metaphor and metonymy mediate between the extremes represented by the other two sets (109).

The reason why clarity, here, can be considered a masterly heuristics, is obvious: whereas famous theorists like Christan Metz, Gérard Genette, Roman Jakobson, Paul Ricoeur, and Jacques Lacan have attempted to sort out the relations between these three pairs of terms on the basis of grand philosophical thought, no one has succeeded in doing so. Silverman, in contrast, endorsing in this passage the persona of a teacher whose mission it is to explain, manages to do so. "Mastery" gains a new content here.

The analysis of the psychoanalytic theories of the subject, taken as basically semiotic theories, is followed by a critique of their inherently closed ideology. The triple meaning of the Lacanian phallus, ostensibly distinguished from the penis yet related to it, provides the *brèche vers une latence* (Delay). Since lack of meaning leads to desire, *and* (male) privilege *and* the mortgaged penis which allows entrance into the symbolic, the concept cannot but theorize as unavoidable the *status quo* of culture. As soon as the primordial lack is denied, all ideal representations, including the Father, can be understood as culturally manufactured (192). This modification of the theory, which is simply based on the refusal of the primordiality of the lack which seals off the critique and change of discursive practice, makes a critical tool out of what functioned as a rigid axiom.

The critical capacities of the psychoanalytic semiotics of subjectivity are tested in the analysis of the film-theoretical concept of *suture,* commonly narrowed down to the shot/reverse-shot technique. The device consists of the succession of a field of vision (shot) and the position from which the field was seen, including the (fictional) viewer (reverse-shot). According to Silverman, the latter is often male or a substitute for him. This device is used in classic Hollywood films to assure the (male) spectator of a means of identification while not inducing his fears. During an analysis of the process at work in two rather disturbing films, the author shows how the device itself holds the means of its own disruption: transgressing certain distinctions, resistance to the system is displayed while the reassuring transparency of the process is broken up into self-consciousness and questioning.

One may wonder whether the discussion could not have been more illuminating had the author not succumbed precisely here to the apparent self-evidence of the antithetic character of the subject-object relation in the shot/reverse-shot device of *suture*. This problem being similar to that of the subject-object relation in theories of focalization, its interest for literary theory is obvious. In agreement with the author's critical attitude toward binarism, I would suggest the relation should be considered as complementary and mutually constitutive in the first place. Like oppositions such as black/white, or good/bad, the one term does not have any meaning without "collaboration" of the other; but unlike these, the subject is subject *by* its relation to/desire of the object, it contains the latter; in other terms, it is the object's displacement. Once this relation is viewed in this way, it becomes more obvious that the scopophilic, voyeuristic tendencies of the viewer *must* react to the fetishization of the female body in Hollywood movies, just as the relation cannot but be disturbed by any displacement of their respective roles. The subject is not the antonym of the object but its complement.

This book is, after all, ambitious: it presents, clarifies, illustrates semiotic theory, it shows its critical capacities, their limits, *and* it contributes to the widening of the latter.

BEYOND QUESTIONING

What is the point of the ongoing questioning of the subject? And what exactly is questioned? One feature the theories under discussion have in common is the assumption of the subject as a human individual, however determined, disrupted and subjected s/he may be. Benveniste and the other linguists preoccupied by a linguistics of enunciation, necessarily a linguistics of subjectivity, aim at a systematic account of the traces of subjectivity in language. As Kerbrat-Orecchioni (1980) states, a linguistics of enunciation cannot but displace its object: interested in the *production* of language, inherently unique and fugitive, its only material is the *product* it seeks to overcome. Hence, the notion of *trace*. The object of study becomes the traces of the production as present in the product, thus spanning the gap it first installed.

The question, then, is whether or not this approach can break radically with a notion of the subject as a unified individual. The subject as open substance and as the agent of signifying activity can exist in language only, the language which signifies it, constitutes it and then effaces it, as in a perfect narrative cycle (Bremond). But as long as one considers the traces of subjectivity in language as a means of returning to the subject as its origin—however questionable, however disrupted—the myth of the origin of language is not yet overcome. This is not, however, the only possible meaning of *trace*. The notion does not necessarily point backwards to some origin it allows one to reconstruct. Rather, the trace, as symptom or index, relates to its co-text by contiguity. Projecting the network of a semantic space onto the continuous parts of the enunciated, it becomes progressive rather than regressive, pointing, not to the outcome of an original activity but to the form of a structure. As such, the notion of subject can only be useful for an analysis of enunciation which is unavoidably semantic, if it is itself semantically broken open. Benveniste points to that consequence when he says that it is the *you* that constitutes the *I*, while the *I* presupposes an even unformulated *you*. This mutuality already holds, in fact, a radical break with the individual subject: losing its stability and continuity, the *I* moves back and forth between the two positions of *I* and *you*. There is no way to join the social individual anymore, and thus linguistic theory has no direct continuity with psychoanalysis and sociology, where the object of study remains the relation between the individual and its environment, however problematic and, in recent views, overwhelming, the latter is to the former.

Once this break is assumed, the possibility of a semantics of subjectivity unhampered by an ongoing search for unmediated social integration is laid open. Narrative theory is one discipline which has already assumed such a possibility, if within an illusory representational framework. It is here that Carroll, for example, could have been more original in his critique of the notion of implied author. Had he not mistaken the formulation, confusing Booth's "resultant image" with his own interpretation as "origin of form," he could have deconstructed the notion because of its personalistic representationalism. In fact, Booth's is a failed attempt to theorize subjectivity *not* because of an originalistic fallacy, but because it sticks to the *unified* subject as a reflection of the individual, human subject. In spite of her attempt at a critique of the Lacanian assumptions on sexualization, Silverman does not quite overcome the unified subject either. Both critics seek illustrations of their points in *representations* of subjects, in characters that is, instead of analyzing subjective positions in their multiplicity and difference.

The direction that seems more promising to me is that of a radicalization of the notion of subjectivity as a certain narrative theory has it, mapping the different subject positions according to their semiotic activities. Kerbrat-Orecchioni (1980) points to the same idea when she assumes the distinction between the speaker/hearer positions and the interpretative competence, fed by ideological and psychological dispositions displayed in the act of interpretation. This distinction joins that between narrating voice/addressee and focalizer/interpreter (Bal 1986). These positions, and those of the represented subjects/diegetic agents being plural by definition, the semantic network of such positions can be mapped for each discursive unit, thus providing the *traces* of subjectivity in the sense of *projection*. It is only at this point that the relations between this discursive subjectivity which is basically semantic, and the social, ultimately individual subjects of writer and readers and their subjecting environment can be rethought as the pragmatic dimension of the semiotic process. The break I have mentioned between disciplines is thus a precondition of their ultimate integration in a theory that is not multidisciplinary but truly interdisciplinary. The very subject-matter of both these books makes such a progress impossible. The limitations the authors imposed upon themselves in their choice of sources have not a little to do with that impossibility.

Both books draw largely upon French theoretical works, and not always the most important nor the most recent ones at that. Both keep silent on Kristeva, whose theory of the subject in process, and the production of the text whose hiding engenders ideology, deserves attention in this context. Fortunately, Silverman deals with Kristeva in a later book, where she conducts a brilliant critique of the latter's gendering of subjectivity (1988). Although in this earlier book Silverman at least tries to go beyond the French seventies in her own attempts, while Carroll offers extended essays on Simon's novels, I feel it is time for American academics to emancipate themselves from this fixation. After all, Barthes' *S/Z,* however stimulating, is better placed at the beginning of such books than at the end. It is given the last word in *The Subject of Semiotics,* which I feel is a regression after the discussion of the critical possibilities of *suture* theory. For *S/Z* is neither a theory, in spite of its theoretical insights, nor concerned with the subject of semiotics. Other work has been done, and remains to be done, to analyze further, not only the subject of speech, but also its relations to other textual subjects in all the aspects of the term. Well analyzed, the ambiguity of Carroll's "subject," not only in his two senses but in the numerous possible others, is worth a theory.

The lines drawn from theory to the critique *of* and *with* theory all converge on the concept in the title of Silverman's book. In fact, and this is the last paradox of this double review, the books should exchange titles. The ambiguity of the word "subject" in Silverman's title is uncalled for, while Carroll's title promises what it does not do: it does not question *the* subject. If I had my way, Silverman's introduction to semiotics would be the central textbook for a required course in all humanities programs.

▪ 6 ▪

Force and Meaning

INTRODUCTION

The enigma of art, creativity, and artistic sensitivity has always intrigued psychoanalysts. Since art is part of the object-domain of semiotics, the psychoanalytic views of the above have also intrigued some semioticians. Semioticians have borrowed psychoanalytic concepts and sometimes its style, while psychoanalysts are sharply aware of the overall importance of symbols and signs for their discipline. The two books that will be discussed here each represent one of the directions of the borrowing. Methodologically speaking, this is about as far as the encounter of semiotics, esthetics, and psychoanalysis has gone. Critics hover between explanation and interpretation and struggle with the problem of the "other" discipline: how to talk psychoanalysts into being less speculative? Semioticians into being less positivistic? Or estheticians, less idealistic? But why try in the first place?

Psychoanalysis is a semiotic theory, in that it works on signs (symptoms, dreams), on codes (condensation, displacement), on the phatic dimension (transference and counter-transference), and, first and foremost, on meaning. It shares with semiotics the imperialism inherent to any hermeneutic "mastercode." Objects of art, or the process of production and reception of art for that matter, consist of, or work with, signs. Any esthetic theory has therefore a potentially semiotic status; it is only a matter of vocabulary whether to speak of brush-strokes, style, or iconographic traditions as codes or not. On the basis of this double semiotic status, psychoanalytic discourse on art cannot avoid at least touching upon semiotic issues. Psychoanalytic theories of art and creativity are of interest, not only because of this semiotic potential, but also because they share with semiotics the attempt to overcome both deterministic, mechanistic views of culture, and idealistic speculations about it.

However, attempts to construct a general theory of what is assumed to be a psychic phenomenon suffer from a number of problems of method that are difficult to solve:

- Premises are vague. The relations between the disciplines are more or less based on an implicit analogy, which leaves room for more specific relations that remain unargued (see chapter 4).
- The concepts of art and creativity cannot be defined without recourse to a theory of the same type; hence, circularity is inevitable.
- There is no reason why one should assume a general phenomenon, like creativity or art, for which a single theory should account.
- The resulting lack of specificity makes such theories virtually irrelevant. On what basis can one expect to illuminate the question of art regardless of its varied forms, media, historical, social, and ideological contexts? Universality narrows empirical content down to very little.
- There is no hope to ever reach falsifiability. There is no way of finding out whether there are subjects with the features that define the creative psyche and yet do not create. Theories remain necessarily speculative.
- The discourse of such theories is strongly metaphorical. Each metaphor used brings in a number of uncontrolled features which travel along with it. Moreover, metaphorical equations tend to replace other relations, like causal, functional, or synedochical relations, while these would make the theory less vague and more falsifiable. Deri's book, for example, draws heavily on metaphors such as behavior of mother = behavior of child, toys = the world, and the like, where a functional relation would have had more explanatory power, or be more easily rejected. The equations are stated, of course, and can hardly be argued: psychoanalysis as a whole is based on a number of such metaphorical premises and they have become so self-evident that we do not question them any longer.
- A last problem is that theories that deal with "good" things like beauty easily become moralistic. Freud tried to overcome this tendency, and managed better than many of his followers, but not entirely. In Kofman's book, this moralism is absent; in contrast, the premise of Deri's book is that creativity is a good thing. The author, then, sets out to explain the origin of that good thing by good origins, by another of these metaphors. The good mother is, not surprisingly, the first and foremost requirement for a creative person to develop. Moralism and metaphor collaborate closely.

These are enough problems to make one wish to give up the attempt to develop a psychoanalytic theory of art. However, from a semiotic perspective, they may not matter so much. Rather than seeking to explain art, in the strong sense, as a genetic theory like psychoanalysis does, a semiotic view of "psychoanalysis *and* art" might specify this ambiguous "and" (Felman 1982) in a hermeneutic framework. The conjunction means "behind" in the sense of "before" for psychoanalysts, "about" or "in" for many pre-post-structuralist critics, "in dialogue with" for deconstructionists; it may indicate "functioning as a go-between in the process of" for the semiotician. The relationship between psychoanalysis and art is, then, neither a master-slave relationship as the arrogance of positivist epistemology would have it, nor an egalitarian dialogue as Felman prefers it. Psychoanalysis could provide, through some of its concepts, tools to semiotize art, to account for the dynamic process of art by mediating the relations between sender, work, and addressee in an otherwise noncommunicative process dominated by fixation and delay.

The assumption that underlies this use of psychoanalytic concepts concerns the problematic relation between genesis and reception through the message that semioticians call a set of signs. In brief, it supposes that the artist's psychic force which leads to the making of a work impresses its traces in that work. Here, force can best be viewed as the interaction between energy, drive, imagination, and symbolization. The result of this process, that translates force into meaning, retains the forcefulness of the process within the meaning. The addressee is somehow sensitive to that aspect; it triggers his or her identification. The expression is the only accessible part of this process: its result and its trace. Through the semiotic status of these traces as signs—or symptoms for that matter—psychoanalytic theory is able to grasp the effect of its concepts of art.

In contrast to an explanatory theory, psychoanalytic concepts are to be situated somewhere between signs and codes. As signs, they signify the background on which the above assumption of the force-meaning interaction rests. As codes, they mediate between interpretation and explanation on one level, and on another between sender and addressee, on yet another between force and meaning. In order to keep the transition between these levels open, I will refer to the concepts discussed in this light as *views*. Since they are identified with familiar concepts from psychoanalysis that function as interpretive tools, interpretations based on these concepts can be integrated as an interdisciplinary enterprise.

In the following pages, I will assess some views of art as interdisciplinary hypotheses. I will illustrate my ideas with reference to paintings by Rembrandt. In our culture, painting is the art *par excellence*, so much so that it influences in an exemplary fashion the institutional and ideological location of art within Western culture as a whole. Rembrandt, in that location, is a most representative figure, if not *the* clearest case. His canvases, then, constitute a challenge to any reductive attempt to analysis. Secondly, this artist belongs to an era still innocent of Freudianism. On the other hand, unlike Sophocles' verbal art, there is, in the case of painting, not such wonderful coincidence of discourse as was possible between Freud and his prestigious model. Thirdly, Rembrandt's art is figurative, which gives us both an opportunity and a problem. Representational art is "about" something, and thus open to reductionism. Therefore, it is appropriate to use it for exploring the ways interdisciplinary analysis can counter the tendency to reductionism. Additionally, Rembrandt belongs to a tradition where skill was considered a primary asset of a painter, more so than the "touch of craziness" that psychoanalytic criticism, as heir to the Romantic tradition, so often presupposes. There is little enough known about his life that wild speculations about his possibly neurotic constitution can only be ridiculous. This protects the enterprise of psychocriticism as viewed in this chapter, against another well-known trap. On the other hand, most Rembrandt scholarship is so exceedingly tedious (see for example Slatkes 1983) that any attempt to renew the approach should be welcomed. Finally, after the many respectful but not always sufficiently distanced studies that escape such tediousness only by replacing it with laudative discourse, Rembrandt's work deserves some attention in which respect is not an issue.

In the present survey, five concepts will be shown at work in the way described above. As tools for a "psychosemiotic" criticism, they will be assessed only insofar as they integrate both disciplines while entailing understanding of both work and effect of the paintings. Numerous other aspects of the views will be left aside. For a much further developed discussion, both to Rembrandt and to the use of psychoanalysis to understand this art, I have to refer to my book on the subject (1991).

SUBLIMATION

A central, yet admittedly vague (Laplanche and Pontalis 1980: 431–433) Freudian concept is *sublimation*. Its most thorough discussion by Freud is in *Three Essays on the Theory of Sexuality* (1905) and, in relation to art, in *Civilization and its Discontents* (1930). Like the other concepts to be discussed here, sublimation is not specific to art; it is meant to explain social life and civilization in general, of which art is a "sublime" extension. The concept points to human activities which have no apparent connections with sexuality but are assumed to be motivated by the force of sexual (or aggressive) instincts. The instinctual force remains, but is diverted toward a new, non-sexual aim. The objects of the sublimated instinctual force are socially valued ones, like artistic and intellectual creativity. Hence the somewhat idealistic term, which should not, however, be mistaken for its everyday correlate "sublime" as used to evaluate the fine arts.

The idea that art comes from the repression of sexual or aggressive instincts, which is what the sublimation hypothesis amounts to, is obviously bound to scandalize many art-lovers. Attempts to counter it with more "positive" views have been numerous, some of them most valuable (Klein 1977, Westlund 1984). Deri's views are clearly motivated by, among other things, the hope, rather than the scientific conviction, that human beings are more elevated, especially when creating beauty. This aspect is not of concern here. As it stands, the sublimation hypothesis has to be evaluated in its capacity for interdisciplinary illumination of specific works of art and their processing.

An analysis of the concept shows that it rests on two tensions. One is that between *force* (instinctual drives) and *meaning* (its sublimated aim). This tension disturbs Deri (83) and I would venture that this is her major motivation in trying to counter the sublimation hypothesis with a different view. The other tension is that between *symbol* (the disguise of the repressed) and *meaning* (the repressed). Deri's polemic stance (43) distorts and simplifies Freud's perspective when she claims that for him an irreducible opposition exists between the poles of the latter opposition. Her alternative, however, is inherent to Freud's semiotic theory. "Only by considering symbols as *revealing* and *communicating as well as concealing* can their full meaning be understood" (44). Freud's interpretative practice shows that he could not agree more happily with this idea. In fact, what distinguishes Freud's semiotics from, say, Saussure's, is the motivatedness of the relation between signs and meaning; it is motivated, precisely, by the force wherein it originates. Concealment is revealing in itself, or can be revealed, in contrast with arbitrariness. Deri's problems with these two tensions are symptomatic of what is the most interesting characteristic of the sublimation hypothesis: its deep interdisciplinarity.

What makes the sublimation hypothesis difficult to grasp and relevant for semiotics is that the tension of force and meaning is dialectic without *Aufebung*. Whenh repression takes place it leaves traces of its instinctual background. Through the indices those traces constitute, the force becomes meaning. The meanings conveyed in the sublimation process, on the other hand, cannot but carry the force that is their signifier; the meaning is force. It is perhaps for this reason that the ambiguity inherent in any semiosis seems to be so vital in art. Ambiguity implies that the ambiguous sign is a case of condensation. Lacan (1966) and many others equate condensation with metaphor; the cluster /one sign-several meanings/. One reason why semiotic theories of metaphor always have some slight inconsistency (as argued by Ricoeur 1979, Silverman 1983) may be due to the illusion that the above equation is valid. If condensation in a semiotic analysis has this metaphoric aspect, its psychoanalytic background implies that it must possess in the form of traces of its instinctual force a metonymic aspect as well. Finally, the meaning revealed and concealed, being metonymically related to the signs of the work of art, the sublimation hypothesis implies that some meaning related to sexuality or aggression must be traceable in the work. According to the semiotic perspective, these meanings are figuratively signified; metaphor subsumes metonymy.

The interdisciplinarity of the concept can best be shown by trying to force its different aspects into two sets of mono-disciplinary concerns, which would result in the following:

psychoanalysis	*semiotics*
force	meaning
trace	ambiguity

metonymic aspect	metaphoric aspect
sex or aggression	work of art

This ordering shows that neither set is self-sufficient. The need to clarify each concern through one or more of the other set is characteristic of interdisciplinarity.

Kenneth Clark finds Rembrandt's *The Blinding of Samson* (fig. 1) "an extremely disturbing picture" and he adds, "Only a man of genius could have done anything so consistently horrifying" (1978: 50). Clark describes the painting in terms such as "ugly," "horrifying," "appalling," "grotesque." Like Deri's disturbances, I take Clark's extreme reaction as a symptom that the processing of the painting requires the sublimation hypothesis. These strong terms, that have negative connotations, have more force than is usual in Clark's discourse. Although their meaning, in context, is acceptably technical, I venture that something happened between Clark and the painting that belongs to the register of shock.

There is even no need to interpret the work with reference to the biblical source. The intertextual relations can only make Rembrandt's choice of subject, as well as his composition, accents, and execution, more disturbing. The sexual meanings that the biblical story hardly conceals (see Bal 1987) are rivaled in the painting by the aggressive violence of the event. Critics have suggested that Rembrandt's conspicuous obsession with blindness refers to his repressed Oedipal castration complex (Held 1969). True, his work is full of blind old men (Homer, Tobit), of old men that seem blind (the artist's alleged father, the father in the Hermitage *Return of the Prodigal Son*) and even of blind old men carefully—or cruelly—operated upon by their son (several of the Tobias drawings). But here, the situation is reversed; it is the men in power that blind the lover Samson who is all but fatherly in position, outfit and behavior.

This painting was not commissioned, but is alleged to have been a present to Rembrandt's patron Huygens and imposed on the latter against his will. It was in order to make up (and how ambivalently!) for the artist's lack of punctuality in the execution of a commission of a series of Passion scenes for the Prince of Orange, Huygens' employer (Rosenberg 1980). Moreover, there was no tradition of representation of this particular scene of the Samson story, of which Rembrandt represented several rarely depicted scenes in the course of his career (*Samson Threatening his Father-in-law* being perhaps the most revealing of the set).

Why did Rembrandt, apparently unable to execute the commission—the best he ever got—and aware of Huygens' reluctance to accept the gift, have to substitute the one suffering scene for the other, while the one was welcome and well paid for, the other hardly acceptable? The opposition between the two suffering heroes is revealing. The passion scene has the victim on the erect cross, his body fully exposed. The innocent victim is willingly accepting

Figure 1: Rembrandt, *The Blinding of Samson*. Frankfurt am Main, Städelsches Kunstinstitut

his suffering. Instead, Samson is guilty of his own undoing, yet in revolt; he is lying down, in a sort of grotto guarded by the woman, formed by hardly recognizable curtains. Instead of the classical style of the commissioned series, he paints here in a wild baroque or Jacobean style (Clark 1978: 53). Indeed, Rembrandt is doing the contrary of what he is expected to do, and this as punctually as he could possibly do it. The violence of the work has not passed unnoticed. The aggression implied in such a gift is obvious. What has passed unnoticed, however, is the striking resemblance between its structure and that of a seemingly entirely different work of roughly the same period; calm, beautiful, erotic—the *Danae* of the Hermitage at Saint Petersburg. The similarity is disturbing, given the difference in subject-matter. *Danae* is an attractively sensuous work, where the reclining body of the woman in the grotto formed by curtains yields self-confidence and power. The grotto is substantially similar in both works. Where Samson lifts his right foot, Danae lifts her right hand, forming a similar line (Bal 1991: 326–345 for details of this comparison).

What can the sublimation hypothesis do for our understanding of this disturbing painting of Samson? Throwing such a work into the face of his benefactor—a father figure—is so obviously aggressive, that no repression of that impulse can be assumed. But when using the sublimation hypothesis we do not want to understand what Rembrandt did to Huygens, what his (consciously signified) message was, although those relations of power have relevance for the artist's psychobiography, but rather, what he did to Clark, and to many others who are emotionally affected by the work and, while disturbed, can hardly do more than call it "disturbing."

The overt aggression goes from the psychoanalytic side to the semiotic side of our analysis of the concept, in order to become a meaning which must contain some trace of its initiating force that may be other than aggressive. In other words, it becomes the sign of the possible other drive. According to the sublimation hypothesis, this may be a sexual impulse. The sexual aspects of the painting are of a different order than the aggressive ones. If the soldiers, for example, *are* aggressive, their weapons *mean*, by their form and direction, the penis; the grotto, and the position of the body in it, represent sexual penetration. The sexual aspects come clearly to the fore when we compare it to the overtly erotic *Danae*. More importantly, however, the sexual aspects signify in their turn another level of meaning where they "conceal and reveal" the relation between aggression and sexuality; the representation of the latter as frightening. The soldiers who do the blinding not only handle their phallic weapons relentlessly, they labor; this is hard work.

The shifter between the two distinct but related isotopies is the structural element that makes the painting deeply ambiguous, in the psychoanalytic and in the semiotic sense. Samson lifts his foot in order to kick Delilah. It is this element that is similar to the arm of the powerful woman of the *Danae*. It resembles two things at once; the struggle of the infant to separate itself from the mother's body, here clearly represented as the womb in the form of the grotto/curtains, and the thigh of the birth-giving woman, suffering and cramped, yet tense with effort. This double similarity suggests that the struggle at stake is that entailed by sexual ambiguity. It is caused by the frightening coincidence of two frightening experiences; the violence perceived in male sexuality, and the emprisonment that female sexuality, through the association with the mother, seems to entail land from which the represented subject has to free himself. As Kristeva put it, the association between sexuality and the grip of the mother causes a struggle of life and death, of existence and annihilation, in which the subject constitutes itself as a sexual being (1982: 12–13).

This suggests why the male subject in the painting is the birth-giving mother and struggles against her in a most unusual reciprocal perspective. We see the grotto, with Delilah as the guardian at the entrance/exit; the reclining body inside this gigantic body, and, at the same time, the inside-body of the baby, being born and giving birth, replacing the mother and fighting her (Kristeva 1982: 64; Kofman 1980: 97). The scene represented here is a strikingly elaborate response to what is, in the biblical story, represented at the clearest in the scene of the destruction of the temple (see Bal 1987).

It is, hopefully, clear that the horribly suffering Samson is a more suitable signifier for this painful experience, this forceful event, than Christ, sublimely erect and already past his suffering, relating to the father rather than to the mother, accepting his fate so that the force of the struggle is gone. The solely metaphoric interpretation, then, would consider aggression as the concealing sign of something else, say, sexual ambiguity. But the sublimation hypothesis also requires a metonymic link. Aggression, then, must be related to the sexual impulse. In the picture, the aggression is directed toward the already powerless man. He is the victim of male (the soldiers and their weapons) and female (the emprisonment in the grotto) sexual impulses. The aggression goes back from the victim to the woman, from the victim as woman/mother, to the woman as victim. The violence of the shock between these two impulses, coming from these different identifications, is what constitutes the trace of the force that disturbs our critic. It is there that lies the "touch of craziness" of this work which signifies the meeting of force and meaning.

The sublimation hypothesis can, then, be used within an interpretive procedure that is reluctant to jump to biographical conclusions. It does, however, integrate such data if one wishes; the gesture toward Huygens certainly enhances the effect of the painting; maybe it adds an element (the father figure absent from the painting) that helps link this work intertextually with the other "blind men." But there is no need to assume that artists are neurotic, or more neurotic than we all are. There is no need either to stick to the overtly instinctual features of the work, which would be going in a sense *against* the sublimation hypothesis, in that it would ignore repression in the concept, and the semiotic detours it entails. Nor do we need to ignore the instinctual features, for the sublimation hypothesis itself requires that the signs be there.

MELANCHOLIA

Compared to the sublimation hypothesis the hypothesis that the process of art is melancholic mourning (see Kofman 1985) is of a different status in both disciplines. Unlike sublimation, melancholia is not an overall decisive factor in culture. If there were no losses to suffer, there would be no need to mourn, and if all mourning were successful, there would be no melancholia. For melancholia is—in Freud's definition—failed mourning. The process of detachment from the lost love object may be hampered by the overwhelming force of the identification of the subject with the object. As a result, the subject cannot free itself from the object, nor can it invest other objects; there is no space left. Given the powerlessness that results from melancholia, the melancholia hypothesis is paradoxical from the outset, not because it relates beauty to sadness but because it relates the creation or investment of an object to the incapacity to relate to objects. Greuze's *Girl Weeping over her Dead Bird* is not, according to Kofman (22), about a girl mourning her dead bird. It is about mourning beauty. Making, or relating to, beauty is an attempt to escape from the elusiveness of all things, which we spend our time mourning. But while seeking consolation in beauty, we discover that beauty is in itself elusive. Art, then, mourns itself. We create beauty that gives us simultaneously the illusion of eternity, awareness of elusiveness, and the mourning of that clash. Hence, Greuze's girl does not mourn anything, she *is* mourning. This is Kofman's central view in *Mélancholie de l'art*.

The semiotic implications of this view are complex, indirect, and difficult to grasp. They touch upon representation. Kofman describes Aristotle's double conception of mimesis as both copying and supplying, but in any case replacing reality, and relates it to fascination with and fear of resemblance. The dead body, the antique colossus (Vernant 1976), and the mirror image each exemplify the surplus meaning (i.e., the *atopia*) inherent to the object that represents, through resemblance, something which it and is not. This *atopia* necessitates that something be done, in order to reinstate the reassuring categories of being, something magic:

> Art concerns, not a simple annihilation of the real (which would still be a way to control it) but its sacrifice in the sense that Bataille says that the sacrifice changes, destroys its victim, but does not neglect it. It concerns a slippage of the real, its suspension where all immediate meaning gets lost. (16)

It is in this sense that Kofman can equate the sacrifice of the subject that loses itself in its overinvestment in the lost object, and the loss of that object which triggers melancholia. Resemblance creates a loss of identity similar to that caused by overinvestment in the lost object by the melancholic subject who, in the process, sacrifices itself.

In spite of the entirely different status of the concept of melancholia in both psychoanalysis and semiotics, the melancholia hypothesis like the sublimation hypothesis has an interdisciplinary background that exceeds by far the simple borrowing of concepts. The psychoanalytic side requires that an object be lost; so we need to identify the object and the event. In Kofman's view, beauty, the ultimate resource for the sufferers of loss, constitutes loss by its elusiveness. Mourning, then, becomes melancholia because the lost object was the last resource, and losing beauty teaches the subject that all objects are lost beforehand. But what is beauty? When is art beautiful enough to trigger this melancholia? The link, here, or maybe the leap, brings us to the semiotic side. The feeling of loss is related to, perhaps is, the *atopia* that characterizes resemblance. The double concept of mimesis, which is described in an almost Peircian language in the *Poetics* (Bal 1982), provides an entrance into the problem. As Kofman rightly says, the duality of Aristotelian mimesis is not an opposition but rather, the opposition is a feature of what it describes, and what constitutes its fictionality. The antithetical interpretation has brought about a stream of fictionally based arguments, traditions, esthetic philosophies, and that displacement onto the concept is precisely its force. Resemblance, then, is both similarity and difference, and the object stands for, but is not, something else. Its status as sign is what constitutes, inaugurates, its being lost.

If we follow the suggestions of the melancholia hypothesis, art is effective when it is self-reflexive. It will, then, represent an object lost by definition, hence signs which stand for something else, and it will also represent the resulting *atopia*. The duality of such works triggers in the addressee that uneasy feeling which uncannily suggests that we are not just looking at one thing, but that something is happening on another level than the one with which we are preoccupied.

The Polish Rider (fig. 2) is one of Rembrandt's most enigmatic paintings. Little is known about the circumstances of its genesis. It stands alone in the work of the artist, although it shares features with several of his "periods." Again, it is Clark's phrasing of his incapacity to articulate a response in his presentation of the painting that occasions the effectiveness of the melancholia hypothesis for the interpretation of the work. He calls it "one of the most personal and *mysterious* of his later paintings," "magical," and "one of the great poems of painting" (1978: 59–60, my italics). Others react equally strongly to its "strange" quality (Held 1969) which is often explained as orientalism (Slatkes 1983; for a critical view of orientalism, see Said 1978). The typical move of critics to set out and naturalize the strangeness (Culler 1975, Campbell 1973) calls for a view of the type under consideration here which should enable us to interpret both the painting and the response through explanation. One feature that, according to Clark (1978: 60), accounts for its strangeness, is the "almost feminine beauty" of the rider. This sexual ambiguity is naturalized by reference to the sitter, who may have been the same as the woman sitting for Potiphar's wife in the two paintings devoted to that subject. Although this reference could lead to interesting intertextual features of the three paintings, it does not at all account for the "strange," because "almost feminine" beauty of this knight—a model of masculinity in the feudal tradition. The other feature that is called upon for an understanding of the strangeness is the gaze of both rider and horse, each directed toward some unattainable object.

These gazes will provide the key to the solution of a problem which Kofman leaves unanswered. Melancholia refers to a story. The loss of the loved object, the attempt to mourn it, the failure of the attempt, the process of investment of the object in the self, and the subsequent fixation which closes off new object relations; it is a process in time. How, then, can art be the loss and its mourning, as well as the failure of the process, at the same time? The gazes of horse and rider are directed, spatially, toward some unattainable object, unattainable because irretrievable, lost—in time. The object is outside the representation itself. Moreover, the gazes diverge. The split between the subject of gazing and the lost object is represented within the representation; the unity horse-rider, one of Freud's favorite metaphors for the unity of *ich* and *id* that is the subject, is broken by the divergence of the gazes. Spatially, the directions differ; narratively, the aims, the objects differ. The contiguous space and the future object are represented negatively, in their loss. In narratological terms, the object of focalization is nothingness. This structure of focalization, divergent and reaching outside the work, represents the limits of focalization itself.

The gazes, in their double relation to time and space, introduce a tension between the narrative and the descriptive modes of representation. As Alpers (1985) argues, Rembrandt explores the limits of the descriptive mode that distinguishes Dutch art in the seventeenth century from Italian art, which was much more narrative. The directionality of the gazes entails description, the mode of representing what is seen. But nothing is seen, the rider and horse see "it" in a different space. The teleology of the gazes, their object-orientedness, entails narration, the mode of representing what has happened, and what will happen. But what happened is loss, the loss of beauty's duration, what will happen is the unattainability of the object. Melancholia, by its fixating and paralyzing power, makes the story into nothingness: into description. It is this tension that allows the melancholia hypothesis to operate; where object and time, implied by loss and mourning, create narration, the unattainability of the object, rendering the gaze pointless, triggers melancholia. For this reason, the knight representing beauty should be beautiful himself, and ambiguously so: through femininity, through otherness. In this way *he* becomes *it*, the beautiful man becomes beauty itself, the represented object becomes representation.

Figure 2: Rembrandt, *The Polish Rider*. New York, The Frick Collection

This "cross-eyed" gaze so characteristic of *The Polish Rider* may shed new light on Rembrandt's blind men, too. The paradox of the blind gaze, the dead eye and the fixated eye, is particularly acute in some of the paintings where the blind men are, perhaps, not quite blind. In the *Danae*, for example, the gaze is as objectless as in *The Polish Rider*, although here the object is as fully represented as possible. But strangely enough, the body of the woman, the mother, nude and exposed to the man's gaze as it is, needs only lift her powerful arm in order to strip the on-looker of his identity. Subjected to her direction, the voyeur whose identity depends on gazing, looks away from the very object that constitutes himself. In the Hermitage *The Return of the Prodigal Son*, often cited as an example of the obsession with blindness, the ambiguity is even greater. At first sight, the father looks down upon his retrieved son. At closer inspection, his eyes are empty, blind. The departure of the son may have had this castrating result, because a father without his child is a father no more. But when we actually look into the father's eyes, he does see, his eyes are not entirely dead, although the result may be equivalent; he looks away from the son. Where the head of the son turns slightly to the right, the father's eyes turn to the opposite direction, signifying the irretrievable loss between them. The consummation of this irretrievable loss turns into the fixation that is melancholia, and blindness.

Through the mediation of the concept of mimesis, the melancholia hypothesis suggests how absence, loss, and the failure to relate to the outside world, can be represented in the gap between descriptive and narrative art, brought about in these cases by the divergence of focus, a divergence which sets the limits to narrativity itself. The melancholia hypothesis, then, is not only less general within psychoanalysis, but also more specific than the sublimation hypothesis within semiotics. It speaks of signs as signifiers of modes of representation. Kofman's account would have been more convincing had it been clearer in its interdisciplinary position between psychoanalysis and semiotics. Where her discourse remains merely suggestive, the view she sets forth can be theoretically enriching if the paradoxical relations between the negativity of loss and the sacrifice of the subject that melancholia entails, and the representation through the breaking of limits of semiotic modes and means, are more explicitly thought through.

NARCISSISM

The assessment of the psychoanalytic and the semiotic impact of the concept of narcissism leads to another paradox. The concept points to a love relationship whose object is the image of oneself. The image one has of oneself is, however, founded on the model of other persons. Here lies the psychoanalytic paradox. The hypothesis that art is a function of narcissism rests on a second one: the amorous captivation of the subject by this self-image which leads to the internalization of a relationship and externalized in the work of art.

The latter comes to stand for, becomes a sign of, the loved self-image. If the self is, first, fully internalized, short-circuiting others, it is, second, fully externalized, made other. This tension reflects back on the concept of narcissism itself: rather than the definition of a specific object, the self, it refers to a relationship.

The concept has come to stand for a number of varied phenomena, of different stages in the development of the subject. Primary narcissism is the phase where the subject has not yet gained awareness of difference. There can be no relation to an object, then, for object and subject still merge in unity. This objectless state is seen as both complete unity and complete *morcèlement*, non-delimited while not whole either; or rather, wholeness does not apply as a category. A subject that is not distinguishable from an object cannot be a subject, for separation is what defines it. In Freudian terms, the ego cannot exist yet because it is not yet distinguished from the *id* which, once distinguished, should allow object relations to emerge. Narcissism as relationship does not apply to this state. The tension which is initiated with the need for separation from the mother is considered by Kristeva (1982) the most archaic form of narcissism which can be the force of art (Kristeva's view, Chase 1983; also Jacobus 1986). At the point where the effort to separate is strong enough to set forth the purely negative relation to the mother, the first relation to the self as non-mother, as m/other; the first form of narcissism features the duality of the representation of self as nothingness, as that which goes away from the mother by becoming one, modeled as this beginning subject is on the only possible object.

The moment, which is one of effort, struggle and pain, may be what is so forcefully represented by the double image of Samson as both baby kicking himself out of the mother, and as mother in pain of labor. The archaic experience burdens the subject, both painter and onlooker, with the trace of being absolute effort, and nothing but effort. Samson's blinding comes to stand in a new light. The moment at stake, the transition from inside the womb to outside, is blinding: there can be nothing but the transition itself, and the purely negative subject cannot have eyes to see. It represents non-existence and, on another level, forgetfulness of that terrible state.

An intermediate form of narcissism, a next and equally transitional stage, has been analyzed by Lacan as the mirror phase (1966). The subject relates for the first time to another, and losing the initial blindness, internalizes the first image: the image of the self. The itinerary can be described as a voyage from the subject-to-be to the other, identification of that other with self, and return to the subject. If relation is there, it is one of imagination rather than of object. Image-forming is the basic experience that follows separation, and this image-forming leads to self-reflection in every possible sense. In art, this stage leads to the sense that there is not so much a represented object but an image, a non-reflexive (Banfield 1982) and yet self-conscious *image* of the self.

We may see this process, this itinerary from the subject to the self, in the series of etched self-portraits Rembrandt did at the beginning of his career. Usually, the set of varied facial expressions, from laughing to anger, through merry, sad, clownish, with an exaggeratedly ugly nose or with an idealized nose, is explained as exercises. The artist was simply training himself, using the cheapest sitter available. This explanation is highly plausible and down-to-earth and its only flaw is in the suggestion that it is exhaustive. It fails to account for the impact the etchings have on their viewers. The uneasiness they evoke is based here on the excess of difference between them which can be accounted for in terms of the transitional narcissism of the mirror stage. The discovery of the self as a first possible object/other to relate to is preceded by the realization of the otherness of the image. Rembrandt's practice of practicing in front of a mirror, then, is not only an attempt to develop his skills, but through that attempt it is a representation of that primal experience of the self as other in the first place.

The third moment of narcissism, referred to as secondary narcissism, is the later, regressive relationship from subject to self as exemplified by the myth of Narcissus. Here, the object-relation identifies the self with the other, or invests the self-image with the features of the love object. The relationship is regressive and as such constitutes a reversed narrative of the formation of the subject. Looking for the love object, Narcissus returns to the mirror, invests the self with the love directed to the object, then discovers the self-image in its contradiction and as a result returns to non-separation, back into the womb where he, and it all, came from. Secondary narcissism, unlike the two other stages, and just like melancholia, implies a story. As such, it subsumes in its reversal the two other moments with which it forms a series of moments, of events whose agents are gradually merging into nothingness. This is painfully contradictory because the subject of secondary narcissism has the awareness of the object status of the self as of others. In myth, the story leads to death; in art, to the sense of alienation—inherent to representation as discussed in the previous section—that affects the viewer who is unsure of what is seen: object or self, self as object.

The very early self-portrait (fig. 3) evokes that uncertainty more than the later self-portraits. The face features the symptoms of vanity that make critics qualify the painting as idealized. If moustaches and mouth, arrogant eyebrows and straight nose are not telling enough, hairdo and hat, gown and light, hardly leave room for doubt that the painting is idealized, not in relation to some "real" model, like the artist's legendary ugliness, but as representation. Its object is a handsome and proud young man, the self. On the other hand, this very feature signals insecurity, as does the hesitant eye directed almost, but not quite, to the viewer, who, insofar as she or he identifies with the subject of the work, functions like a mirror.

Of what, however, does the self consist in the case of a beginning ambitious artist? The idealization of self and the insecurity about it do not refer only to the self as image, but also to what this subject wants to be; a subject making objects, a subject whose identity is the work. The painting has the features, not only of the presentation of a proud and insecure young man, but also of the masterpiece of a proud and insecure young painter, who applies through this work for the status and the identity of the master-painter. It has the carefully accomplished strokes that display his skills—the varied substances of the hair, the feather, the scarf, and the chain, the velvet, and the jewel, the slightly shiny reflection on the nose, the tender wrinkles—and it has the daring novelties through which this particular painter will create his image: the empty background, the decentered light, the near absence of colors.

The representation of the self is, here, that of the self as being and as doing, as conforming to the standards of quality—handsome and skilled—and as different—insecure and original. It places the artist as a disclosing subject—beginning, still soft moustaches, and good, still over-skillful details—that strives for a place in relation to the world, to others. His is an attempt to acquire inter-subjective status, in order to establish his existence. As such, the portrait has the contradictions of narcissism itself. It constitutes the relationship with the self in otherness, and the resulting object, the work, displays by its sheer existence as object that the narcissistic subject loves an *image* of the self that is inter-subjectively acknowledged as other.

The semiotic aspects of narcissism are based on the relation of representation that the image of self as other entails. Where melancholia is based on the relation to the other who becomes, after the loss, internalized into the subject—so that, mediated by representation, the object becomes part of the subject—the narcissistic subject relates to an outside object, but this object is represented as the self. The relation of melancholia is synecdochical; that of narcissism is metaphorical. What is lacking in both cases is the metonymic relation based on existential contiguity. The different types of narcissism, however, entail different motivations of the metaphorical relation (Genette 1972: 41–66). Only secondary narcissism leads to full representation of the self, since the self is formed through the mirror stage. The self-portraits relating to that stage represent the self as other rather than self. But even within the broad category of secondary narcissism, the image can be based on what the subject is, what it used to be, thus introducing time, what it would like to be. Only in the first case does the relation remain fully metaphorical. In the second case, the temporal relation, virtually narrativizing the image, motivates the metaphor metonymically. In the third case, a temporal relation that points to the future insinuates itself, remaining slight and overwhelmed by the descriptive urge to give form to fantasy. Schafer (1967) distinguishes a fourth possibility: the image is modeled on what was once part of it. The resulting motivation of the metaphor is, then, synecdochical. If at all, it is doubly so: the stage at which the limits of the subject were different is that of primary narcissism, and then there was not yet self-image, there was not yet image at all. This relation can only be established through the reversed narrative of secondary narcissism regressing toward the pre-separation moment and its struggle. The narcissistic metaphor, then, not only represents the self as what was once part of the subject, but it does that through a previous part of its story.

The self-portrait is a socially and historically specific form of artistic self-expression. As such, it exemplifies possibilities that can choose other modes to reach a similarly significant double self-reflexivity. It is no coincidence that Rembrandt, who painted, etched, and drew his own image as other and as self in an amazing number of works, lived in the era of rising bourgeois self-consciousness. The genre could flourish in the context of social attitudes that make the urge for the contradictory self-expression through the object/other in inter-subjectivity into a typical phenomenon of the cultural environment. The artist who hovered between social classes all his life accommodates this particular mode with more than just conventional enthusiasm. Social factors may account for the mode (Wolff 1984), but not necessarily for the ambiguity and the insistent feeling of alienation that these self–portraits convey, nor for the onlooker's feeling of recognition of the urge and the archaic experience it rests upon. In other eras, artists will use different modes (Kristeva 1980; 1982; Jacobus 1986) to deal with the need and the strength of the persisting experience; but the viewer who is socially embedded in the conventions whereof the modes are a part, will still recognize, and hence acknowledge, what happens.

The power of the narcissism-hypothesis is twofold. It relates specifically to social attitudes, thus discriminating between the different forms of art they accommodate. The correspondence between the three forms of narcissism within psychoanalytic theory, and, through the different relations to the self/object, the semiotically pertinent figures that those relations subsume, allows for specification of semiotic motivations within representation.

IDEALS AND IDEALIZATION

The self that becomes the object of relational investment in narcissism can be described as the "aggregate or organization (so far as it exists) of all the self-representations" (Schafer 1967: 145). The plural form of the latter noun is to be kept in mind. Self-representations are numerous and changing and occupy different roles in the psychic system. They are constantly tested to standards the subject holds and to the latter's representations of reality. The hypothesis that the process of art derives its dynamic from the tensions brought about by the confrontation between representations of self—and of objects, for that matter—and standards the subject holds may partially subsume the narcissism-hypothesis, that is, when the idealization the confrontation often leads to concerns the self.

Ideals are standards of, for example, perfection, beauty, excellence, gratification. They concern all possible functions of the mind. They are morally and socially neutral. One may maintain standards that are socially unacceptable,

Figure 3: Rembrandt, *Self-portrait*. Boston, The Isabella Stewart Gandener Museum

like standards of "pure blood" or of absolute lust-gratification. Standards are defined by the tension between them and actuality; they are almost always impossible to meet. In trying to do something about that tension, one can change the standard, or one can change reality. Pushing toward the limits of reality in order to make ideals meet it more closely is different from changing (one's representation of) reality in order to make them coincide. In the first case, one is pursuing an ideal and trying to get the best out of it; in the second case, one is idealizing. Hence ideals may or may nota lead to idealization. A subject in a narcissistic stage will idealize itself by constructing self-representations that meet the standard. The standard defines the requirements for an investable love object. A less narcissistic subject will idealize another object: constructing representations of the other that are better than reality in order to make the object meet the standards set to it.

The idealized self-portrait, or portrait, shows the possibilities. The self is made better, that is, more impressive or beautiful, than reality. The quality of the portrait as representation, the insistence invested in making it as good as one possibly can, is not idealization: one can idealize one's image, but one's performance tells the truth of one's real limitations.

Rembrandt's numerous self-portraits suggest that some features of his looks did not meet his standards. The most noticeable is the nose. The nose is what he seems to have had the most problems with accepting as his, if we judge by the series of early etchings. In the light of narcissism, the ugliness of his nose seems to have made the artist feel "other" more than any feature. The idealization hypothesis suggests an antithetical relation between these etchings and the painted early self-portrait at the Gardener museum. The experience of alienation at the moment of the mirror stage leads to the standard of physical beauty that implies a straight nose. The etchings, then, signal the failure to meet that standard, and the cynical mocking of that failure; the painting, in contrast, represents a solution to the tensions through idealization. The ambition to be a good painter that this work so ostentatiously displays fulfills the function of making good for the lack of realism. Pursuing the ideal of excellence in painting successfully, the artist "deserves" the idealization of his face. Whether or not the pride in the young man's face is realistically justified is not our concern; there is no way to judge. But the fusing of the beauty of the face and that of the painting as such, which has been discussed already, points to the attempt to compromise between ideal and idealization. The good artist manages to meet the standard of excellence closely enough to allow himself to idealize his face without going too deeply into illusion and delusion. The excellent painter cannot but produce beauty, and the nose is part of that beauty: that is what the perfect matching of both ideals signifies as is visible in the work.

Another interesting case of this tension can be perceived in the painting *Samson Threatening his Father-in-law*, in which he represents himself as the young Samson, the ideal image of masculinity, beautiful, confronting an ugly old Jew. Here, the nose problem has been solved in an even more extreme way; keeping his striking eyes, he gives himself beautiful hair and a slightly "Jewish" nose, attributing to the father-figure the other side of what he so much desires: a caricatural aquiline nose. This suggests, as other works confirm, that the artist's interest in the Hebrew Bible pertains not only to religious or social interest in the growing Jewish community in Amsterdam. The story of the Jews must have appealed to him for reasons of self-representation.

Ideals originate in varied sources. For a semiotic study of what they bring about, it is not enough to notice that ideals are at stake in the production of a work. The reason why the work works, why the process, of which the work carries the traces, affects the addressee is, according to the idealization hypothesis, to be situated in the force with which ideals and reality clash, so that idealization and the pursuit of limits become so urgent that they become part of the representation. The force of the clash in its turn is entailed by the variable force with which the ideals are held up, for reasons that concern their origin. One reason why a subject can experience an unusually intense need to idealize can be the urge to repair for extremely ambivalent feelings and the destructiveness they entail. The craving for "something extremely good" (Klein 1977) as "reparation" for damage done in the past, which artist and addressee share, can then account for the positive response to an idealized self-portrait like Rembrandt's, while a mere display of vanity would rather irritate. The Kleinian concept of reparation integrates the two aspects of standards mentioned above into a convincingly harmonious whole: the idealization of the self-representation and the pursuit of the standard of excellence in the execution of it, which draws idealization nearer to reality, and reality nearer to ideal. Westlund (1986) explains the effect of Shakespeare's comedies by this aspect of the idealization hypothesis, thus interpreting the genre of romantic comedy as a whole. Whether or not such a genre will, in the cases of specific works, be effective or not—in other words, whether they will be experienced as a successful specimen of the genre—depends on the intensity with which the above clash has been turned into (idealized) representation. Not just any idealized representation will be appealing to the need, in the addressee, to go about repairing him or herself; yet sharing this appeal between artist and addressee is indispensable for the effect of art. The force of the clash between pushing and transgressing the limits that the work can plausibly display becomes ramified into all aspects of the work as its central meaning. It is only in this doubleness that the idealization hypothesis, subsuming both ideal setting and idealization, as well as the relations between them, can successfully account for the process of art.

SYMBOLIZATION

The concept on which Deri's book focuses seems the most appropriate one for a semiotic approach of the psychoanalysis of art. It is through symbolization that any aspect of the problematic becomes semiotically relevant at all, and therefore open to analysis. In this sense, symbolization is a general concept useful for the elaboration of the other, more specific hypotheses. The very generality of the concept is, however, what makes it difficult to use as a function of the artistic process. Therefore, Deri tries to argue how the general capacity for symbolization, indispensable for human life, relates to specific creativity as it is at stake in art. Although the problem of the transition from the general to the more particular use of the concept has not been solved by the author, I will discuss here the way in which symbolization can be useful as a hypothesis in the same sense as the other concepts. The symbolization hypothesis suggests that the process of art is brought about by the capacity of encoding and decoding experiences that are usually beyond symbolization. This is, however, still too broad a view, since it subsumes all the hypotheses discussed so far, as well as many other similar ones. One of the basic problems with Deri's book is indeed the lack of specification. At one point, she tries to solve it by focusing on the concept of transitional objects (Winnicott 1971) and it is there that the symbolization hypothesis, coming to stand on the same level as the other hypotheses discussed, seems to begin to make sense.

The work of art considered as a transitional object fulfills the function between the internal and the external world that had, for the infant, the "thumb or the fist, later a piece of soft material," and "these objects do not simply belong to the external world of objects, nor are they purely wishful hallucinations; *they are both at the same time*" (254). The capacity to "mend the gap" in the infant's lifespace produced by the absence of the gratifying mother develops creativity, and the artist retains this capacity: "The artist's lifespace is not disrupted by an empty gap separating self from world" (289). The tension inherent in the very creation of transitional objects—the gap left by the absent breast, and the need, rather than the desire, to stretch the self out until it can reach the world in contiguity—is lost out of sight when Deri simplifies further: "Truly creative people have a 'horn of plenty'—a 'magic bag' into which they can dip for creative ideas. . . . This 'magic bag' is their unusually extended preconscious, which contains well formed and 'ready-to-use' symbolic forms" (289–290). This quotation shows that, paradoxically, the apparently most semiotic view fails to grasp both psychoanalytic and semiotic premises. Psychoanalysis cannot accept anything as static and readily available as the contents of this magic bag, since the "magic" that brings forth the content of that bag is the force which, all but magic, produces meaning in and through tension, in the unconscious, and through time. Similarly, semiotics cannot accept the idea of ready-mades. It would require that the "symbolic forms," signs that is, be grounded in some intersubjective rule in order for them to produce meaning.

Deri's book has many theoretical flaws, such as a lack of specificity and also semiotic naivety; these are aggravated by excessive eclecticism and a striving for harmony and adequacy that entails moralism. This is not enough reason to dismiss either Deri's book or the symbolization hypothesis as a whole. The intrinsic problem of the hypothesis' stronger claim that works of art are transitional objects is in its internal logic. Characteristically, transitional objects serve their function of mediation, because at the stage where they originate the infant is not capable of symbolization. They represent pre-semiotic self-communication. The child typically clings to the object and will not separate from it, nor will it allow the object to be a sign, intersubjectively meaningful. The work of art, in contrast, although bridging the gap between the subject and the world, is typically semiotic and given up by the artist whose most urgent desire is to reveal its secret. If transitional object status is involved at all, it is rather on the part of the addressee, insofar as art-collectors sometimes show an infantile possessiveness that makes them hide the work, explicitly for safety reasons, implicity in order to keep it for themselves—in other words, to prevent its semiotic function. Hence, the symbolization hypothesis' stronger claim rests on a variant of the intentional fallacy: it attributes the consumer's reaction to the maker, without other logic than reversal of perspective. Unlike the other hypotheses discussed here, it disposes of the problematic relation between sender and addressee by leaving it unarguably specular, assuming a simple analogy where a complex process is at stake. The tension between force and meaning is eliminated by the metaphor of the magic bag which cannot be on both sides of the communication model. If the artist has this bag, the viewer cannot have the same ready ideas.

The broader, and weaker, claim of the symbolization hypothesis that art is produced by the exceptionally successful attempt at symbolically expressing, hence, making inter-subjective, utterly subjective experiences, loses contact with psychoanalysis, becoming vaguely psychological, hardly surpassing everyday clichés on art, unless it narrows down those experiences to those repressed into the unconscious. But then again, it becomes a comprehensive account of the already discussed hypotheses which are each more specific. In some cases of highly self-reflexive art, however, the symbolization hypothesis allows us to make more specific sense of a work. It is, then, the process of "reaching out" to the world through symbolization, the attempt to break the chain of primary narcissism in overcoming, through acknowledgment of them, the limits of the self that is thematized in the work and lends it forceful meaning. The tension between timeless self-confinement and narrative construction of the image charged to bring the self into the exterior world—that becomes the meaning which grows out of the need and the force it sets forth. This seems to happen in the representation *The Artist in his Studio* (fig. 4). This small painting is one of the very earliest of the artist's works, and the virgin state of the palette hung on the wall even suggests that it represents his very earliest attempt to paint. In that case, we catch Rembrandt at the moment of "stretching out" to the world. The work is striking for its strange perspective which is considered out of balance in the room. What can the symbolization hypothesis suggest about the work?

There is a confrontation between the young painter, the self who wants to identify himself as a great painter, and the canvas. The already typical chiaroscuro technique stresses the canvas as the source of light. The work itself is small; the represented work is outrageously large. The man is tiny. But the light enlightens him. To the narcissistic question whether the self can be more important than the work, the answer given here is no. But the artist whose face is given light, hence, visibility by the canvas, turns his eyes to the viewer. It is he, not his yet unfinished work, that seeks contact with, and acknowledgment from, the spectator. He is not yet painting; holding a pencil, the empty palette still unused, he is just about to begin. Once the canvas is filled, his face may be more clearly illuminated. Whether it will be filled with a self-portrait or with some other representation, we do not know. In both cases, however, the answer to the urgent question of where the self-as-other is situated is, for the artist, in the work that extends the self, contiguously related to him and providing him with the intersubjective status. In this work we will never know the answer because it is not the issue. Perhaps the work shines because it is already finished. The work we are looking at is not the small panel we think it is, but the great canvas we see represented, and which predicts the greatness of this tiny artist, when the proleptic narrative of his fulfillment becomes narratable.

CONCLUSION

If there is one thing that psychoanalysis cannot do for art, it is to explain how it came about. This is not only so because, as Krauss (1985: 241) points out, the poverty of the reading of art it leads to, and the questionable conception of causality it rests on make the enterprise both futile and fragile. Given the semiotic status of art and the communicational aspects it entails, the causal explanation is in the last instance beside the point. What psychoanalysis can do for art depends heavily on the interdisciplinary perspective that integrates semiotics and psychoanalysis. Only within such an integration can it escape the poverty that characterizes causalistic psycho-criticism as well as non-psychoanalytic criticism like iconography and biographism. What these approaches have in common is the search for what is *not* the surprising quality of the works as art; rather, they try to explain the works as anything but art.

Freud, Deri, and Rembrandt each use a metaphor which illuminates our findings. Freud describes the "team" of *ich* and *id* as horse and rider. Deri rejects that metaphor. She finds it too much based on a split. It is, also, an instrumentalist view, which suggests that in spite of Freud's insistence to the contrary, the *ich* is the master in its own house. It is a rationalist vision of the

Figure 4: Rembrandt, *The Artist in his Studio*, Boston, Museum of Fine Arts, The Zoe Oliver Collection

relationship. As a return of the repressed, the desire for mastery keeps recurring in the Freudian view. It does, however, imply the dynamic aspect of the relationship. However hard the *ich* tries, the horse may run away with it, and that danger is part of what Freud wanted to express through the metaphor. The meaning of riding a horse is in that tension between the two partners.

Deri's alternative metaphor is the centaur. She describes it as follows: "Here the intense instincts (the id, the horse) blend into the human figure (the ego, or rider) so that instead of two antagonistic gestalts one has a complex *whole*" (292). The split between two partners is replaced with the recurring ideal of unity. The Freudian metaphor has two components, but Deri seems to forget that as horse-and-rider they represent a whole. The price Deri pays for unity—if such would be desirable at all—is double. The tension between the subject and the world which, in her own view, provides the motivation for symbolization, disappears. The centaur regresses back into primary narcissism; it is a self-sufficient and self-contained, but also, *fictitious* creature. The unity, moreover, makes any change in the relationship between what are now two parts impossible. Narrativity has been eliminated through the back door of the metaphor.

The Polish Rider underscores the role played by ambiguity and condensation in the use of such metaphors. Here, there are, as in the Freudian text, two partners. The split between them is even stressed by the divergent gazes. But they share the relationship they have to each other, to beauty and to the representation of their melancholic striving, to narrativity and descriptivity. They do a better job for unity than the centaur, because, being two, they remind the viewer that unity is brought about and not naturally there. The same holds for the relationship between disciplines in the interdisciplinary enterprise.

The psychoanalytic concepts that have been discussed here each fulfill specific hermeneutic functions. They allow the relation between the disciplines to be thought through without losing, through excessive eclecticism, their place within each theory from which they derive in different aspects. The last discussed view has more difficulty in accomplishing this, while being also less fruitful in the interpretation of the dynamics of art. I would like to finish by venturing that this had to be so because in the last case, there was a deceptive—apparent, but not integrated—terminological similarity between psychoanalysis and semiotics: a centaur.

Interdisciplinarity is not the obvious result of any attempt at addressing a question that concerns more than one discipline. The insights shown by Kofman, though less theoretically argued, are by far more integrated than the loose ends displayed by Deri, which unsuccessfully hide a strict and limited mono-disciplinary obsession. Where Kofman provides new views, if not of theory, at least of the works of art she discusses, Deri's attempt to conciliate Freudian, Jungian, Gestalt, and Winicottian psychoanalysis does not lead to a consistent, let alone revealing, approach to art or creativity. The ambitions of such theory building are far too high, the scope too broad, the results too meager. Concepts used as heuristic tools for interpretation may not counter the problems of the interdisciplinary attempt as outlined in the beginning of this chapter; stripped of the ambitions of generalizing theory, however, they can become powerful, enriching, interdisciplinary.

PART III

Semiotics and Art History

co-author: Norman Bryson

Initially the three chapters collected in this series were written as a survey article for the *Art Bulletin*, the official organ of the College Arts Association of America. This journal has been publishing a series of introductory articles into a field relevant to art history, but not familiar to many art historians. The article was commissioned to Norman Bryson, and he asked me to join in. Writing with him was a challenge and a pleasure, and we had much to exchange on the basis of a fundamental common ground in two inclinations: to problematize commonplace conceptions in our fields of study, and to continuously confront theoretical insights with concrete objects.

As a result of those inclinations the article became too long for the journal. Among other more or less painful cuts, we were asked to excise a section particularly dear to us, the one here entitled "Semiotics as a Theory of Subjectivity." The opportunity to publish the entire piece here made that excision slightly more acceptable.

But there is another reason why these chapters have their due place here. In the development of my intellectual itinerary which the essays of this volume chart, an increasingly intense collaboration, not only with other disciplines than my own, but with colleagues from other disciplines, has a large place. The creation of the Comparative Arts Program at Rochester was at the core of that development. The set-up was beautifully symmetrical: with Michael Ann Holly, chair of the department of art and art history, and Norman Bryson, appointed in both comparative literature, like myself, and art history, like Holly, we were able to start up a program that was serious in its interdisciplinarity. These chapters came out of that collaboration, and if Bryson and I wrote them, Holly commented on the drafts and thus contributed her indispensable insights and knowledge. I wish to acknowledge her presence in these chapters as well as, in fact, in the whole volume.

The following presentation is intended for a non-intiated audience, but assuming such basic knowledge as the introduction to this volume provides. Although primarily written for art historians, much of what is presented can be transferred without much trouble to any other humanistic discipline. That is why it seems appropriate in this volume. In chapter 7 the major positions of the communication model are discussed in order to problematize them. The discussion holds for other disciplines as well: wherever cultural objects—texts, documents, visual images—are studied, the problems of context, of authorial intention, of readership inevitably arise. Chapter 8 is a short retracing of our steps to the roots of twentieth-century semiotics in the ideas of Peirce and Saussure. Chapter 9 goes into a few specific interactions between semiotics, art history, and a third discipline: psychoanalysis, feminist theory, narratology, history.

■ 7 ■

Visual Communication?

THE SEMIOTIC CRITIQUE AND ITS USEFULNESS FOR ART HISTORY

The basic tenet of semiotics, the theory of sign and sign-use, is an anti-realist one. Human culture is made up of signs each of which stands for something other than itself, and the people inhabiting culture busy themselves making sense of those signs. The core of semiotic theory is the definition of the factors involved in this permanent process of sign-making and -interpreting, and the development of conceptual tools that help to grasp that process as it goes on in various arenas of cultural activity. Art is one such arena, and it seems obvious that semiotics will have something to contribute to the study of art.

From one point of view, it can be said that the semiotic perspective has long been present in art history: the work of Riegl and Panofsky can be shown to be congenial to the basic tenets of Peirce and Saussure,[1] and key texts of Meyer Schapiro deal directly with issues in visual semiotics.[2] But in the past two decades, semiotics has been engaged with a range of problems very different from those it began with, and the contemporary encounter between semiotics and art history involves new and distinct areas of debate: the polysemy of meaning; the problematics of authorship, context and reception; the implications of the study of narrative for the study of images; the issue of sexual difference in relation to verbal and visual signs; and the truth-claims of interpretation. In all these areas, semiotics challenges the positivist view of knowledge, and it is this challenge which undoubtedly presents the most difficulties to the traditional practices of art history as a discipline.

---

1. See Christine Hasenmueller, "Panofsky"; Margaret Iversen, "Style as Structure 66–7; and Michael Ann Holly, *Panofsky*, 42–5.
2. See, for example, Meyer Schapiro's semiotics reflections (1969).

Because of semiotics' theoretical skepticism, the relationship between contemporary semiotics and art history is bound to be a delicate one. The debate between the critical rationalists and the members of the Frankfurt school, earlier on in this century, may have convinced most scholars of the need for a healthy dose of skepticism in their claims to truth; nevertheless, much "applied science"—in other words, scholarship that, like art history, exists as a specialized discipline—seems to be reluctant to give up the hope of reaching positive knowledge. While epistemology and the philosophy of science have developed sophisticated views of knowledge and truth in which there is little if any room for unambiguous "facts," causality, and proof, and in which interpretation has an acknowledgedly central position, art history seems hard pressed to renounce its positivistic basis, as if it feared to lose its scholarly status altogether in the bargain.[3]

While art history as a whole cannot but be affected by the skepticism that has radically changed the discipline of history itself in the wake of the "linguistic turn"—which, to be more precise, should be called the semiotic turn—two fields within art history are particularly tenacious in their positivistic pursuit: the authentication of *oeuvres*—Rembrandt, Van Gogh, Hals, to name just a few recently and hotly debated cases—and social history.[4] As for the former, the number of decisions which have, after all, an interpretive rather than a positive basis—stylistic, mainly—has surprised the researchers themselves, and no wonder, therefore, that their conclusions remain open to debate.[5] In section 2 ("Senders") we will pursue this question further. But, one might object, this interpretive status concerns cases where positive knowledge of circumstances of the making of an artwork is lacking, not because such knowledge is by definition impossible. Attempts to approach the images of an age through an examination of the social and historical conditions out of which they emerged, in the endeavor of social history, are not affected by that lack.

The problem, here, lies in the term "context" itself. Precisely because it has the root "text" while its prefix distinguishes it from the latter, "context" seems

---

3. The clearest and most convincing overview of epistemological currents in the nineteenth and twentieth century is Habermas' *Erkenntnis und Interesse* of 1968 (1971). Habermas' work has been challenged by psychoanalysts who find that he misunderstood their discipline in his idealized view of psychoanalytic practice as a constraint-free communication. See e.g. Jacqueline Rose, (1986). It is also under pressure from the side of postmodern philosophy, most pertinently by Jean-François Lyotard, e.g. *The Postmodern Condition* (1984). These challenges do not, however, affect Habermas' argument against positive knowledge, but rather his hope for a rational society. If anything, they are more skeptical than Habermas.

4. For the "linguistic" or rather, rhetorical turn in history, see Hayden White (1973) and especially, for a brief and convincing account of the fundamental rhetorical and semiotic nature of historiography, "Interpretation in History" in *Tropics of Discourse* (1978). The most detailed and incisive analysis of the rhetoric of historiography remains Stephen Bann's remarkable *The Clothing of Clio*, 1984.

5. See, for example, the Rembrandt Research Project, in J. Bruyn, B. Haak, S.H. Levie *et. al.*, 1982, 1987, 1989.

comfortably out of reach of the pervasive need for interpretation that affects all texts. Yet this is an illusion. As Jonathan Culler has argued,

> But the notion of context frequently oversimplifies rather than enriches the discussion, since the opposition between an act and its context seems to presume that the context is given and determines the meaning of the act. We know, of course, that things are not so simple: context is not given but produced; what belongs to a context is determined by interpretive strategies; contexts are just as much in need of elucidation as events; and the meaning of a context is determined by events. Yet whenever we use the term *context* we slip back into the simple model it proposes (1988: xiv).

Context, in other words, is a text itself, and thus consists of signs which require interpretation. What we take to be positive knowledge is the product of interpretive choices. The art historian is always present in the construction she or he produces....[6]

In order to endorse the consequences of this insight, Culler proposes to speak not of context but of "framing":

> Since the phenomena criticism deals with are signs, forms with socially constituted meanings, one might try to think not of context but of the framing of signs: how are signs constituted (framed) by various discursive practices, institutional arrangements, systems of value, semiotic mechanisms (1988:xiv)?

This proposal does not mean to abandon the examination of "context" altogether, but to do justice to the interpretive status of the insights thus gained. Not only is this more truthful; it also advances the search for social history itself. For by examining the social factors that frame the signs, it is possible to analyze simultaneously the practices of the past and our own interaction with them, an interaction which is otherwise in danger of passing unnoticed. What art historians are bound to examine, whether they like it or not, is the work as effect and affect, not only as neatly remote product of an age long gone. The problem of context, central in modern art history, will be examined further from a semiotic perspective in section 1, while the particular problem of the reception of images, and of the original viewer, will come up in section 3 ("Receivers").

In the following three chapters we intend to conduct two inquiries simultaneously. On the one hand, we will examine how semiotics challenges some fundamental tenets and practices of art history. Although permanently present, this aspect will receive greater emphasis in chapter 7. But, perhaps more importantly for many, on the other hand we will demonstrate how semiotics can further the analyses that art historians pursue (this aspect will be increasingly central in chapter 9). The parallel presentation of a critique and a

---

6. Similar arguments within the social history of art, explicitly articulating art history with semiotics, have been put forward in a number of places by Keith Moxey (1989; 1989; in press).

useful set of tools conveys our view that art history is in need of, but also, can afford, impulses from other directions. Since semiotics is fundamentally a transdisciplinary theory, it helps to avoid the privileging of language that so often accompanies attempts to make disciplines interact. In other words, rather than a linguistic turn, we will propose a semiotic turn for art history. Moreover, as the following chapters will demonstrate, semiotics has been developed within many different fields, some of which are more relevant for art history than others. Our selection of topics is based on the expected fruitfulness for art history of particular developments, rather than on the—futile—attempt to be comprehensive, at the cost of persuasiveness. This perspective needs to be distinguished from an altogether different possible approach: this article does not present a survey of semiotic theory for an audience of art historians, nor a semiotics of visual art. The latter has been provided by Fernande Saint-Martin. Some of the specialized semioticians (e.g. Greimas, Sebeok) might see an intolerable distortion in our presentation. On the other hand, some of the theorists discussed here, like Derrida or Goodman, might not identify themselves as semioticians. In order to make this presentation more directly and widely useful we have, however, opted for a treatment of semiotics as a perspective, raising a set of questions around and within the methodological concerns of art history itself.

Chapter 7 deals centrally with the semiotic critique of "context" as a term in art historical discussion. From questions of context we move to the origins and history of semiotics, the ways in which these tools and critical perspectives have grown out of initial theoretical projects. The limits of space force us to consider the ideas of just two early figures: Charles Sanders Peirce, the American philosopher, and the Swiss linguist Ferdinand de Saussure will be presented in chapter 8. In chapter 9 we will present a variety of "semiotic and" approaches: the ways in which semiotics can be mustered for the interdisciplinary analysis of visual art in conjunction with a few of the main disciplines or intellectual currents in the humanities: psychoanalysis, feminism, narratology, and history. First, we will present a semiotic view of psychoanalysis, demonstrating a variety of ways psychoanalysis is bound up with semiotics and can be useful for art history, and then going on to discuss the most relevant concept, central in art history, that of the gaze. Psychoanalysis connects semiotics with an awareness of gender differentiation as pervasively relevant, indeed, as a crucial basis for the heterogeneous and polysemous nature of looking. Feminist cultural analysis has been quick to see the relevance of semiotic tools for its own goals; we wish to acknowledge that efficacy and demonstrate the inevitable "feminist turn" in semiotic theory itself by presenting the intersections between feminism's theorizing of gender, semiotics and art history in the section ("Semiotics as a Theory of Subjectivity"). Following that presentation we go on to show the interpretive and descriptive, but also critical value of a semiotically based narrative theory or narratology for the study of images which frequently have a narrative side to them which is not necessarily literary in background. Instead of rehearsing the language-centered view of history painting as basically illustrative of prior stories, we will demonstrate the specifically visual ways of story-telling that semiotics enables one to consider. At the end of chapter 9 we will offer a few reflections on the status of meaning in relation to historical considerations so important for art history, but also for the other disciplines in the humanities.

One further question concerns the relation between the disciplines. Interdisciplinary research poses specific problems of methodology, which have to do with the status of the objects and the applicability of concepts designed to account for objects with a different status. Thus a concept mainly discussed in literary theory—for example, metaphor—is relevant to the analysis of visual art, and refusing to use it amounts to an unwarranted decision to take all images as literal expressions. But such use requires a thinking through of the status of signs and meaning in visual art, for example, of the delimitation of discrete signs in a medium that is supposed to be given over to density.[7] Rather than borrowing the concept of metaphor from literary theory, then, an art historian will take it out of its unwarranted confinement within that specific discipline and first examine the extent to which metaphor, as a phenomenon of transfer of meaning from one sign onto another, should be generalized. This is the case here, but not all concepts from literature lend themselves to such generalization. Rhythm and rhyme, for example, although often used a propos of visual images, are more medium-specific and their use for images is therefore more obviously metaphorical.

Semiotics offers a theory and a set of analytic tools which are not bound to a particular object domain. Thus it liberates the analyst from the problem that transferring concepts from one discipline into another would entail. Recent attempts to connect verbal and visual arts, for example, tend to suffer either from unreflected transfers, or painstakingly translate the concepts of the one discipline into the other, often inevitably importing a hierarchy between them. Semiotics, by virtue of its supra-disciplinary status, can be brought to bear on objects pertaining to any sign-system. That semiotics has been primarily developed in conjunction with literary texts is perhaps largely an historical accident, whose consequences, while not futile, can be bracketed.[8] As a supra-disciplinary theory semiotics lends itself to interdisciplinary analyses, for example, of word and image relations, which seek to avoid both hierarchization

---

7. For the distinction between discrete and dense sign-systems, see Nelson Goodman, 1968. This theory is much indebted to Wittgenstein. See Allen Thiher, 1984.

8. The intimate connection between semiotics and linguistics is a problem in Saussurean semiotics, which developed out of linguistics rather than the other way around; not so much in Peircean semiotics, which came out of logic. See chapter 8.

and eclectic transferring of concepts.⁹ But the use of semiotics is not limited to interdisciplinarity. Its multi-disciplinary reach—as journals like *Semiotica* demonstrate, it can be used in a variety of disciplines—has made semiotics an appropriate tool for monodisciplinary analysis as well. Considering images as signs, it sheds a particular light on them, focusing on the production of meaning in society, but it is by no means necessary to semiotic analysis to exceed the domain of visual images.

CONTEXT

One area in which the semiotic perspective may be of particular service to art history is in the discussion of "context"—¹⁰ as in the phrase "art in context." Since semiotics, following the structuralist phase of its evolution, has had to examine the conceptual relations between "text" and "context" in detail, in order to ascertain the fundamental dynamics of socially operated signs, it is a field in which analysis of "context" as an idea may be particularly acute. Many aspects of that discussion have a direct bearing on "context" as a key term in art historical discourse and method.¹¹

When a particular work of art is placed "in context," it is usually the case that a body of material is assembled and juxtaposed against the work in question in the hope that such contextual material will reveal the determinants that make the work of art what it is. And perhaps the first observation on this procedure, from a semiotic point of view, is a cautionary one: that it cannot be taken for granted that the evidence that makes up "context" is going to be any simpler or more legible than the visual text upon which such evidence is to operate. The observation is directed in the first place against any assumption of opposition, or asymmetry, between "context" and "text," such that here lies the work of art, waiting for context to order its uncertainties, and over there is the context, as that which will act upon the work of art and transfer to the latter its own certainties and determination. For it cannot be assumed that "context" has the status of a given, or of a simple or natural ground upon which to base interpretation. The idea of "context" invites us to *step back* from the uncertainties of text to context, posited as platform or foundation. But once this step is taken it is by no means clear why it may not be taken again; that is, "context" implies from its first moment a potential regression "without brakes."

---

9. Examples of analyses of word and image interaction or comparison can be found in Wendy Steiner, 1982; 1988. See also the special issues of *Poetics Today*, 10, numbers 1 and 2, edited by Steiner. Also A. Kibédi Varga, 1988; 1989. For a critical examination of the hierarchies implied in many of these attempts, see W.J.T. Mitchell, 1985 and Bal, "On Reading and Looking," in *Semiotica*.

10. The inverted commas round "context" ("text," "artwork," etc.) are meant to designate that at this place the word appears as an object of methodological reflection.

11. The points in this section and in section three ("Receivers") are worked out in more detail in Norman Bryson, 1992.

Semiotics, at a particular moment in its evolution, was obliged to confront this problem head-on, and how it did so has in important ways shaped the history of its own development. We will discuss later on the different conceptions of semiosis in Saussure and in the work of post-Saussureans such as Derrida and Lacan. Suffice it to say, for now, that in its "structuralist" era semiotics frequently operated on the assumption that the meanings of signs were determined by sets of internal oppositions and differences mapped out within a static system. In order to discover the meanings of the words in a particular language, for example, the interpreter turned to the global set of rules (the *langue*) simultaneously governing the language as whole, outside and away from actual utterances (*parole*). The essential move was to invoke and isolate the synchronic system, putting its diachronic aspects to one side; what was sought, in a word, was structure. The critique launched against this theoretical immobility of sign systems pointed out that a fundamental component of sign-systems had been deleted from the structuralist approach, namely the system's aspects of on-going semiosis, of dynamism. The changeover from theorizing semiosis as the product of static and immobile systems, to thinking of semiosis as unfolding in time is indeed one of the points at which structuralist semiotics gave way to post-structuralism. Derrida, in particular, insisted that the meaning of any particular sign could not be located in a signified fixed by the internal operations of a synchronic system; rather, meaning arose exactly from the movement from one sign or signifier to the next, in a *perpetuum mobile* where there could be found neither a starting-point for semiosis, nor a concluding moment in which semiosis terminated and the meanings of signs fully "arrived."[12]

From this perspective, "context" appears to have strong resemblances to the Saussurean signified, at least in those forms of contextual analysis that posit context as firm ground upon which to anchor commentaries on works of art. Against such a notion, post-structuralist semiotics argues that "context" is in fact unable to arrest the fundamental mobility of semiosis for the reason that it harbors exactly the same principle of interminability within itself. Culler provides a readily understood example of such non-terminability in his discussion of evidence in the courtroom (1988:139–52). The context in a legal dispute is not a given of the case, but something which lawyers precisely make, and thereby make their case; and the nature of evidence is such that there is always more of it, subject only to the external limits of the lawyers' own

---

12. Jacques Derrida, 1982. For a discussion of Derrida's theory of signification, see Stephen Melville, 1986. Umberto Eco, an important semiotician who draws upon Peirce but is also well-versed in the Saussurean tradition, warns against a confusion between theoretical polysemy and actual interpretation, where limits are obviously in place. See Eco 1979; 1984; 1990. But the point is that these limits are socially and politically motivated, putting a practical stop to a theoretical polysemy. Thus the very thesis of polysemy provides clearer insight into the limits of interpretation and their motivations.

stamina, the court's patience, and the client's means. Art historians, too, confront this problem on a daily basis. Suppose that, in attempting to describe the contextual determinants that made a particular work of art the way it is, the art historian proposes a certain number of factors which together constitute its context. Yet it is always conceivable that this number could be added to, that the context can be augmented. Certainly there will be a cut-off point, determined perhaps by such factors as the reader's patience, the conventions followed by the community of art-historical interpreters, the constraints of publishing budgets, the cost of paper, etc. But these constraints will operate from an essentially external position with regard to the enumeration of contextual aspects. Each new factor that is added will, it may be hoped, help to bolster up the description of context, making it more rounded and complete. But what is also revealed by such supplementation is exactly the uncurtailability of the list, the impossibility of its closure. "Context" can always be extended; it is subject to the same process of mobility which is at work in the semiosis of the text or artwork that "context" is supposed to delimit and control.

In case misunderstanding arises at this point one should, perhaps, remark that while the consideration that contexts may be indefinitely extended makes it impossible to establish "context" in the form of a totality—a compendium of all the circumstances which constitute a "given" context—semiotics does not in fact follow what may appear to be a consequence of this, that the concept of determination should be in some way given up. On the contrary, it is only the goal of totalizing contexts that is being questioned here, together with the accompanying tendency towards making a necessarily partial and incomplete formulation of context stand for the totality of contexts, by synecdoche. Certainly the aim of identifying the total context has at times featured prominently in linguistics (among other places). Austin's remark concerning speech act theory is a case in point: "the total speech act in the total speech situation is the *only actual* phenomenon which, in the last resort, we are engaged in elucidating."[13] Semiotics' objection to such an enterprise focuses primarily on the idea of mastering a totality that is at work here, together with the notion that such a totality is "actual," that is, that it can be known as a present experience. However, this by no means entails an abandoning of "context" and "determination" as working concepts of analysis. Rather semiotics would argue that two principles must operate here simultaneously: "no meaning can be determined out of context, but no context permits saturation."[14] Though the two principles may not sit easily together, or interact in a classical or topologically familiar fashion, context as determinant is very much to the fore in semiotic analyses, and particularly those that are *post*-structuralist.

13. J.L. Austin (1975: 148). See also John Searle 1977; and Derrida, afterward to the paperback edition of *Limited Inc* (1988).
14. Derrida, 1979: 81.

As it has tried to work through the complexities of the text/context distinction, semiotics has developed a further caveat, concerning the stroke or bar (/) between the terms "text" and "context." That mark of separation presupposes that one can, in fact, separate the two, that they are truly *independent* terms. Yet there are many situations within art historical discourse which, if we consider them in detail, may make it difficult to be sure that such independence can easily be assumed. The relation between "context" and "text" (or "artwork") which these terms often take for granted is that history stands prior to artifact; that context generates, produces, gives rise to text, in the same way that a cause gives rise to an effect. But it is sometimes the case that the sequence (from context to text) is actually inferred from its end-point, leading to the kind of metalepsis which Nietzsche called "chronological reversal."[15] "Suppose one feels a pain. This causes one to look for a cause and spying, perhaps, a pin, one links and reverses the perceptual or phenomenal order, *pain...pin*, to produce a causal sequence, *pin...pain*" (Culler 1983:86). In this case the pin as cause is located after the effect it has on us has been produced. Does one find comparable instances of such metalepsis or "chronological reversal" in art historical analysis?

The answer may well be, yes. Imagine a contemporary account of, say, mid-Victorian painting, one which aims to reconstruct the context for the paintings in terms of social and cultural history. The works themselves depict such social sites as racetracks, pubs, railway stations and train compartments, street scenes where well-to-do ladies pass by workmen digging the road, interiors in which domestic melodramas are played out, the stock exchange, the veterans' hospital, the church, the asylum. It would not be thought unusual for the art historian to work from the paintings out towards the history of these sites and milieux, in order to discover their historical specificity and determination, their detailed archival texture. Just this sort of inquiry is what, perhaps, the word "context" asks for; such reconstruction would be fitting and, one might say, *indicated* by the nature of the visual materials to hand.

But there are senses in which the procedure is still strange, despite its aura of familiarity. A primary difficulty is that those features of mid-Victorian Britain which do *not* find themselves pictured by mid-Victorian painters do not necessarily feature here as part of the context that is to account for the works of art. A social history which sets out, unassisted by pictures, to discover the social and historical conditions of mid-Victorian Britain might well attend to quite other milieux, different social sites, and indeed many other kinds of historical objects that do not readily lend themselves to pictorial represen-

---

15. "The fragment of the outside world of which we become conscious comes after the effect that has been produced on us and is projected *a posteriori* as its 'cause.' In the phenomenalism of the 'inner world' we invert the chronology of cause and effect. The basic fact of 'inner experience' is that the cause gets imagined after the effect has occurred." Friedrich Nietzsche, 1986: 3, 804; cit. Culler, 1983:86.

tation. A harder social analysis might treat the pictures incidentally, in passing, as one sort of evidence among many—if one is going to do social history, why privilege works of art in such a way that the findings of historiography must be bound to the *mise-en-scène* of painting? There are a number of observations that might be made at this point: for example, concerning the relations between art history and social history as disciplines both intertwined and impelled by different kinds of momentum; or concerning the role played by synecdoche in the rhetoric of art historical discourses.[16] The point that concerns us here, though, is that in the example chosen, the pictures have in some sense *predicted* the form of the historian's portrayal; that the work of art history is "anticipated by the structure of the objects it labors to illuminate."[17] If that is so, then the "context" in which the work of art is placed is in fact being generated out of the work itself, by means of a rhetorical operation, a reversal, a metalepsis, which nonetheless purports to regard the work as having been produced by its context and not as producing it. Moreover, in a further rhetorical manoeuvre, the work of art is now able to act as evidence that the context that is produced for it is the right one; the reversal can be made to produce a "verification effect" (the contextual account must be true: the paintings prove it).

In cases of this kind, elements of visual text migrate from text to context and back, but recognition of such circulation is prevented by the primary cut of text-stroke-context. The operation of the stroke consists in the creation of what, for semiotics, is a phantasmic cleavage between text and context, followed by an equally uncanny drawing together of the two sides that had been separated. The stroke dividing "text" from "context" is the fundamental move here, which semiotic analysis would criticize as a rhetorical operation.[18] From one point of view, as Derrida has argued, this cut is precisely the operation that establishes the aesthetic as a specific order of discourse. From another point of view, the cut (text/context) is what creates a discourse of art historical explanation; it is because the blade can so cleanly separate the two edges, of text and context, that one seems to be dealing with an order of explanation at all, with explanation one side and *explanandum* on the other. To see this separation of text from context, then, is a fundamental rhetorical move of self-construction in art history.

Semiotic inquiry has a further reservation about procedures of this kind;

---

16. On synecdoche in historiography, see Hayden White, 51–80; on synecdoche as it functions within the rhetoric of art history, see Mark Roskill (1989: 3–35). See also David Carrier's study of the rhetoric of art history and art criticism, *Artwriting*, 1987.

17. Michael Ann Holly, 1990: 373. Holly's essay examines the general problem of "chronological reversal" in relation to the historiography of Burckhardt.

18. The stroke is what Derrida critically describes as "the *sans* of the pure cut, a cutting of the field that will be so sharp as to leave no traces of its own incision; a conceptual blade so acute that when the two sides of the cleavage are brought together the edges will perfectly rejoin" (1987: 83–118).

since it is concerned with the functioning of signs, it is particularly sensitive to the fact that in our example (a contextual account of mid-Victorian painting) the status of the paintings as works of the sign has in fact largely been effaced. This need not happen with all contextualising accounts—and our example is, of course, only an imaginary case. What the example depends on is the idea of a number of contextual factors converging on the work (or works) of art. The factors proposed may be many; they may belong to all sorts of domains; but they all finally arrive *at* the artwork, conceived as singular and as the terminus of all the various causal lines or chains. The question to be answered was, "what factors made the work of art what it is?" And in order to answer such a question, it is appropriate and inevitable that some *narrative of convergence* will be produced. The question casts itself in just this convergent form: n number of factors, all leading towards and into their final point of destination, the work of art in question.

What semiotics would query here is the idea, the shape, of convergence. Certainly the model is appropriate if the object of the inquiry is assumed to be singular, complete in itself, autotelic. All the clues point towards the one outcome, as in a work of detection. But the problem that is overlooked here is that in so far as works of art are works of the sign, their structure is not in fact singular, but *iterative*.[19] Singular events occur at only one point in space and time: the guest at the country house party was murdered in the library; the Magna Carta was written in 1215; the painting was autographed and framed. But signs are by definition repeatable. They enter into a plurality of contexts; works of art are constituted by different viewers in different ways at different times and places. The production of signs entails a fundamental split between the enunciation and the enunciated: not only between the person, the subject of enunciation, and what is enunciated; but between the circumstances of enunciation and what is enunciated, which can never coincide.[20] Once launched into the world, the work of art is subject to all of the vicissitudes of reception; as a work involving the sign, it encounters from the beginning the ineradicable fact of semiotic play. The idea of convergence, of causal chains moving towards the work of art, should, in the perspective of semiotics, be supplemented by another shape: that of lines of signification opening out from the work of art, in the permanent diffraction of reception.

It may be that scholars in certain other disciplines are more at ease than art historians with the possibility of a work of art that constitutively changes with different conditions of reception, as different viewers and generations of viewers bring to bear upon the artwork the discourses, visual and verbal, that construct their spectatorship. Admittedly, the openness of such a text or work of art can and has been appropriated and used in the name of a number of

---

19. On "iteration," see Derrida, "Signature Event Context," in *Limited Inc*, 1–23.
20. See Paul de Man, 1983.

ideological exercises: the rehabilitation of the concept of the canon in literary criticism is one (the open text turning out to coincide with the shelf of masterworks, the rest remaining ephemeral and merely *readable*); the cult of the reader as hedonistic consumer is another (a consumer who never reflects on the pre-conditions of consumption). But obviously the plurality attributed so selectively to the "classic" text (whether visual or verbal) is not an excess it has because it is a masterpiece. Rather the opposite: its openness is the result of that fundamental lack it shares with all texts, masterworks or not. It is the consequence of the fact that the text or artwork cannot exist outside the circumstances in which the reader reads the text or the viewer views the image, and that nothing the work of art is able to do can fix in advance the outcome of any of its encounters with contextual plurality. The idea of "context" as that which will, in a legislative sense, determine the contours of the work in question is therefore different from the idea of "context" that semiotics proposes: what the latter points to is, on the one hand, the unarrestable mobility of the signifier; and on the other, the construction of the work of art within always specific contexts of viewing.

When "context" is located in a clearly demarcated moment in the past, it becomes possible to overlook "context" as the contextuality of the present, the current functioning of art historical discourses. Such an outcome is something which semiotics is particularly concerned to question. It hardly needs remarking that the referent of "context" is (at least) dual: the context of the production of works of art, and the context of their commentary. Semiotics, despite frequent misunderstandings of precisely this point (and especially of semiotic "play"), is averse neither to the idea of history, nor to the idea of historical determination. It argues that meanings are always determined in specific sites in a historical and material world; even though factors of determination necessarily elude the logic of totality, "determination" is recognized and indeed insisted upon. Similarly, in recommending that the present context be included within the analysis of "context," semiotics does not work to avoid the concept of historicity; rather, its reservations concern forms of historiography that would present themselves in an exclusively aoristic or constative mode, eliding the determinations of historiography as a performative discourse active in the present. The same historiographic scruple which requires us to draw a distinguishing line between "us" and the historical "them"—in order to see how they are different from us—should, in the semiotic view, by the same token urge us to see how "we" are different from "them," and to use "context" not as a legislative idea but as a means that helps "us" to locate ourselves instead of bracketing out our own positionalities from the accounts we make.

SENDERS

"Context," then, turns out to be something very different from a given of art historical analysis. But no less problematic is the status of the concept of "artist" (painter, photographer, sculptor, and so forth; to avoid some of the connotational baggage that comes with the label "artist," we will use here the more neutral word "author").[21] It might seem at first that the idea of the author of a work of art is, again, a natural term in the order of explanation, and one which is now much more substantial and tangible than "context." As the context-idea is probed and tested, various disturbing vistas open up—regressions, mise-en-abyme, multiple or folded temporalities; but "author" seems much more stable. We may not be able in the end to point to a context, since in so many ways the context-idea involves lability and shifting grounds; but the author of a work of art is surely someone we can indeed point to, a living (or once living), flesh-and-blood personage with a palpable presence in the world; as solid and undeniable as any individual bearing a proper name, as reliably there as you or me.

Yet, as Foucault points out (1977), the relation between an individual and his or her proper name is quite different from the relation that obtains between a proper name and the function of authorship. The name of an individual (as they say in Britain, J. Bloggs)[22] is a designation, not a description; it is arbitrary in the sense that it does not assign any particular characteristics to its bearer. But the name of an author (a painter, a sculptor, a photographer, etc) oscillates between designation and description: when we speak of Homer, we do not designate a particular individual, we refer to the author of the *Iliad* or the *Odyssey*, of the body of texts performed by the rhapsodes at the Panathenaic Festivals, or we intend a whole range of qualities, "Homeric" qualities that can be applied to any number of cases (epics, epithets, heroes, types of diction, of poetic rhythm—the list is open-ended). "J. Bloggs" is in the world, but an "author" is in the works, in a body of artifacts and in the complex operations performed on them. Like "context," "authorship" is an elaborate work of framing, something we elaborately produce rather than something we simply find.

Some of the processes of this enframement can be seen at work in the strategies of attribution.[23] Perhaps the first procedure in attribution is to secure clear evidence of the material traces of the author in the work, metonymic contiguities that move in a series from the author in the world, the flesh-and-

---

21. Though the term "author" has some advantages over the term "artist" in this discussion, it too has its own baggage of connotations. In some types of literary criticism "author" is no less hagiographic than is "artist" in some types of art history; but we hope that the change of context here, from literary criticism to art history, will enable this range of meanings to be discarded. "Author" has the further disadvantage that, as a term brought into art historical discussion from literary theory, it carries with it a connotation of "linguistic imperialism"; a name for the *verbal* artist being used for the *visual* artist. We are aware of this coloration, and wish to state expressly that in our discussion the term "author" is meant to designate a function, or set of functions, not particularized by medium.

22. In fact what they say in Britain is likelier to be "Joe Bloggs"; for us, though, Bloggs can be a woman.

23. Our description of attribution is not, of course, meant to be exhaustive.

blood J. Bloggs, into the artifact in question. The traces may be directly autographic—evidence of a particular hand at work in the artifact's shaping; they may be more indirect—perhaps documents pertaining to the work, or the physical traces of a milieu (as when an artifact is assigned to the category "Athenian, circa 700 BC"). At this level, the most "scientific" stage of attribution, all sorts of technologies may provide assistance: X-rays, spectoscopic analysis, cryptography. What is assumed is that the category of authorship will be decided on the basis of material evidence, and what "author" names here is the work's physical origin. The techniques employed are essentially the same as those that would be used by a detective[24] to establish whether J.Bloggs is guilty or innocent (whether the artwork is authentic or fake); and to this extent there is nothing as yet peculiar to art historical discourse about the construction of authorship—the techniques are part of a general science of forensics. But attribution in art history involves further operations that lead away from science and technology into subtler, and more ideologically motivated, considerations concerning quality and stylistic standardization. Before, the "author" referred to a physical agent in the world, but now it refers to the putative creative subject. In the drastic change-over from scientific procedures built on measurement and experimental knowledge, to the highly subjective and volatile appraisals of quality and stylistic uniformity, one already sees how multifarious are the principles which "authorship" bring into play. Not only are the principles diverse, which would make "authorship" an aggregated or multilayered concept, they are also contradictory; though the essentially unificatory drive of the concept of authorship as a whole will work to mask this, and to conceal the joins between conflicting elements from view.

If a certain measure of arbitrariness is already evident in the principles of quality and of stylistic standardization, a further and quite different range of the arbitrary is found in the procedures for "setting limits" to what counts within authorship. J. Bloggs, under the forensic principle, is origin of all the physical traces that point to Bloggs' presence in the world, every one of them, however minute; forensics can consider all possible evidence, even the most unpromising. But "authorship" is an exclusionary concept. On one side, it works to circumscribe the artistic corpus, and on the other it works to circumscribe the archive. If the author were the physical agent J. Bloggs we should have to count among Bloggs' authorized works every doodle, every jotted diagram, that Bloggs left in the world. Similarly, in defining the archive for Bloggs, we would have to admit into it the traces of every circumstance that Bloggs encountered in his life. As a concept, "authorship" turns out after all to entail the same regressions and mise-en-abyme involved in "context." And as

---

24. On the relation between detectives and art historians (and psychoanalysts), see Carlo Ginzburg, "Morelli, Freud and Sherlock Holmes: Clues and Scientific Method," in Eco and Sebeok 1983.

it operates in practice, "authorship" manages these receding vistas through many variations on the theme of non-admission.

Excluded from "authorship" one finds whole genres, and the decisions regarding such genres are historically variable to a degree. In our own time, graphic art occupies a mysteriously fluctuating zone between authorship (many graphics in magazines bear signatures) and anonymity (many others do not). Photography is similarly divided, with sometimes an expectation of authorship (for example, when photographs appear in museums—but museums centrally depend on authorship operations; where would they be without them?), and sometimes not (most photographs in daily newspapers). Among the forces which patrol these borders one must obviously include those deriving from the economic matrix, since "authorship" in the modern sense has historically developed in conjunction with the institution of property. Here the concept becomes a legal and monetary operation, closely bound up with the history of copyright law. And the forces must also include the protocols of writing and the rules governing what is to count as a correct mode of narration. For instance, a *catalogue raisonné* would be breaking those rules if it wandered into the realm of an author's doodles and napkin sketches; just as a biography of the author would be breaking them if it widened the aperture of relevance to the proportions of a *Tristram Shandy*. That such deviant narratives are rarely encountered is proof of the efficiency of the "authorship" operation, which is designed to prevent such aberrations. By a rule of correct narration or "emplotment," only those aspects of an author's innumerable wanderings through the world which may be harmonized with the corpus of works will count as relevant; while, on the other side, only a certain number of an author's traces will count as elements of the authorized corpus. The exclusionary moves are mutually supportive, and "correct" narration will set up further conventions, which vary from period to period, from Vasari to Francis Klingender,[25] concerning exactly how much latitude may be permitted in describing the perimeters.

Authorship, then, is no more a natural ground of explanation than is context. To paraphrase Jonathan Culler, authorship is not given but produced; what counts as authorship is determined by interpretive strategies; (1988:xiv) and in the disparities among the plural forces that determine authorship are seen lines of fissure that put in question the very unity which the concept seeks, contradictions that the concept must (and does) work hard to overcome.

(B) physical agency

(A) property   "author"   (C) creative subject

(D) narration

25. On "emplotment," see Hayden White, 1978, 66–7; and Mark Roskill, 1989, 7–10.

Interdependent, these various pressures take different forms in different sites: in museums and auction houses, for example, (A) and (B) assume more centrality, and are subject to more exacting differentiation, than in departments of art history, where (C) and (D) may be more pressing than questions of monetary value or of forensics. In art history, modes of narration are of capital importance. And according to the view of many writers, from Barthes to Preziosi, the whole purpose of art historical narration is to merge the authorized corpus and its producer into a single entity, the totalized narrative of the-man-and-his-work; where the rhetorical figure *author=corpus* governs the narration down to its finest details.

What these writers find unacceptable is that such narratives are saturated with a romantic mythology of the full creative subject. Barthes: "the author is never more than the instance writing, just as *I* is nothing other than the instance saying *I*. . . .We know now that a text is not a line of words releasing a single 'theological' meaning (the 'message' of the Author-God) but a multi-dimensional space in which a variety of writings, none of them original, blend and clash."[26] Preziosi:

> The disciplinary apparatus works to validate a metaphysical recuperation of Being and a unity of intention or Voice. At base, this is a theophanic regime, manufactured in the same workshops that once crafted paradigms of the world as Artifact of a divine Artificer, all of whose Works reveal. . .a set of traces oriented upon a(n immaterial) center. In an equivalent fashion, all the works of the artist canonized in this regime reveal traces of (that is, are signifiers with respect to) a homogeneous Selfhood that are proper(ty) to him (Preziozi 1989:31).

The concept of "author" brings together a series of related unities which, though assumed as given, are precisely the products and goals of its discursive operations. First, the unity of the Work. Second, the unity of the Life. Third, out of the myriad of accidents and contingent circumstances, and the plurality of roles and subject positions an individual occupies, the discourse of authorship constructs a coherent and unitary Subject. Fourth, the doubly reinforced unity that comes from the superimposition of Work upon Life upon Subject in the narrative genre of the life-and-work; for in that genre, everything the Subject experiences or makes will be found to signify his or her subjecthood. The mythology of this Subject is not only theophanic, it is also—as Griselda Pollock and others have shown—sexist: "(In a male-dominated art history) Women were not historically significant artists. . .because they did not have the innate nugget of genius (the phallus) which is the natural property of men" (Pollock 1988:2).

There can be little doubt that the discursive operations of authorship have been appropriated by ideologies with a heavy investment in the kind of Subject described here. In art history, and particularly through the formula of the monograph, the narrative genre of the man-and-his-work has exercised a hold

---

26. Roland Barthes, "The Death of The Author," in 1977: 145–6.

over writing that is perhaps unparalleled in the humanities. To the extent that this has been the case, the author-function has enjoyed a hegemonic influence within the discipline, naturalizing a whole series of ideological constructs (among them: genius, genius as masculine, the subject as unitary, masculinity as unitary, the artwork as expressive, the market or cash value of the authentic work). But however much one may recognize the forcefulness of the critique of the author/Subject, it may now be just as critical to realize the strategic limitations operating upon it.

In those—by no means all—art historical discourses that remain colored by romantic ideas of artistic creativity, the "death of the author" thesis may come as a shock, but in others it is old news indeed. Perhaps a rough and provisional distinction between "humanist" and "modernist" may be useful here. In humanist art historical discourses, the author-function remains essentially sacramental. Doubtless it would be wrong to underestimate the persistence of this view, or to imagine that somehow progress had swept it away.[27] Yet many modernist discourses in art history have defined themselves exactly by shedding this baggage of mythified authorship. Getting away from romantic suppositions concerning the creative, plenary subject has been the very badge of their modernity. Their goal has been not to perpetuate Michelangelism but to be rid of it; instead of rendering monographs of the author-genius, to describe the limiting conditions that make the myth of genius impossible; to move, for example, from creators to patrons; from patrons to the competing interests within patronage; from popes to committees, and from committees to the raw documents that the archive supplies. Where the humanist discourses spoke of a full, creative subject, modernist discourses modernized art history precisely by emptying that subject, by evacuating its plenitude. In many ranges of its modern practice, the charge that art history is a theophanic regime accordingly falls rather flat; there the analogue might be, not *Lust for Life*, but perhaps the *nouveau roman*.[28]

In modernist discourses, the author-function fulfils quite other purposes. It is not necessarily the central focus of analysis; it may even be incidental. Imagine a project of the following kind. Let us say that the art historian wishes to investigate the possible role played in a particular painting by an idea first stated away from art, in a philosophical treatise on perception.[29] A humanist

27. We cannot, for example, consign it to the nineteenth century. Rosalind Krauss' essay on "The Originality of the Avant-Garde" has shown how central the discourse of authorial self-origination has been to modernism: "The self as origin is the way an absolute distinction can be made between a present experienced *de novo* and a tradition-laden past. The claims of the avant-garde are precisely these claims to originality" (1984: 18).

28. In Preziosi's *Rethinking Art History* the 1956 film *Lust for Life*, based on the life (or the life-and-work) of Van Gogh, is presented as a distorting mirror in which art history may (or may not) recognize its own features. For detailed discussion of Preziosi's book, see the review by Whitney Davis, *Art Bulletin* LXXII, Number 1 (March 1990), and for a more polemical one, Max Marmor, *Art Documentation*, 1990.

29. See Michael Baxandall's extraodinarily scrupulous account of Chardin's relation to Lockean ideas of perception, (1985: 74–104).

procedure here might be to posit a third term, such as the unity of the "period" or of the "culture," that would guarantee in advance that the philosophical treatise and the work of art are mutually related. But here the art historian is skeptical of such holistic moves, and seeks more concrete relations. A certain ascesis is evident. There must, for example, be proof of actual contact between the treatise and the artist, whether directly (the artist read the treatise) or via "middle-men" who relayed the ideas of the treatise to the artist. And it must be established that this particular idea, and not another, is present in the work of art; the idea must satisfy a condition of representability, which it will do if—to further specify the example—the philosophical idea concerns perception. As the analysis proceeds, visual properties of the work—its way of transcribing perception—are brought out; proof of contact is forthcoming; the place of middle-men, relays between the treatise and the pictures, is clarified. Nowhere has there been any mention of genius; in fact there has been little mention of the artist beyond what has been necessary to the causal narration linking treatise, middle-men, artist, and picture.

In a case like this, the "author" is obviously not part of the hagiography of the man-and-his-work; it satisfies quite different narrative needs. The governing figure is no longer that of synecdoche—the part standing for the whole—but that of metonomy,[30] the linking together of contiguous events into a narrative continuum. The "author" is not an origin, but just one link in the chain. It is a link that cannot be dispensed with—the narration requires an agent to operate the chain that runs: treatise—middle-men—author—work. But the agent required can be a "man without qualities." The only quality required is provable participation in the series of causation. The "author" is essentially transparent, like a window through which we look to see the causal factors that resulted in the work; essentially empty, like a funnel; penultimate, like the *neck* of a funnel. What the author-function enables is the closure of the chain; the function is defined not by theophanies, in the archaic way, but by the "shape of convergence" that constitutes metonymic accounts. The idea of contextual factors that all eventually converge and terminate in the artwork is what produces the "author" here: an usher gathering in the various causal strands or chains, before the work. The author is needed not to open the work but to close it.

---

30. Jakobson defined metonymy on the syntagmatic axis of language, the "horizontal" movement that links one word to the next in a sentence (or one link to the next in a causal chain); he opposed metonymy to metaphor, a relation involving the "vertical" substitution of one element for another. A rough analogy for metonymy might be melody (as opposed to harmony) in music. This is the sense of metonymy in the present discussion. "Metonymy" in our discussion is used in Jakobson's sense, as a series of contiguous (syntagmatic) relations. See Roman Jakobson, "Two aspects of language and two types of aphasic disturbances," in 1971, volume 2, 239–59; P. Pettit, 1975: 7–10; and Roland Barthes, 1967, 58–61. For a clear comparison between various concepts of metaphor and metonymy, see K. Silverman, 1983. The rhetorical implications of metonymy for historiography are explored by Hayden White in "Interpretation in History," (1978: 51–80); the implications of metonymy in art historical narration are explored in Roskill, 1989, 31–4.

If the critique of the plenary subject is heard by many art historians as not referring to them, but as it were to their grandfathers, this may be because in certain ranges of disciplinary practice art history's modes of narration have shifted away from the trope of synecdoche (of totality, of the great unities of period, style, and culture, art history's early dreams). What has replaced synecdoche is the trope of metonymy, of contiguous elements, a trope whose presence is the mark of modernization within art historical discourses. The issue here is not to deny the viability of metonymy-based narration (or of any other kind of narration), only to see some of the consequences of the trope as it is used. The particular problem for metonymic narration stems from the logic of the figure itself, for metonymy is endless. Contiguities go back in time forever, one chain joining another, ramifying outwards like the branches of a vine, a vine the size of the universe. And contiguities also travel forward in time, the artwork becoming contiguous with many contexts and discourses, touching them, travelling on with them, along plural paths that branch their different ways (how many ways we cannot know, for only the trope of totality will tell us that). To be narratable, metonymy requires two moments: inauguration, and closure. Inauguration is the privilege, and also the essential function, of the narrator, the art historian: to open the discourse, to broach the subject, to start the metonymic chains. Closure is the privilege, as well as the essential function, of the "author"; through this figure the chains will be brought together in a movement of convergence and penultimacy, before "the end" finally appears on the screen.

The "death of the author" thesis in art history does not, then, apply evenly throughout art historical practices. In regions where the "humanist" discourses of the full creator-subject have sway, the thesis may still have considerable moment as a critique of prevailing assumptions. In "modernist" discourses, where the "author" as creator-subject has already been evacuated, and where it exists more as a stripped-down narrative function, the thesis may be much less persuasive. One should remember that the space of a disciplinary field is not homogeneous; the same arguments mean different things in different places. Here the gendered organization of discourse becomes an important factor, for the "death of the author" thesis may not mean the same thing for men and for women.[31]

When Barthes or Foucault first presented the "death of the author" thesis, for many male critics it spelt release from the paternal powers of the master-creators, the totemic fathers who, ruling the canon, also ruled criticism; for now the male critic could propose a different kind of activity, one that no longer assumed the heavy, guiding hand of those paternal ancestors.[32] But for

31. See Janet Wolff, 1983, and Kaja Silverman, 1988, 187–234.
32. "The author is reputed the father and owner of his work: literary science therefore teaches *respect* for the manuscript and the author's declared intentions, while society asserts the legality of the relation of author to work (the *'droit d'auteur'* or 'copyright,' in fact of recent date since it was only really legalized at the time of the French Revolution). As for the Text, it reads without the

feminist critics, the same thesis could appear in another light. The demise of canonical authority might not be experienced as the same process, by those who had never stood much chance of being included in the canon in the first place. The decade that saw the rise of the "death of the author" thesis, the 1970s, was the same decade in which the "first generation" of feminist art historians[33] began demanding a place for women artists in the canon. It might seem that as soon as authorship for female artists was called for, the rules of the game changed so that "authorship" could appear as an archaic concept, and the demand could be construed, by male critics, as "regressive." In a non-homogeneous field, "progress" is not always to be measured by the same co-ordinates. To the male advocates of the "death of the author" thesis the appropriations of Sherrie Levine, for example, might be taken as a critique of the Subject, where "Subject" has no connotations of gender; but to a feminist, Levine's refusal of authorship could be taken as "a refusal of the role of creator as 'father' of his work, of the paternal rights assigned to the author by law."[34]

Similarly, the "death of the author" evident in "modernist" art history could be taken as "advanced" by those art historians who were working against a "humanist" background of hagiography of the Author. But the procedures involved in "modernist" work can be take in another sense if one's situation is different. For instance, it is part of the "scientific" quality of "modernist" causal narratives that the position of the analyst is not included in the narrative account. The narrator of the metonymic chains stands apart from those chains, "behind a glass wall;"[35] the narrator occupies a point of knowledge outside the field, a point that is supposedly without qualities or investments.[36] The narrator's non-implication in the narrated sequences guaranteed by the fact that the causal chain ends penultimately with the "author" and finally with the artwork, in a clearly demarcated moment in the past. The metonymic narrative is third-person and aoristic, an overview from a place quite separate from artworks, authors, or causal chains. Against a background of "humanist" art historical discourse, such separation might count as progress; but from another point of view this apartness and this "objectivity" might be taken another way, as non-recognition and as disavowal of the creative authorial function of the art historian.

The moment of narrative closure, when all the metonymic chains draw to a convergent close, can also be read as a denial of the actual continuation of the

---

inscription of the Father." Roland Barthes, "From Work to Text," (1977: 160–61).

33. Thalia Gouma Peterson and Patricia Mathews propose the distinction between "first generation" and "second generation" feminist art historians in their survey article on feminist art history (1987). Our inverted commas indicate distance from such familial metaphors.

34. Roland Barthes, "From Work to Text," (1977: 160). Craig Owens applies Barthes' remark to the work of Sherrie Levine (1983, 73).

35. Preziosi (1989: 35).

36. "The position of the analyst, in this panoptic regime, is a tacit space (that may be filled by similarly equipped or invested persons)—an ideally neutral Cartesian zero point..divested of its own history, sociality, and conditions of investment and establishment. . . ." Preziosi (1989: 39).

contiguities in which the narrator stands. The movement of contiguities in fact passes on from the artwork into the art historian's own situation; the work of art is also contiguous with her or him. But the modernist discourses, which foreclose metonymic movement by getting the chain to end with the artwork, can work to deny this, making "contiguity then" eclipse and elide "contiguity now." The draining of hagiographic qualities from the "author" in the past can also be said to justify a corresponding emptying-out of the qualities of positionality, motivation and investment present in the author of the art historical narrative, making the positionality of "modernist" art historical discourse in general that much harder to think through.

The problem of the "author" is not, then, so different from the problem of "context." Semiotics assumes that not only artworks, but the accounts we fashion for them, are works of the sign; it especially attends to the governing tropes of art historical rhetoric (where "rhetoric" does not, of course, imply "ornament" or "embellishment," but names the fundamental conceptual shapes of art historical accounts). From the viewpoint of semiotics, the modernist no less than the humanist discourses are constructed in such a way as to prevent realization that when we confront works of art, we enter the field of the sign and of semiosis, of potentially infinite regressions and expansions; and that we deal with this situation by delimiting it from the place where we stand "now." In this process of concealing where we stand, the concept of "author" plays a crucial role, if as a result of its operation "author then" comes to mask—and to mask the masking of—"author now."

RECEIVERS

Semiotics is centrally concerned with reception. As Barthes puts it, semiotic investigation "will not teach us what meaning must be definitively attributed to a work; it will not provide or even discover a meaning but will describe the logic according to which meanings are engendered" (1966:63). Semiotic analysis of visual art does not set out in the first place to produce interpretations of works of art, but rather to investigate how works of art are intelligible to those who view them, the processes by which viewers make sense of what they see. Standing somewhat to one side of the work of interpretation, its object is to describe the conventions and conceptual operations that shape what viewers do—whether those viewers are art historians, art critics, or the crowd of spectators attending an exhibition. Modern art history has developed a number of ways to describe the role of the viewer and the "beholder's share." How do these accounts appear to the semiotics of reception?

It may be useful to begin by drawing a distinction between "ideal" and "empirical" spectators, since the distinction has been highly influential in directing art historical discussions of reception. Empirical spectators are the actual, living and breathing viewers of the sort we see in Rowlandson's cartoon

Viewing at the Royal Academy (figure 1), walking through the exhibition space alone or in couples or in groups, looking at the pictures around them and discussing what they see. The ideal spectator is a more abstract figure; broadly speaking the term refers to the various roles ascribed to viewers by the paintings they see, the set of positions or functions proposed and assumed by each of the images on display. Within modern art history, the ideal spectator has been a continuing focus of interest, from Riegl's *Dutch Group Portraiture*,[37] through the reception studies of Wolfgang Kemp[38] to the work which more than any other has brought the question of the spectator's modes of implications in paintings to the forefront of art historical discussion in English, Michael Fried's *Absorption and Theatricality* (1980). Bringing empirical spectatorship into sharper focus has been the goal of a far more materialist analysis which begins by investigating the actual traces left by actual encounters between viewers and works of art. As Nikos Hadjinicolaou puts it: "We must put forth another conception that sees the work of art as a relationship...between an object and all the ways it has been perceived through history down to the present day, ways of perceiving that have untiringly transformed the work in a thousand and one ways. The work of art we have before us is the history of its consumption which has been determined 'each time' by the aesthetic ideologies of each present, these being in turn conditioned by the ideologies of contemporary social groups."[39] From the point of view of the semiotics of reception, this project and its approach accord closely with semiotics' own understanding of the concreteness, materiality and sociality of sign-events: "communication and the forces of communication may not be divorced from the material base."[40] Nevertheless, the phrasing of the formulation here brings into play a number of difficulties. The clauses "the history of consumption which has been determined, . . ." and "conditioned by social groups" involve a complex problematic, which we may be able to grasp if we attend to the word "groups."

Let us suppose that analysis of reception discloses particular social groups, whose visual responses to particular works of art vary in semiotic terms; that different groups (however these are defined) possess different codes for viewing even the same work. But the idea of *possession* of codes of viewing cannot be taken for granted: if one is really going to address reception, it must be recognized that possession of codes of viewing is a process, not a given, and that members of groups acquire their familiarity with codes of viewing, and their ability to operate those codes, to varying degrees. Access to the codes is a matter of unevenness: codes have to be learned and their distribution varies

---

37. A. Riegl, 1931. Michael Podro provides an illuminating analysis of Riegl's theory of spectatorship (1982: 81–95).
38. Wolfgang Kemp (1983). See also Kemp's article (1985); and A. Neumeyer, 1965.
39. Nikos Hadjinicolaou, quoted in Kemp, *Der Anteil des Betrachters*, 30.
40. V.N. Voloshinov, 1973, 21; see also Robert Hodge and Gunther Kress (1988: 37–78).

(and changes) within a group, even in those cases in which a group defines itself through its ability to manipulate visual codes in distinct ways. That is, even when attention to the conditions of reception discloses a particular group, which operates codes of viewing in a unique way, analysis of reception must still distinguish between degrees of *access* to those codes. If it does not do so, it is substituting an ideal case (full possession of cultural skills, expertise, naturalness) for what is in fact an uneven process. The danger here is that the term "group" may function as an unacknowledged, and undetectable, synecdoche: in fact members of the group have different levels of access to the group's codes, varying degrees of competence and expertise; but the condition of expertise is generalized to all of them.

Let us think, for example, of Rowlandson's cartoon of viewers at the Royal Academy. They are a motley crew: a gouty clergyman admires a bust; fashionable ladies point with their fans; some spectators bend over to quiz a nude, another stands with his hands in his pockets looking lost. Or consider the crowd in Martini's engraving of the French Salon of 1785: men, women and—surprisingly—children, gesticulating and craning to see, admiring or criticizing what is around them, talking, arguing, moving on. How much of this commotion has entered the historical record? Not much. What *has* entered it are highly specialized responses to exhibitions of this kind, literary productions which promoted or defended particular artists and schools, and entered into various running debates about questions of taste. Such traces do not speak of their viewing in a straightforward manner. Constrained by often highly restrictive literary conventions, which left little room to register the viewing response of their authors in any detail, they become expressive only when "enhanced" by reading between the lines, and between those lines, and by carefully sounding their turns of phrase, their ellipses, to determine what by implication they may be giving voice to. If we meet with such obstacles within the public and recorded responses, and if we wish to develop further our concept of reception, what of all the other microscopic acts of viewing, each local and infinitesimal, which in their unseen trajectories failed to give rise to a discursive configuration that could survive? If such difficulties arise even with the molar groups that reception analysis is able to identify, what of all those other practices of looking, those swarms of viewers who left no trace of their ways and moments of seeing? There are many other viewers besides the ones who compose a treatise, publish pamphlets, or pen their memoirs. Those are only a fraction, the smallest percentage, of actual reception. And how should we view this immense reserve?

In answer to this question, from the point of view of semiotics it might be said: by beginning to remember it is there, even when it cannot be retrieved; by noticing the absences in the record as much as what survives; by shifting the terms of analysis from the actually documented viewers to the way the latter's discourses produce their own exclusivity. For example. . . the absence of women. In the cartoon of the Royal Academy and in the engraving of the Salon, women are a visible and active presence. Yet, as a group without access to the machinery of the aesthetic treatise and of official taste, the archival traces of women's spectatorship are slight. The difficulty here is that identification of "reception" with the archival traces left by the small fraction of male viewers who wrote their treatises, pamphlets and memoirs is a synecdoche that can only re-enact those exclusions which the archive has already performed; it can even naturalize them further, while a critical analysis of the codes in those documents can avoid such repetitiveness. This points to an extension of the archival project, to a more comprehensive history of reception that would ideally and eventually uncover the hidden traces of other codes of viewing than those we are currently attuned to. As a canon has its exclusions, and can be countered by making it now admit those whom it had set aside, so has an archive; though we may need to look away from the obvious, the official records of reception in order to do so.

What semiotic analysis draws attention to is the plurality and unpredictability at work in contexts of reception. Surrounding those forms of looking that have given rise to discursive configurations that actually figure in the archive are other, submerged series of procedures that addressed other needs, procedures whose traces can still be derived from the forcefulness of the attempts to repress them. Such series will include codes of viewing that represent residual practices edged out by the rise of those later codes which come to replace them; and, conversely, codes which are hardly yet formed, emergent ways of seeing whose coherence has not yet been established and whose energies have not yet taken root, still tentative and faltering configurations that still have to find each other and lock together to form a configuration that may be seen emerging into the historical record.[41] Staying just with those fully configured codes of seeing, the ones which have made it into the arena of public taste and debate, there will be those which also exist in "debased" versions of the official protocols of viewing. On one side, there is the practice of viewing works of art that seeks, but has not yet attained, confidence within a dominant visual discourse, which stammers and is not yet there, does not fully grasp which responses do and which do not fall within the orbit of the sanctioned, yet seeks instruction and admission. On the other side are decaying versions of dominant practices of viewing, those which drift from the official model, through lapses of memory, disaffiliation, random variation, memory lapses, and so forth. As to the practices of resistance to dominant regimes of viewing, we know these are legion, and perhaps—comparatively— they are better understood: they range from polite parody to outright defacement, from the clandestine inversion of existing rules of viewing to the invention of wholly new sets of rules, from subtle violations of propriety to blank

---

41. See Raymond Williams' discussion of "residual" and "emergent" cultures (19)

refusal to play the game.⁴² In a separate category are complete idiolects of viewing, private languages of memory and habit which re-order the dominant codes into secret configurations of desire and identity, codes which may or may not be revealed to another human being, whose nature may or may not be consciously recognized.⁴³

Alongside the official records of reception one must posit another world of looking, even before it can be specified in order to make it legible; against the "monotheism" of synecdoche, and its molar constructions, analysis has to assume the persistence of a "polytheism" of hidden and dispersed practices of looking at works of art, which while never giving rise to the consolidated forms of the review, the essay, the treatise, nevertheless constituted "reception" and "context" as historical realities.⁴⁴ One cannot know in advance what might enter into reconstructions of silent practice. What counts as much as what might eventually fill the space of the "reserve" is that such a space be conceptually created. It is not enough to escape the enclosure of synecdoche if the archive is simply extended towards as yet silent groups, for as each of these is identified and brought in, the logic of the "representative sample" is not yet challenged, only confirmed. In the same way that extension of canons to include, for example, the work of women or black artists, nevertheless stays within the bounds of canonicity, so the discovery of previously unrecognized modes of visual practice stays within the logic of synecdoche unless the trope is deliberately confronted.

Among other things, this confrontation takes place where the study of reception confronts the dimension of semiotic play. Until it does, in fact, reach that point, "reception" risks (in the critique of semiotics) being made over into a primarily repressive and legislative idea, like so much of the context-idea in which it plays a conspicuous role. Semiotics argues that it is only in concrete material circumstances that signs operate; but it also raises a number of questions concerning the tracing of these operations in reception-analysis. Reception of works of art is certainly an aspect of the general category of consumption; but the nature of consumption cannot be discerned by looking into the mirror of production.⁴⁵ Production may appear to be a highly determinate process, with a distinct sequence of stages and a clearly demarcated outcome, the product, although that, too, is a simplification. But reception is a work with signs that opens on to the "polytheism" of hidden and dispersed practices that make up semiotic play. Even in the chamber and season of its first appearance (the Royal Academy, the Salon), the work of art enters networks of semiotic transformation as volatile and as tangled as the glances of a

42. On "local resistance" to dominant regimes, see Michel de Certeau, 1984.
43. On private "idiolects" of reception, see Roland Barthes' discussion of the *punctum* (1981). Victor Burgin provides an interesting discussion of Barthes' text in "Diderot, Barthes, Vertigo," in *Formations of Fantasy* (1986: 85–108).
44. On "monotheism" and "polytheism" see De Certeau (1986:89; also 1984: 48).
45. See Jean Baudrillard, 1975.

crowd in any given minute of its life. Nothing can stop the movement of signifier to signifier in a visual text as it is actually being viewed by empirical spectators. To do so one would have to be able to overcome something that cannot be eradicated from texts—whether visual, verbal, written, or the "general text"—that at the moment when a text is made, enunciation and enunciated cleave at the most fundamental level, and the visual text sets out on its numberless trajectories of seeing, none of which will exhaust the mobility of signification.

Is the argument of a visual semiotics, then, that attempts to retrace or reconstruct reception be abandoned as a goal? No—what it seeks is to add a question and to shift the claim. For visual semiotics, the better question to ask would be: from where, from what position, is the reconstruction being made? Art historical discussions of reception seem to move between two poles: the plural, dispersed, often submerged "polytheism" of actual, empirical reception; and the delimitations of a discourse on viewing that produces out of this plurality a cast of viewers whose responses are said to follow the most determinable contours. Out of the welter of concrete reception is distilled a character, "the viewer" whose attributes vary from one narration to another. But however this figure is defined, the viewer is essentially a character, a personification, in stories of viewing written in the first place according to the disciplinary norms of the narratives they work within.

A plain example will make this clear. How is it that female spectatorship has not been, from the beginning, a primary object of art historical inquiry into visual reception? Can it be said that it was because the archive was lacking in evident traces of women viewers, that because incidentally the representative sample typically concerned only male viewing, that the latter was extrapolated from the archive and presented as the self-evident context of reception? But obviously this is an insufficient explanation. It suggests more innocence that is plausible: it is as if "the fault lay in the archive, not in ourselves; had the traces been those of some other privileged group, we would have privileged them instead!" It is only by seeing from within the present context that institutional forces within art history have worked generally to silence the whole question of the roles played by gender and sexuality in the field of vision, that art historians are able *now* to begin to see the ellipses and silences within the archive. The present context of reception has latterly enabled art historians to realize different modes of reception, and that it is art history that establishes them. Which should, rationally, lead to investigation of the institutional forces that identify reception with some groups rather than others, and the narrative pressures that impound the welter of empirical viewing into stories of clear delineation. Until this occurs, art historians are probably at the mercy of the narratives that seem, within disciplines, naturally to explain things; stories of "reception then" serving to mask "reception now," in the same disciplinary ecology or episteme that makes "context then" and "author then" eclipse and elide "context and author now."

▪ 8 ▪

Peirce, Saussure, and Visual Art

Thus far we have been discussing a single set of issues concerning context, author and reception, and we have attempted to outline the semiotic critique of these terms. But in order to understand how semiotics has reached a position from which to form that critique, one needs to know something of semiotics' own development. Restrictions of space oblige us to keep our discussion of the history of semiotics to a minimum; in this short intermediate chapter we shall single out just two traditions within semiotics, the first stemming from Peirce, and the second from Saussure.[1]

PEIRCE

The semiotic philosophy of Charles Sanders Peirce (1834–1914) is a complex logical system, much of which is relevant only to specialists. A few of his concepts, however, have had an important bearing on developments in semiotic criticism. Peirce's theory is characterized by a trichotomistic structure which accounts for the ways signs function. Peirce's view is primarily dynamic; it describes the process of signification, which is called *semiosis*. This process involves the production and the interpretation of signs, both equally fundamental. Hence, this theory provides a logical basis for a reader- or reception-oriented theory of art.

The process of semiosis works through three positions: a perceptible or virtually perceptible item—the sign or *representamen*—that stands in for something else; the mental image, *called the interpretant*, that the recipient forms of the sign; and the thing for which the sign stands—the *object* or

---

1. For more discussion of the contribution of Peirce and Saussure to visual semiotics, see Margaret Iversen's article "Saussure v. Peirce: Models for a Semiotics of Visual Art," in *The New Art History*, ed. A.L. Rees and Frances Borzello (1988).

referent. When one sees a painting, say a still-life of a fruit-bowl, the image is, among other things, a sign or representamen of something else. The viewer shapes in her or his mind an image of that something with which she or he associates this image. That mental image, *not the person shaping it*, is the interpretant. This interpretant points to an object. The object is different for each viewer: it can be real fruit for one, other still-life paintings for another, a huge amount of money for a third, "seventeenth-century Dutch" for a fourth, and so on. The object for which the painting stands is therefore fundamentally subjective and reception-determined.

Peirce's famous and often misquoted definition of the sign runs as follows:

> A sign, or *representamen*, is something which stands to somebody for something in some respect or capacity. It addresses somebody, that is, creates in the mind of that person an equivalent sign, or perhaps a more developed sign. That sign which it creates I call the *interpretant* of the first sign. The sign stands for something, its *object*. It stands for that object, not in all respects, but in reference to a sort of idea, which I have sometimes called the *ground* of the representamen.[2]

The structure of address of the sign has been taken up by speech-act theory; the "more developed sign" points at the complex acts of interpretation, e.g. in scholarly work; the "ground" can be seen as the basis on which the interpretation takes place, and comes closest to the more common concept of *code*.

As for the process of interpretation that this definition implies, it is obvious that the interpretant is constantly shifting; no viewer will stop at the first association. As soon as the mental image takes shape, it becomes a new sign, which will yield a new interpretant, and we are in the middle of the process of *infinite semiosis*. None of the aspects of this process can be isolated from the others, which is the reason why this theory is incompatible with any dichotomistic theory of the sign, such as Saussure's pair signifier/signified. Peirce insists that the thing that becomes a sign only does so when it begins to evoke its interpretant: "A *Sign* is a Representamen with a mental interpretant." This view is consistent with standard aesthetic theories, e.g. the German phenomenological school of Rezeptions-Aesthetik[3] which stated that a work of art only becomes a work of art in its *concretization* by a recipient. The Prague school *of semiotics adopted Mukarovski's distinction between artifact*, the mere object, and *aesthetic object*, the work when processed as work of art by readers or viewers, which is another aesthetic account similar to Peirce's more general account of semiosis.[4]

---

2. Charles S. Peirce, "Logic as Semiotic: the Theory of Signs" in Robert S. Innis (1984:5). Innis has selected the most representative passage for our purpose here. See also his bibliographical notice for further references.
3. A representative collection in this vein is Wolfgang Kemp (1985b).
4. In spite of the different epistemological backgrounds, there is a strong similarity in this respect between Peirce's and Lacan's concepts of the sign. Both concepts entail the notion that the fixation of the meaning of a sign is endlessly deferred, as is also held by Derrida. The major

The interpretant is a crucial concept in Peircean semiotics. As we said earlier, it should not be conflated with the person doing the interpretation. A good example of the representation of an interpretant is Vermeer's *The Artist in His Studio* (Vienna, Kunsthistorisches Museum). Because Vermeer cannot have seen this scene while painting it, we must conclude that he imagined it, as an outsider would see it, for example. "The scene was nowhere but in his head."[5] Hence, the scene of the painting artist presented from the back is in the first place and emphatically a sign or rather, a sign of its own sign-ness.

Peirce elaborates this basic trichotomy of the semiotic process in at times exasperating detail. A primary division of the field of semiotic inquiry is based on the relations between the elements of semiosis. The relation between the sign and the ground lead to grammar, whose most commonly studied aspect is syntax. The relation between sign and object leads to questions of meaning or semantics. The relation between sign and interpretant can be linked to questions of rhetoric as part of pragmatics by virtue of the idea that one thought brings forth another. This division into three fields of inquiry is more common in linguistics than in art criticism, but certainly deserves consideration. Pragmatics would be the dimension where the affective efficacy of a work is examined; semantics includes any hypothesis about the meaning of a work, e.g. iconography; syntactics studies the relations between elements of the image to codes or ways of meaning-production.

Although many of Peirce's elaborate typologies of signs derived from this basic theory have not been commonly taken up by art critics, the most famous of these, *icon, index, symbol*, deserve further investigation. We quote Peirce's own definitions, because this typology is frequently misunderstood.

> An *icon* is a sign which would possess the character which renders it significant, even though its object had no existence; such as a lead-pencil streak as representing a geometric line. An *index* is a sign which would, at once, lose the character which makes it a sign if its object were removed, but would not lose that character if there were no interpretant. Such, for example, is a piece of mould with a bullet-hole in it as a sign of a shot; for without the shot there would have been no hole; but there is a hole there, whether anybody has the sense to attribute it to a shot or not. A *symbol* is a sign which would lose the character which renders it a sign if there were no interpretant. Such is any utterance of speech which signifies what it does only by virtue of its being understood to have that signification. (Innis 1984: 9–10)

---

difference seems to be that Lacan insists on the social formation of the practice of interpretation (his concept of the *symbolic order*). But as De Lauretis rightly argues, Peirce's interpretant, although presented as a mental image and therefore carrying the burden of mentalism, can be redefined as radically social in origin. For the Peircean *ground* without which no interpretant can occur, is, precisely, a *common ground*. See De Lauretis, 1983. De Lauretis presents an integration of Peirce's and Kristeva's semiotic theories, the former mediated through Umberto Eco's rethinking of Peirce in *A Theory of Semiotics* (1976). For further comments see the section on "semiotics as a theory of subjectivity.".

5. Brian Rotman (1987: 35).

First of all, any identification of icon and the entire domain of the visual is wrong.[6] As Peirce clearly states, the iconic is a quality of the sign in relation to its object; it is best seen as a sign capable of evoking non-existent objects because it proposes to imagine an object similar to the sign itself. Iconicity is in the first place a mode of reading, based on a hypothetical similarity between sign and object. Thus, when we see a portrait by Frans Hals, we imagine a person looking like the image, and we don't doubt the existence, in the time of Hals, of such a person; we don't demand substantiation of that existence by other sources. Similarly, we think we know the face of a self-portraitist, say, Rembrandt, even though other painters have presented a face of Rembrandt quite different from his self-portrait, just because we adopt the iconic way of reading when we look at Rembrandt self-portraits.[7]

But the example of portraits might wrongly suggest that the icon is predicated upon the degree of "realism" of the image. An abstract element like a triangular composition can become an iconic sign whenever we take it as a ground to interpret the image in relation to it, dividing the represented space into three interrelated areas (Leo Steinberg, for example, makes this division in his paper on *Las Meninas*; 1981). Instead of visuality in general, or realism for that matter, the decision to suppose that the image refers to something on the basis of likeness is the iconic act, and a sense of specularity is its result. A romantic sound of violins accompanying a romantic love scene in a film is as iconic as the graphic representation of Apollinaire's poem about rain in the shape of rain. Neither is realistic.

The concept of index has been brought to bear on visual art primarily by Rosalind Krauss.[8] Peirce's description of the index emphasizes its symmetrical opposition to the icon: while the icon does not need the object to exist, the index functions precisely on the ground of that existence. His example suggests that real, existential contiguity between indexical sign and object (or

---

6. This is the grave error of Louis Marin's influential papers (1988; also 1983). For Marin, the "iconic text" is the visual text. Thus the sign-status of the icon is obscured, while the importance of the other two signs in visual art, the index and the symbol, are underestimated. And an ontological distinction between verbal texts as symbolic and visual texts as merely "natural" inevitably returns.

7. This example is mentioned by Svetlana Alpers (1988). For a study of Rembrandt's self-portraits, see H. Perry Chapman (1990). A semiotic perspective on his self-portraits, related to psychoanalysis, is proposed by Bal in *Reading "Rembrandt"*.

8. "Notes on the Index," two parts, in *October*, 3 and 4. These papers have had a decisive influence on the art history of modernism. Krauss gives many examples, one of which we cannot resist quoting:
> To actually place one's tongue in one's cheek is to lose the capacity for speech altogether. And it is this rupture between image and speech, or more specifically, language, that Duchamp's art both contemplates and instances. (206)

The play of indexicality is double here: Duchamp indexes the loss of speech by representing the tongue in the cheek as concretely hampering speech; and Krauss reads this representation as an instance, a concrete case, of the loss of speech, which turns the representation as a whole into an index of speechlessness.

meaning) is indispensable. But that existence need not be confined to "reality"; the indexical sign and its meaning can entertain such a contiguous relationship within the image itself. The many recent publications on the gaze and the look which take the represented look of the figures in the painting as their starting-point, for example, implicitly state that there is an indexical relationship between the look and what is looked at. The represented voyeur looking at the nude body of a woman is an effective figure precisely because he stands for a real, objectifying contiguity between look and object defined by looking as a real act. The index functions here in conjunction with the icon: the figure directing his eyes somewhere is taken to stand for a similar figure, a man looking at a woman. In the same way, the open mouths, iconically suggesting screams, of the popes in Francis Bacon's early portraits after Velazquez, function iconically because they also function indexically; the contiguity between screaming and the pain which induces it enhances the effectivity of the works.[9]

The most obvious use of the concept of index is the pointer. Pointing elements in an image are the most convincing case against the notion that the image is still and can be "read" in a momentary, punctual act. Pointers make us aware of the way our eyes move about the surface in different directions, some of which are suggested by indexical signs. When a figure points a finger in a certain direction, our look will follow the figure's directions.

One category of indexical signs gives the illusion of expressivity. Those are all the signs which refer to the maker of the image, ranging from the recognizable "hand" of the artist, the will to be expressive as in expressionist painting, to the signature. But the index functions in very different cases, and the most plausible one is not necessarily the most reliable one. The signature of the artist, for example, is an index of the person of the maker, even if it is a false signature; that is precisely why it is a sign, a stand-in for an absent other. From the perspective of the sender, a false signature is an icon (of the real signature) parading as an index. This possibility of falsification of the most materially grounded of the three signs is fundamental. As Eco has written with his characteristic philosophical insight parading as a joke, the sign can be defined as everything that can be used in order to lie (1976:10). For in a Peircean view, the sign stands for something else, and that something is logically absent from the scene.

The signature has been the occasion for fascinating philosophical reflections in the work of Derrida. It is the most typical case of the Derridian *trace*, the indexical sign which refers by contiguity, not simply to the past (the maker of the image) but more importantly, to the future, the reading of it (1976). The act of writing, which for Derrida is much more than graphic writing alone, is precisely the production of traces, and painting, drawing, and most emphati-

9. See Ernst van Alphen, 1992.

cally, etching are also acts of writing in this sense.[10] Therefore, the notion of the index suggests that we do not only account for images in terms of their provenance and making, but also of their functioning in relation to the viewer: their structure of address. In a discussion with John Searle, Derrida insisted on the impossibility of determining exactly which speech-acts are performed, as Searle would like to do in his logic and typology of speech-acts. Instead, he emphasizes the constant interaction between the reader or viewer who tries, but in vain, to fix meaning and point down the act as a one-time, predictable performance.[11]

Finally, the symbolic sign in Peirce's theory must not be confused with the many different and often vague colloquial meanings of the word "symbol". As the definition in the quoted passage makes clear, it is dependent even more strongly than the two other terms on the act of interpretation which brings it to life, because without that interpretation it simply does not exist—as a sign, that is. What is not specified in this passage is the ground on which interpretation of a symbol comes about, which is the conventional rule of correlation between sign and object or meaning. The interpretant formed by the reader is possible because the latter knows what things usually mean in the culture in which the sign functions. The idiom of a particular language is conventional in the same sense as the idiom of iconographic traditions. "Translation" from one language into another, from an image into words that explain it, from one image into another image, all work by virtue of the knowledge of such idioms. These conventional signs are always also involved when we read iconically and indexically. We only come up with an iconic interpretation of a portrait because we know the convention of portrayal.

Symbolic interpretation, which always underlies other kinds of interpretations, is the most convincing evidence of the cultural specificity of pictorial traditions and styles. Even when we think the image is "realistic," we are in fact imbued in the convention which suggests that certain kinds of pictorial signs stand for "reality" more clearly than others. With the help of iconicity, which suggests that the image *must* have an object in the real world, and indexicality, which makes us aware of the real contiguities between elements of the image, and between those elements and ourselves, symbolicity by virtue of its very arbitrariness is the most deceptive code. In every day life, we tend not to question what is conventional; we don't even notice it. Much of art historical work aims at denaturalizing these conventions, and to bring forth insight into the historical changeability of conventions. This kind of work can be seen as analysis of the symbolic as a code. Iconography is in this sense a semiotic approach.

10. For a collection of literary analyses in this Derridian vein, see Peggy Kamuf (1988).
11. The clearest account of this debate can be found in the Afterward to the paperback edition of Derrida's *Limited Inc* (1988).

Peirce's semiotic theory is relevant for the study of art because it helps us think about aspects of the process of art in society, in history, in a way that is not bound up with the artist's intention. It can contribute to the explanation of why certain elements of an image are particularly seductive or deceptive, suggesting depiction of something real while specularity, a return to the self away from the real, is in fact the basis of the seductiveness. The mix of iconicity, indexicality, and symbolicity which every image presents emphasizes the other side of the illusory unity that the image is so easily assumed to be: its fracturedness, the "difference within" which allows for a view of image-seeing that is dynamic and positioned in time.

SAUSSURE

If Peirce's view of the way signs function is primarily dynamic, that of Ferdinand de Saussure (1857–1913) involves far more stasis. In order to understand how the words in a language (*langue*) function, Saussure argues that we must set to one side both the aspects of historical change within particular languages over time, and actual utterances or performances of language in local situations (*parole*). What is sought is the global set of rules governing a language; the *state* of a language as a whole at a given and, as it were "frozen" moment. Isolating the total body of rules allows investigation of the internal relations between the signs of a language which, Saussure proposes, are what determine the meanings of those signs: the meaning of a word derives from its "diacritical" differences from other words; "red," for example, acquires its meaning from the ways in which it is not "green," not "blue," not "yellow," and so forth. Although, as a linguist, Saussure's primary task was to elucidate the operations of verbal language, he also put forward the view that his method could be generalized: "One can conceive of a science that studies the life of signs at the heart of social life.... Linguistics is only one part of this general science" (1983:33). Later analysts have extended the Saussurean model towards what is indeed a great variety of cultural systems. Roland Barthes, to take only one figure from this tradition, proposed the systematic study of "any system of signs, whatever their substance and limits: images, gestures, musical sounds, objects, and the complex associations of all of these...." (1967:9). In *Elements of Semiology* Barthes set out to explore the operations of signs in the fashion system, the food system, the car system, the furniture system;[12] in *Mythologies* his analyses ranged even more widely.(1972)

Images are obviously included in this extended project,[13] and it may be useful to see how semiotics, in its structuralist phase, tackles a particular work of art. Our example is Edmund Leach's analysis of the Sistine Chapel ceil-

---

12. On the semiotics of clothing, see also Barthes (1983); on the semiotics of food, see Claude Lévi-Strauss (1969); on the semiotics of consumer goods, see Jean Baudrillard (1968).
13. See, for example, Barthes' investigations of the image (1977; 1985).

ing.[14] Leach concedes the multiplicity of factors that may have influenced the way Michelangelo carried out his task, but argues that among these should be included the internal logic of the scenes and narratives depicted in the nine central panels. These can be divided, Leach suggests, into three groups. The first shows God in the Cosmos without Man: *God dividing Light from Darkness, God creating the Sun, Moon, Stars and Planets, The Spirit of God moving on the Waters*. The second group shows the Garden of Eden story in which God and Man are together in Paradise: *The Creation of Adam, The Creation of Eve, The Fall and Expulsion from Eden*. The third group relates the story of Noah, where sinful Man is in this World separated from God: *The Sacrifice of Noah, The Flood, and The Sin of Ham*. The primary opposition governing the disposition of the ceiling panels is between This World, where Man is impotent, mortal, sinful; and the Other World where God is omnipotent, immortal, sinless. Equally important, in Leach's view, is the liminal space in between the terms of the polarities: "In any binary pair of the type 'A'/'not-A,' the boundary layer which is neither the one nor the other but both at once, 'both A and not-A,' is especially 'interesting' because it is 'repressed.' This is where the theory of structuralism ties in not only with psychoanalysis but also with anthropological theories about magic and primitive religion. The boundary, the interface layer which separates categories of time and space, is the zone of the sacred, the forbidden, that which is taboo; God when seen from one side of the fence, Sin when seen from the other" (1979:20). Leach's decision to concentrate on the *central* panels stems from his Lévi-Straussian (1974) understanding of the importance of the "mixed" space in between the poles of the opposition, for here one finds complex and transgressive figures: Eve, who is shown in states of both innocence and "corruption" (her face echoing both the sinless uncreated Eve seen in *The Creation of Adam*, and the serpent who brings about the Fall); Adam, both pristine first man and ruined, post-lapsarian figure of sorrow; the tree and serpent of Eden, which coil both towards and away from Paradise, the ambiguity assuming visual form as the spiralling and torsion in the center of the panel of *The Fall*. Pursuing such sacred ambiguities in other scenes Leach finds further evidence of complex, contradictory figures: Cain, the first murderer, but also the founder of cities and culture-hero; Haman, a transform of Judas but also of Christ, in the same way that the figure of Holofernes is cross-referenced to John the Baptist, and Judith to Herodias.

This brief sketch, which does not begin to do justice to the complexity of Leach's interpretation, is enough at least to indicate how Saussurean procedures became elaborated within structuralism. There are perhaps three essential moves. First there is the drawing of a boundary round a distinct, enclosed corpus (Leach excludes the large nude male figures, the Sybils, most

---

14. Edmund Leach (1979). An earlier version of Leach's interpretation appeared in the *Times Literary Supplement* for March 18, 1977, 311 ff.

of the Prophets, the Tree of Jesse, and the medallions). Then there is the segmentation of that corpus into signifying units (here derived from the primary oppositions of "This World" and "the Other World," as well as the "trickster" zone produced by their merger). Finally, the segmented units are related syntactically, through a logic of transformation and condensation (Eve metaphorically connected with Mary, Esther, and Judith; Noah with Christ and Adam). All these have their parallels in Saussure's own methods: the drawing of a boundary round the *langue* (setting *parole* to one side); the segmentation of the *langue* into units (morphemes, phonemes, and so on); and the mapping of the units in terms of oppositional syntax.[15] But each of the moves is problematic, and in post-structuralist semiotics within the Saussurean tradition (but moving ever more remotely away from Saussure) quite different steps are proposed.

Derrida's text *Truth in Painting* is probably the most systematic answer to the kind of visual analysis proposed by structuralism. The first move, the drawing of a non-permeable perimeter around the work of art, is the subject of Derrida's lengthy excursus on "framing" ("The Parergon").[16] It may be essential to the structuralist project, as well as to many others (including "formalism" in art history) to maintain the fiction that the work of art is characterized by its apartness, that it inhabits an area of autonomy and separation from "extrinsic" concerns. But for Derrida semiosis is a process that can never be placed within a logic of enclosure: "*There is* frame, but the frame *does not exist*" (81) (il *y a* du cadre, mais le cadre *n'existe pas* [93]). Where Saussure theorizes the sign as a fixed and static entity, with each signified stitched to its stable signified, Derrida argues for the dynamism of signs: that a sign is not (as in Saussure) the conjunction between a signifier and its single, univocal signified, but the movement from one signifier to another, the *motion* between them. As motion, visual signification is therefore incompatible with the ideas of boundary, threshold, frame; it is a "passe-partout."[17] Investigating the conceptual structure of the frame in aesthetic discourse, Derrida finds that it is both fundamental to that discourse, and at a profound level absent from it. Fundamental, because without the idea of frame, there can be no object of aesthetics:

> . . .we must know what we are talking about, what concerns the value of beauty intrinsically and what remains external to an immanent sense of beauty. This permanent demand—to distinguish between the internal or proper meaning and the circumstances of the object in question—organizes every philosophical discourse on art, the meaning of art. . . .It presupposes a discourse on the boundary between the inside and the outside of the art object, in this case a discourse on the frame (1987:45).

---

15. Similar procedures are to be found in an interesting, if neglected, study of a painting by Paris Bordone, Jean-Louis Schefer (1969).
16. Derrida (1987) section 2. For a lucid commentary, see Jonathan Culler (1983: 193–99).
17. Derrida, "Passe-Partout," *Truth in Painting*, section 1.

Yet even though it is the idea of the frame which calls the discourse of aesthetics into being—for without it, that discourse could not open itself, could not define what it is that it discusses—that discourse, according to Derrida, cannot adequately theorize the frame, or describe its opening move. What it can, of course, discuss is the "outside" of the work of art, which comes into being as outside once the concept of frame is in place; and equally well it can discuss the "inside," what is proper to the work of art. But the frame itself is consigned to a kind of conceptual limbo, for the reason (Derrida argues) that the frame is the one thing in the discourse of aesthetics which escapes the categories of "inside" and "outside."

In fact the frame is both at once, a hybrid, a categorical aberration—which might be manageable if the discourse within which the "frame" operates, and which it also establishes, could permit a mediating zone between its two extremes (perhaps in the manner of the "trickster" category discussed by Leach). But the discourse of aesthetics, exemplified for Derrida by Kant, cannot allow such a zone of aberration to be admitted, since that would be to call into question its own primary move, the division of the field into "inside" and "outside." Instead, the frame is conceptually disavowed and repressed, becoming an ornamental supplement, an unnecessary and optional accompaniment to the work of art. Nevertheless, this relegation of the frame to the place of a mere incidental in aesthetic discourse cannot conceal, in Derrida's analysis, that the latter's central area of interest, the "inside" of the work of art, depends for its very being on the conceptual operation of the frame; that is, on an operation which threatens the clean separation of "outside" and "inside" to its foundations, since the concept of the frame is the undoing of the relation of "inside" to "outside" on which all else is predicated. Derrida's argument aims to expose the persistent logic of enclosure that allows there to be found in painting the stasis of transcendental contemplation (Kant), stabilized reference (Meyer Schapiro), or onto-theological presence (Heidegger). Against such a logic, and by pressing hard on the contradictions and incoherences of its fundamental moves, *Truth in Painting* shows visual semiosis to be a matter of dis-framing: an unending dissemination which, nevertheless, as Derrida himself but also Eco and many others have repeatedly pointed out, always occupies specific social and historical sites.[18]

If enclosure is impossible, so is segmentation. When one falls, so does the other: it is only within the confines of an enclosed and tabular space that internal oppositions can be established and "geometrized," and from those oppositions the "significant units" be derived. By the same token, the relation of opposition (which in Leach's analysis lies behind all the units of sig-

---

18. Derrida insists on this qualification, most emphatically in the Afterward to *Limited Inc*. It is precisely because of the theoretically overriding effect of dissemination that we are forced to interrogate which social and political pressures do check the actual dissemination.

nification he isolates, including those of the intermediary "sacred" zone) cannot survive the dissolution of the aesthetic boundary: as soon as the idea of a delimiting frame is questioned and the possibility of dynamic semiosis is admitted, the relation of opposition must give way to that of non-oppositional difference. The image becomes what it is by being traversed by flows of signification that cut across the boundary, making the image part of a general circulation of signs and codes within the social formation as a whole.

While Derrida's revisionary work within the Saussurean tradition may have resolved some of the difficulties of structuralist methodology, it might be objected that the Saussurean legacy is of limited use in furthering understanding of *visual* art, since all of its models are verbal ones.[19] Saussure's projected science of signs may have called for an expansion of inquiry beyond the domain of language, but in practice the term "signifier" is modeled on the linguistic case. If this is so, it is right to wonder to what extent the "expansion" proposed by a "general" science of signs may in fact be an attempt at appropriation, the absorption of the visual domain into the empire of linguistics. For obviously there are a great number of aspects of visual art and visual experience that cannot be "translated" into language at all. As Michael Baxandall has put it, "In fact, language is not very well equipped to offer a notation of a particular picture. It is a generalizing tool. . . .the repertory of concepts it offers for describing a plane surface bearing an array of subtly differentiated and ordered shapes and colours is rather crude and remote."[20] The vocabulary of our languages is able to scan for only a fraction of the hues that a painting presents us with; the lexicon for shape is not much better. If the word "signifier" is modeled on the verbal case, surely everything that makes up the visual as a specific domain will be lost from view?

While such apprehensions are well based, in principle semiotics is well equipped to respect the specificity of visual and verbal discourses: not only does its key term, semiosis, embrace both visual and verbal practices of the sign, its attention to sign-types forces it carefully to distinguish between those which belong to the linguistic domain and those which do not. In our "Narratology" section of chapter 9, for example, the narratives described are specifically visual ones; and the distinctions made by Peirce between symbol, icon and index supply a firm basis for fine-tuned description of the differences between verbal and visual modes. But Peirce is one thing, Saussure and his

---

19. Some readers of Derrida sometimes cite as an indication of the persistent "verbal imperialism" of Derrida's project a certain impoverishment in his dealings with the visual domain, perhaps related to the poverty of the works of art discussed in *Truth in Painting* (setting to one side those that relate to Van Gogh). One might agree—but there after all is no reason to believe that such impoverishment, if there, is necessarily the result of Derrida's *method*. Moreover, if the arguments in *Truth in Painting* are accepted, the secure autonomy of a "visual domain" cannot be simply taken for granted.

20. Michael Baxandall, (1985: 3).

tradition another: the question remains, whether the semiotics of Saussure is adequate to the specificity of works of visual art.

Take, for instance, the problem of the "significant unit." In language, the minimal blocks are abundantly clear: we all know what is a letter, a word, a sentence; we can pick out the fundamental "atoms" of language without difficulty. But with an image the nature of what is to count as a unit is far from obvious. We might try to say that below a certain threshold, perhaps roughly corresponding to phonetics in language, there are marks which contribute to, but which do not yet produce, signification—individual brushstrokes or lines, or dots or pixels; and that above that threshold these as yet non-semantic marks emerge as productive of meaning. But can we say that the marks below the threshold are "units"? Or above the threshold? Particularly in the Saussurean tradition, the positing of meaning-bearing units—signifiers—seems essential.[21] But a painting is a continuous surface, with marks that blend together inextricably. If no minimal units for images can be found, then a visual semiotics, deriving from Saussure, must be an impossible endeavour: we cannot establish where the "signifier" actually is.

The objection is understable, but it may be misplaced. The problem of mismatch between words and images can, in fact, lead us in rather a different direction, towards the question whether the individual word actually is language's *prima materia*. In Saussure's view, a certain "atomism" of language undoubtedly prevails, a confidence that, if we want to exemplify what language is, the individual word can stand in for all linguistic operations. Yet it is not obvious why this synecdoche should be accepted. The problem and source of the atomistic view could be said to be the semiotic positivism that claims ontological status for signs. If the sign is a *thing* that is *there*, then signs must be numerable, hence, discrete and intrinsically static; and the quest for the significant unit is on.[22] That quest is a reflection of a philologically derived linguistics that posits meaning as occurring at the level of the word or the sentence, but does not consider the larger aggregates, the bonding together of words and sentences in social practice, as discourse.[23] At this level, signs are not discrete but "dense:"[24] individual signs become molar, consolidated, fundamentally inseparable. If a visual semiotics pitches itself at this level, which is that of discourse and interpretation rather than of taxonomy, the difference between verbal and visual discourse is no longer one of the status and delimitation of the signs that constitute them. To think of semiosis as

---

21. The Saussurean tradition, we note, is famous for its proliferation of "-emes": mythemes, semes, monemes, lexias, etc.

22. The points briefly stated here, concerning "minimal units" in language and in images, are argued at greater length in Bal, *Reading "Rembrandt"*, Introduction and Chapter 1.

23. See Colin MacCabe, "On Discourse," (1985: 2–112). For a full elaboration of the theory of discourse in semiotic terms, see Robert Hodge and Gunther Kress (1988).

24. With apology to Nelson Goodman for this reversal of his term "density" (in *Languages of Art*).

process and as movement is to conceive the sign *not as a thing but as an event*, the issue being not to delimit and isolate the one sign from other signs, but to trace the possible emergence of the sign in a concrete situation, as an event in the world.

Whether such a dynamic conception of the sign can still be called Saussurean is an open question: from one point of view, there is a certain continuity with Saussure, and for Derrida especially it was in part as a result of critical engagement with the stasis and fixity of the Saussurean sign that his own version of the dynamic view came into being;[25] from another point of view, the changeover may be a genuine mutation, a break with the Saussurean legacy. But the problem of the "significant unit" is only one of the places at which Saussure's conception of the sign makes it hard—without drastic modification of the system—to see how a visual semiotics might be developed from a Saussurean framework. Equally challenging is what Saussure (speaking of language) referred to as the "arbitrariness" of the sign.

For Saussure, the relation that obtains in language between a signifier (a word) and a signified (its corresponding concept)[26] is a matter of conventional agreement: "apparently nothing would prevent the association of any idea whatsoever with just any sequence of sounds."[27] There is nothing about the idea of a tree, for example, that would indicate that the sound "tree" be made to correspond to it; but can the same be said of images? To take a difficult case, is the "realism" one might find in a Renaissance painting when comparing it with, say, a Chinese literati painting, a matter of convention, or is it a result of the fact that the Renaissance painting more directly reflects the natural world? [28] For if the Renaissance painting involves representational "directness," an uncoded access to nature, to the extent that it does so, its realism stands outside conventions and codes; it is not a product of sign-activity at all, and therefore is not available as an object of semiotic inquiry.

Let us take two figures who have argued that there are no limits to the conventionality of representations: Roland Barthes and Nelson Goodman. It is part of Barthes' project, in many of his works, to take what might be thought to be a "natural" phenomenon, and to show that it is in fact a cultural construc-

---

25. Though there are certainly other, non-Saussurean or obliquely Saussurean traditions that argue for the dynamism and the social embeddedness of signs and discourse, notably that which stems from Voloshinov/Bakhtin: see V.N. Voloshinov, (1973); M. Bakhtin, *Rabelais and his World*, (1968); Gary Saul Morson, ed. (1986); Gary Saul Morson and Caryl Emerson, eds. (1989). On Derrida's engagement with Saussure, see Robert M. Strozier, (1988: 160–288).
26. "The linguistic sign unites, not at thing and a name, but a concept and a sound-image." (1974: 66).
27. Saussure (1983:76). The parallel between Saussurean "arbitrariness" and modernism's break with mimetic representation is developed by Yves-Alain Bois (1987).
28. See E.H. Gombrich (1984: 84–6). For Nelson Goodman, however, European painting is no more able to justify the claim to realism, as defined by Gombrich, than any other sort of painting; its system of perspective, for example, is only a series of conventions (1968: 10–19). See also Hubert Damisch (1987); and Norman Bryson (1981: 1–28).

tion, a product of history and not of nature; the idea of "nature" being, in Barthes' view, a myth or a mystification of the workings of culture and history.[29] In *Languages of Art*, Goodman writes against the common sense view that lifelike representations are "realistic" because they copy real things in the world, arguing that the effect of lifelikeness is a product of a certain kind of denotation, and that in the case of pictorial representations it is the result of the particular form of notation that pictures use (the notation of pictures, as opposed to that of schematic diagrams, being "dense" and "replete").[30] With both Barthes and Goodman, realism is entirely conventionalized, and the *vraisemblance* of an image is described as a quality that can be accounted for without reference to a criterion of fidelity to a natural world.[31]

It is often said against such conventionalism that it flies in the face of the fact that human viewing is not only a matter of codes and conventions but of inborn perceptual capacities, irreducible to cultural factors. Certainly an extreme form of conventionalism is contradicted by the admission of a natural human capacity to process imagery, but one may not be convinced that all forms of conventionalism are threatened by this to the same degree. Discussing the drive (*Trieb*), Freud proposes (in the *Three Essays on Sexuality*) a model in which a biological or hard-wired program (for instance, the infant's need to suckle) becomes the support for forms of symbolization that deviate from the drive and transform it; these forms are said to be "propped" on the instinct (*entsteht in Ahlehnung an*), and also to swerve away and to produce effects in human subjectivity that are irreducible to instinct.[32] Freud here is far from being a pan-conventionalist, and his model in fact depends on the instance of a biological program; but he also suggests something highly relevant to the discussion of conventionalism in art, that the model he proposes "represents the model of every drive," including the scopic drive (1976: 8; 11). To the extent that the recognition of images depends on a prior, hard-wired program, it stands outside semiosis; but recognition of such limits to semiosis does not exclude the possibility that the most complex forms of symbolization, for example of the kind we associate with visual art, may be propped superveningly upon the non-semiotic base.

29. On the unmasking of social myths, see Barthes, "Myth Today," (19: 109–59); and Jonathan Culler (1983b: 33–41).
30. On "density" and "repleteness," see Goodman (1968:225–32).
31. See Barthes, "The Reality Effect," in Tzvetan Todorov, ed. (1982: 11–17). For an incisive critique of Goodman's account of the "reality effect," see Richard Wollheim (1973).
32. Freud, *Three Essays on the Theory of Sexuality* (SE VII, 125–243). See also the commentary of Jean Laplanche (1976:8–24).

▪9▪

Art And...

The call for interdisciplinary collaboration in the humanities has been heeded for quite sometime already in a variety of areas. Humanists have made use of, considered, integrated, misunderstood, and misused, such different disciplines as sociology, anthropology, history, philosophy. Whereas methodological problems are often severe in such endeavors, semiotics has been an extraordinarily powerful discipline to help understand where those problems come from, and how they can, if not solved, at least be attended to in a responsible way. In this chapter we will present a few of the most successful integrations of art history with another discipline through the mediation of semiotic theory.

PSYCHOANALYSIS AS A SEMIOTIC THEORY

Psychoanalysis is a mode of reading the unconscious and its relationship to expression, and as such it is a semiotic theory. Using this theory for the study of visual art assumes that art bears traces of the unconscious. Moreover, many of the key concepts of psychoanalytic theory have a specific visual status (the imaginary, the gaze), or refer to visual experiences (castration anxiety, the mirror stage), refer to sign-making (condensation, displacement), or refer to concepts we tend to visualize (the breast, the phallus). When used to read visual art or literature, however, the transfer of a method for curing subjects to a method of reading a work poses the problem of the nature of the relationship between the theory and the work of art. Psychoanalysis is a "talking cure" in which the patient does the talking, the interpreting; in psychocriticism the work cannot talk, so who is the patient? If psychoanalysis tends to take on the status of a mastercode that can be "applied" to art, one can also argue that the critic is the patient who does the talking (s/he is the only one who talks), while the work of art is the analyst who orients the analytic work (the analyst is typically silent, but strongly structuring of the analytic work). One can even argue that the discourse of psychoanalytic theory is the patient whose unconscious is uncovered by the slips it produces when confronted by the visual work (many recent analyses of Freud's texts follow this lead). Without prejudging the nature of the relationship, then, we assume here that the relationship between the work and psychoanalysis is an interaction between two discourses, conducted among three subjects: the psychoanalytic theorist, the work, and the critic.

With this in mind, we can think once more of the basic methodological models that have been discussed in chapter 4. The most common one in classical psychocriticism is the *analogical* model, based on an assumed analogy between the processes and products of the practices of psychoanalysis and visual art. Our position as outlined means that we hardly have a place for a *diagnostic* reading that would focus on the symptoms of psychic pathology or disease. But the questions Freud raised a propos of Leonardo, and also of Michelangelo's *Moses*, can also be seen primarily in terms of a reader-oriented commentary. Freud's and Jones' interpretations begin with a Morelli-like detail—the little finger in the *Moses*, the question why Hamlet does not kill his uncle right away—that becomes an obsession of the critic. Thus, the relationship between critic and work, which Freud and Jones took to be that of analyst to patient, can be reversed. The process that made them think they were the analysts applying their master-code to the work can be called transference, a projection on the work-analyst of roles the critic-patient needs to work through.[1]

The second comparison the analogical model works with is between the work and psychoanalytic theory itself. The use of either of the two comparisons does not protect the work against arbitrary interpretations. In fact, the theory and its interpretive schemas have been taken as a whole, as a story in themselves, which is superposed on the work. Such doubling presents the inconvenience of leading invariably up to allegory. And allegory is a flight away from the signifier toward an elusive, logocentric meaning outside. The work can be appropriated for ideologically dubious uses, and no check on this appropriation is possible.[2]

The goal of interpretations according to the *specification* model, in contrast, is not to confirm the psychoanalytic content of the material, but to make explicit in what ways the presumed subject exposes itself as existing through various psychoanalytically theorized problems.[3] For instance, the famous and

---

1. Jane Gallop (1984). Gallop continues the line proposed by Shoshana Felman (1977). Felman's later book (1987) is of crucial importance for those interested in the connections between semiotics, art, and psychoanalysis.
2. On allegory, the key text remains Walter Benjamin (1977). Joel Fineman (1980) is also relevant. On allegory in contemporary visual art, see Craig Owens (1984).
3. This is, for example, how Ellen Handler Spitz discusses the relevance of psychoanalysis for art (1985).

over-quoted woodcut by Dürer, *Draughtsman Drawing a Recumbant Woman* of 1525, invariably alleged as a statement on the technique of perspective, can be argued to represent the fear of women: the standing ruler, not without phallic overtones, also protects the draughtsman from the proximity of the woman who is, in addition, doubly screened off, by the screen which works like the bars of a prison window, and by the veil that covers her body, otherwise exposing her genitalia to the stern gaze of the man. The woodcut does not display *the* psychoanalytic concept—say, castration anxiety—but a unique instance of it, which turns the work into the attractive instance for scientific demonstration that it aims at being, and has in fact become as the critical responses demonstrate, but now loaded with gender issues that problematize the very statement it is making. The psychoanalytically informed interpretation supports the technical one, but it also foregrounds its importance and explains the urgency that is betrayed by its insistent quotation. Thus the psychoanalytic concept informs the analysis but does not reduce the work to what it is not; it is not allegorical. This feature distinguishes the specification from the analogy: analogy summarizes while specification expands the realm of meaning.

The point of psychoanalysis is then neither the diagnosis of a psyche, nor its contribution to the interpretation itself, but the possibility it offers to gain access to issues of visual art. In the Dürer example, the "denotative" meaning of the work—the statement on perspective—does not disappear but gains more depth, becomes culturally framed, and shows the complicity of scientific development and gender relations.[4]

As was explained in chapter 4, what is designated here as the *semiotic* model is different from the preceding models in that it does not use the content of psychoanalysis to inform the work but, instead, draws upon psychoanalytic assumptions and axioms such as its theorization of repression, its views on semiosis, its theory of the subject, and uses these as descriptive concepts. This approach draws less upon the developmental theory and more upon Freud's and Lacan's semiotic intuitions. The procedure is not so much interested in traces of the Oedipal drama or the pre-Oedipal conflations, but rather in traces of the unconscious and the forms these take, disturbing coherence: forms of censorship such as condensation and displacement, contradictions and incoherences and their status in relation to the coherent, "conscious" propositions the image offers. This procedure can yield relevant views on the work in relation to the more common interpretations of its overt semiotic system.

Condensation occurs when one sign—any detail of the work—refers to different meanings, mutually unrelated or even inconsistent. Thus two stories

---

4. On the complicity between science and gender politics, see Evelyn Fox Keller (1985). Alpers (1982) is one of the rare commentaries on the Dürer woodcut which pays attention to the gender aspect.

are represented at once, one of them often inavowable. Margaret D. Carroll demonstrates, for example, that Rubens' *Rape of the Daughters of Leucippus* of 1615-1618 represents a pernicious collusion of two different events: a violent rape and a pleasurable heterosexual encounter (1989). This collusion is, of course, culturally coded in the discourses surrounding rape, which contribute to the perpetuation of the idea that women enjoy rape. Thus it connects to an ideological condensation while its status as a condensation in the psychoanalytic sense needs further examination. And this meaning is included in this overt and pernicous condensation: the exposure of the women in the most graceful poses, while the bodies of the two abductors although "coming down on" the women, are hidden and confused with the bodies of the horses. While the latter confusion may be read as an indication of the idea of male sexuality as bestial, hence, irrepressible, the hiding of the male bodies is symptomatic of an insecurity about their own grace. Thus, reading the work as an unconscious condensation, its sexual violence receives a new light: as compensation for the lack of confidence in the seductive power of the two males. As in the case of the Dürer woodcut, then, the psychoanalytic semiotic helps to provide the more obvious interpretation with an explanatory dimension that gives it more depth, more nuance, and more ideological relevance.

While condensation and its twin concept in Freudian rhetoric, displacement, both concern semantic complexity and the plurality of meaning, displacement is often helpful in revealing a hidden "other side" of an overt meaning. In Picasso's response to Velazquez's *Las Meninas*, for example, the central positions of the proud painter on the one hand, and the reflected king and queen on the other, have been displaced on to two other figures: the man in the background and the little princess (Picasso, *Las Meninas*, 181 x 57, Museo Picasso de Barcelona).[5] Already spatially central in the Velazquez, in the Picasso the princess is now also central in the work's distribution of attention through color, light and space. The yellow of this figure, which sets her off against the rest of the work, rhymes with the yellow surrounding the man in the open doorway; the square form of her dress repeats the rectangular space of the open door; and her arms are in the same position as his. This displacement of emphasis can be seen as pointing towards an aspect of the scene already present in the Velazquez but screened off, there, by the crowded stage: the vulnerability of the little girl. Leading the work away from the class issue and the dignification of the art of painting, this displacement of attention reveals the less avowable sexual concerns that the older work displays only subliminally, if at all. So far, Picasso's work proposes a reinterpretation of Velazquez' statement on class, shifting power relations in the direction of sexuality. There is nothing unconscious in this yet; rather, sexual explicitness was a fashionable topic in Picasso's time. But the explicit sexual reorientation

---

5. The painting is reproduced on the cover of Culler's *Framing the Sign* (1988).

escapes full coherence. Although the other figures can be discerned, their cubist treatment, usually emphasizing presence, here hides them, reducing them to mere eyes, and the only other striking figure is a red shape at the bottom right with a distinctly phallic head. With that figure as an index, metonymically pointing towards the issue of sexuality, the man in the doorway suddenly becomes threatening, and the girl, frontally exposed to the viewer, is helplessly surrendered to the violence of vision. The other figures now uncannily repeat that violence, like phantoms in dark corners, rather than protecting the girl; but this meaning displaces the threat from sex to visuality, contaminating the painting as well as sex with guilt. Reading the Velazquez back from the perspective of the Picasso, we realize that there, too, the presence of the other figures merely exposed the girl more emphatically, enhancing her loneliness; but from the overt drama of court life, the threatening aspect of vision is displaced on sexuality.[6]

This psychoanalytic hermeneutic can be brought to bear on art critical discourse as well. Thus Sander Gilman's use of visual illustrations in his article on "Black Bodies, White Bodies," juxtaposing images of monstrosity in women of color to representations of a clitoris with a phallic form, displays an ambivalence toward his own sex which his discursive comments also suggest.[7] In T.J. Clark's discussion of Manet's *Olympia* (Louvre, Paris) the contrast between the two women obscures similarity in their figuration; Gilman, taking up Clark's analysis, sees Olympia as skinny and the black woman as plump, setting up a problematic contrast so that he does not have to see the similarity which indicates the genitalia as "flourishing," signified in the bouquet.[8]

The examples quoted here are all related to a problematic of vision, and that is, of course, no accident. The most central concept that links psychoanalysis and visual art is that of the *gaze*. That centrality could, however, also be a problem, as we will suggest at the end of this section.

The psychoanalytic description of vision has been a particular focus within the work of Jacques Lacan. Two texts in particular, in which vision is described, have become highly influential in film studies, though their implications for the study of painting, sculpture and photography are in principle no less powerful than for the cinematic image. *The Four Fundamental Concepts of Psycho-analysis* lays down a general theory of the role of signification in

6. The literature on *Las Meninas* is abundant and well known. Key texts are Foucault's introduction to *The Order of Things* (1973), which proposes a semiotic reading. Precisely the semiotic nature of this reading—its readerliness—has been misunderstood. John Searle attempts to explain Foucault's reading through speech act theory (1980), while for Foucault the painting exemplified his own theoretical view of classicism. Joel Snyder and Ted Cohen misunderstand both Foucault and Searle and counter their readings with scientistic calculations on the "real" rather than the semiotic point of view (1980).

7. This text by Gilman has been analyzed in some detail in Bal (1991).

8. T.J. Clark (1985). Sander Gilman, "White Bodies, Black Bodies: Toward an Iconography of Female Sexuality in Late Nineteenth-Century Art, Medicine, and Literature," *Critical Inquiry*, 12, 1985.

shaping visual subjectivity (1979), while the essay "The Mirror Stage as Formative of the Function of the 'I'" deals more specifically with the formative stages of visual experience (1977).

In *The Four Fundamental Concepts* Lacan extends into the sphere of vision an argument central to his project in psychoanalysis, that human subjectivity is profoundly and constitutively shaped by the institution of symbolism or sign-activity in its largest sense. To the sum of cultural processes in which symbolism occurs Lacan gives the name, the *symbolic* (or the symbolic order), a term meant to designate the entire domain brought into being by the social circulation of signifiers. In other Lacanian texts, more concerned with the role of linguistic structures in determining subjectivity, it may seem that the symbolic order is identical to language; one may come away with the impression that the human being's entry into the cultural field of semiosis occurs at the moment when speech is acquired, and that "the signifier" whose operations Lacan proposes as determining the structures of subjectivity is simply another name for "the word." But in *The Four Fundamental Concepts* Lacan assumes that the signifier can be visual as well as verbal, and that just as the signifier in the domain of language produces a speaking subject, so in the domain of vision it produces a "seeing subject," that is, a subject whose mode of seeing is the product of the signifier as it operates upon vision.

One aim of Lacan's discussion is to dislodge the Cartesian notion that the subject stands at the center of vision, in a position of mastery over its visual field; this conception has no more validity, in Lacan's view, than the corresponding notion in the theorization of language, that the subject possesses mastery over speech. Learning to speak involves an insertion into pre-established systems of verbal discourse which lay down in advance the paths or networks which the speaker's words are obliged to follow. In the same way, once the subject learns to "see" it is obliged to orchestrate its personal visual experience with the socially agreed descriptions of the world around it; thereafter, deviation from this social construction of visuality can be named and dealt with, variously, as hallucination, misrecognition, or "visual disturbance." What is seen is formed by paths or networks that pre-exist the subject and continue to operate in the social formation long after the individual's demise. The visual field therefore has the character of a "ready-made." In the "Tyche and Automaton" section of *The Four Fundamental Concepts* Lacan describes the mechanisms of repetition which give visuality its coherence. Once installed in the symbolic order, the subject must refer all new visual "data" to the chains of signifiers which now cut across and organize visual experience. To these chains or tracks, pre-established in the social formation and then internalized by the subject, Lacan gives the name the gaze (*le regard*).

To expose the pre-fabricated character of the visual discourses into which seeing subjects are inserted is, however, only one aim of Lacan's discussion. The subject's entry into the various visual discourses that make up the gaze might, after all, be a simple and pacific process, no more a matter of conflict or anxiety than the programming of a computer, or the acquisition of any human skill. What makes both the entry into the gaze, and the subject's subsequent occupancy of the field which the gaze forms, into a complex and conflictual process, is the subject's systematic misrecognition of the externality of the visual discourses through which it organizes sight: for unlike a computer programmed to manipulate chains of signifiers, the human being is, according to Lacan, also structured in such a way as to produce a continuous sense of itself as autonomous headquarters of signification, an "I" that looks out at the world from a central vantage point, experiencing the visual field as a horizon always composed around itself.

The register of psychic processes in which this sense of centralized identity is produced Lacan calls the *imaginary*, a term which may, however, lead to considerable confusion unless glossed further. In both French and English the terms *imaginaire* and *imaginary* carry connotations of illusion or fictionality, as though the ego were unreal or in some way a mirage. Lacan's point, though, is not that the Imaginary is a realm of illusion, as against the "real" and objective structures which make up the gaze or the symbolic order in general. Lacan reveals his debt to post-Kantian thought in his assumption that the human subject has no direct access to reality; all transactions with the kind of objective world postulated, for example, by the physical sciences, are mediated, he argues, on the one hand by the work of the symbolic order (producing signification), and on the other by the work of the imaginary (producing identity): the *real*, in Lacanian theory, is a logically empty category. It is not that the sense of self generated within the imaginary is false; Lacan's emphasis is rather on its instability, and on the vicissitudes of the imaginary as it attempts to generate a sense of centralized ego in the face of a symbolic order which does not of itself produce, or even require, the notion of center for its operations to proceed.

At this point some examples may help to clarify the discussion; we shall move from a case in mathematics, to language, to the image. When I perform a mathematical calculation, the symbols I manipulate make no reference to my situation; they are impersonal in the sense that the numbers are no "nearer" to me before or after the calculation; though the numbers have not spontaneously re-arranged themselves, and I am without doubt the operator who works with them, they bear no traces of my personal activity or existence. To enter into the realm of mathematics is, accordingly, to risk being effaced as "I."[9]

The signifiers in language seem at first sight less personal; for instance, language hospitably provides the personal pronoun "I," through which one may enter into verbal systems as one cannot with mathematical ones. But,

9. See 1988, 294-308.

again, the personal pronoun "I" is, in fact, impersonal: anyone may use it, so that the "I" of language actually refers no more to me, in my specific situation and identity, than it does to anyone else—even a computer or an auto-teller may use the signifier "I."[10] And similarly with the gaze, though I may experience the visual field around me as a horizon whose center I always occupy, so that all of the vision appears to unfold inside me ("somewhere behind the eyes"), the signifiers of sight can no more be my unique possession than the symbols of mathematics can, or the "personal" pronoun "I." And in so far as the social coherence of the visible world requires me to submit my visual experience to the operations of the visual and the verbal signifier, it obliterates me as the center of my lived horizon at the very same moment when I seem, to myself, to occupy its heartland.[11] Holbein's *The French Ambassadors* is the work chosen by Lacan to demonstrate this simultaneous process of possession and dispossession in the field of vision. The ambassadors are masters of symbolism, in possession of all the codes of knowledge, of science and art, fashioned in their social milieu: but their visual field is cut across by something they cannot master, the skull which casts itself sideways across their space, through anamorphosis. For Lacan, the subject's entry into the networks of signification involves a force of decentering so profound that the metaphors for the process are necessarily those of death; the skull is emblematic of the fate of sight as the latter is subjected to the work of the symbolic order.

Evidently Holbein's painting is not the only work of art in which this Lacanian dialectic between the symbolic and the imaginary orders might be discovered: the structures that Lacan describes are in principle capable of manifesting in a wide variety of instances (which raise a methodological problem that will be discussed below). For example, in her Lacanian reading of the work of Francis Bacon, Brenda Marshall argues that Bacon's work draws the viewer into complicity with a structure of perversion in which Oedipal law is both asserted and denied. In her essay on Edward Hopper, she finds that although Hopper's images show what is in some respects a world of resolute mundanity and ordinariness, they are nevertheless shot through with the affect of death.[12] This thematics of loss opens up a rich field of possible interpretation, and in film studies the Lacanian emphasis on what might be called the "mortification" of sight has influenced a number of analyses of cinema's capacity to engulf the viewer in its imaginary world (so that everything unfolds before the masterful witness of camera and spectator), and to interrupt that centering of sight around the viewing subject in order to expose the workings

10. On the relations between the first person pronoun and its operator, see Emile Benveniste (1971: 195-246).
11. The topic of the decentering of the vision in Lacan (and Sartre) is examined in N. Bryson (1988).
12. Brenda Marshall (1990). Marshall's study is perhaps the most systematic attempt so far to bring the Lacanian understanding of the unconscious, and of vision, to bear upon painting; besides Bacon and Hopper her analyses include works by Frieda Kahlo and John Singer Sargent.

of the cinematic apparatus and its symbolic codes, producing a thematic loss, separation, and nostalgia.¹³

Yet there is an obvious problem of method here—one that has nothing to do with the accuracy or inaccuracy of Lacan's account of visuality. What Lacan offers is a theory of visual subjectivity in general, not in the first place a theory of visual art, and in fact his discussion of *The Ambassadors* follows what was earlier described as the *analogical* model, where the work of art serves primarily as an allegory of the terms used in psychoanalytic theory. One might well raise the objection that the painting predictably ends up in a subservient and colonized role, as the mere illustration or staging of the theory. And one might further object that such allegorical instrumentalism might be served just as well, not by Holbein's *Ambassadors*, but by any picture whatsoever; or, for that matter, by any visual phenomenon or scene that could be made to allegorize the gaze (there is nothing in the theory that requires its illustration to be a representation, a picturing).

It may seem that such objections severely qualify the usefulness of Lacan's terms in discussing works of art. The difficulty is not that of finding other examples besides *The Ambassadors* that might accord with the terms of Lacan's description of vision; the problem is just the opposite, that—if Lacan's general view is accepted—all pictures (or photographs, or sculptures) would do just that. The principles of curtailment and of counter example seem absent from the argument. This does not mean, however, that there is no way that Lacan's discussion can be made to intersect with individual works of art in all their complex particularity. Following the specification model earlier described, it remains possible to use Lacan's terms (the symbolic, the imaginary, the real, the gaze) not in order to allegorize them through art, but to make explicit those features in a given work which these terms, and perhaps only these terms, describe.

The *specification* model has the further advantage of being able to provide principles of resistance and counter-example. That is, it may well prove to be the case in practice that Freud's or Lacan's terms will undergo revision in the light of particular works. A clear example here is Leo Bersani's analysis of Assyrian sculpture, which depends on a radically revisionist reading of Freud's texts on repetition and sublimation.¹⁴ A similar instance of major revision occurs in film studies, where certain theorists have been obliged to insert into Lacan's account a political elaboration of the qualification that the gaze does not structure the field of vision in the same way for both male and female subjects: since the most powerful visual discourses have been created, historically, by men and for men, the gaze should be theorized, they argue, as a male construction; it cannot be separated, as it is in Lacan, from questions of

13. See Christian Metz (1982); Kaja Silverman, "Suture" (1983:194-246); and Silverman (1988: 1-41).
14. Leo Bersani (1986: 67-79); and Bersani and Ulysse Dutoit (1985).

sexual domination.¹⁵ The application of Lacan's general theory of visual subjectivity according to the specification model has, in fact, resulted in a number of compelling interpretations of individual works. An excellent example here would be Rosalind Krauss' analysis of early Surrealist works by Max Ernst (1989). What a collage (more precisely, an overpainting) such as *The Master's Bedroom* explores, Krauss argues, is exactly the "ready-made" nature of the visual field; and Surrealism's interest in automatism may in certain cases need to be thought through, Krauss implies, not as the pursuit of spontaneity and randomness but in the opposite direction, as dramatizations of the pre-fabricated and machinic nature of visual subjectivity (it may well be that Lacan himself encountered the idea of the visual "automaton" in the Surrealist circles to which he belonged in Paris in the twenties and thirties). The Lacanian model of the gaze is able to pick out, searchlight fashion, a host of signifying details in Ernst's image and to integrate them into a powerful interpretation of the work as a whole. And if it is objected that of course Lacan's "Surrealist" theory fits Surrealist art, since both come—so to speak—from the same stable, one can point to many other Lacanian-inspired readings in which the question of "circularity" does not arise: Kaja Silverman's work on Fassbinder (1989), Jacqueline Rose's analysis of Leonardo (1986:225ff), certain investigations of David and Ingres, and Michael Fried's account of Thomas Eakins.

SEMIOTICS AS A THEORY OF SUBJECTIVITY

Those recent development in semiotic theory which connect with psychoanalysis have strongly shaped semiotics' engagement with issues pertaining to gender as well as other aspects of the subject.¹⁶ Indeed, there are three key issues in semiotic theory which have been grounded in differentiation, the relationship between individual subject and social pressures, and power relations: the issue of ideology, that of subjectivity, and that of the relation between the latter and interpretation. All three represent aspects of the key-concept of Peirce's semiotic theory, the *interpretant*, which anchors the

---

15. See, in particular, Laura Mulvey (1975); Mulvey's position is criticized from a Lacanian point of view by Kaja Silverman (1989; esp. 59-60). In this article Silverman offers a seminal revisionist analysis of Lacan's theory.

16. Two relatively recent surveys of feminist approaches to art history have made available to the general art-historical audience the increasing number of works in this vein. Thalia Gouma Peterson and Patricia Mathews (1987) discuss feminist art history in terms of generations, beginning with a first generation identified primarily with Linda Nochlin's early work which is not always treated fairly. We also have problems with the family metaphor implied in the use of generation as leading principle. Lisa Tickner (1988) divides the field according to three views of sexual difference: as an experiential category, a category in discourse, and in psychoanalysis. In this section, we will avoid overlap with these two articles which we highly recommend. Instead of arguing the relevance of semiotics for feminism, we focus here on the relevance of feminism and other theories of gender and of ideology for semiotics' theorizing the subject.

production of meaning both in the subject's *hic-et-nunc* agency and in the social field where ideology shapes the imaginable priorities.

The most obvious issue is, of course, that of ideology. Visual art, just like literature and other forms of discourse, provides representations that are laden with ideologies, notably regarding gender. From a semiotic perspective ideologies are codes that suggest or even impose particular interpretations which they present as "natural" or otherwise inevitable. This happens in the production of visual images, but also in the readings of them which circulate in a given culture. The self-evidence of the link between virility and domination in early twentieth-century art as analyzed by Carol Duncan is a case in point.[17] Because ideology is in place not only in the images themselves, but also in their art-historical interpretations, the discourse of art history partakes of the distribution of power that organizes our culture. Thus Svetlana Alpers argues that the privileging of narrative Italian art over the more descriptive art of the low countries is informed by a gender ideology that emphasizes heroism and discounts the descriptions of everyday life (1982).[18]

Ideology becomes more acutely operative, and the question of its semiotic status urgent, when we think of images representing certain themes that are somehow characteristic of both Western art and dominant views of gender, such as images which represent sexual intercourse as rape, or female beauty as publicly available as in the nude, and tainted with racial overtones as in orientalism.[19] Other themes which lend themselves well for a semiotic analysis of ideology are the connections between gender and class, those between gender and danger as in the *femme fatale*, and the theme of looking itself.[20]

But representing ideological views does not automatically convey the ideology itself. Yet, if so many contemporary analyses of visual art focus on the gaze and the representations of the look in the images, it is because a directiveness of representation is assumed. In order to understand how the ideological *effect* of art can be produced by ideological representation, it is necessary to account for the formation of subjectivity in culture, a topic to which we will turn in a moment. Representation is not neutral because it offers ideological positions from which to interpret the world around us. When looking is

17. Carol Duncan, In "Virility and Domination in Early Twentieth-Century Vanguard Painting," in Norma Broude and Mary D. Garrard (1982).
18. For a further inquiry into the gender ideology in still life painting, see Bryson (1990).
19. John Berger's classic account (1972) has had many followers. A critique of the ideologies involved in the nude does not necessarily entail a global condemnation of representations of nakedness. Rosemary Betterton (1987) discusses the differences between a nude coded as self-evident appropriation and one that emphasizes nakedness as a consequence of particular circumstances. The key text on orientalism remains Said's *Orientalism* (1978). Orientalism in art is discussed by Linda Nochlin (1983). Nochlin discusses typical absences (of history, of the observer, of manipulation) in orientalist works, thereby implicitly analyzing ideology as code. On orientalism in photography, see Sarah Graham-Brown (1988).
20. On gender and class, see e.g. Nathalie Boymel Kampen (1982); and her book (1981). On the *femme fatale* see Bram Dijkstra (1986). Also Susan Casteras (1982).

constantly represented as an exercise of power and domination, then it will be practiced as such. This is why ideological coding is such a pernicious mechanism.

The point of analyses of these instances of gender ideology is not so much to denounce ideological motivations for representation, although that denunciation needs to be constantly rehearsed. Rather, by demonstrating the ideological underpinnings of the images of the history of art, semiotic critics make a strong case for the non-obviousness of western art as it is. Moreover, ideology is neither whole nor singular; there will always be conflicting and fracturing clashes between ideologies. The plurality of ideological codes makes it easier to train our sensitivity to local resistances and alternatives, which have been present, but nevertheless systematically overlooked. In order to control the profileration of ideologies, discursive practices (and, we might add, images, since they constitute, or at least partake of, a discourse) ensure the domination of certain social interests.[21] The ultimate rationale for the examination of gendered semiosis is itself anchored in semiotic conceptions of the place of the subject in culture. Semiotics rests on assumptions concerning the subject and a subjectivity grounded in difference, with gender difference as a central one.[22] As will become clear in the section on narrative, an image does not represent a single subject-position, but rather an organized plurality of these, thus suggesting what Berger called "ways of seeing" to the viewer. Here lies the power of manipulation of images—as well as the site of local resistance to it. This power is complex rather than simple. Yet, at the same time, it is hierarchized rather than dispersed. Semiotic inquiry will be particularly sensitive to the ways in which these networks of subject-positions are related to gender divisions.

Subjectivity is particularly relevant because it is a dynamic category. A subject is constantly in movement, developing from one state to another, and bringing in constantly shifting foci of attention and centers of interest. Therefore it makes sense to project this dynamic view of the subject also onto the images it produces or perceives. Looking is a time-consuming activity, not a pointed, singular act. Looking, therefore, is mobile and changing, and involves an on-going interaction between the image and the viewer. But once we face the fact that the look moves about the image, the looking positions represented therein do influence and structure the ways that moving takes place. Although every spectator has a certain amount of freedom to ignore or endorse represented positions, the response to what the image suggests is not neutral and will be, precisely, a response, which can vary from endorsement

---

21. On discursive practices and their relations to ideology, see Michel Foucault (1972). On the relation between ideological manipulation and the formation of the subject, which will be discussed shortly, see Foucault, "The Subject and Power," in Hubert L. Dreyfus and Paul Robinow (1983).

22. In this respect, Tickner's article mentioned earlier is particularly relevant.

through indifference to resistance, but evidently the first is the easier, more obvious response. The response when faced with, say, Manet's *Olympia* will most probably be different for, say, a black woman, a woman with experience in subaltern positions, or a man with experience of heterosexual domination. For each of these subjects, the painting begins by suggesting particular subject-positions, which can be endorsed, refused, or indifferently ignored, but in each case at a price. The activity of looking has to be thoroughly different accordingly, with the first less demanding but possibly more damaging to the subject itself.

This semiotic view entails the secondary place attributed to the author, in favor of the interaction between image and viewer. Indeed, the semiotic perspective may not quite kill the author, as some would have it,[23] but it surely deprives him (sic) of his primary position of power (see chapter 7). Once the individualistic concept of the artist has been bracketed, the intertextual artist can come to the fore as a social force. That a semiotic view of subjectivity needs gender specification for the conditions of production of art to be accounted for is convincingly demonstrated by Griselda Pollock among others.[24]

The rhetorical structure of subjectivity in a work of art includes its address, which is highly political, as the example of *Olympia* showed. Address, the ways in which a viewer is invited to participate in the representation, is perhaps the most relevant aspect of a semiotics of subjectivity. According to the linguist Emile Benveniste, language inscribes the subject of discourse as the implicit "I" who speaks. Certain linguistic categories, like, precisely, "I" and its correlate, "you," but also other elements such as pronouns and adverbs like "here" or "yesterday," have no referential value but only mean in terms of the discourse itself. Thus the subject of discourse is defined by these *deictic* words, whether or not s/he is the same person as the speaker who conveys the speech, say, the narrator. The non-coincidence between the speaker and the subject of the discourse is precisely the condition of possibility of narrative.[25]

The equivalent of "I" in a painting is often the figure whose act of looking is represented, thereby suggesting participation in a story: "I" takes the shape of an "eye." But that story involves the onlooker as well. If *Olympia* scandalized its contemporary viewers, we now say it was because, precisely, the woman participated too fully in her own display; rather than contenting herself with being the "third person" whose body was objectified for the sake of the onlooker, this woman looks actively at the viewer, so much so that her objectification is nullified, and the viewer, who is now no longer the "I" who can take possession of the woman, is offered the position of the "you" hailed by the

23. Foucault (1977) and Barthes, "The Death of the Author" in (1977: 142 ff). Barthes' position has been moderately revised by Janet Wolff (1984, ch. 6).
24. Pollock (1988) In her earlier work, Pollock discussed the artist in more experiential terms; see Pollock and Parker (1981) and Pollock (1983).
25. Emile Benveniste (1971).

woman and held accountable for his act of looking. For any "I" implies a "you" whom it addresses. The French philosopher Louis Althusser claimed that this address, this "hailing," constitutes the subject in ideology: it forms the subject as what the "ideological state apparatuses" wish the subject to identify with. Thus a woman looking at *Olympia* may identify with the male viewer traditionally addressed by the nude, without questioning that alienating identification; she has been trained to "read as a man." Or she may go along for a moment, and *then*, say, wink at the woman, applauding her insolence, or turn away, or shake her head indignantly.[26] However much autonomy a particular viewer may have (or assume to have) in front of a painting, according to this theory subjectivity is always produced at least by the interaction between the "I" of the work and the "you" this "I" addresses.[27]

This relationship between "I" as speaking subject and the spoken "I," and the ambiguous relationship of the "you" to these two "I" and the subsequent formation of subjectivity in representation, has been particularly well articulated in film theory.[28] Precisely because, as Silverman argues, the speaking and the spoken subjects remain rigorously on opposite sides of the screen, the "you" is especially vulnerable to ideological hailing. For the viewer responds to the spoken "I" set up for response, while the speaking subject can manipulate the latter at will without being caught in the act.

One way to unravel this production of the spoken subject is by a rhetorical analysis, which is part and parcel of semiotics to the extent that rhetoric is considered a particularly effective and pervasive, often pernicious way of producing meaning. Subjects "spoken," set up, that is, as constituted in relation to violence (Picasso), racial sterotypes (Gauguin), nature (Cézanne), threat (Rembrandt), can be analyzed in their metonymic associations. Rather than just being what they seem to be, soliciting a response to their bare essence, they can be exposed as the products of rhetorical choices and the ideological codes that assign these essences to them as their primary meaning.

Metonymy, the rhetorical figure which signifies by proximity, is perhaps the most powerful, for the least obviously theoretical, figure of signification. Next to metaphor, the figure which replaces one item by another, thus transferring the one meaning to the other on the basis of a perceived or suggested similarity, metonymy is a frequently used and powerful figure that should be more systematically mobilized for the critique of visual art. Meton-

---

26. The expression "reading as a man" is the equivalent of "reading as a woman," put into currency by Jonathan Culler in his famous section of this title in *On Deconstruction* (1983: 43 ff.) Culler distinguishes three moments in feminist criticism which may have their parallel in art history: identification with the roles of women, re-evaluation of the traditionally female roles, and deconstructing the oppositions on which these value-systems are based. In a mitigated manner, all three approaches can be seen in Gill Saunders (1989).

27. Louis Althusser (1971; 1977).

28. Most central are Kaja Silverman's studies (1983) and, for specific analyses which focus on the intimate connections between the voice and the image, (1988).

ymy is based on the code of indexicality. A third figure is synecdoche, where an element is suggested or read to stand for the whole of which it is a part. Thus synecdoche can, for example, be seen as the rhetorical figure *par excellence* which has operated or naturalized the exclusions in art historical discourse. Synecdoche as a readerly device, in converse, can bring back into view what had been excluded; not only the women who have looked at paintings in the past without being considered as "empirical viewers," but also elements omitted or repressed from the images themselves. Any representation of the suicide of Lucretia, for example, will gain much by being read synecdochically, suicide standing as the (final) part of the whole story, which begins with the violent appropriation of her by her rapist. That rhetoric is far from neutral shows immediately when we replace such a synecdochical reading by the more usual metaphoric one. Suicide, then, stands for the rape, on the basis of similarity, and the idea is not far that Lucretia did "it" to herself, that she is somehow accountable for her undoing.[29]

In a seminal essay which demonstrates the inherent bond between semiotics and subject theory, Teresa de Lauretis addresses the difficult problem of the relationship between the social experience which constitutes "women" as a group of subjects (not identical but identically "hailed," and thereby ideologically produced), and the semiotic practice of meaning production. Unlike many attempts to theorize the subject in meaning production, which fail because they stay on either side of the divide between sociological and psychoanalytic approaches, De Lauretis takes the difficult but rewarding avenue of Peirce's concept of the interpretant.[30] Leaning on Peirce on the one hand, and on Lacan on the other, she describes subjectivity as an effect of meaning, "a semantic value produced through culturally shared codes" (1983:167) and experience is the process wherein that happens. Obviously, looking at representations, or making them, is part and parcel of that experience. In a Peircean view, the production and reception of signs are basically a similar activity with a similar result: both receiver (interpreter, reader or viewer) and producer form interpretants. These are not arbitrary, individual or idiosyncratic; interpretants are new meanings resulting from the signs on the basis of one's *habit*. And habits, precisely, are formed in social life. "The individual's habit as a semiotic production is both the result and the condition of the social

---

29. For an extensive discussion of Lucretia and the rhetoric of rape, see Bal (1991: ch. 2).
30. "Semiotics and Experience," in (1983). This article is an example of the gain that both semiotic and feminist theory can draw from the integration of both through subject theory. De Lauretis defines experience as "a *process* by which, for all social beings, subjectivity is constructed. Through that process one places oneself or is placed in social reality, and so perceives and comprehends as subjective (referring to, even originating in, oneself) those relations—material, economic, and interpersonal—which are in fact social and, in a larger perspective, historical" (159). De Lauretis elaborates her view in a polemic with Umberto Eco (1976; 1979) and with Julia Kristeva (1980). The best critique of Kristeva's theory is Silverman's in *The Acoustic Mirror*, ch. 4, which is an indispensable addition to De Lauretis' necessarily brief treatment of it.

production of meaning." (179). Thus, not only is experience a legitimate basis of interpretation, it is the only possible one. If those who have hitherto believed that they can reach universal validity, are willing to see the general validity of this view and therefore, to abdicate their illusionary claim in favor of semiotic specificity, much indispensable scholarly as well as political progress can be gained.

Rather than speaking of the context in which art is produced, such a semiotic view of art will speak of the ways signs are framed. Framing is something active, something people do, not a static and fixed condition out of which art emerges as if automatically. Among the framings that have been practiced on visual signs are those of intertextual and iconographic allusion, of narrative (narrative representation as well as reading), the use of rhetorical figures, the logic of scholarly discourse and the expertise of connoisseurship. These framings have subjects accountable for them, and are open to revision. A dynamic view of the sign, including the signs that constitute visual art and the discourses about it, can help to de-naturalize the exclusions that have resulted from those particular framings, as well as, conversely, use framings to counter these exclusions without falling back into positivistic truth claims. One such framing that can be used for a more open and equitable interpretation, is narratology, which will be the subject of the next section.

NARRATOLOGY AND VISUAL ART

Accounts of narrative in visual art tend to focus on the question of how images are able to narrate stories.[31] Although such accounts have great usefulness, the underlying presupposition seems to be that images are a priori handicapped in this competition; narrating is primarily a matter of discourse, not of visuality. Hence, attempts to overcome the limits of the visual, brave as they are, will have to be considered with indulgence. But from a semiotic perspective, various theories of narrative have been developed which can be brought to bear on visual art, without presupposing that narrative is somehow a foreign mode in visual art. Perhaps the best known example of such a theory is the one implied in Barthes' famous book *S/Z*.[32] Barthes develops an interpretation of Balzac's short story "Sarrasine" through an analysis of five codes which the reader allegedly activates when reading this story. The essay is attractive because it is reader-oriented while placing the act of reading within cultural constraints.

31. Recent examples are A. Kibédi Varga (1989) and (1989b); Wendy Steiner (1988).
32. Barthes (1975). Barthes' initial, structuralist theory of narrative can be found in *Elements of Semiology* (1976). Barthes essays on visual images not bound up with his narrative theory are mostly in *Image-Music-Text* (1977). On photography he published *Camera Lucida: Reflections on Photography* (1981). His *Empire of Signs* (1982) offers a semiotic interpretation of Japanese culture, which is implicitly a semiotic of ethnocentrism. Two of Barthes' older texts deal with visual material, albeit in a linguo-centric way: *Mythologies* (1988). *The Fashion System*, 1983. A most accessible introduction to Barthes' work is Jonathan Culler (1983).

The *prorairetic* code is a "series of models of action that help readers place details in plot sequences: because we have stereotyped models of 'falling in love,' or 'kidnapping,' or 'undertaking a perilous mission,' we can tentatively place and organize the details we encounter as we read" (Culller 1983:84). In a way this is a narrative version of an iconographic code.[33] The *hermeneutic* code presupposes an enigma and induces us into seeking out details that can contribute to its solution. Although this code may seem less relevant for visual art, we claim that there is a hermeneutic code at work for the viewer, precisely when an image's subject is hard to make out. The *semic* code inserts cultural stereotypes, "background information" which the viewer brings in to make sense of figures in the image in terms of class, gender, ethnicity, age, and the like. With the help of the *symbolic* code the viewer brings in symbolic interpretation to read certain details, e.g. "love," "hostility," "loneliness," or, for that matter, "theatricality," "*vanitas*," or "self-referentiality." Finally, the *referential* code brings in cultural knowledge, such as the identity of the sitter for a portrait, the program of an artistic movement, or the social status of the figures represented. Together, these (and other) codes produce a "narrative," as a satisfying interpretation of the image in which every detail receives a place. This narrative is emphatically produced by the reader to deal with the image; it produces the story through the processing of a strange image into a familiar mindset.[34]

The intertwining of codes produced by prior discourses of a culture makes Barthes' approach congenial with Bakhtin's theory of narrative.[35] Barthes starts from the receiver, the reader (or viewer) of the work. Bakhtin's concept of polyphony, the intertwining of different voices in the novel, resulting in *heteroglossia* or the cacophony of incongruous strands of cultural discourses, takes the same issue up from the other side, the side of the sender or writer—in our case the maker of the image. The major gain this view of semiotics yields for our purposes is the awareness that the image is not unified. Indeed, classical art criticism and history has tended, just like literary studies, to seek the interpretation that accounts for each and every detail of the work within the same framework. Thus details that don't fit are ignored or set aside as unimportant or as "mistakes," evidence of a foreign hand, of studio practice, ultimately discounting the work as non-autographic rather than contributing to a heteroglossic view of the work. Bakhtin helps us to accept that even when the image is made by one artist, the inherent hetero-discursive nature of the

---

33. Eco analyzes *Casablanca* as a "cult film" because of the predominance and intertextual play of the stories projected by what Barthes calls the prorairetic code (1986). A comparison between iconography in visual art and literature is undertaken in M. Bal (1991: ch. 5).
34. An discussion analysis in this vein of Francis Bacon's work is published by Ernst van Alphen (1992).
35. Mikhail Bakhtin (1981). Ken Hirshkop and David Shepard, eds. (1989) offer a wonderful collection of critical essays on the usefulness of Bakhtin in a perspective of cultural studies. A good introduction is Tzvetan Todorov (1984).

culture of which this artist is a product necessarily brings in elements of alterity, if only to be repressed to the margins. Thus an image that overtly represents the intervention of women in a fight between men such as David's *Sabine Women* (Paris, Louvre) cannot help inserting indexes of homosexual interest.[36] Velazquez's *Las Meninas* has been argued to present a visual heteroglossia in that it is at the same time narrative and descriptive, displaying the act of painting within the description of courtly life as still life.[37] This mix of modes is fundamentally different from the famous self-referentiality (Foucault), paradox (Searle), or unity (Snyder and Cohen) proclaimed by other critics, who ultimately gave the painting a unity it so stubbornly refuses to yield.[38] Paradoxically, Alpers' refusal to appropriate the entire painting for the narrative mode enabled the critic to do more justice to the painting as narrative than the other, simple narrative readings.

In spite of the importance of Barthes' and Bakhtin's insights into the various factors that collaborate or compete to produce narrative, the one factor that keeps slipping away is the traffic of meaning from source to destination and back. In traditional narrative theory, the concept of the narrator as the source of information or the utterer of the speech act of narrating has favored a model of a unified voice: one narrator determines what the reader is going to get.[39] Replacing the author by the narrator, or the artist by an implied orchestrator of the image, does not really help in understanding the various signs at work in an image.

Attempts to atomize the informational sources of narrative in view of a semiotic conception of texts may be more useful. One such attempt distinguishes between three narrative agents: the *narrator* or speaker, source of the utterance, the *focalizer* or source of the vision presented in the utterance, and the *actor* or agent acting out the fabula (the sequence of events presented).[40] This model allows for integration of two important views: the idea that signs

---

36. See Norman Bryson (1984).

37. Svetlana Alpers (1983). Leo Steinberg also interprets the painting as an interplay of different forms, although his interpretation ends up unifying the image. See Leo Steinberg (1981).

38. Michel Foucault (1973:3-16); John Searle (1980); Joel Snyder and Ted Cohen (1980).

39. The best known book in English is Wayne C. Booth (1961), which introduces the concept of *implied author* as a fictional stand-in for the author and orchestrator of the narrative as a whole. Booth's attempt to rid literary studies of the moralism that blames the author for any unacceptable ideological statement in the text was important in its time, but only half successful. The unified nature of his implied author only displaced the problem from "real" author to implied author, still not managing to account for hetero-discursive strands and ideological disjunctions.

Exceptions to this unified model not influenced by Barthes or Bakhtin are Gerald Prince's speech-act theory of narrative (1983), and Ann Banfield's linguistic theory of narrative (1982). Gérard Genette, (1980) begins to differentiate between narration and focalization (a term which replaces the muddled traditional term of point of view, far less technical in narratology than in visual analysis) but fails to account for it in semiotic terms, and thereby falls back into the older privileging of the narrator.

40. The following is drawn from Mieke Bal (1985), further elaborated in Bal (1988). This theory is used for visual analysis in Bal (1991).

are organized, and the possibility of "the difference within."[41] Precisely because the narrators of a text hold discursive power, they are also able to embed the vision of somebody else, like in the phrase "She saw that he noticed that the lipstick on his collar had not escaped her." Here one narrator conveys three views, embedded like Russian dolls, and each based on signs positioned on different levels: in the fabula, two actors are confronted, one of whom, the woman, constructs on the basis of a sign of facial expression that the other, the man, has in turn constructed on the basis of the sign of her own facial expression, a third construction, the sign of lipstick on his collar which he may up till then have been unaware of himself.

In this structure of embedding one voice conveys in a single discourse a visual dialogue which seems typical of language. In fact, something like Free Indirect Discourse, where not just the vision but even aspects of the voice of another figure are embedded in the narrator's monological voice, might seem impossible in visual images where this hierarchical ordering is replaced with the presence of all elements of the configuration of subjects on the one surface. Yet this is a deceptive unification of the status of the various elements. Imagine the story of Susanna surprised by the Elders. In a traditional painting of *Susanna and the Elders* by, say, Rubens, the figure of the naked woman is presented to the viewer, exposed for sight and delight (Munich, Alte Pinakothek). The elders, the represented focalizers, provide a position from which the viewer can interpret the woman's body; in other words, they offer a point of identification. The woman, either looking away or looking at the viewer in compliance, does not counter the voyeuristic position offered. This is, then, a simple, one-strand narrative. In contrast, Artemesia Gentileschi's *Susanna* (Pommersfelden, Schloss Weissenstein) is claimed by Mary Garrard to suggest discomfort at the situation of voyeurism, implying a critique of it.[42]

What are the narrative signs of this critique? To give one example, Garrard mentions the uncomfortable stone bench Susanna is sitting on. As opposed to the lush foliage that, alluding to the garden of earthly delight, traditionally represents the cheerful focalization of the Elders, this stone bench foregrounds the experience of the threatened woman. The structure of focalization in this painting is more complex than in the Rubens: the men exchange glances, "telling" each other visually their scheme; Susanna looks away, refusing to interact with her assailants; and the hard and unpleasant features of the Elders counter any tendency to identify with their viewing position: spying on Susanna. Instead, Susanna's distressed look, although not directed at the viewer so as to preclude the idea of compliance, and not directed at the men either with a similar effect, suggests that the unpleasant men we see are as she sees them:

41. This phrase is used by Barbara Johnson in her book *A World of Difference* (1987).
42. See Mary Garrard, "Artemesia and Susanna," in Norma Broude and Mary D. Garrard, eds. (1982). See also Garrard's monumental book on Gentileschi (1988).

Susanna, here, focalizes her assailants, and the result of that focalization is signified to the viewer, before the latter reaches their focalization, which in its mutuality excludes the viewer. Thus, within the single "discourse" of voyeurism, so prevailing in the western tradition, instead of a narrative of voyeurism we have a counter-narrative of anguish and vulnerability.

Between Rubens' and Gentileschi's Susannas we can read Rembrandt's *Susanna* in Berlin, of which more in chapter 10, where one Elder is sitting on a throne while the other is busying himself with Susanna differently. On the one hand, the female nude, vulnerable, young, and iconographically recalling the Venus Pudica, hence, evoking eroticism, looks at the viewer, who can read her as helpless and calling for sympathy, or as an object of sadistic lust. But the Elder who is with one hand undressing her, is with the other hand signifying the direction of his look, which literally overlooks Susanna's body. With the help of another iconographic reference, to Dürer's *Melencolia I*, we can construct a narrative that complicates and critiques voyeurism. This effect is produced, not so much with reference to the woman's focalization but rather to the man's failed focalization. Once a viewer identifies with this man, he or she is struck by the failure of looking and the resulting paralyzing melancholy. Again, the image presents three figures looking in different directions and different modes, breaking up the unity that would cast this work in the too-encompassing category of "the nude."

What this view of narrative suggests, then, is that the act of looking at a narrative painting is a dynamic process. The viewer moves about the surface to anchor his or her look at a variety of positions. These positions are not just alternatives as a pluralistic view would have it, but they are interrelated and embedded.[43] Whichever position one chooses to endorse in the Rembrandt, the other two cast their shadow over it. If one looks with the man in the upper right, comfortably sitting and watching the scene, one's eye travels with him to his colleague, and once that embedded position is occupied, the failure to see happens. If one responds to Susanna's look, her experience of already being attacked then leads to the awareness that the man undressing her is also emphatically not looking at her. In Bakhtin's terms, the discourse of melancholy and the discourse of rape are in dialogue with each other and with the discourse of voyeurism. But that view does not account for the embedding of the former two into the overall concept of the latter. Therefore, we would rather contend that both melancholy and rape, as well as the opposition between these two, are embedded within the discourse of voyeurism, embodied by the man at the upper right.

---

43. Bakhtin's radical view of heteroglossia, as well as Derrida's account of polysemy in the concept of dissemination, are often followed up as liberal pluralism. This is a mistaken interpretation of both theorists' positions. On Bakhtin's critical edge, see Hirschkop and Shepard, eds. (1989); on Derrida's disavowal of the pluralistic position, see Derrida (1989).

The semiotic nature of this model emphasizes the sign-status of the elements involved in this reading. As we abandon the illusion of unity, the focused eye of the active Elder, engaged in an act of looking unrelated to the nude body, stands out as a sign of a whole range of meanings which include the ideas about melancholy as an index of artistry. And these meanings are close to losing any connection with the Susanna theme. In competition with this cluster of meanings stands the allusion to the Venus pudica in Susanna's left hand. But this sign is in turn overruled by the slight shift backwards, turning the sign of statuesque display into that of a narrative agency pushing back the threatening presence.

This example also demonstrates that the atomization of narrative within a discursive order—the integration of pluralization with embeddedness—allows for an account of ideology that breaks away from monolithic readings without falling back into an "innocent" relativism. Thus those paintings by Anselm Kiefer which have disturbed some viewers because of their allusions to Nazism, while being hailed by others as a critique of fascism, can be seen as a debate with Nazism. This dialogic approach refuses to silence, ignore, repress and thereby conserve fascism today. By integrating another partner in this debate, the tradition of linear perspective, that emblem of realism and objectivity, Kiefer's works also signify the complicity of art with politics. The suggestion is that perspective and the scientific pursuit it stands for, collaborate with the fascist tendencies that an obliteration of the Nazi past facilitates. The resulting narrative presents a highly complex account of both fascism and painting, within which the various possible focalizers take their share in the production of meaning. The narrative of the paintings is constituted by the tensions between these focalizers.[44]

Another aspect of this semiotic narratology, inherent in any semiotic, is the integration of the viewer/interpreter. The signs indicating narrative subject-positions need to be interpreted, activated by the viewer or they will not work. The narrative, therefore, is constructed by the viewer as an interpretant of the image. The viewer uses the various codes analyzed by Barthes, for example, bringing in the expectations of the prorairetic code so as to order the events—say, voyeurism, threat, resistance, sympathy—and/ or the hermeneutic code anticipating the ending—will she be saved? will they manage to rape her?—and constructs characters with the help of the semic code—the nasty rapists, the innocent victim, placed within the set of cultural stereotypes of the referential (or rather, ideological) code—"she must have asked for it." The viewer also activates the grounds defined by Peirce. One can take the represented focalizations as so many indices directing the construction of the

---

44. On the question of Kiefer's position toward recent German history, see Andreas Huyssen (1989).

narrative, but also less conspicuous details embedded therein, such as the pompous hat, potentially ironic, of the acting Elder as an index for his position of power and his abuse of it. One will assume the iconic status of elements like the female body and the water which confines her space. And the symbols of the competition between compliance and resistance, of which the bare foot and the empty slipper are just one example, denoting fetishism for a Freudian reader, compliance for an iconographic reader, and helplessness for a feminist reader, complete the survey of Peircean signs. Thus a variety of narratives will be constructed by different viewers, according to their own subjectivity, historical position, and political alliances.

Narrative semiotics, then, does not merely identify subjects within the image and their relations of embedding; it also permits specification of the nature, place, and effectivity of each subject's agency. It provides a possibility for reading images against the grain of the alleged opposition between discourse and image by interpreting elements as signs of negation, like in the Elder's not-seeing; as signs of syntactical connection, like in the bench in the Gentileschi shifting focalization from the Elders to the victim; as signs of causality, like the anguished look of Susanna in the Rembrandt as caused by the physical attack on her person by the man. Most importantly, narrative semiotics provides insight into visual narrative, as distinct from visual allusions to verbal narratives.

HISTORY AND THE STATUS OF MEANING

The preceding sections have each presented questions of visual art from a semiotic angle, and in each case our readers may have continued to worry: but what about history? How do these approaches account for the historical status of the images, their origins and their original intentions, and the ways they were interpreted by their contemporary audience? As we have announced in the introduction to chapter 7 and emphasized all along, we are less sure than many colleagues about the possibility of reconstructing those origins and the relevance of the attempt to do so. In addition to our previous remarks on this topic, we wish to point out that semiotics involves three issues which complicate the historical search: intertextuality, polysemy, and the location of meaning. In this section we will wind up our presentation by briefly outlining the problems these issues entail for the certainties and relevances of the historical search for origins.

The term *intertextuality* was introduced by the Soviet philosopher of language Mikhail Bakhtin. It refers to the ready-made quality of linguistic—and, one can add, visual—signs, that a writer or image-maker finds available in the earlier texts that a culture has produced. For art historians, this concept may seem to overlap with that of iconographic precedent, and to a large extent it does; in crucial aspects it does not, however. Iconography seems nothing but the examination of just this re-use of earlier forms, patterns, figures. Three features, and crucial ones, distinguish the two, however. In the first place, iconographic analysis tends to take the historical precedent as the source which virtually dictated to the later artist what forms can be used. By adopting forms from the work of a certain artist, the later artist declares his allegience and debt to his prestigious predecessor.[45] Michael Baxandall has already convincingly proposed to reverse the passivity implied in that perspective, and to consider the work of the later artist as an active intervention into the material handed down to her. This reversal, which also amounts to a deconstruction of the relation between cause and effect, already challenges the idea of precedent as origin, and thereby makes the claim of historical reconstruction problematic.[46]

A second difficulty in the juxtaposition of intertextuality and iconography is the place of meaning. Iconographic analysis frequently avoids statements about the meaning of the borrowed motifs. To borrow a motif is not a priori also to borrow a meaning. The concept of intertextuality, in contrast, implies precisely that: the sign taken over, because it is a sign, comes with a meaning. Not that the later artist necessarily endorses that meaning; but she will inevitably have to deal with it: reject or reverse it, ironize it, or simply, often unawares, insert it in the new text. This is how Mary Garrard uses precedents in her—basically iconographic—analysis of Artemesia Gentileschi's *Susanna* (1982). Thus, referring to Dürer's *Melencolia I* in the pose of the aggressive elder in his *Susanna* in Berlin, Rembrandt cannot help bringing in the quite unsettling meaning of that precedent, suggesting that illegitimate and abusive looking paralyses the transgressor.

A third difference resides in the *textual* character of intertextual allusion. By re-using forms taken from earlier works, an artist also takes along the text out of which the borrowed element is broken away, while also constructing a new text with the débris. Re-using a pose used earlier in a self-portrait, Rembrandt inserts the discourse of self-portraiture into his *Bellona* of 1633 (New York, Metropolitan Museum).[47] The new text, say, a mythography, is contaminated by the discourse of the precedent, and thereby fractured so to speak, ready at any time to fall apart again. The fragility of the objectifying, distancing device of mythography is displayed by this taint of "first-person" subjectivity. In Benveniste's terms, the historical narrative is infected by subjective discourse. Such a view has obviously consequences for the interpretation of this painting in terms of gender.

    45. This is how H. Perry Chapman explains Rembrandt's use of forms taken from Raphael and Titian in his self-portraits of the middle period. See Chapman (1990).
    46. Michael Baxandall (1985: 58-62).
    47. The reference is put forward by Gary Schwartz (1985).

One can push this reflection of the implications of intertextuality further, in the direction of the kind of self-reflection advocated by Habermas.[48] For the art historian, just like any viewer of images, cannot help but bring to the pictures her own legacy of discursive precedents, and reading images entails the inevitable mixture of these signs with those perceived in the work. The allusion to *Melencolia*, for example, occurred to us for reasons Habermas would wish us to explore further, and of which it is immediately obvious that they have to do with contemporary gender issues. This input from the present is emphatically not to be taken as a flaw in our historical awareness, or a failure to distance ourselves from our own time, but as an absolutely inevitable proof of the presence of the cultural position of the analyst within the analysis, which, from a semiotic point of view, is not surprising. To take that presence into account makes the analysis, in fact, more rather than less historically responsible.

This leads to the second issue, that of polysemy. Since readers and viewers bring to the images their own cultural baggage, there can be no such thing as a fixed, predetermined, or unified meaning. Attempts to fix meaning provide, in fact, the most convincing evidence for this view. The field in which struggles over meanings are fought is a social arena where power is at stake. A good example of this mechanism is allegory, the interpretation of, say, a mythical story and all its representations as referring to something outside itself. On the one hand, allegory demonstrates the fundamental polysemous nature of signs. If stories can mean something entirely outside of themselves, then there is no constraint. This freedom is viewed positively by Paul de Man, for example.[49] We wish to express some caution, though, which is warranted by the same cases that come up again and again: the allegorical interpretations of mythical stories of rape as "really" dealing with tyranny and the establishment of democracy. Intertextual analysis will bluntly refuse such abdication of the meaning imported by the sign: if rape means political tyranny, then the bodily, subjective experience of the woman raped cannot be divorced from the politics at stake. The myth of Lucretia, then, is allegorical, but with a vengence. The *allos* of allegory is, after all, not only "other," but also "within."

This problem we have with allegory is, in turn, allegorical for a larger problem implied by polysemy. For the dynamism of signs implied in this view might be mistaken as an abdication of the scholarly position altogether. Derrida's concept of dissemination is the most radical endorsement of the view that no interpretation can be privileged over any other (1982). In spite of the

---

48. Habermas (1971). His concept of self-reflection has been demonstrated to lead easily to an idealistic "purity" of power-relations. See J.-F. Lyotard (1984).

49. Paul de Man (1979). De Man develops his argument around the root *allos*, other, and thus allegory becomes itself an allegory for the acceptance of otherness within. In the wake of Walter Benjamin, a whole school of allegorists have written positively about allegory, in addition to the seminal article by Owens, quoted earlier.

attraction of this idea, especially as a corrective to the remants of positivism still pervasive in the humanities, we wish to advocate some caution here again. For the play of interpretation is surely not entirely free, or else there would be no cause for chagrin about power relations and exclusions in academic practice. In agreement with Wittgenstein's concept of the language game, semiotics proposes to see signs as active, and requires them to be both deployed according to rules and public. A sign, then, is not a thing but, as we have said, an event which takes place in a historically and socially specific situation. Sign-events take place in specific circumstances and according to a finite number of culturally valid, conventional, yet not unalterable rules which semiotics calls codes. The selection of those rules and their combination leads to specific interpretive behavior. That behavior is socially framed, and any semiotic view that is to be socially relevant will have to deal with this framing, precisely on the basis of the fundamental polysemy of signs and the subsequent very possibility of dissemination. In the end, there is no way around considerations of power, inside and outside the academy.

PART IV

Discourse and Image

In the preceding section, Norman Bryson and I pleaded for an encounter between semiotics and art history. While that discussion was primarily internal to art history as a discipline, it was at the same time an attempt to break up the boundaries of the monodisciplinary study of art. Art, we argued there, is a cultural practice involving social positions and relations of power. The consequence of that section was meant to be a reflection on the untenability of these disciplinary boundaries semiotics could challenge.

It seems obvious, then, that an interdisciplinary practice of cultural studies informed by semiotic principles has to emerge out of this discussion. In the following section such a practice is attempted. In the first, primarily theoretical chapter of this section which bridges the gap between art history as a monodiscipline and a more radically interdisciplinary semiotic in which art has its place among other cultural forms, I explore the current state of what I call "visual poetics": the study of visual art from a literary perspective. Trying to move beyond the principle of "illustration" often focused on in so-called "word-and-image studies," I dramatize in this chapter the literary aspects of visual images—their "verbality" or "wordness." This verbality should not be confused with logocentrism, that concept used in deconstruction to indicate the assumed presentness and priority of meaning. On the contrary, "verbality" or "discursivity" points at surface, not depth; at signifiers, not signifieds; at rhetorical or narrative structurings, not the meanings derived from them. The chapter argues for such a verbality as a device for reading art through a detailed analysis of a few publications within the most recent developments in art history. It foregrounds the ways in which the authors of these publications, sometimes unawares, enter the domain of visual poetics, or struggle with its limits.

As the analyses in chapter 10 demonstrate, the attention to the surface of discursivity in visual images entails insights into the politics of representation.

My emphasis on this kind of estrangement from art historical dogma is precisely motivated by this political element. But now it is time to argue for the opposite as well, lest an ideology of discursive primacy reinserts itself. For the point is not that verbality or the discursive strategies of representation are more subliminally effective than the plain visual ones; rather, the participation of the image's "other" in the event of representation is the complicating element. hence, the reverse is also the case. Close attention to the visuality of language and of the forceful participation of visual representation within literary texts brings to the fore a politics of representation which is strongly bound up with gender. In the remaining three chapters of this section this political element is analyzed through detailed discussion of the interchange between discursive and visual strategies in representation, with a more emphatic focus on the literary texts under scrutiny.

The discussions about the canon and its exclusions are by now too common to dwell upon here. But it may still need some emphasizing that semiotics is particularly apt to help overcome the sense of randomness that might obtain once the doors have been opened, and studying computer hacking, t.v. serials, and museum displays has become as legitimate as studying Rembrandt or Racine. In other words, it is not the object studied that determines the focus and coherence of the analysis, but the questions raised and the context brought in.

The second of the essays in this section is quite old; I wrote in over ten years ago. It was, in fact, one of my first academic pieces, and it came straight out of my high school and freshmen teaching experience. Teaching a French reading course, soon turned into a consciousness-raising class as they came in those days, I was always desperate for texts selected by the sole criterion of readability. In this frantic search I stumbled into the gossip article on Farah Dibah and Constantine. It gives me some pleasure to realize that I can easily combine in this section both one of the oldest and two of the newest pieces of my work.

In chapter twelve I analyze texts wherein the female body is used as a stumbling block, a scandal, that resists the naturalization of the moralistic meaning. In this chapter, visuality undermines logocentrism, and the female body is the locus of that subversion. The texts studied are a wildly anachronistic set, Rousseau taken to respond to twentieth century criticism, the Bible to Rousseau, and the latter again to Rembrandt. This anachronism is part of the argument; for the inevitibility of misreading I argue for in this chapter also holds for chrono-logic. The reader of this book is confronted with the impossibility to escape reading from the present, thus realizing, it will be hoped, that the circulation of images has no beginning and no end.

Chapter thirteen continues this provocation of chrono-logic by proposing Rembrandt, not as a gloss on the Book of Esther but as a version of that text without which the "original" cannot be read. This chapter foregrounds a theme that has not only been put forward as centrally problematic in our culture by Derrida, but that also sits at the intersection of visuality and discursivity: writing. The Esther scroll has been taken as an emblem of the ties between cultural politics and gender through the act of writing, crucially decisive in the book, and in the end appropriated by the woman whose subjectivity had been challenged from the start. Together these four chapters offer a strong plea for the analytical and hermeneutic productivity of a systematic refusal to heed disciplinary boundaries.

■10■

Visual Poetics

INTRODUCTION: THE CRISIS OF ART HISTORY?

It is fashionable today to speak of Art History as a discipline in crisis. At first sight, the symptoms of such a crisis are overwhelming but, as I will argue in this chapter, deceptive. Events interpreted as symptoms of such a disciplinary crisis are the following: Books with titles like *The End of the History of Art?* (Belting 1988) find eager publishers and buyers; scholars from adjacent fields invade the field of art history to propose alternative approaches to art because they consider current approaches dead ends (e.g. Bryson 1981, 1983, 1984) or to deconstruct the art historical enterprise itself (e.g. Melville 1988); some of the most fascinating art historians disclaim their allegiance to the discipline (e.g. Fried 1987:10); and, most significantly, alternative fields emerge, under various headings, which propose the study of art in relation to other disciplines. The headings quoted in the title of this chapter, terms that seem to be around more and more, are testimony of the attempt to revitalize by expansion to another field a discipline considered, without such an emergency measure, in danger of being rigidified, impoverished, dying if not dead.

These symptoms are deceptive and, when looked at more closely, point at something quite different from a crisis. They arguably indicate an astonishing vitality, perhaps even an all but overwhelming predominance of art history within the humanities today; indeed, perhaps a shift, from linguistics in the sixties and early seventies, via anthropology in the early eighties, to art history as the central discipline on which other fields draw heavily for their *own* revitalization. One can argue that, if art historians are willing to challenge their discipline, they provide evidence of its strength: the discipline can afford the challenge. If scholars from other fields are attracted to the study of art, one can assume that there is something attractive going on there that they miss in their home fields, and if a field is worth deconstructing, every good deconstructionist knows that the deconstructive enterprise remains basically immanent to the thing deconstructed.[1] And if strong art historians take some distance from what they consider less interesting or tenable in their home-field, they are by the same token contributing themselves the new perspective that was lacking; for in spite of their disclaimer, they, too, are art historians, and unless they wish to give away the field to those whose practice they don't like, their own practice *is* art history. If new fields are created, art history is expanding its boundaries, not giving them up. Art history itself, then, is not in crisis; it is challenging, explicitly addressing, and thereby overcoming, the threat of its foreclosure.

This is not to say that all is fine in art history, and that those who think the discipline is in crisis are out of their minds. Of course, to the question if art history is sick or blooming, the answer will be: neither, or both. Something is happening, thus far we can be sure. In this chapter, I am speaking from within the cracks produced by the opposition between the "art-history-in-crisis" and the "blooming-of-art-history" views; as one of those "aliens" coming to visual art from a literary background, with what some may want to call the arrogance of ignorance and others a fresh—or at least different—perspective, and enthusiastically participating in the creation of the integrating discipline in which the studies of words and images are no longer separated. I am also speaking as one who is fascinated by the quality of some of the work done in the field of "straight" art history.[2] The question if, for example, literary criticism has so much more to boast in terms of quality, that is, new insights and understanding, both of particular works and of the workings of art in context, than art analysis as represented by Leo Steinberg (e.g. 1985), Svetlana Alpers, Michael Fried, to name just a few contemporary, "straight" historians of older art, remains to be answered. That a scholar coming from literary studies like Bryson is able to bring in a new perspective and a new method for art historical analysis based on *his* background gives evidence of his own quality more than of art history's inherent lack of it.

More to the point, these "aliens" have been able to enter the adjacent field thanks to semiotics, a multidisciplinary methodology, which is in no way the property of literary studies, as the very existence of semiotic journals show.

---

1. This is even the case on the institutional level: if the College Art Association invited, as it did in 1988, an "alien" (Norman Bryson) to organize a panel on deconstruction in the visual arts, an "alien" approach to be introduced to the most important gathering of art historians in the United States, what happened was a recuperation, an embedding of deconstruction within art history, not a challenge put to it from the outside.

2. And also, to be sure, as one being put off by the less interesting products of an art history which uncritically continues the trend of iconography, set decades ago. But the drawbacks of mediocrity are present in any discipline, and uncritical, automatic continuation of a once promising approach hampers development only if it remains unchallenged, which is hardly the case in art history today. Moreover, iconography itself is neither pointless nor, for that matter, without interesting relations to the "word" component of the endeavor of "Word and Image Studies."

The place of semiotics as a method, a paradigm, a perspective, or just an eye-opener, in relation to the sense of crisis and the new, exciting events in and around art history, is worth assessing.

Part of this analysis originated in an attempt to understand my own present interest in visual art,[3] and I would hope for the reader's indulgence toward this personal motivation. I do have, of course, a professional justification for it. In *Tradition and Desire*, Norman Bryson takes up the issues raised by Harold Bloom in *The Anxiety of Influence* (1975) and brilliantly shows how the dialectical relationship between the wish to follow and the desire to outdo great models of influence, establishes the unique interaction between sameness and difference that characterizes each work of art in its own way. These interactions can be properly called a dialogue, in the specific Bakhtinian sense, referring to the many-voicedness of any work, but including the tensions that Bakthine's slightly embellishing concept tends to underwrite. The tensions between, as Bryson phrases it, tradition and desire, are generative of *new* work, of renewal of work, and of re-working newness, with the very newness, of course, being relativized in the very process of analysis.

There are two contexts for this dialogue that I wish to actualize in this inquiry. The first one is that of the relations between scholars. It is well known that scholars, just like everybody else, need to establish their own difference from others by lumping together all the work they wish their own to differ from. The very label, so often misused, of "new" as opposed to "old" if not to "ancient" works to disqualify that from which the distance must be sketched, yet whose difference is never unproblematic (e.g. "Les anciens et les modernes," where the oldness was less easy to define than the newness; the New Historicism in literary studies, just a little too close to the old one to gain a clear profile; the New Art History, too busy disqualifying great predecessors to emerge itself as detached from them.) This tension is productive, as it motivates the "new" people to radicalize their positions, which is in turn an efficient way to maximize newness and, for the "ancients" challenged, to renew or to reclaim their newness. But also, it is partly responsible for the continued defensive conservatism among large contingents of art historians who rightly refuse to recognize their work in the caricatures set up by the "new"-ers.

---

3. This interest, which has been latent all along I suppose, became more urgent during my study of the biblical Book of Judges. At a few crucial moments of my work, visual images brought me the insights I needed to overcome a blockage, a *tedium*, a frustrating inconsistency. The cognitive value of the images became a challenge to biblical scholarship—another field "in crisis"—and led me to claim Rembrandt as a supreme biblical scholar. These illuminating heuristic moments allowed me to question commonplace ideas about the relations between word and image. This development can be seen in my *Death and Dissymmetry: The Politics of Coherence in the Book of Judges*. I have since then published a book entitled *Reading Rembrandt*, which is a more systematic exploration of the relations between words and images in (our dealings with) cultural artifacts.

A second context for the tension between tradition and desire is the dialogue between word and image, actualized in two ways. First, mirroring the preceding context, Word & Image works tend to suggest that "straight" art historians neglect the verbal aspects of visual art. This can hardly be the case in a field whose strongest tradition is today icono*graphic*, that is, based on *reading* images as what, visually, they are *not*, and which has, moreover, always been strongly anchored in verbal sources. Over-emphasis on newness encourages the repression of the verbal aspects of traditional art history, hence, of the insertion of traditional work within the new paradigm. Second, the very phrase Word & Image suggests that two different things are to be brought together, thereby neglecting the common aspects of the two. Here, too, a distinction is set up and maintained in the very move of overturning it. I will argue that this dichotomistic fallacy continues to weaken even the renewing enterprise.

My own position becomes clear now: having learned so much from art history, I am caught in the very tension Bryson demonstrated in *Tradition and Desire*, both in relation to the works I will discuss here and in relation to the very endeavor, they, and I, are involved in. But considering these issues, things have to grow even more personal. Having been working on a project of "word and image" concerning Rembrandt and "verbality," I want to briefly discuss, not a general trend but some of the recent works from which I personally have drawn major inspiration in my desire to overcome limitations in my own field which I felt were arbitrary and confining. Again I am tempted to say that the personal choices and the inherent degree of randomness such a review entails is part of the argument, for I would like to contend that the limitations, imposed by scholarly traditions, are in some sense more arbitrary and artificial than other limitations, e.g. those imposed by a personal route of inquiry which brings in its own inquiries, urgencies, and perspectives, hence, coherence. Yet I will also argue that disciplinary input is indispensable in order to prevent importing old problems into new attempts. By doing this, I hope to show to both outsiders and insiders of art history one side of my thesis, explored elsewhere, that "verbality" or word-ness is as indispensable in visual art as visuality or image-ness is in verbal art.[4] I wish to emphasize from the outset

---

4. Although I prefer to emphasize that my Rembrandt book is basically *not* art historical because it is more reception-oriented, literary, and theoretical, I also feel the need to specify what I mean by "art history." By that I mean the whole range of activities of departments traditionally named so. This includes some sort of history—be it of the institution of art, including ecomonic and social history; of particular works or styles, including the analysis of works, more or less emphatically placed historically, or of the discipline itself, in a kind of metahistory in the Hayden White fashion. The most interesting representative of the latter approach seems to me Michael Holly (1984, 1988). I agree with Holly that art history should not be distinguished from art analysis: no analysis can be entirely a-historical, nor can historical explorations do without some sort of analysis of works. The term art criticism, not exactly parallel to literary criticism, usually refers to the more journalistic mode of reviewing art currently on exhibit.

that the following remarks are not to suggest that reflections on word-image interaction are absent from the traditional disciplines; nor that the analyses of paintings I will propose differ in kind from, say, formalist analysis. My goal is not to claim more "newness' than is there, but to systematize currents, or even, perhaps, undercurrents, "tropisms" in Nathalie Sarraute's sense, in extant work, and thus contribute to more thorough relations between fields, and more self-confidence for each, which is a precondition of acceptance of otherness.

I will begin by a brief presentation of recent work by three authors: Svetlana Alpers, a "straight" art historian whose work is crucial for an evaluation of where the best of art history is today;[5] Michael Fried, who is trained as an art historian and a literary critic; and Norman Bryson, who came to art history as a trained literary scholar. This presentation is merely meant to place the subsequent discussion of the field and its approaches. Next, I will proceed by drawing a few lines between the words "word" and "image" in order to replace that awkward conjunction "and" which seems highly unfit to define a discipline or approach, with some more specific links. As Shoshana Felman has demonstrated for the equally unsatisfying phrase "Literature and Psychoanalysis" (1977), such an apparently neutral conjunction or linking word often hides an unwarranted hierarchy which precludes the connection's enriching potential. I will argue that this is indeed the case here. Such a rethinking of the phrase must lead, I will contend, to a name change, and the two remaining section headings are two different possibilities to rebaptize, hence, to reorient the enterprise.

FLOWERS IN A FERTILE FIELD

Svetala Alpers published in 1985 a successful book, *The Art of Describing: Dutch Art in the Seventeenth Century* in which she undertook no less than a revision of the concepts with which we approach the art of the past. Her argument against an art historical bias privileging narrative art in the Italian mode, thus obliterating the specificity of Dutch art, is forceful, though its force is less in its conclusions than in its argumentation and in its heuristic usefulness. She demonstrated the latter aspect, for example, in one of the most interesting pieces of the recent flow of publications on Velazquez's *Las Meninas*, where she showed that the sense of paradox this painting seems to produce (e.g. Foucault, Searle, Snyder and Cohen) stems from an integration of narrativity and descriptivity. Drawing upon contemporary documents, both verbal and visual, concerning the "visual culture" in the Netherlands—ideas about vision, about scientific reliability, the invention, and the impulse to invent, of instruments for the perfection of vision, the impulse to documen-

---

5. I would have liked to include Leo Steinberg's work in this review, as his is the fourth body of art historical work that has greatly influenced my own interest in visual art. The topic of this chapter, however, did not make such a choice consistent.

tation, to visualize structures e.g. in maps—Alpers analyzes in the book a large number of works of art, of various genres, in order to demonstrate the descriptive impulse in that art. What is at stake, then, is the input of a verbal context, a diffuse cultural text, on the visual art of the time; an episteme à la Foucault, which eventually pervades the culture as a doxa à la Barthes. It is this aspect of the study—its roots in contemporary verbality, in diffuse rather than pointed sources, that makes the study a good case for art history's inherent "word & image-ness."

The book concludes with two case-studies, of Vermeer and of Rembrandt, where the former fits the concept of descriptivity, while the latter escapes it, or takes it to its limits. Interestingly, Alpers' later book *Rembrandt's Enterprise* begins by challenging this conclusion. Here, the author takes Rembrandt not as an exception in his time but as an artist who greatly contributed, within the habits of his time, to change these. It is a surprisingly creative response to current debate on (dis)attribution, authenticity, and the sense of loss entailed by the non-autographic status of many of Rembrandt's masterpieces. Rather than deploring the loss or stopping the debate at the resolution of the authenticity question, Alpers produces an argument—convincing, and quite satisfying in other respects as well—why it is that these paintings have fooled us so long. This study is almost materialistic in an unorthodox sense of that word, analyzing both the materiality of painting and the economic activities of the artist, the economic organization of art traffic and Rembrandt's eccentric and founding place in it. The four chapters each deal with a different aspect of Rembrandt's active intervention in the status of art: the relation to the materiality of paint, the use of theatricality, the direction of his studio, and his way of creating value on the market. I will only return to the first two in this review.

Michael Fried's 1980 book, *Absorption and Theatricality: Painting and Beholder in the Age of Diderot* declares its object to be painting-plus-commentary. Diderot's writing on painting in the *Salons* is not taken as a secondary metatext, but as an inherent part of the art production of the time. The interaction between critic and artist is dialectic rather than hierarchical. As the title indicates, the central theme of the study is the relation between painting and beholder which, in the period Fried discusses, becomes more and more problematic and paradoxical. Fried begins at the moment when the central interest is in characters so absorbed in their own mental occupations that the visual representation of their states of mind is the ultimate challenge painters have to face. The twenty or so years he studies show a shift from this challenge to a seemingly opposed one which is in fact a response to it: the representation of dramatic movement. This preference for the theatrical is the diegetic[6]

---

6. The term diegetic comes from French narratology (Genette 1972; Bal 1985) and refers to the level of the represented objects—for narrative, a fabula consisting of actors and events—as distinct from the level of representation, where the specific ordering of the fabula-elements yields the particular structure of the work. In painting, the depicted actions of the figures are diegetic, as are the figures themselves in relation to the events the actions constitute.

consequence of a representational preoccupation with unity. This concern for unity can be seen as a response to the absorption tradition, where unity remained thematic—all figures were absorptive—but could not be diegetic—they don't interact. Fried argues, however, that the concern for unity is in turn grounded in a specific view of the relationship to the beholder, which is paradoxical from the start and, as we will see, bound to break the unity itself. Theatricality addresses a beholder willing to identify with positions offered, and most of these paintings include a figure representing that identification diegetically. Yet the theatrical mode also implies an awareness and acceptance, even a demand, of the viewer's absence from the scene of (the) painting.

In his later book *Realism, Writing, Disfiguration*, Fried focuses only indirectly on these issues, his main theme being a kind of deconstructionist self-representational quality in a major painting by Thomas Eakins, *The Gross Clinic*, and in the writings of Stephen Crane. The self-representations in both cases are paradoxically intertwined; simplifying Fried's complex and nuanced thesis one could say that Eakins' preoccupation is with writing, Crane's with drawing. Yet the analysis of Eakins' work, which is the part of the book I will limit myself to here, works its way to that thesis through an analysis of the relationship to the beholder as suggested by two major figures in the painting, the master surgeon Gross and a seemingly secondary figure, usually taken to be the patient's mother. The paradox of theatricality takes on a twentieth century affective quality that is related to familial roles and becomes the acute dilemma of intense seeing and intense not-looking. Although in this book Fried presents himself thematically as a "word & image" scholar, since he focuses on writing in painting and on visual representation in writing, it is within the former that I wish to take up his work.

Norman Bryson has published three books within a few years' time: *Word and Image, Vision and Painting*, and *Tradition and Desire*, already mentioned. The first and the third book deal with a historical body of painting, from Lebrun to Delacroix. The second is a shorter essay, largely a polemic against realism in art history, of which Gombrich's schemata are taken to be the last remnant. In the first of this series, Bryson addresses "word & image" issues in more than one way, representative of the various steps, to be outlined in this essay, from word & image via visual poetics to comparative arts. He analyzes paintings and texts—two chapters are on Diderot. This belongs to "straight" "word & image" approaches. He confronts texts with their pre-textual background (Lebrun) or with their post-textual responses (Watteau) and shows the interaction between them, a bit in Fried's mode. To the extent that he is able to demonstrate how the texts interfere both with the painting and with its perception by the viewers, that textuality determines the rhetorical effect of paintings; Bryson comes close to what I will call visual poetics. Most characteristically, throughout the book he works with a distinction, within the paintings, between two modes of representation, both visual and both present in each of the works discussed, "discursivity" and "figurativity." The distinction draws upon French semiotics, and it is related, in not always very clear ways, to pairs like paradigm and syntagm, denotation and connotation, signified and signifier, and realism and narrativity. The theoretical foundation of this concatenation of pairs is somewhat shaky but the heuristic value of the basic distinction is immense. As such, it is an example, to be developed further methodologically, of what I will call comparative arts.

At moments, Brysons' distinction seems to come close to Peirce's symbolicity and iconicity, but such a conflation would be fallacious, as iconicity—in the vulgar sense of pictorial resemblence—is precisely what all three books are out to challenge. Figurality is used in the etymological sense of form-ness, materiality; discursivity as propositional content. The most extreme figurality is what Bryson calls the painterly trace, the deixis of a work of art which is, of course, closer to indexicality than to iconicity.

This idea of using the linguistic concept of deixis to get away from realism is the major focus in the second book, a theoretical and polemical, not so much historical book. The idea of deixis leads to a plea for a kind of materialism[7] that would foreground the trace of the work of painting over the transparency of realism. The latter appeals to the a-historical, disembodied gaze; the former to the more engaged, bodily glance. This pair seems quite helpful to me, notably for a discussion of the feminist hot issue of voyeurism, although it is not always clear, in Bryson's own analyses, whether he is speaking of the interaction between painter and beholder, or of the diegetic representation of that relation in the work; yet the very term diegetic belongs to his negative term. The integration of the linguistic concept of deixis or, to stretch Bryson's theory a bit, of the opposition, established by Benveniste, between *discours* and *histoire* or first-second person and third person modes of language use, and two modes of viewing, is a good example of comparative arts as a discipline.

As already indicated, the third book is inspired by Harold Bloom's *Anxiety of Influence*, and analyzes, through often fascinating discussions of major works, the tension between various trends in art throughout the period, and in particular, between specific painters—chapter 4: "Ingres in the atelier of David"—or painters and their context—chapter 6: "Desire in the Bourbon Library." Methodologically, Bryson renews his previous proposals by drawing more upon psychoanalysis.

Paradoxically, the three authors are presented here in an increasing allegiance to literary studies, and also an increasing commitment to an analysis of visual art. Bryson's own development shows this same itinerary: from a heavy input from literary studies and distinct focus on verbal texts, via a discussion of art (only) criticism through the body to critical texts, to a work of art history *pur sang*, albeit with a difference, which is the methodological

---

7. I am not sure the concrete proposal should go under the name of materialism. I guess there is some sort of Tradition & Desire problematic at stake here.

background from (psychoanalytic) literary studies. If I confine myself to these authors, it is not only because of my personal gratitude for the inspiration I drew from them, but also, precisely, because I can only address one side of the issue of visuality and verbality; not because it is the only interesting one. This is another limit of my essay that the reader should keep in mind.

WORDS IN IMAGES: BEYOND ILLUSTRATION

Let me begin with the obvious. One of the more traditional approaches to Word & Image, which has yielded sometimes fascinating results, is the study of texts and their illustrations, preferably done by the same artist or, conversely, images and the captions that "illustrate" them. Blake is a favorite author/artist studied in the first approach (Guest & Barrell 1988); seventeenth century emblems a favorite genre apt for the second (Gelderblom 1988). The theoretical question of what can be rendered in which medium is central for this approach (e.g. Kibédi Varga 1988). The most obvious conclusion drawn over and over again is the inexhaustibility of the one medium in terms of the other. Poems will never be fully illustrated, nor are the plates ever fully understood with reference to the poem. Image and caption hardly quite match, not only in terms of exhaustibility of meaning, but also in terms of coherence of the messages. Yet reading the image without the lines can lead to hilariously erroneous interpretations. Text and image even when presented as a whole do not match, do not overlap, can neither do with nor without one another.

The study of images supposedly meant to illustrate well-known stories, e.g. biblical episodes, shows the same obvious fact. Although those images, especially when painted on walls or windows of churches, did function as a replacement of texts in partly illiterate societies (Miles 1984), they did so on the basis, not of total redundancy but, to the contrary, of overwriting the previous text. Images are readings, and the rewritings they give rise to, through their ideological choices, function in the same way as sermons: not a re-telling of the text but a use of it; not an illustration but, ultimately, a new text. The image does not replace a text; it *is* one. Working through the visual, iconographic, and literary traditions that produced it, these images propose for the viewer's consideration a propositional content, an argument, an idea, inscribed in line and color, by means of representation. By means, also, of an appeal to the already established knowledge that enables recognition of the scene depicted. And paradoxically, this recognition is an indispensable step in the communication of a new, alternative propositional content.

One example among many is Rembrandt's biblical history paintings.[8] Take

---

8. I will draw upon an extremely reduced set of examples, for various arguments. One recurring example will be the two paintings Rembrandt did in 1655 of the episode, in Genesis 39, of Joseph's accusation by the wife of Potiphar, another, the Berlin *Susanna and the Elders*. The decision to dwell repeatedly on the same examples is, again, part of my argument: the works are

Figure 1: Rembrandt, *Joseph Accused by Potiphar's Wife*, 1655. Washington D.C., National Gallery of Art

Figure 2: Rembrandt, *Joseph Accused by Potiphar's Wife*, 1655. Berlin-Dahlem, Gemäldengalerie

his two paintings of Joseph accused by Potiphar's wife (figures 1 and 2). In Genesis 39, the story told, in turn a rewriting of an ancient mythical tale, runs more or less as follows.[9] Joseph, a slave in Egypt, escapes a seduction attempt by the wife of his owner. He refuses, alleging Potiphar's total trust in him. Having entered the house as a nobody, his master has given him everything, and he feels he could have it all except his master's wife. The woman grabs his coat, which she later uses as evidence that Joseph tried to rape her. The story belongs to a tradition commonly referred to as "lustful stepmother seducing innocent young son" (Yohannan 1982).

If words and images could be separated, it should be possible to read the two paintings without reference to this tradition, as will be done by people who lack the knowledge and are therefore unable of recognition. It is hard to predict what kind of response such ignorance would produce, and to what extent it would still partake of the obvious psychoanalytic flavor of the problematic represented in the tradition. However, this would be a thoroughly ahistorical reading, since no seventeenth century Dutch person would possess this happy ignorance. The paintings are immediately recognizable as Josephs, both as a whole, in character cast, and in detail, through iconographically readable signs.

The three characters and their postures are read on the structural level: the woman's action of pointing is easily decoded as accusatory, while the age difference between the two men and the intermediate age of the woman complete the plot. An iconographic detail is for example the key hanging at Joseph's waist in the first work, which represents the notion that Potiphar has trusted his entire house into Joseph's hand.[10]

Interestingly, this "immediate" reading, based on recognition of the subject, finds only partial support in the verbal story. Bryson uses the concept of

---

not meant as mere (visual) illustrations of a more important (verbal) argument, but constitute an argument in tension, in a relation of non-overlapping, with the propositional argument.

9. Obviously, this summary is less than reliable, which cannot be helped. See Bal 1987 for a fuller account of the case. In that paper, I have discussed the Genesis story in relation to Freud's *Totem and Taboo*, to Thomas Mann's novel *Joseph and his Brothers*, and to Rembrandt's etching of 1634. I will not repeat the argument I made there for the inherent impossibility of myth as stable meaning.

10. This is a case where the iconographic detail works connotatively, although denotation is required for the connotation to work. Visual or verbal, the problem of this pair remains the same.

I chose to consider the Washington painting the first work, the Berlin one the second. There is no historical reason to do this: it is likely that both works are from 1655, but no more is known (Schwartz 1985). There is, however, a narrative reason—which brings my argument into the "word-and-image" endeavor. In the Washington piece, the gesture of accusation seems primary; in the other one, we see Joseph's reaction to the accusation already. If the two works were to be considered as a sequence, as a kind of comic strip, this would then be the "logical" sequence. Schwartz relates the works to Vondel's play *Joseph in Egypt*, written in 1640 and successfully performed in 1655. The repetition of the theme could be due, according to Schwartz, to a change in cast (275). On Rembrandt and theater, see the following section. I don't find the facts alleged by Schwartz relevant for a discussion of the paintings in relation to reading them, although they do shed some light on the context of their making.

recognition to distinguish denotative signs from connotative ones. Denotation is for him iconographic, and in semiotic terms, that identification makes sense. It is the opposition with connotation, for him equivalent to the seemingly irrelevant (in realistic terms) painterly detail, that seems more problematic to me. Although the difference between recognition and decoding, or rather, between direct recognition of the image and indirect recognition of the code, has some differentiating value, it encourages falling back into a naive notion of visual iconicity that is hard to substantiate and misleading. The pair denotation-connotation does not solve the problem raised by the question: why is it that viewers recognize the works as Josephs while they differ from and in some sense contradict, the biblical story?[11]

The biblical story does not present the three characters at the same time, and there is no mention of keys. There, three confrontations follow each other: Joseph versus the woman, the woman versus her husband, the husband versus Joseph. Given the obvious psychoanalytic aspects of this story, the direct confrontation between the three characters, due as it may be to the needs of visual simultaneity (see Kibédi Varga 1988), brings about a major change in the reading of the story. Briefly and provisionally summarized: the three-fold confrontation increases the anxiety and enhances the position of the woman who, in the Genesis story, is merely a pre-text[12] for the main confrontation, the scapegoat whose rejection strengthens the inter-generational bond between the men. Rather than one of two single-episode oppositions, her position becomes central both structurally—the apex of a triangle—and sequentially—the three episodes are conflated into one. Hence, the knowledge of the verbal story partakes of the reading of the painting, but in doing so it brings about a radical change in its meaning.

The paintings respond to the story, but they do not copy, illustrate, or visualize it *as is*. To the interpretation proposed by Genesis they propose a counter-reading, a displacement, a shift in emphasis and affect.[13] Although the paintings are, on an obvious level, totally visual, they function on a combination of modes which includes various levels of verbality: of the pre-text—Genesis 39, globally known—of the new structure, referring to prop-

---

11. Even if, for simplicity's sake, I will focus on the visual signs which contribute to recognizability, it is clear that prior knowledge of some version of the story is indispensable. Stories like this, circulating in allegorical and other modes, are part of the cultural common knowledge, or background, or they will not be representable in painting. But this is not a priority for the verbal; this common cultural knowledge is not in itself verbal. What circulates is the interiorized imagination of the story, including its visuality.

12. The word pre-text is meant to be ambiguous, referring to the previous "text," the desire and anxiety toward the mother-figure who proposes sexuality to the initiate-son, as well as to the occasion, the excuse for the central confrontation between father and son for which the woman is used.

13. So far I have treated the two works as similar. Later on I will propose radically different readings for each, but here that differentiation is beside the point. The relation between a shift in meaning and a radical change in affect is itself problematic. I will return to this issue.

ositional contents—psychoanalysis, a theory and practice verbal par excellence—of the new meaning—the increased and shifted affect, arguably mediated through verbal conventions of emotional expression.

The iconographic detail of the keys, on the other hand, represents in itself a different level of verbality. It requires reading stricto sensu to relate the keys to the biblical expression "he gave everything into my hand," to which this visual sign has no *visual* connection. The semiotic perspective makes this remark commonplace, but it needs pointing out: reading is a semiotic activity broader than literate reading, yet narrower than interpretation in general. On the visual level, a painted key refers to a "real" key, by a combination of iconicity, indexicality, and symbolicity, the first and the third modes of signification dominating, the second indispensable nevertheless; on the verbal level, a represented key "stands for" trust, in a precise, because material, interpretation of both sign and interpretant, by a combination in which the indexical is predominant. It is only by virtue of conventions of reading that this mode of reading is literary rather than just verbal; some would say metaphorical or symbolic, rather than literal.[14]

This shows us something about the "pure" visuality of visual art but also about the difficulty to speak of paintings in terms of "word & image." There are neither pure words—no verbal caption is visible—nor pure images—if by that we understand images readable without recourse to words—while materially as well as according to clichéd norms of "word & image" distinctions,[15] the works are entirely visual. An interpretation[16] of the works cannot confine itself within a traditional art historical perspective, as the input of verbality would remain unnoticed. On the other hand, a problematic of "word & image" would tend to assess the relationship between the biblical text and the paintings in terms of the priority of the one and the derivative nature of the other. The dichotomy inherent in such an endeavor would preclude the *visibility* of the interaction of more than two modes simultaneously operating.

Norman Bryson means something in this spirit, it seems to me, when in his first book on painting he tries to assess the relative degrees of discursivity in French painting of the *Ancien Régime*. I am quite happy with the enterprise of this fascinating book, but its title is thoroughly problematic. His analyses are mostly wonderful: rich, dense, subtle, original; and at least for me as an

14. But that distinction itself is ideological, and subject to deconstruction, as any attempt to sharply delimit the realm of the literal will show. See Van Alphen 1987b for a semiotic concept of ideology; 1987a and 1988 for a deconstruction of figurative versus literal.

15. I mean notions like spatial versus temporal, simultaneous versus sequential, etceetera. The problematic status of these distinctions which invariably turn, first, binary, and, next, hierarchical has been sufficiently demonstrated. See e.g. Mitchell 1986.

16. I insist on the particular status of interpretation. I can imagine art historical approaches which would (try to) refrain from interpretation in the semiotic sense, and limit themselves to the study of commissions, material state of the canvases, attribution etc. To what extent interpretation can be totally bracketed is, of course, questionable; neither Schwartz, who claims to do so, nor Alpers, who seems to desire to do so, can do without interpretation.

outsider, they strike as convincingly historical. As a work of "new" art history—but for the newness, his *Tradition and Desire* is self-instructive—the book is extremely valuable, evidence of the discipline's blooming state.[17] But to the extent that it is on "word & image," it is confusing. The trap of simplistic binarism is inescapable. Even though Bryson's account of discursivity is subtle and pluralistic, the very mode of binarism takes its toll.

Bryson exploits his dichotomy admirably. He does not stop at the analysis of Diderot's prose on painting in visual terms, and its relation to the paintings reviewed,[18] nor at the visual implications of the double meaning of history as event and representation. Of the many facets of discursivity, the interpretation of visual representations of propositions commonly known through verbal accounts, e.g. the notion of *gloire*, known through Corneille,[19] is convincingly exploited and related to a theatrical mode of spectator address (38). Yet the work suffers slightly from the lack of structure that results from binary overstructuring: since the various facts are subsumed under the one heading "discursivity," it remains hard to grasp the argument otherwise than simplistically. For example, in the theoretical introduction I miss a specification of the different modes of discursivity as outlined re Rembrandt's Josephs, like the distinction between pre-textual and intra-textual discursivity or verbality as I prefer to call it: between the image as response to a text and the image *as* text. Not that Bryson neglects these specifications; he only fails to name them. Discursivity is now equal to semiosis and opposed to realism (10), then equal to verbality and opposed to visuality (passim), sometimes equal to syntax and opposed to paradigm (10), equal to relevance and opposed to realistic persuasiveness (10–11). All these meanings make much sense. I wish to suggest that Bryson is doing much more, rather than less, than his title promises. The point of my problem is that the very *name*—or word, for that matter—Word & Image does not help clarity, and puts subtlety and complexity in danger of getting lost between confusion and simplicity. It is the very book that carries

---

17. Of which Bryson is one of the leading critics—see his *Vision and Painting*. I consider this theoretical and polemical book the least convincing of the three, precisely because of the tradition & desire problematic. If it provides evidence of anything, it is primarily of the necessarliy personal motivation of scholarly work, which I take as an excuse for my own as displayed in the present review. The impulse to claim radical newness precludes clarity, and thus obscures some of the most interesting ideas forwarded. For example, the idea of relating the semiotic concept of deixis as a specific form of indexicality to painting in a kind of first person / third person distinction is fascinating and should be taken up; the connection between deixis and bodiliness remains unnecessarily unclear, thus resulting in a failure to persuade due, in my view, to a desire to break more radically with predecessors than is substantiated.

18. Just to show the inescapability of his own point in the later book: his scarce references to Fried's *Absorption and Theatricality: Painting and Beholder in the Age of Diderot* subtly display a "tradition & desire" problematic.

19. Although in Corneille, too, this notion is problematic, and precisely because of the oedipal tradition & desire problematic. See Verhoeff 1983 for a psychoanalytic analysis of Corneille's tragedies and the concept of *gloire* in that framework.

this problematic title, that shows convincingly that we have to move beyond the terms of a "word & image" enterprise.

WORDS ON IMAGES: FROM ART CRITICISM TO EPISTEME

A different relationship between word and image, also present in Bryson's books, is that between art and the verbal dealings with art: words on images. When Michael Fried set out to study the changing relation between painting and beholder in the age of Diderot (1980), in the age of the invention of art criticism that is, he promised to study the paintings as paintings-plus-commentaries. The connection between art and commentary is, however, not the simply hierarchical one we have been accustomed to through methodological positivism and its rigorous distinction between object and meta-language. Fried's argument about the relation is more subtle than that: interactional, rather than hierarchical. The art critic is a beholder in the first place. Painters who listen to what art critics have to say will learn about the other side of the relationship between painting and beholder. The thematization of beholdership in Diderot's commentaries supposedly furthers the painters' thinking about, and acting upon, this crucial position.

The key position in Fried's thinking, in this book, is the beholder, his own position that is, which is mediated through the critic's construction and the subsequent artistic shifting of it. The concept of the beholder is obviously central to art analysis, but no less problematic. On one level, it is, as Fried and others (Alpers 1988 is a case in point) convincingly show, it is a basically historical notion, and any serious art historical study must account for historical beholdership, both actual and constructed by the period's episteme. This is what Fried is doing: he tries to reconstruct the historical position of the beholder in a specific historical period (roughly, from 1755 to 1781) through an analysis of word and image interaction.

The intellectual itinerary resembles somewhat that of recent reader-response theory in literary criticism, which shifted from text to reader but remained caught in the dialectic of historicism in its attempt to reconstruct contemporary readership, a legitimate focus but not one that was going to account for the critic's own position.[20] In Fried's study, the appeal to contemporary criticism provides a surprisingly convincing reconstruction of the beholder's historical position in the age of the author of both the *Salons* and of *Le paradoxe sur le comédien*, described as uneasiness between absorption and

---

20. Two collections of essays on reader-response theory are Suleiman and Crosman (1980) and Tompkins (1980). See Jauss' concept of horizon of expectation as an attempt to reconstruct contemporary readership; Iser's concept of gap as an attempt to construct an ahistorical, ideal model of readership; Culler's (1983) analysis of the paradox theories of reading get caught in; and Van Alphen (1988) for an attempt to solve the paradox systematically, with an in-built account of historical readership. The latter account seems so far the most plausible, comprehensive, and non-contradictory one.

theatricality. I will return to these terms in the next section; here, it seems useful to realize that Fried bases his reconstruction of the beholder on the words of the critic and on the images of the painters, which serve as support and substantiation more than as source of the words.[21] Arguably, then, Fried's implicit argument is for a double predominance of words over images: the words of the critic who encourages the painter to follow his lead, and those in which the beholder is constructed as the relevant position in the construction of images. But this also implies, through a deconstruction of the conventional communication dogma in literary theory since Jakobson, that the reception of art precedes, generates, and confines its production.

Similar positions can be read, equally implicitly, in the other works under discussion here. But I sense that a slightly defensive historical claim is also forwarded to obliterate the other claim, implicit and for me more interesting, but probably for art historians unacceptable. Bryson relates the political events around, and the critical events in, the *Académie* to the art production. And in fact, the psychoanalytic framework of the thesis of the third book is, of course, verbal in precisely the same implicit, yet pervasive sense, inevitable in the discussion of the visual in a thoroughly verbal culture.

What I mean by this perhaps unconscious level of "word & image" relations can best be illustrated—with apologies for this less than innocent word—with the difference between Svetlana Alpers two recent books, which are also part of my personal sources of inspiration. In *The Art of Describing*, Alpers leans heavily on written sources of a philosophical and epistemological tradition, to substantiate her claim that Dutch art in the seventeenth century is descriptive rather than narrative. Although the more diffuse relation between these sources and the works of art is less direct, the argument is not fundamentally different from Fried's in *Absorption*: here, too, contemporary writing provides evidence of the (verbal) construction of the horizon of expectation against which the art of the time sets itself off, and without which, the explicit claim runs, it cannot be understood. Although Alpers' sources cannot be dubbed words *on* images in the same way as art criticism, they certainly fit the idea of meta-language; hence, of language on the visual ("language" of) images.

For art historians, yet not for them alone, but arguably for Western culture as a whole, the relationship is problematic, and this leads sometimes to repression of the inevitable verbal side of the argument. The repressed verbality of Alpers' argument in *The Art* is visible in the absence of definitions of, and even of explicit reflection on, the very concepts of description and narration. This is not surprising, and the author can hardly be blamed for it. Seemingly obvious, these notions suffer from a conspicuous lack of convincing definition within

---

21. This particular relationship between words and images is frequent, especially in the sites of cultural leadership where canonization is effectuated. Studying this relationship is a very relevant, though of course not exclusive approach.

their "home" field, literary theory, as well.[22] This, in turn, is not surprising either; they constitute one of those ideological dichotomies that almost automatically turn hierarchical, and that can only be undone by a stepwise deconstruction.[23] Reversing the hierarchy, as Alpers does in this book by showing the value of descriptive art,[24] is a first, powerful but not sufficient step. Its insufficiency shows in the solution to the dilemma of the non-fitting "exception." As she states herself in her later book, categorizing Rembrandt as culturally exceptional—as a more narrative artist than the rest of the Dutch—undermines the reversal: classifying one of the greatest artists outside the emancipated class come close to reinstating the dominance to be undermined, while the potential subversive power of exceptionality remains unexploited as long as the dichotomy stands, reversed or not. Any serious attempt to define the terms of such a suspect pair leads to a questioning, not of the order of the hierarchy, but of the very opposition underlying it.

In her following book, *Rembrandt's Enterprise*, Alpers takes issue with her previous position regarding this artist. Within her project, which is a continuous struggle to define the difference of images in a verbal culture, she has no reasons also to take issue, as from my perspective I would, with the (verbal) dichotomy that led to his exceptional position in the first place. Nevertheless, the relation between paintings and historical context, and between words and images becomes more diverse, and for me more interesting, in this fascinating study. Although the precedence of words is more problematic, Alpers rightly states, since in the preclassical age when artists did not follow a body of theoretical writing, she manages to show a more complex relation to writing in which now the paintings, then the texts generate the other. For a typical "tradition & desire" artist, full of ambivalence towards predecessors, this relationship becomes even more complex.

And inevitably, the modern critic partakes of the problems produced by that complexity, and the subsequent need for simplification. Where art critics wrote about that other deceptive distinction, between "fine" and "rough" (*fyn*

---

22. See my account of this problematic, and a typology of description in the context of rhetoric, in "On Meanings and Description," (*On Story-Telling*, 1991). Hamon's book (1981) remains the only major work on description from a literary-theoretical perspective. On narration, Alpers' most relevant source is Banfield 1982.

23. For the notion that apparently semantically empty codes like dichotomies constitute ideologies, see van Alphen 1987b.

24. Alpers gives herself a powerful argument on the impossibility to distinguish the two modes in her article on *Las Meninas* (1983), one of the best analyses of that over-analyzed work. The special status Alpers assigns to Velazquez's painting, which also holds for Rembrandt, would appear less special if it was not built on the pre-established dichotomy. This paper, incidentally, also provides evidence of the primacy of words: it is through the activation of the concepts of descriptive versus narrative, a distinction and its deconstruction, that Alpers is able to *see* the painting differently from those who remain unaware of the steering agency of words in their account. This is an instance of the as yet termless symmetrical counterpart of visual poetics: a verbally informed, yet basically visual, seeing, perhaps "poetical vision."

and *grof*) painting, it is tempting to discuss Rembrandt's works, divided or not in "periods," in terms of that distinction but taking it a step further, into semiotics. The terms then indicate not just manners of painting but meaningful signs. Paint-handling becomes a statement, and the propositional content of that statement moves from self-reference to affective attitudes. Alpers leads this semiotization of manner in a very original and exciting manner, in emphasizing the materiality of paint and its relation to sculpture, to touching as a specific way of seeing, and to a problematization of representation; in short, to self-reflection. Her analyses of particular paintings are subtle and mostly convincing, and her general point is well taken. For example, she establishes an illuminating relation between paint-handling and impasto on the one hand, and a small etching, *The Goldsmith*, in the Pygmalion tradition. Here, handling becomes domination, and the choice of motifs turns the etching clearly misogynistic. Defending "rough" painting or the famous late-Rembrandtish impasto by making it so much more interesting and meaningful in the semiotic sense, the critic carefully stays away from binary valuation.

It is in the (verbal) interpretation of the (visual) particularities of the works that I find the return of the repressed hierachy to occur. This happens when the focus on material seeing—touching—is rephrased in the idealizing terms of love, understanding, human relation (e.g. 23, 29). For an artist with a clear predilection for subjects wherein the contiguity between seeing and touching is thematized in terms of power and sexuality—Bathsheba, Susanna, Lucretia—this seems a problematic stance to take. The viewing seems to be informed, here, by a certain humanistic discourse.

What does this problem have to do with "word & image," and specifically with the subject of the present section, words *on* images? I would submit that the unawareness of the input of verbality in this interpretation, which presents itself as based on distinctly visual observations, obscures the extent to which words take precedence over, even produce, the construction of the image. Only, the words taking precedence here are less easy to see, obscured as they are by the more explicitly alleged contemporary texts. The words constructing the (=Alpers') images here—as distinct from the sharp critique of *The Goldsmith*—are those of the doxa of our culture which, as I have argued elsewhere, condones rape with reference to the implicitly alleged "natural" continuity between seeing and touching,[25] which in turn allows the members of that culture to construct touching as caring and love, rather than as power and taking possession. Interestingly, Alpers' chapter title, "The Master's Touch," can be given an unintended second meaning in this context.

---

25. See chapter two of *Reading Rembrandt*, an extended version of which has already been published in Dutch (1988). Of course, I am not suggesting that Alpers shares these misogynistic views that condone rape; only that she borrows its ideologies unawares, as we all do, inevitably, to some extent.

I would like to see the relation between these two issues, the more technical one of Rembrandt's impasto and its relation to self-reflection through emphasis on the tactile dimension, on the one hand, and the ideological one of the representation of sexual power, on the other, in a particularly rich painting. In one of his two paintings of Susanna, the more complex one in Berlin, the subject is, on one level, the abuse of power through the extension of seeing to touching (see figure 3). This subject is related to the verbal pre-text in a manner similar to the Josephs. In both the Joseph and the Susanna cases, the attractiveness of the subject for painting is in the thematization of vision: power and the abuse of it is related to seeing: for Joseph, the physical presence of the coat as material though deceptive evidence, credible because embedded in the woman's derivative social power position; in the Susanna, the lust to touch aroused by seeing, and the power to touch warranted by social power. Visuality or rather its epistemological potency, visibility, are decisive factors that generate the narrative. The fact that the one Elder, in the Susanna, touches his victim, is less important than the specific part of her he touches: her clothes, thus by undressing her enabling *visibility* of her vulnerability—her touchiness, so to speak. According to Alpers' argument, the man's hand is thematically related to the painter's touch as well as to the diegetic hold on the woman, but the isotopy of touching is clearly related to a theme more negative than love. Of course, as her interpretation of *The Goldsmith* suggests, Alpers would agree with this.

But the case becomes slightly more interesting as soon as we notice, thanks to Alpers' semiotization of it, the dealings with impasto, the handling of paint, in this particular painting. Large parts of the work are done in the manner Alpers is analyzing, although not very strongly: "rough" or, as I would call it in Alpers' line, touchy; Bryson would say deictic, rather than "fine" or transparent. But amazingly, and undermining the dichotomy, not all of it is "rough." The one detail done in the "fine" manner is Susanna's hair, triply "refined": as opposed to the alleged model, Lastman's *Susanna* where the victim's hair is lose, the hairdo is complicated; the hair is intertwined with a velvet ribbon, a string of pearls, and a scarf; and the execution of these refined details is exceptionally "fine." The transparency of realism is here doubled by and commented upon by the deictic indexicality of the painterly manner. From a semiotic perspective, that is, taking these striking details as signs, one is led to ask: what do they, and their manner, mean?[26] The answer to this question must be anchored in the visual image presented. The position of Susanna's hair within the structure of the image is crucial: it is the object of the

---

26. In a personal communication, Svetlana Alpers argues that hair does not have for Rembrandt the relevance I attribute to it in the following interpretation. I am not convinced by the objection, but more to the point is the difference in focus. For Alpers, images in this art are more maker-oriented than viewer-oriented, while I maintain this is not the way to put it. For me, the difference lies, not in the artist's intention but in the approach.

Figure 3: Rembrandt, *Susanna Surprised by the Elders*, 1638. Berlin-Dahlem, Gemäldegalerie

Elder's gaze—Bryson's critique of the gaze applies here quite strongly. Surprisingly, this man is not looking at all at the body he is busy unveiling, but, looking above it, he is doubly overlooking it. He is staring at the one location in the work where "fine" takes precedence over "rough." This is a compelling confirmation of Alpers' claim that the handling of paint works for self-reflection and self-representation of the work of painting. Further details confirm this interpretation, the most astonishing one being the right hand of this man. This fist seems to be clutching around an object, but no object is represented. Hence, we might conjecture, the object held is a fiction. Representing fiction through emptiness, but an emptiness emphasized by the fist; such is Rembrandt's semiotic masterstroke here.[27]

In combination with the represented line of vision and the place of "fine" painting therein, the obvious object to take into consideration is a magnifying glass. Alpers' *Art of Describing* has amply demonstrated the obsession with techniques of vision as a central episteme in Rembrandt's days. Techniques of vision broaden the scope of the power gained by means of vision. This power is not unrelated to what later becomes positivism: a sheer unlimited confidence in observation. This ideologeme[28] is thematized in the verbal pre-text of the *Susanna*, where the Elders threaten to denounce Susanna for adultery with a (fictitious) young man they pretend to have *witnessed*.

In this painting, I propose to interpret this strange detail as a double statement on vision. On the one hand, and according to Alpers' thesis, the fictitious magnifying glass refers to the refinement of vision a good artist is able to call forth. On the other, and countering the positive interpretation of seeing as touching Alpers proposes, it denounces the contiguity between these two actions. Visually enjoying the beautiful or "fine" is what the good artist enables one to do; and this enjoyment is contrasted with bad seeing, with the wicked abuse of power that the automatic collocation of seeing and touching encourages.

The difference between this interpretation and Alpers' positive view of the seeing-as-touching complex in some of her statements—with the analysis of *The Goldsmith* to contradict it—is not so much a matter of disagreement as of shift in focus. The works Alpers discusses are focuses on the production of art; this one is more geared toward its reception. If Rembrandt often recommends

27. The sign produced by, or projected upon, the tensely clutching but empty fist is a good example of a Lotmanian *zero priëm* as described in *The Structure of the Artistic Text*.

28. The term ideologeme, which, analogous to sememe and phoneme, indicate the smallest unit of ideology, has been proposed by Jameson (1981). In agreement with van Alphen's semiotic reworking of the concept of ideology (1987b), I suggest such ideologemes are structures rather than contents, codes rather than semes.

Since I rely on Alpers' work here, it is suitable to say that she is not convinced by the fictitious magnifying glass I am bringing up here. On the other hand, it must be clear that I am not projecting this object onto Rembrandt's conscious intention. For me, the glass is a possibility of reading an awkward detail, hence, an act of reception. The fact that the detail is there does not prove my interpretation, but it does allow it.

"rough" *painting* as an artistically validating mode of self-reflection, as I agree he does, he also recommends[29] "fine" *seeing* as an ideologically commendable mode of practicing gender-relations in a culture so fascinated by vision. From the relation between painter, paint, and painting, my interpretation has shifted in Fried's direction: the relation between painting and beholder, but with a difference. The subject, that is, the ideo-story,[30] verbal by virtue of its medium—the text—of by its structure—narrative—is neither an incidental choice exclusively motivated by commission or market as Schwartz would argue, nor an underscoring of the artist's personal obsessions as one might misconstrue my present argument. I take it as evidence of the inseparability of images and words, and of the impact of words on images. It is a reference to a verbal—philosophical as well as practical, ideological, and political—discussion going on in the society that generated the work: the token of an episteme.

WORDS AS IMAGES: THEATRICALITY AND VISUAL POETICS

Fried's earlier book established a tension between two modes of the painting-beholder relation: absorption, where the figures are ostentatiously engaged in an inward activity, seeing being one of the possibilities, and theatricality, where they are acting out their relationship to one another, drawing the viewer in. This tension is then studied in the late eighteenth century, and one of Fried's great qualities is that he remains so carefully historical, yet opens up the possibility to use his systematic semiotic[31] for works from other periods, but given the historical precision, not unproblematically. He exemplifies this in his later book.

Before discussing that study, I would like to demonstrate the validity and relevance of the distinction between absorption and theatricality as a systematic device by returning to the two Joseph paintings. The Berlin canvas has a typically theatrical device, often used by Rembrandt, the "speaking hands." The woman's hand pointing to Joseph is so clearly indexical that its effect does

---

29. Again, I am not claiming, of course, that this was his conscious intention. I am shifting the discussion from intention—Alpers' focus—to reception, and in this shift, Rembrandt the individual person becomes an historical man, representative of his time and also differing from it in surprising ways; but I would claim that this Rembrandt, just like Alpers' Rembrandt, is a fiction, a product of the viewer's interpretive activity. Alpers was right, then, to propose an image of Rembrandt as exceptional in the *Art of Describing* book, and equally right in proposing the opposite in the new book. Both are her constructions, and both help us dealing with the works, as criticism should.

30. I have proposed this term to indicate stories that are apt to promote ideological investments by virtue of their binary structure, even if this structure itself is ideologically empty. See Bal 1989.

31. Fried does not claim to be semiotician, but I would argue that his distinction is at the heart of semiotic thinking. On the one hand, he is writing about signs: signs of the relationship at stake, at the crossroad of semantics and syntactics. On the other, he is discussing these signs in use, in their effect on the viewer, thus bringing in the pragmatic perspective. The interpretive impulse becomes self-reflective as we realize that the semantics of painting and beholder include our own pragmatic position.

not go beyond explicit signalling. With her left hand, she seems to protect her breast from the attack by a violator. As a "speaking hand," that gesture is part of the speech: she is telling, in a theatrical manner, that Joseph tried to violate her. Potiphar's right hand is resting on the chair, slightly behind the woman, thus creating the sense of intimacy between the two which excludes the accused.

The Washington painting is different. The narrativization is much more ambivalent. The hand with which the woman supposedly accuses Joseph does point, but not at him. It points perhaps to the red garment, the token of Joseph's misbehavior, but even that direction is not clear. Instead of gesticulating in despair, Joseph is standing still; he does not participate in the scene. This painting is so much more enigmatic that it is worth trying a different approach, not from Joseph's side but from the other side of the bed, and not from Genesis but from the image itself. Potiphar's hand is not, here, behind the woman but slightly in front of her, as if on its way to grasping her. The woman protects her breast again, but in combination with the lesser distance between her and Potiphar, his grappling hand, and his determined face, it seems as if *he* was approaching her sexually against her will.

The work of light is much more subtle than in the other painting. The light falls on the bed and on the woman in both, but here, Joseph is also, very subtly, illuminated. The light produces a pattern in which the woman and the young man are illuminated to the exclusion of the older man. Joseph's face has an intense, but unclear expression: desiring, anxious, admiring? The curtain, much more clearly indicated in the Berlin painting as the (realist) representation of a bed-curtain, is here so vaguely indicated that its only function seems to be to set off Joseph as standing in a space, lighter and further away, *at the other side*. The lower seam of his garment forms a figural line: his body seems to end there.

The eyes of each protagonist thematize a specific concept of visuality. Each figure looks intense, but inwardly. No one looks at a clear object. The woman does not look at her husband; she seems to stare at an inner vision; the vision of her desire. The older man does not look at the woman; he, too, seems to concentrate on his desire. Joseph's look, not directed anywhere either, is even more inward than that of the two others. The separation between Joseph on the one hand, and the couple on the other, is radical; when viewed from the other side of the bed, his image is almost detached, like a portrait on the wall. He takes on a different ontological level. The image is itself the inner view, the preoccupation of the two others. When viewed in isolation, Joseph seems full of feelings, yet not involved in any event.

If we wish to consider these paintings in terms of absorption and theatricality, they seem to fit almost too perfectly. The Berlin painting is highly theatrical, with the interaction between the figures grounded in the liveliness of their movements—the speaking hands—and in the unity of the scene. No special relation to the beholder seems to be thematized, however. The Washington painting is entirely absorptive, and as a consequence, there is no unity based on the interaction between the figures. There is, however, a much more profound unity, based on the phantasmic character of the representation. Ontologically, Joseph does not belong to this fantasy as a figure but as an image. But in order to see the paintings in this way, we must get away from Genesis, from "word & image" that is, and be ready to reverse the traditional perspective and reconsider Genesis on the basis of the paintings. In the story, there is no moment where all three characters are present, and the Berlin painting therefore presents itself as a theatrical condensation of different scenes. The Washington painting, apparently more removed from the Bible, shows an interesting though repressed aspect of the story in which the woman's lust gets full attention—the story as her fantasy, that is.

In *Realism, Writing, Disfiguration*, Fried characterizes Eakins' *Gross Clinic* as a painting that is hard to look at, yet impossible to look away from. The thematics of surgical violence and the representational practice of making key details invisible, together appeal to this ambivalence in the viewer, which Fried relates to the psychoanalytic framework of father-son relations in Eakins' life. This shift to a more personal problematic does not, however, do away with the complex of absorption and, and versus, theatricality. The woman/mother figure in Eakins' painting, with her strange gesture of refusing to look, yet expressing horror at what she sees, is a powerful representation of precisely the kind of theatricality discussed in the earlier work. What is the status of this figure in terms of the word-image problematic as outlined so far, and how can it take us beyond that problematic into one of a slightly different kind?

The woman in *The Gross Clinic* is, literally, the image of a concept. The concept she represents, makes present, is a specific relation between painting and beholder which Fried has proposed to call theatricality: engagement in action played out with the other figures; it refers to a mode of looking, a mode of composition, and a mode of representation. This concept shows that it is no longer possible to base the discussion on the distinction between words and images, nor to return to an illusionary "pure visuality." Although the theater uses words—text—and images—e.g. backdrop, costume, staging—the theatrical collapses words and images. It does so through the three modes of looking, of composition, and of representation.

Theatricality as a mode of looking is based on identification: the viewer wants to see what the other figures are engaged in seeing so intensely—here the violent and healing operation on the sick body—but cannot quite see—the inability being both visual and psychological. The intricate connection between the visual and the psychological colors the concept of theatricality with a historically specific nuance. It takes the early twentieth century to produce such a connection, exemplified by, but not exclusive to, the work of Freud.

Of all the figures represented, that of the "mother" mediates between the play and the spectator. Spectator herself, she is also an actor. She is an embedded, diegetic spectator symmetrical to Brecht's staged narrators.[32] Fried is careful to spell out the different beholder positions to be distinguished, in order to avoid what I would call the diegetic fallacy, the collapse of represented, proposed, and actual looking that is. There are several passages in *Absorption* that suggest this care (e.g. 104–105; 121). On the basis of Fried's suggestions I would systematize these distinctions as follows. The actual viewer chooses his or her position on the basis of, first his or her own desires and competences, and, second, on the basis of the various positions offered by the painting. They can be differentiated as follows: the *addressed* viewer is the equivalent of the *narratee* in narrative (Prince 1982). This position is defined, in the *Susanna*, by the female figure's appeal to the viewer as represented by her eyes and lips, expressing vulnerability and need (Garrard 1985). The position, then, demands sympathy. The woman in Eakins' painting addresses this viewer by her gesture of hiding her face as well as blocking her sight. Here, the position demands identification with the mode of (non)vision. The *implied* viewer would be slightly differently defined as the kind of viewer the painting as a whole seems to call for. For the *Susanna* the implied viewer would be the voyeur who is attracted by her exposure. The "mother" in the *Gross Clinic* as well as the hidden-and-exposed body of the ambiguous[33] patient imply a viewer fascinated and repulsed. The *represented* viewer is diegetic, partakes of the represented scene that is. In the *Susanna*, the Elders are represented viewers. Their act of viewing is embedded in the story about it. In the *Gross Clinic*, various viewers are represented: the four visible doctors, watching their object unambivalently;[34] the woman who displays the impossibility of looking, and Gross, reassuringly mediating for the benefit of the external viewers.

The woman, then, stands for theatricality, but as Fried claims this very concept to imply unity, she cannot represent it by herself. She is the sign of problematic vision that the one Elder in the Susanna painting also was, but the mode of the problematic has shifted since Rembrandt's time and place,

---

32. The narratological term of *focalizer* does not coincide with either of these two functions. Both the Brechtian narrator and the represented beholder *also* function as focalizers, mediating the represented *view* of the diegesis proposed for the reader/viewer's adoption.

33. Fried calls attention to the fact that, strictly speaking, the sex of the patient is indetermined because the sexual organ is invisible. I suggest that the shape of the thigh suggests he is male, but I agree with Fried that the invisibility of the organ as well as its replacement by the probed wound turn the male son into the ambivalent son under threat of castration. Hence, the organ is not blocked from sight to keep the gender indistinct but to show the male gender at the moment of danger of dissolution into indistinctness, identified with femininity. This is something entirely different.

34. Although the looking of the doctor at the lower right is ambiguous, as he could be looking at Gross as well as at the wound, or at the mother. If we take it that this polyvalence is a sign in its turn, this man's eyes are shifters between the three levels of diegesis: that of the primary action of the operation, that of the female outsider, and that, intermediate, of the resting master surgeon.

through Diderot's, to Eakins'. The mode of looking at stake here is gender-specific, as was the case in Rembrandt's *Susanna*, and, equally unconscious, it is radically different in this respect as well. Eakins' painting stages an exclusively male world, where tensions are at work between fathers and sons, and played out in terms of (medical) technology—as distinct from the technology of vision thematized in the *Susanna*—and of life giving (healing). More strongly than Fried I would suggest that these roles are themselves problematic. This becomes obvious when we realize that the father figure par excellence, the master surgeon, is not doing anything. Although displaying the bloody knife he has, by implication, been wielding—and Fried's discussion of the motif of castration is highly plausible here—he is at this very moment just looking, possibly at the theatrical woman, possibly at the audience she stands for, turning away from the acting sons toward the diegetically excluded woman and the equally excluded audience. Being, himself, unable to look, he takes the unexpected side of the viewers, both diegetical and external, whose power of judgment is, in fact, paternal.

The exclusion of the mother from the medical scene is thus broken by her identification with the master surgeon-painter. The mother figure thus also signifies the unifying mode of composition. On the basis of what precedes I must use this idea of unity as a means to relativize it. The paradoxical position of the woman who, standing for theatricality, would be excluded from the unity theatricality implies, is broken by Dr. Gross' pose. This pose is symmetrical to hers: while she makes a clawing gesture, he quietly displays the bloody knife, and while she violently refuses to see that whose seeing constitutes her horror, he quietly looks at her horror, but away from its object. This complex interaction between these two figures almost absorbs the theatricality of the entire scene. The operation, the audience in the background, the writers, seem an embedded painting, an object of vision for the two parental figures whose sole interaction constitutes the unity of the theatrical scene, breaking, by the same token, the unity of the work as a whole.

The break in the compositional unity implies a statement about theatricality as a mode of representation. For the basic break is that which links painting and beholder, drawing the latter within the former, and thus challenging the autonomy of the work. The theater itself is the non-autonomous art par excellence. For most of us, a performance without an audience is more obviously unthinkable than a text without readers, or a painting without a beholder; yet, the case of performance makes the case for the other two. Theatrical painting draws attention to that extreme position of the theater and, by implication, claims the same status for painting. It is not a coincidence that the theater is also the art in which word and image can neither be ignored nor separated. What is at stake, in Fried's concept of theatricality, is an analysis of painting in terms of a *poetics* of painting: of a conception of visual representation as working toward an ever-changing problematization of the relations between the work as sign and the work's working as pragmatic event, of a rhetoric of visual art—in other words, a visual poetics, beyond the word-image opposition. In this context, Bryson's interpretation of *gloire* as necessarily ostentatious, as void without spectatorship (1982:37–38) becomes acutely relevant as a plea for just this kind of visual poetics.

I wish to stress at this point that my exploration of modes of analysis beyond the word-image opposition implies no negative evaluation of either art history or "word & image" at all. I am trying to make room for work based on a shift in focus, not to replace other approaches. The dialectic of the pursuit of insight entails temporary and strategic emphasis on what is, temporarily, underemphasized. By claiming a notion of visual poetics and, below, of comparative arts, I wish to make more visible some aspects already inscribed in traditional art history and "word & image" studies. Theatricality in this discussion becomes a metaphor for my pursuit of non-oppositional relations between verbality and visuality—but at other times, oppositional relations may be called for, even if not the hierarchies they so often entail.

Alpers' later book also devotes attention to the theatrical model. Rigorously historical without following older, rather superficial historical views in which theatricality was merely associated with gestures, light, and dress (35), the author shows convincingly how Rembrandt drew upon the popularity of the theater of his time, the discussions about acting, and what Diderot would later call the paradox of the actor—the fundamental unnaturalness of acting as imitation of nature—to confine his practice of painting to the domain where he alone reigned: the studio. Here, he had models act out scenes and actions to be painted. The discussions about the theater focused, precisely, on the relationship between word and gesture—hence, image—and between oral and visual presence (48).

Discussing the represented viewer, so frequently present in Rembrandt's works, Alpers proposes to see this idiosyncratic feature as *spectatorial*, rather than *voyeuristic*, and this remark joins Bryson's criticism of the use of the term voyeurism for cases where the privacy characteristic of voyeurstic looking is not only absent but by definition excluded (1982:37) because spectatorship is part of the meaning of the display. Rembrandt's preference for scenes involving spectatorship point indeed in this direction. Beyond this thematic argument, Alpers interprets other aspects of Rembrandt's work as theatrical as well, like the unconventional movement of his figures which have no sources in the pictorial tradition, and which bear comparison with Delacroix as Bryson discusses him. The movement of figures, in turn, works beyond their own mobility. In a subtle and wonderful discussion of one of the only written phrases in which Rembrandt expressed his views on art (49–51), Alpers shows that the movement of the figures was linked, by the artist, to another kind of movement. It reaches an effect, according to the double sense of the word

Figure 4: Rembrandt, *Samson's Wedding-Feast*, 1638. Dresden, Gemäldengalerie

moving, which belongs to the rhetorical model of visual poetics, and of which theatricality is the central mode.

FROM VISUAL POETICS TO COMPARATIVE ARTS

Let me pursue the vein of theatricality a little further. As in the case of Alpers' discussion of "the master's touch," I am fully convinced by the overall argument Alpers makes about Rembrandt's theatricality; and although most of her discussions of actual works are wonderfully illuminating, I have a problem with one of her subsequent interpretations; indeed, again I would play off the argument against the interpretation. I can be blamed, of course, for choosing my example too well, and I am aware of the unjustice I am doing Alpers by foregrounding the case which is secondary for her. As it happens, the case has an interesting bearing on the problematic of this essay, the attempt to overcome the word-image dichotomy, that is. In this section, and with the help of this example, I will try to rehearse and wind up that attempt by proposing the study of comparative arts as a fruitful academic venture, not instead of, but in addition to, or rather, integrated within, art history and comparative literature.

Among the two first examples Alpers discusses is an early *Judas Returning the Pieces of Silver* of 1629, where the theatrical gestures of the figure emphasize the untrustworthiness of his intentions. Once a traitor, always a traitor is what the painting's excessive theatrical movement seems to say, by the same token addressing the paradox of acting—and, we might say, opposing words (of repentance) to image (of hypocrisy). The link between representational and moral opposition suggested by this example is not inherent; yet it is, I fear, a rhetorical trap. The second example is a work of a decade or so later, *Samson's Wedding-Feast* of 1638 (fig. 4). The author gives a visual description of the work, immediately followed by an account of its verbal background:

> To the one side we see Samson posing his riddle to the Philistines, while just off center, behind the festive board, is the self-conscious, stiffly posed figure of his new wife, identified in the Bible only as the woman from Timnah. It is she who will betray Samson to her people after tricking him to tell her the answer to his riddle. Posed in the posture of a bride . . . she is a woman who will contradict her appearance as a newly wedded wife by doing her husband in. Once again, at the center of his picture, Rembrandt has focused on a betrayer—on one whose appearance or actions must be understood as being a performance. And this fact is underlined here by the compositional echo of Leonardo's *Last Supper*, in which Rembrandt placed Samson's wife, his betrayer, in the place of Christ (37).

I quoted this passage at length because of the interaction of word and image it displays and which, I assume, go largely unnoticed, and because this interaction entails a view of the painting in which the visual is overruled by the verbal. The first sentence describes the painting ("we see"), while its final clause introduces the verbal source. The assimilation between the two is marked by the words describing the bride, a narrative shifter which bears evaluation of the figure on the basis of a verbal account. The words "self-conscious, stiffly posed" are quite concretely shifters: self-consciousness and stiffness are each semantically double, but differently. The self-consciousness is so strongly related to the relation to the addressed viewer—the woman literally addresses the viewer—that the very content of "self" calls for identification between figure and viewer through the implied viewer the very contrast between the woman and the other figures calls forth. The stiffness of the pose, in contrast, inserts the figure in the theatricality which it alone challenges. The figure is isolated from the other actors, all ostentatiously engaged in interaction with each other, excluding the viewer who can enter the scene by identification alone.

The problem can be summarized as follows: why is the "stiffly posed" bride chosen to represent theatricality, while the other figures, engaged in busy action with each other, seem to qualify much better?[35] If it is the connection with Judas that motivates this focus, the verbal—the notion that both characters are traitors—has overruled the visual. This is why I suggested above that the example was a rhetorical trap. But Judges 14 mentions neither tricks nor betrayal; only blackmail, only life-threatening intimidation of the woman by her kinsmen. Hence, it is not the specific text that is brought in here, but a more diffuse and by no means universal doxa, a cultural commonplace which has it that this bride is a prelude to Delilah.[36] In order to claim that Rembrandt has represented this particular doxa, contemporary views on the story need to be checked, which I cannot undertake here.

The visual allusion to Christ, taken as evidence that a (theatrical) betrayer is intended, seems to me to prove rather the opposite. The woman is compositionally taking the place of Christ. For me, the ironic reversal of values implied in Alpers' interpretation is unwarranted. Rather, the woman is depicted in this honorable position because she is about to be sacrificed, just like Christ at the Last Supper. The wedding feast is, so to speak, *her* last supper. And that is much more likely, in a seventeenth century fond of so-called typological interpretation, where characters of the Old Testament are taken to

35. The other figures are engaged in interaction and constitute a unity from which the bride is emphatically excluded. Fried's book is not mentioned in this chapter on theatricality. Alpers uses the concept in a way opposed to Fried's: for her, theatricality in Rembrandt "is not engaged with addressing the viewer but with constituting a self by performance and by commanding performance." (Alpers, personal communication). The opposition between the two uses of the term does not change my view, that the men, not the bride, are being theatrical, in both Fried's and Alpers' sense.

36. Who, strictly speaking, also neither tricks nor lies. See my *Lethal Love* for a detailed analysis of Judges 14–16. This is the second case where Alpers borrows a misogynistic element of the doxa. This is unfortunate, as she has showed elsewhere (1983b, 1985) a fine sense of gender problematic and its exclusions.

prefigure Christ. What makes the case special, and shows Rembrandt's ambivalent relationship to women in an interesting light, is the fact that it is not Samson but the woman who is—we must not forget this fact—his victim who is here presented typologically.

In terms of theatricality, according to Alpers' own criterion—movement and a sense of performance—as well as Fried's—interaction, unity, and the relation to the beholder—I would suggest the painting does appeal to a notion of theatricality, but through a questioning of its status. The figures busy performing on the mode of genre painting, all engaged in role-playing, contrast with the one figure who is *not* acting, and who is, ostentatiously, outside of the scene. Alpers senses this exclusion when she places her "behind the festive board," which, in strictly visual terms, is not so convincing, but rings nevertheless true. Fried's criterion unity is, then, not disobeyed but "explicitly" foregrounded: by breaking it. The relation to the beholder is, indeed, comparable to that in *The Gross Clinic*. Although the issues connected with it are different, due to differences in historical context, the figure who, like a Brechtian narrator, steps out of the play, here does so in order to address the viewer and ask for help, or at least, for an opinion.

I am not presenting this dissident view as a simple difference of interpretation, nor am I out to quibble with an otherwise fine study. I want to argue that the concept of theatricality, presented, in the previous section, as an exemplary meeting place for verbality and visuality, as the token of visual poetics, has hit its limits before we know it, and that this entails yet another turn in my case for an approach beyond the word-image opposition. Its limits are bound up with its implicit relation to word and image, its historical exclusivity, and its methodological isolation. The exploration of these limits will help bring the present argument to a provisional close.

The concept of theatricality is so fit for a visual poetics precisely because it establishes a unification of word and image in one, composite sign. A theatrical unit, be it diction, gesture, movement, can only artificially be confined to either verbality or visuality. This unity, however, is implicit. For students of the theater, the very word-image opposition does not even make sense. It is to some extent because of this implicit unity that the colonization of the image by the word passes unnoticed. Alpers' description of the *Samson* showed a domination of the visual image by the diffuse verbality that informed the interpretation. The specific form this verbality took was double: on the one hand, the doxa surrounding the biblical story; on the other, the pre-established status of betrayal as the syntagm of role-playing. The concept of theatricality came in only after these two verbal pre-texts had been given relevance. This turned out to be too late: it was unable to correct the verbal dominance and to assert its own specificity. In contrast, Bryson's distinction between discursivity and figurality offered the advantage of its explicitness. Thus it worked heuristically—the analyst knew what to look for—and it made the analyses accountable. What interpretation did each of the terms yield?

In general, the historical approach is easily seen as in conflict with a systematic approach; this dichotomy is in my mind among the most powerful and paralyzing ideologies in the humanities today, together with that between theory and practice, literal and figurative, form and content, text and context. One can only agree on the necessity to study a historical object in context, and I find the research underlying this study as well as the other studies discussed, admirably solid and interesting. The lack of reference to a systematic concept of theatricality made for a line of argument which led, in spite of the author's overt disavowal of the dichotomy truth-falsehood, to a syntagm in which role-playing was connected to the stiff pose, rather than to the movement of the other figures; to the opposition between "appearance" and "reality." If, as the author claims, "taking the part of another . . . is the measure of success" (37), it requires a unification of historical and systematic perspectives to answer the question: whose part is this woman playing—that of Christ, compositionally present through the prestigious predecessor and historically present through contemporary exegesis, or that of Judas, verbally present through the modern doxa? In other words, what address is proposed to the viewer by the woman's stiff, anxious eyes? Working the systematic perspective proposed by Fried—unity and engagement of the beholder—into the historical one—Alpers' point about performance in the studio, *and* that of contemporary theology, would have led to a different, and in my view more challenging, interpretation. This is exactly what Bryson does in his two historical books, and the result shows the importance of such an integration. Bryson, even less than Alpers or Fried, is emphatically *not* opting for systematic against historical work.

Methodological isolation, finally, is the result of these two problems. It is by remaining within the art historical paradigm, although exploiting it admirably, that Alpers cannot take the concept of theatricality to a level of discussion where the input from the verbal and the visual perspectives are both acknowledged in their respective potential and overcome in their limits. Semiotics, providing the perspective of a theory of signs, could have helped to recognize which phenomena were taken as signs and given meaning. But it takes more than just a semiotic toolbox to do this. To be sure, it would be helpful to realize what the sign status of the stiff pose is, and how it overlaps with or deviates from the compositional sign that is Christ's place.

The input of indexicality—the metonymical relation to the earlier painting and the synecdochical relation to the doxa—in the overruling of iconicity—the (com)positional identification of the woman with Christ—raises the question of relative power of sign systems. Is it because index overrules icon, or because words overrule images, that the concept of the theatrical did not bring the interpretation beyond the implicit domination of verbality? Precisely because it is a general theory of signs, semiotics cannot answer this question.

The semiotic perspective raises questions that can be answered more specifically within an interdisciplinary framework in which semiotics serves to let the traditions and methods of the various disciplines be consciously confronted with one another. Although all three scholars discussed are aware of disciplinary differences and of the importance of a balanced integration, Bryson goes further than the two others in taking this necessity at heart. Visual poetics can be placed within such a framework, and within it, theatricality can still be a privileged term. But one step between general semiotics and visual poetics must not be skipped. It is the step where disciplines take themselves and each other seriously.[37] Declaring one's own or the interlocutor's discipline in crisis is less helpful—even if more helpful than unwarranted self-congratulation or over-admiration of the other—than a recognition of limits, in order to overcome them.

37. The reflections proposed in this essay have institutional backgrounds. The verbal & visual integration is much in the air, and various journals devote special issues to it (*Style, Poetics Today*) or discuss such integrations as a matter of fact (*Semiotica, October*) while new journals have emerged that explicitly address these issues (*Representations, Word and Image*). More importantly, universities are starting to adopt programs in this line, like the undergraduate majors Woord en Beeld at the Free University of Amsterdam (Director S. Kibédi Varga; see Varga 1984, 1987, 1988; forthcoming) and Visual and Cultural Studies at the University of Rochester (Director Janet Wolff). Research groups are active in various European universities (see Muckenhaupt 1986; Bätschmann 1977; Bonnefis et Reboul 1979; Guillerm 1987).

I owe much of the thought that led to this essay, in addition to the authors of the books discussed, to Ernst van Alphen. I thank Michael Holly for helpful comments on an earlier version.

▪11▪

Love-Story

FARAH ACCUSED OF ADULTERY

Let me now turn to an entirely different realm of the traffic of images: from High Art to gossip. However suspicious we may in effect be, a newspaper article pretends to a referential function. The context in which it is published confers on it the status of truth. Not that it *is* true; but it has truth value, can be endorsed or denied, solicits yes or no. The truth of the message is concerned with some elements of the world. The credulity in principle of the reader of the newspaper gives the journalist an ideological power without equal. What kind of use does he or she make of it? Many critical analyses of news, t.v., journalism, have demonstrated how manipulation occurs. One aspect in all this deserves a little more specific attention. The analysis which follows demonstrates that the narrativity itself, inherent in all reportage or news items is a very effective tool for the subliminal conveyance of ideological values. Paradoxically, these values are enshrined in images that narrativity constructs.

Here is the standard view of discursive practice: reportage is devoted to the transmission of knowledge whereas argumentative discourse aims at the transmission of opinion. Since these generic conventions are known to the reader, she is prepared to react with the requisite competences. Reading a discursive text, she is prepared to weigh the arguments advanced. In front of a narrative text he means to expand his knowledge and is less likely to question the truth of "facts" presumed to be "true." These conventional attitudes constitute the fertile soil in which the manipulator sows his ideology. But for the latter to grow, ploughing, watering, and other labor, like the extirpation of weeds, is necessary.

Ideology: "a collection of ideas, beliefs, and doctrines peculiar to an age, to a society, or to a class" (social or sexual). Manipulation: "underhanded dealings; an arrangement, a dubious scheme." Here, the *Petit Robert* is too vague. Let's be more precise: to manipulate is to impose elements of an ideology *without forewarning*. To argue is to persuade openly. To manipulate is to do it in secret. The difference does not lie solely in the moral sphere, which is less relevant here. There is also a difference in technique. I will restrict myself to the second point. The question is not: is there manipulation? but, how does one manipulate? A lesson, also, not in writing (there competence is already too widespread) but in reading. The trick above all is practice. The text will be followed as it unfolds, because readerly chronology, often ignored in literary analyses, should be taken into account when analyzing the reading of a text designed for rapid consumption. A newsreel is not a poem. One does not stop to go back, retrace the steps of the narrative, analyze the rhetorical devices. The case at stake in this essay is a text written for rapid consumption. Even if, in its genre, it is a masterpiece of disquieting quality and, in fact, deserves to be treated like a literary text.

Farah Accused of Being Unfaithful

This time, passions have been unleashed around the throne of Iran. The enemies of the imperial couple are multiplying their attacks, seeking to strike the fatal blow at the Shah and even, today, at the Empress Farah herself.

This started with an unbelievable smear campaign shrewdly orchestrated. A campaign which was aimed at the Shah. His enemies had not hesitated to claim that he had secretly remarried. They had even gone so far as to insinuate that he had produced a legitimate child outside his union with the Empress.

Today things have gone much farther still. The enemies of the imperial couple have dared to take a further step into slander. It's the turn of the Empress Farah herself to be directly the target—she whose reputation, nevertheless, one knows to be without stain, and whose devotion as wife and mother are well-known.

Of what has she been accused?

Quite simply—of being unfaithful to her husband the Shah!

The rumor has moreover widely crossed the frontiers of Iran—to spread over the whole of Europe like wildfire. In Germany, in England, in France even, it is the subject of impassioned conversations in all the Iranian colonies abroad.

On what does the terrible accusation which today has Farah in its sights *rely*?

For the last three months, one has observed that one man never leaves Farah's side. It's *true*: wherever she goes, he is always there dancing attendance. Ten days ago he even went to rejoin her secretly in Teheran.

It was last October when he made his appearance at the side of the Empress.

Last October 17, *in fact*, they took a drive, just the two of them, in the blue Mercedes of the Iranian embassy to the Ile Saint-Louis in Paris. There, they went to have dinner together at L'Orangerie, Jean-Claude Brialy's restaurant. They stayed there from 9 o'clock to 1 o'clock in the morning.

The next day, it was almost the same scenario: at 1:30 P.M. the Mercedes parked in front of the famous Right Bank restaurant Lassere. Farah and her faithful companion lunched there and left at 3:45. The Mercedes next took them to the Rue François Premier, to a famous optician. For one hour Farah tried on several pairs of dark glasses, and her companion advised her on her choice.

Friday the 19th, a day consecrated to Farah's official receptions, while she—among others—dined at the Elysée Palace with the President and Mme. Pompidou, the man remained invisible.

But that night he took a special airplane to Orly to welcome Farah Saturday morning at the Nice airport and to act as tour guide during her stay on the Côte d'Azur.

He first accompanied her to the Hotel Negresco where they each had a suite on the same floor.

Then they went out to visit the Chagall Museum at Saint-Paul-de-Vence.

To her aunt, Mme. Louise Ghotbi, the Empress then confided: He's attractive, lively, merry, athletic, dynamic. In short, all that I lack in Iran.

It needed no more for the enemies of Farah to crow triumphantly: "Look how she flaunts herself with the man! She even goes so far as to avow he pleases her."

The truth is completely different: *France-Dimanche* has uncovered the astounding identity of Farah's white knight. And this revelation puts the Empress above all suspicion. The man who accompanied her everywhere for three months is none other than . . . the former King of Greece, Constantin.

Attacks

Ah, but even this has not unhorsed the Empress' detractors.

"Constantin's house has its ups and downs," they insinuate, *"and besides, the ex-King knows full well now he no longer has any chance to remount the throne of Greece . . ."*

The slanderers in their blind hatred are simply forgetting one essential fact: that is the Shah himself who asked Constantin to accompany Farah in her travels, in the capacity of Steward of the journeys of the Court.

They also forget that despite the clouds which have often darkened their union, Anne-Marie and Constantin are husband and wife. Moreover Ann-Marie came to join her husband and Farah on the Côte d'Azur.

> *And above all the Shah's enemies forget the respect which Constantin shows for Farah—it is not he who at the time of their first meeting said to her, when she only the little commoner fiancée of the Shah:*
>
> "Protocol would demand that I call you 'Mademoiselle' still. Permit me to call you 'Majesty' already, because you are the breed of Chiefs of State."
>
> Well then, in the face of the repeated attacks which are aimed at Farah and the Shah one can only conclude: it's a question of an odious plot. A plot to topple the Shah and Farah, to chase the Empress from the throne.
>
> This plot, it must be said, has surfaced at the worst moment for the imperial couple. At the moment when the Shah is leaving for Vienna to have made a serious examination of his health, which is troubling him. At the moment when Farah herself is very depressed by the slanders and is crushed by rumours which say the Shah wants a divorce.
>
> Baron d'Urdal
Extract from France-Dimanche
December 1974

The text, then, is referential. Just as a fictional text contains signs indicating that the question of truth should be suspended, the referential text presents itself explicitly as true. The question true-or-false is pertinent, and the true ought to carry the day. This text, which was published in a material frame—the daily paper—already referential, contains moreover the following indications:

- verb time: the present.
- other deictic elements establishing contact with the contemporary reader (December, 1974). Example: "this time."
- elements of history: the former king of Greece, the Shah, Farah, Paris, Tehran, Nice.
- the thematization of the question true-or-false.

This text self-reflexively reasserts its truth-claim.

WHAT IS IT ABOUT?

Taken as a whole, the text treats two themes. The content is composed of two layers which are in a hierarchical relationship.

1. A *slander*. The title indicates this already: Accused! The slander is attacked by the text. The journalist gives his opinion: what a scandal, this slander. The slander is the object of narration, and the narrator denounces it. While the text is developing an opinion, it is *discursive*. That

is the first layer of meaning. It involves an argumentative discourse which defends a thesis: the slander is false. Very much as it should be.
2. The second layer is hierarchically subordinate (in the technical sense of pragmatic narratology) to the first meaning. It is the content of the slander. This layer is a series of events, caused and experienced by the actors: a fabula. The text of the slander is *reported* (indirectly). This reported text contains a story: it is *narrative*.

A primary layer, discursive, and an embedded layer, narrative: the relationship between the two will be determinative for the semantic effect of the text. It is often supposed that in general a primary text dominates semantically an embedded text (see, among others, Doležel 1980). Thus, in a novel, the text of the narrator dominates the dialogue of the characters. He is able to comment on them, question their meaning, relativize them, make them the objects of his irony, even disown them. When, as in our text, the primary text is in addition discursive, it has, even explicitly, the goal of convincing the reader to follow the opinion of the first narrator (let's call him, for terminological convenience and by analogy with narrator, "the discourser") concerning the second content. Thus, we already have two reasons for supposing that the first text determines the meaning of the whole: one narratological, the other argumentative.

Starting from this hypothesis, which I propose to put to the test in an analysis of the article on Farah, I will attempt to extend it to a generalization. The general hypothesis will thus be:

> Narrativity confers on a text a greater force than discursivity confers. Its force resides in its surreptitious nature. Narrativity raises the question of denouement. Suspense—"how will this turn out?"—makes us forget the question true-or-false. Discourse persuades, narration seduces. Why, you may ask? Because the narrative text, presenting "slices of life," makes us think of life, of *our* life: it's always, among other things, an *iconic* sign. Discourse is the domain of the symbolic, narration the domain of the iconic. And icons seduce: specular reflection tends to undo discursive reflection.

To verify the hypothesis, it is necessary to reformulate the initial question: what is recounted in the second layer? what does the whole of the text signify? what is the function of narrativity in the ordering of the signs of this global message?

THE FRAME

In the second paragraph the question of imperial infidelity is raised. The *on-dit* is not contradicted. By his tone (slander, enemies) the journalist distances himself from the rumor. The result is ambiguity. An example: the slanderers pretend that the Shah might have a legitimate heir elsewhere. Without even taking into account the mechanics of "whatever printed is true," in other words the credibility of the daily paper as a cultural object, one can ascertain that the tone contradicts this fact. But the theme emphasized might very well shift in the process of this indirect denial. The possible conclusion might thus be: the Shah does not have a *legitimate* child anywhere else. That leaves open the possibility of illegitimate children. The idea is taken up again near the end: the Shah would like a divorce.

The frame, then, is: possible (probable) infidelity of the Shah.[1]

I call it a frame because there are no direct connections with the events to prepare the reader. The infidelity of the Shah renders that of his wife plausible. At the same time, paradoxically, this frame arouses sympathy for Farah-the-victim: a poor deceived woman. The two attitudes put in place, sympathy for the heroine and an opening for the possibility of her downfall, are indispensable for the reading of the narrative text. We ought to let ourselves be swept along, and for that it is necessary to be morally reassured.

INTRODUCTION OF THE CHARACTER

In paragraph three, still in the discursive portion, the character is presented. This introduction serves as a narrative hinge: within the discourse, the principal element of the fabula of the embedded text is presented to us, furnished with a number of attributes. Literally immaculate ("without stain"), a mother and devoted spouse, the heroine presented to us corresponds exactly to a literary and mythological image: the Holy Virgin, rehearsed throughout the history of western literature as the Lady of the chivalric romance. Whatever stereotypical attributes are conferred on her by this association are taken away from her from the realistic point of view, according to the convention that the "vraisemblable" and the true are opposed.[2]

As is well known, (stereo-)typing fictionalizes. As a result, the paradox is reinforced. On the one hand, Farah is of the type of the innocent woman, incapable of the betrayal of which the character is accused. On the other hand, she is a *type*, encircled with the halo of the literary tradition, with all that the tradition evokes (*sex, suspense, and sensation*). Thus the reader is set up to endorse a fundamental ambiguity: the woman of the story is interesting because literary, and at the same time already redeemed morally, and thus the way is cleared for the narrative portion of the article and *its* ambiguities.

---

1. The concept of frame is used here in a technical sense, as in "frame-story"; for this use, see my analysis of Duras' *Le vice-consul* in *On Story-Telling*. But the reader is well advised to keep in mind the impossibility to distinguish this technical sense from the social one as defined by Culler in *Framing the Sign* (1988). This essay is, precisely, about how technical pressures entail ideological pressures.

2. See Genette's seminal essay "vraisemblance et motivation" in *Figures II* (1969).

THE THEME OF THE STORY

Finally the content of the slander is revealed, or so it seems. In fact, suspense will be produced precisely through the gradual revelation, never completed. The exclamation point, suggesting moral indignation, absorbs the impact (discourse), all the while underlining the anecdotal character of the facts (with the meaning: this is important!). The reader may be unaware that in this key paragraph the accusation is not contradicted. Quite the contrary. This indecision, indispensable for the suspense that carries the reader along, must also remain unnoticed for the moral reassurance of the reader.

The paragraph which follows emphasizes the force of the rumor with the help of a *literarizing* and *personifying* metaphor. Thus, the rumor, having become a character, comes to play a part in the story which is its very own content. The semantic hierarchy is turned topsy-turvy. A second important point to be raised here is the fact that this paragraph comes *in place of* the contradiction promised and awaited, and, by this fact, lends support to the rumor. Hence, thirdly, such an expansion is an argument in favor of the rumor, following the cliché "There's no smoke without fire." These three points collaborate to bring about the transition from an expressed opinion, claiming the woman's innocence, into the opposite opinion whose subject is lost sight of.

The reader is now well prepared to receive the narration of a *story*, a compelling one. The desire for narrative has been sufficiently put in place. The question of paragraph six, sporting the verb "rely on," indicates the possibility of a stain, a defilement, a blot on the woman without stain. Apparently there is something on which the accusation might *rely* for support.[3]

The possibility of denial is no longer raised. Insofar as the argumentative line of the text has not been eliminated—indeed, the story replaces an argument within that line—the line of reasoning should be readjusted in light of the elimination of denial. Forced by "circumstances" of not circumstantial evidence, the subject of writing proposes that the facts be not denied, but, eventually, rendered futile.

Starting from paragraph seven, the series of events which constitutes the narrative portion of the text will only be interrupted at the end. The story is situated in time; the situation is laid out; the second actor takes the stage. The action is marked as durative, an aspect which is in addition accentuated by "no longer leaves" and "always."[4]

The story lasts three months and continues up to the present. This narrative technique has been familiar to us since Flaubert.

The temporal situation, so exact, combined with the absence of an *end*,

---

3. The French verb is "reposer" here. I read the verb as literally as possible.
4. For the concept of durative narration, see Genette 1980 and Bal 1986.

reinforces the realistic effect (which benefits from the polysemic nature of the term, see Hamon 1973). Indeed, coevalness seems to be achieved, historical reality evoked, and the reader is positioned in a temporal present in which this fabula takes place.

The theme of the story (adultery) is elaborated.[5]

From this point, three groups of signs are going to direct the reading. I consider their collaboration to be crucial for the effect of manipulation in the tabloid press:

- truth signs
- signs of suspense
- signs of romance

These three types of signs, all indexical, weave a web of intertextuality throughout the text.

Truth signs ("it's true") maintain the journalistic pretense of veridical reportage. Through them the reader remains tied to the argumentative text. Thus "ideally"—insofar as she is an ascenting reader—she will be protected against the insight that the content of the truth is slowly being transformed into its opposite. Let's call these signs *realistic*.

Signs of suspense reproduce the atmosphere of the mystery novel. "A man," for example, evokes the quest for the identity of a "culprit." All the signs which point to crime and sin, to secret and mystery, form a part of this group of signs of suspense, arousing the desire for discovery and detection.

The third type contains the signs which, less specifically linked to a literary genre, harken back to the romantic attitude which recurs throughout much of the western tradition, from romance to gothic, from fairy-tale to realist novel, in "popular" as in "high" literature—if there is any reason to give up that distinction, it is the equal importance of romance in both.[6]

These are the signs of the chivalric romance, of the sentimental novel, the signs of the prince-charming code of masculine conduct, which has a clearly defined place in reality as well. The effect of these signs is two-fold. Reality is fictionalized and vice versa; into fiction an illusion of reality insinuates itself, founded on déjà-vu. Whoever reads many novels of this genre is going to expect the same conduct on the part of men, and, inversely, she/he will be content with such conduct because it is romantic. The falseness is doubled. These are the *romance* signs.

Signs of these three types are found in many a text of this journalistic genre. They have great manipulative force: they transmit very effectively ideological

---

5. Adultery is obviously a theme loaded with ideological trickiness. In the history of western literature adultery is routinely performed by women, and men, being saddled with horns, are the victim. See Tanner's classical study of adultery in the novel.

6. An attitude by now critically analyzed by a host of feminist critics.

values which are already established but which need to be constantly reaffirmed and readjusted to a changing reality. These signs, especially those of the second and third types establish together a *literary* effect. This effect exculpates the credulity of the reader, because this literature is meant to be believed. This effect works only in combination with the realistic effect; otherwise it is useless. The theme of adultery is specified thus: the theme of love (romance) and the theme of crime and guilt (mystery) guarantee sympathy and suspense respectively; both are provided with a nuance of realism. We can cry with Emma Bovary and investigate with Maigret, and all this while reading the news of the day for our own edification and instruction. This is the traffic of images of today's doxa.

NARRATIVITY

The possible definitions of the narrative text are too well-known to dwell on them here. Up to this point I have been a proponent of the minimal definition of a semantic nature (Bremond 1966): a text whose content consists of a series of events caused and experienced by the actors. But there are other factors. Thus, from the pragmatic point of view, the narrative text is above all *constative language*, or, in Benveniste's sense (1971), *story* (that is to say "in the third person," having for object the one who is absent), while the discursive, argumentative text is first of all *performative language*, or in Benveniste's sense, *discourse* (that is, language which *does* something, which brings about a change, however slight, in the relationship between the "first and the second person"). As Derrida keeps insisting (e.g. *Limited Inc.*), this distinction is an impossible one to maintain in any ontological sense. No text is "pure" narrative nor "pure" argument. The distinction is crucial, however, to assess the various effects of discursive strategies. Hence, this distinction concerns here the starting-point of my hypothesis which posits exactly the contrary. But this does not contradict the pragmatic hypothesis in the sense that it supposes a result of *doing* which is effective through its secret, dissembled nature. This narrative language *does*/acts to the extent that it speaks "in the third person" *about* someone.[7]

A very important factor for our discussion is the concept of *focalization*. The narrative content is focalized. This is a characteristic so general that its efficiency goes without saying. In the present case, it is legitimate to suppose that the focalizing agency rests with the first narrator identifiable to the discursive subject. As soon as this subject transmits the actorial focalization, located with a diegetic actor, the first subject escapes his accountability to realism to the extent that the focalization enters the shadowy realm of semifiction that makes up the tabloid paper.

---

7. For its place in structuralist pragmatics, see Ducrot (1978).

In paragraph seven we read "one has observed." The choice of verb, a textual feature, is self-referential in referring to the pretense of realism. Observation implies the reality of the thing observed. It is the verb of perception referring to the most reliable kind of perception, charged as it is with the positivistic truth-claim of empiricist methodology. The choice of this verb, a realistic sign, is confirmed by the "it's true" which follows. But there is also the "one": there is a *one*, an anonymous subject of the focalization, a subject not yet named but virtually actorial, diegetic. This technique of the transition of focalization from outer to inner level reinforces the narrative character of the text. At the same time, paradoxically, the realistic effect is again reinforced: the focalizer, diegetic and therefore half-fictional, is also a *witness*.

THE EVENTS

The title *scenario* confirms the fictive character of the narrative text. There is a man. He has no name. His sudden appearance is a sign of mystery, his conduct ("at the side of") of romance. The insistence on the social status of the heroine signifies romance as well: the world of romance swarms with princesses and countesses. The exact date, the phrase "in fact" indicate realism.

The incredible complexity (*refinement*) of this text goes a long way. The journey in the blue car, apparently innocent, is not lost on a French audience which, as a result of an exorbitant school system, knows its classics, and has already been programmed to activate it. It recalls the mad course through Rouen during which Emma and Léon consummate their adultery. The allusion is two-fold: by literarizing the narration, in general at first, then in the romantic sense, the precise facts to which the sign refers can also enter into the journalistic content. Farah and her companion go to an island (called so; even if it is simply a neighborhood of Paris, yet historically significant), just as Emma and Léon pass their honeymoon on the island near Rouen (a city which, in addition, represents Paris for Emma).

Let me make it very clear at this juncture that the reader of this text will not enter into the detail of the intertextual interpretation. Yet that textual indifference does not alter a global effect based on *déjà-vu*, on the contrary. The effect of this intertextual web is dependent on the reader's vague sense of recognition that will not be tested against specific interpretation. Images emerge.

The designation "chic" of the car signifies the romance of the *beau monde*; the exact information on the restaurant and its owner reinforces realism. The focalizer is sketched in in some more detail here; he is well informed, credible, and plays a part in the world recounted. An ideology of class becomes very clear at this point. The atmosphere of wealth is associated with the still proclaimed innocence, the love of truth, and of other beautiful things. The anonymous focalizer's allegiance to this world give him a status beyond doubt.

The temporal precision shows to what extent the different signs are revealed. A reality sign in the first place, the detail "1 o'clock *in the morning*" is also a very effective sign of sin. Although the suspicious reader is able to note that the dinner only lasts four hours, it also lasts from evening to morning: the night.

Here comes into play the phenomenon of repetition. The word "scenario" recalls for us once again the fictive nature of the events, and also, perhaps, the bad faith of the actors whose role-playing is conduct intended to deceive—see Alpers (1988). Having remained convinced that the couple spent the night somewhere, the reader sees transformed in the telling, by the repetition, a unique escapade into a durative affair; the fact that the next day the visit to the three-star restaurant takes place in the afternoon becomes a useless detail which changes nothing about the facts: the two "go out together" regularly.

Cut to the disguise scene. Very clearly a mystery sign harking back to the crime to be concealed, the effect of fictionalization is also reinforced by the gallantry of the companion: romance. More subtle here are the signs of wealth ("a famous optician") and the specification of the focalizer. He/she is apparently an intimate acquaintance of the actors. He must have been in attendance near this event which took place in presumably a small boutique and lasted a full hour. For the whole passage depends, so far as focalization is concerned, on the verb "to observe" whose effect has not been annulled by any sign of disengaging. And the focalizer does not observe only the prolonged stay in the store, but also the contribution of the Man in the choice of dark glasses.

Lotman (1973) insists on the signifying force of the foiled expectation. Hamon (1977) points out that there is however a difference between "the notation of an absence and the absence of a notation." It is true that the scarcely remarked absence of an anticipated meaning can constitute a sign, but the case is clearer and the sign more powerful when the presence of the meaning is explicitly denied. In paragraph ten, printed in capitals for emphasis, this semiotic possibility is exploited. The absence of the Man reinforces his mystery. He is invisible (sign of mystery) but mentioned; his presence haunts the text.

The official events, a sign of romance referring to the *haut monde*, reaching back perhaps even to the world of classical tragedy to evoke the imminent catastrophe (there are no more vague princesses but historical personages), contrast with the absence of the Man who conceals himself without doubt for good reason. The names Pompidou and Elysée Palace are obviously also realistic signs.

We have already seen several examples of illogical oppositions. Above all the inflection of the pretension to truth functions in this sense. Here the word "but," marking the opposition between temporary absence and permanent presence, has not appeared to acquit the couple. The timing is again interesting: evening. The Man hastens to rejoin his Lady at the hour of love; the fact that he does not find her until the morning of the next day is just barely enough to avoid tedious juridical charges of slander, but hardly undoes the effect of the remarks which precede. The reception, the guided tour enter perfectly into the frame of romantic expectation, semi-realistic, centered on the conduct of the sexual classes. The "suite on the same floor"—it is unnecessary to say more—is, in this context, a sign of sin.

In narrative literature, the theme of the voyage as setting for the high points of a story is well-known. In Agatha Christie the murder is often committed during a voyage: on a train, on a plane, on a ship. I have already evoked the ride through Rouen and the journey on board ship in *Madame Bovary*. Anna Karenina meets her lover on a train. Thus, the stay on the Côte d'Azur, the plane trip, the grand Hotel, all enter into the two systems of meaning—mystery literature and romance provide plentiful images.

THE MALE CHARACTERS

In paragraph thirteen the actor the Man is furnished with individualizing features; he is becoming a character. The information is not given this time by the anonymous diegetic focalizer, but by the heroine herself. The direct discourse implies that she also chose the words with which the image is painted. This reinforces the pretension to realism. But the anonymous focalizer who has dominated the observations up to this point does not truly give up his power. In the first place, the very fact of the citation proves that he has access to the words cited; he has therefore access to the fairy-tale world where the story is played out, he forms a part of it. But at the same time the process of citation of a private conversation belongs to the process of fictionalization. Theoretically, the embedded text or hypotext is subordinated to the influence of the primary text wherein it is inserted, unknown to the secondary locutors (see Pelc 1971). It has then a functional place, in fact and in principle, with regard to the primary text, where it supplies a complement. Only the heroine can complete the image of the Man, since the core of the story is her relationship with him. The positive character of the underlying premises provided does not contradict the suppositions of the story—quite the contrary. Thus the expectation that Farah will supply something to contradict the rumor is once again foiled.

Six characteristics of the Man are mentioned of which the sixth ("all that I lack in Iran"), a summary of the five others, in making explicit the comparison permits us to compare thus the semantic axes of the two men, the Man (Lover?) and the husband (cuckolded? we still don't know for sure).

	attractive	lively	merry	athletic	dynamic
The man	+	+	+	+	+
The Shah	—	—	—	—	—

Since the two men are so radically opposed, it is legitimate to suppose this opposition to be general, which is justified by the final comparison. One can therefore fill in also the trait which has been marked for the Shah and not (yet) for the Man: fidelity. The Shah, with the suggestion of an illegitimate son, is not faithful; the Man will therefore be faithful. This hypothesis collides with another expectation: the conduct of the male in general, in opposition to the conduct of women, and that of the scandal in the particular case which occupies us. I will return to this.

OTHER SHIFTS

The hypotext of paragraph fourteen, spoken by the enemy, would seem, then, to contradict the content of Farah's text. Once again, this expectation is overturned, and one glides from one isotopy to another. Enemy and victim seem to be altogether in agreement. She goes all the way to a *confession* ("that he pleases her"). We see here the semantic power of the attributive verb (Prince 1982). Farah's opinion on the subject of the Man is not sufficient to draw a conclusion: the verb "avow," a sign of mystery, turns a favorable opinion into a crime. This kind of *glissement* has been a constant resort of the semantic dynamic of the text from the beginning. The following case is the clearest and shows the importance of an elementary habit of logic for the education of the reader. "The truth is completely different": this contradicts what precedes. Logically, what follows should contradict the notion that the Man pleases Farah, because this had been stated in the preceding phrase. The expected line of reasoning, then, is:

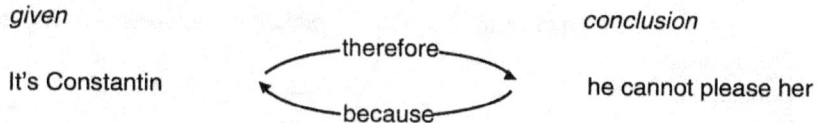

The reasoning is absurd, but the logic of the text implies it. "In truth" it happens otherwise. The discursive argument, that is to say, the beginning of opposition which is called up to reassure us, is quickly lost sight of for the reader who is drawn along by the narrativity, where the revelation of the identity of the culprit (sign of mystery) evokes suspense. The pretension to argumentation is not therefore gratuitous; it is a very effective method of reassuring the reader, of convincing him of his own good faith and that of the journalist.

The relationship between discourse and narration continues according to this model: apparent oppositions, whose first term belongs to the argument and whose second term is replaced by a narrative element which is not at all opposed to the first term. The "arguments" corroborate, the literary signs are employed to great effect. For example, the fact that it is the Shah himself who has appointed Constantin "steward of the travels (!) of the court" only renders his "cuckolding" more probable. The problems between Constantin and Anne-Marie reinforce the probability of the affair. Constantin's *respect* transforms a "porn" scandal into a romance. This transformation is necessary to resolve a fundamental contradiction.

FIDELITY NEUTRALIZED

The opposition between the Shah and Constantin can carry over also to the motif of their respective fidelity. This creates a problem. If Constantin is an opponent worthy of the Shah—which is necessary for romantic justification— he should be faithful. But in this case he would not be able to respond to the exigencies of the fabula, i.e., to have an amorous relationship with Farah—he is married.

This problem is neutralized by another opposition, implicit but ever present, which permits another distribution of the characters' features. This division does not reapportion the good and the bad, but the males and the females. The men are unfaithful, can afford to be within certain limits (the limits of discretion); the women are victims, of the infidelities of their husbands, and of untruthful rumors. Thus, the infidelity of men is no longer negative but neutral (permitted but not prescribed, see Hamon 1977: 152). The semiotic axes will therefore be:

	attractive (the 5 traits)	*faithful*	*aggressor* (⇔victim)
The Shah	—	—	+
Constantin	+	—	+
Farah	Ø	Ø	—
Anne-Marie	Ø	Ø	—

Several conclusions can be deduced from this division of features. The opposition between the two men deals with only one aspect, which is decisive for the morality of the text: attractiveness, charm justify infidelity. The last axis is indissolubly linked to masculinity. We observe also how unimportant the semantic content of the female characters is. They are marked in the same manner, both negatively, as the very features which determine the events are not marked for them.

IDENTITIES REVEALED

We have seen that the identity of the Man was an important springboard for the effect of suspense in the narrative text. This is strikingly obvious if we take into account its lay-out on the page. Not only have capitals been used to put in relief the factors which promote suspense; more than that, the page contains a photograph of Farah and Constantin, represented arm-in-arm, roaring with laughter. Although such a photo does not prove anything like a sexual affair, this photo obviously contributes to the credibility of the facts recounted, and of the scandalous conclusion they suggest: this is circumstantial evidence of another kind. More to the point for this discussion of the powers of narrative is the odd futility of this photo. Although it had been glaring the readers in the face for the whole duration of their reading, the question of the identity of the Man, visually revealed, is verbally kept unanswered.[8]

But the narrative desire is so powerful that the photo does not at all prevent the question of identity from functioning. This has been tried out with a group of freshmen students. These students did not form the public for whom the text was intended. They were better educated than the average reader of *France-Dimanche*. They were aware that they were taking the class to learn the techniques of reading against manipulation; it was a class in resistant reading. They were thus forewarned as much as possible. Despite this privileged position, only one person of fifty assumed the author's intention to be more complex than to innocent Farah, the message being transmitted to have more ideological strands than one. She formulated the message as she understood it thus: "The journalist pretends to contradict the rumor that Farah and Constantin have an amorous attachment, but in fact he is confirming this rumor." The others formulated the message across the whole text in variations of this formulation: "The journalist would prefer that this were not true, he does everything to deny the scandal, but the facts speak for themselves." Thus success lay totally at the feet of the journalist, and my teaching had come to naught up to that point.[9] Focalizer, anonymous but diegetic, observer of the events, intimate friend, on enviably close terms with people in high places: the signatory of the text, Baron d'Urdal, complete with his title of nobility. The title justifies the supposition that the focalizer has a place in the world in which the story unfolds. The title upholds the pretense of realism just as it supports the romance. One can go so far as to interpret the name itself, recovering from it an anagram of the name Landru, murderer of women much romanticized, or

---

8. Most students in the class where I worked with this text were quite confused when I confronted them with the visual evidence; they had been fantasizing, not really about the identity of the Man, but about his mystery.

9. The question the students were asked to answer in writing was: "what is the author's message, and what do you believe?"

of the name Durrendal, the blade which in the Middle Ages cut straight to the truth of a question. But these associations, by definition a little gratuitous, are not indispensable to the interpretation of the focalizer as real and fictional, the mysterious Mr. Harley Quin who helps the reader to see the truth by means of images.[10]

ACTANTIAL MODELS SUPERIMPOSED

An actantial analysis of the various levels of the text permits us to bring to light once again the forces in play in this hypothetical reading. Let us take first of all Constantin. His actions are all directed at his reunion with Farah. I am using the model from 1966. Greimas himself later abandoned the opponent and helper actants, in order to make of them competitive subjects. I am not altogether happy with this modification. It deprives us of the possibility of distinguishing between autonomous and embedded subjects. Autonomous subjects each pursue an object of their own and can each cross in his/her enterprise the enterprise of a rival subject. It remains difficult to say who is subject and who is anti-subject?—are there other criteria than chronological priority or moral approbation, neither very satisfactory? Embedded subjects are better referred to as helpers or opponents, for whom no narrative program is presented in the story. The problems emerge clearly in Greimas' own sample analysis (1976). So I will keep to the earlier model. Here is my analysis of the first diegetic level:

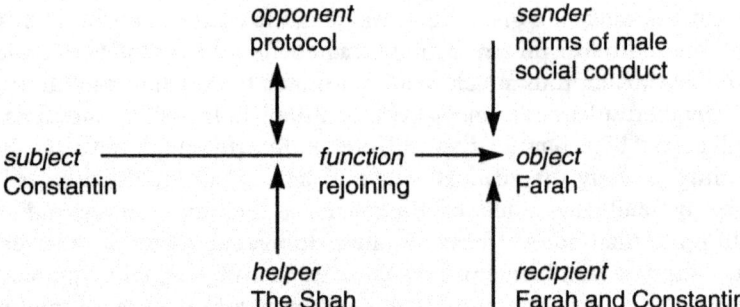

This model accounts for the facts which are least contested, least hidden ("it's true") in the content of the rumor, which is authenticated by them (Doležel 1980). The success of this enterprise gives rise to a new subject, a double subject this time: Farah and Constantin who should, in order to avoid scandal, protect their secret.

10. The allusion is to the figure of Mr. Harley Quin in a collection of short stories by Agatha Christie. Quin is an embodiment of the function of the focalizer: by showing what there is for the reader to see, he enables the latter to make his own discoveries. He does not tell, as an authorial narrator would do, but shows. Christie (1984).

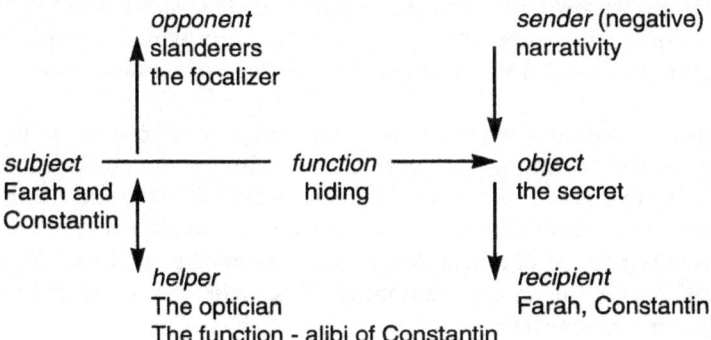

This second model takes into account the thin line between argumentative discourse and narration. The enterprise fails because the sender (*destinateur*), the narrativity, does not sustain it except in appearance. According to convention, a narration embedded in a discourse serves as support, as proof, as verification ("the facts speak for themselves"). Here, as in a number of texts of the genre which we are examining, this principle serves as an alibi for the opposite enterprise. It seems to me helpful to apply the actantial model to the ultimate enterprise as well—the one in which the two others are embedded: that of Baron d'Urdal, the super-detective.

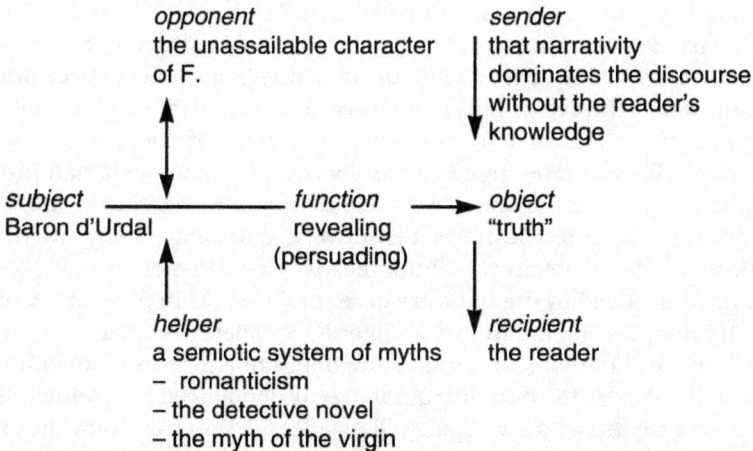

The success of this enterprise is obvious. Every detail counts. Thus, the sentiments of the reader, who is in effect the receiver of the enterprise of which only the object remains hidden, give him confidence in the journalist: the journalist works "for his good." Even the indiscretion and the futility of pursuing a question which concerns the private lives of others does not enter into the case.

The hypothesis which I wished to put to the test in this analysis concerns the techniques of manipulation proper to narration which are found in the journalism of news-items. This question has been examined many times before.[11]

The justification for reexamining so familiar a subject resides in the restrictions which I have imposed on myself. I have limited the analysis to locating certain narrative processes in the interaction between text and reader: intertextuality (direct and indirect citation), suspense, focalization, and the teleological enterprise. A key position in the assemblage of these processes is occupied by the concept of hierarchy. This centrality of so problematic a concept requires a remark.

The misunderstandings born of the use which Genette makes of the notion of hierarchy have revealed a regrettable confusion. Genette, speaking of the embedding in *Manon Lescaut*, says simply that the speech of the Chevalier Des Grieux is narratively subordinate to that of the marquis-narrator of *Mémoires d'un homme de qualité*, something altogether obvious to anyone who has read the novel. To be sure, the very idea of hierarchy is a bit suspect because of its authoritarian connotations. But strangely enough it, has merely been criticized in the name of tradition (Bronzwaer 1970). One commentator supports the opposition with the statement, also obvious, that the text uttered by Des Grieux is the more important of the two, and cannot therefore be secondary. Let's not play word games. Genette had in mind a hierarchy of technique.

The first locutor of the text, having the choice of citing others in it, has in fact a power which influences, without altogether being able to determine, the meaning of the entire text. This is not to say that the meaning of the embedded text would not be able to dominate semantically that of the primary text. The analysis conducted here suggests the contrary. But between narrative and semantic hierarchies, the one fixed, the other mobile, there is no *indifference*. The meaning is proposed, never definitively, but solely, and partially, in a situation which is precisely communicative, hence, not monologic. The meaning is proposed by the interplay of semiotic factors in play. In the present case, the narrative hierarchy which affords complete confidence in the first locutor, is put into place to produce the opposite effect, the semantic domination of the second locutor, the rumor overtly denounced with which the first locutor is surreptitiously associated. This effect is achieved from the start by the reassuring setting of the authority of the morally *good* journalist, by the collaboration of appeals judiciously orchestrated to the preconceived ideas of the reader, couched in terms from the common store of myths and proverbs.

---

11. See, for example, Niel 1973: 70–98; see also Van den Heuvel 1980, who was inspired by an oral version of the present essay.

The processes mapped out are without efficacy whatsoever if the reader:

- does not recognize the myths and texts in question (here, a member of a society which does not venerate chastity would not be familiar with the image of the virgin; to a lesser extent, whoever would not recognize *Madame Bovary* may miss the allusion to adultery in the ride through Paris);
- is not sensitive to the effect of suspense, linked to the mystery novel which, let us remember, is an authoritarian genre predicated upon the protection of the established order;
- is provided with a competence in logic sufficient to thwart the power of the narrativity.

It is necessary, then, in order to manipulate, to have a manipulable addressee. But these appeals—and I return once again to the confusion between technical processes and ideological meaning—function *by means of* such processes as the diegetization of the focalizer, oppositions set up between the characters, suspense, and actantial enterprise. These are the processes which realize the effective meaning, which transmit it in the process of semiosis.

The use of the actantial analysis also requires a brief note. Certain commentators (among others Zima 1979) have denounced its ideological character, and they are not mistaken. The reification of persons is not, in so far as it is an ideological act, very different from the personification of things. By installing as actants mountains, ideas, classes, Greimas set himself up for this attack. But it is possible not to give in to a naive faith in the scientifically objective status (a contradiction in terms in every other context) of the model, and to make use of it altogether differently. Seen as a model not of the ultimate truth of the narrativity, but, more pertinently, as the model of a teleological enterprise, itself ideological which can be seen to function in narrative texts and sustain their effect, the actantial model can be a conceptual tool well fitted for bringing to light ideological aspects in a text as they fit the map of this mastercode of ideology: teleology and dualism. It is in this way that the model is used here as it was in chapter 3.

The linear reading I have carried out, and my reluctance to come up with a preliminary exposition of my methodology have the same source. I wished to demonstrate the progressive construction of a possible world which represents the ideology to be promoted. It was necessary therefore to follow the unfolding of the text and to point out its strategies step by step. By the same token, a pre-established theoretical model, a rigid procedure would be less convincing in this case in which I aimed to give an account of *what happens*. The restrictions discussed above show I do not, however, request my reader to presume innocence of the analysis. Just like the Baron d'Urdal I was, on my part, busy *persuading*.

▪12▪

Body Politic

A paradoxical sketch in the corpus of visual art called "Rembrandt"[1] represents the central scene of Judges 19 (see figure 1). The sketch is paradoxical because it is a statement about death signified by the movement of the dead body. This paradox can be understood as we shift attention from the represented content to the mode of representation. Then, by the incongruous twist which brings death itself to life, the pictorial sign of movement becomes a crucial token of self-reflexivity. But reversing this perspective, we can also say that reflection on pictorial representation is in an important way focused on death. And the dead, here, is a woman.

In this essay, I would like to consider a few relationships between death, women, and representation through an analysis of cultural objects chosen from the four bodies of texts I have been working with up till now: French literature, my initial field; Biblical narrative, a field I encountered when trying to historicize narrative; critical texts, which I began to examine when I discovered *their* use of narrative as a form of argumentation; and visual images, my most recent interest, where forms of narrativity occur which challenge the linguo-centric assumptions of much literary theory. The common ground is narrative, used whether the medium is verbal, visual, or bodily. Narrative as a mode of implicit argumentation is the line which runs through my work on all these different bodies of writing. Narrative as a mode of representation is a tool of manipulation, a figure of rhetoric, and that is my obsession.

---

1. I put the artist's name in quotation marks to emphasize that I consider this work as a text, comparable to "Shakespeare" or "the Bible." I am not interested in the currently hotly debated issue of authenticity and authorship. The body of work that Western culture has considered throughout the past two centuries as "Rembrandt" constitutes a cultural construct, which in my view includes writings about it/"him," borrowings from it, and creative responses such as poetry inspired by it. The quotation marks, then, are a shorthand rendering of my view about "the artist" in our culture.

264 ■ ON MEANING-MAKING

Figure 1: Rembrandt, *The Levite Finds His Concubine in the Morning*. Berlin-Dahlem, Gemäldengalerie

It took me a while to see the connection between this obsession and my other one, with death. Death is a challenge to representation to the extent that the experience of death is a moment that nobody can describe, an event that nobody can escape, a process that nobody can narrate. Representation partakes of the attempt to quell the fear of death and to compensate for the loss of identity and material existence death entails. The representation of death as both gendered and representational, therefore, can shed new light on the diverse aspects of the ideological positions toward gender that texts and images enable their readers to project. This is possible because of death's centrality in the definition of life.

I will begin with a story of an episode in the life of a secular biblical reader, social critic, and educator, whose work was the subject of the first paper I wrote as a beginning student in Amsterdam, someone who, had he lived today, would be an academic, but would have trouble getting tenure because of personality problems. On June 9th, 1762 the Parlement de Paris had issued a *prise de corps* against Jean-Jacques Rousseau, author of *Emile ou l'Éducation*. Rousseau fled Paris at night, suspecting a woman friend, la maréchale de Montmorency, to have precipitated the decree. During his flight he wrote a short story, "Le Lévite d'Ephraim," a rewriting of the most horrible story of the Hebrew Bible, Judges 19 through 21. It is the story of the rejection, gang-rape, murder and dismemberment of a young woman whose body is subsequently used as writing. After her death or as an act of murder, her husband cuts her body into twelve pieces which he sends to the tribes as a call for war. Asking why Rousseau wrote this particular story and how, and what the "why" has to do with the "how," is to raise questions of criticism as an act motivated by and performed in a gendered context.

Rousseau feels good about his tale. He writes that he never rereads it without an "interior satisfaction" that stems from a decent, even glorious feeling.[2] This feeling mirrors the one that motivated him to write it, which he describes thus:

> Drowning in a sea of misfortune, crushed beneath the evil deeds of my ungrateful and barbarous contemporaries, the only one from which I escape and which remains with them to avenge me is that of hatred.[3]

This sentence is deeply ambiguous because of the nominalization of the verb "to hate"; it does not enable us to know who could hate whom but doesn't

---

2. He wrote in the first project for a preface to a volume which was to include this tale:
... je ne le relis jamais sans une satisfaction intérieure, non par une sotte vanité d'auteur, dont l'ineptie en ce point seroit inexcusable, mais par un sentiment plus honnête et dont j'ose même me glorifier. *Oeuvres complètes* II,(Paris: Editions Gallimard, 1961), 1205.
3. "Noyé dans une mer d'infortune, accablé de maux par mes ingrats et barbares contemporains, un seul auquel j'échappe en dépit d'eux et qui leur reste pour ma vengeance est celui de la haine." The ambiguity of the sentence has been preserved in the translation.

("escape").⁴ This conflation of the position of the critic and the view projected from that position onto the story is the phantom that lurks behind every attempt at description through writing. It happens precisely at the point where the disentanglement of self from other is most emphatically claimed. It is this ambiguous starting point, the question of hatred and its subjects, that guides our reading of the story which it mirrors, and which is a reading of the biblical story which *it* mirrors.

Rousseau's reading of Judges triggered a brilliant reading by Peggy Kamuf in the chapter "Author of a Crime" in *Signature Pieces*. Kamuf discusses how Rousseau's text is a mediation between three levels of occupation for his mind: his flight from Paris, the story of vengeance, and his writing. The first level is already ambiguous. Is Rousseau a criminal escaping justice, as his "barbarous contemporaries" doubtlessly considered him? Then his need to write the story of the Levite allows identification with this character. Or is he a victim of *in*justice, as he clearly sees himself? Then he might identify with the woman in the story, who is so utterly innocent and so utterly victimized. The second level, the story supposedly of a vengence which goes awry and which, as Kamuf demonstrates, cannot but *repeat* the crime it is supposed to avenge, engages the critic to assess the "deviations" from the Judges text, and perhaps try to explain those deviations with reference to Rousseau's own preoccupations. This is the role I cast Kamuf in. The inevitable narrative entanglement of the critic in the text is staged from the start when Kamuf repeats Rousseau's emphasis on *vengeance*. Rousseau's repressed and denied desire for vengeance motivates his distortion which appropriates the woman's plight, and I would speculate that Kamuf's endorsement of this distortion is motivated by her argumentative agenda, which is to focus on writing.

The intermediate level of occupation, the writing of Rousseau's reading, mirrors my own occupation as a scholar, and that of most people engaged in criticism or scholarship. Although critics are not often fleeing arrest by the police while writing, at least not in contemporary Western societies, they *are* engaged in writing, in reading, in struggling for a mediation between these two; they are engaged in defending stakes which vary and intersect between political, gender, ethnic, religious, and academic interests. Among these stakes, the claim to pursue and find the "truth" is both the basis and the problem of the academic endeavor.

Rousseau's struggle with the "truth" of *his* story, acted out in his position between reader and writer involves at least eight different mediations (I am

---

4. Nominalization of the verb is one of the means of ideological manipulation, working to obscure the subject responsible for the action. See Günther Kress and and Robert Hodge, *Language as Ideology* (London: Routledge and Kegan Paul, 1979). I have discussed Kress & Hodge's theoretical categories and their usefulness for a critical narratology, in particular for a literary and biblical interpretation, in my book *On Story-Telling: Essays in Narratology* (Sonoma: Polebridge Press 1991). In Rousseau's sentence, the resulting ambiguity concerning the subject and object of hatred is part and parcel of the flabbergasting complexity of Rouseauian discourse on moral values.

expanding here Kamuf's comments). First, Rousseau presents writing as a way to distract his mind from level one: his situation of flight. He phrases the distraction as "donner le change," an ambiguous phrase that Derrida makes an emblem of his concept of the *supplement* in *Of Grammatology*.[5] The expression "donner le change" refers to distracting, in hunting, not the self but the other, the victim, not the hunter. Hence, the use of this expression suggests that Rousseau feels split, and wishes to consider his worries as the enemy. The phrase thereby suggests that split as the subject is, he cannot rid himself of his other, enemy self. But rather than splitting his enemy off, he incorporates it/them/her. In order to do that, he must make the woman guilty of her *prise de corps*.

Second, the writing mediates between the first and the second level, between Rousseau as fleeing criminal or victim, and the Levite and his "concubine," the people in his story. Needless to say, their moral status mirrors his, and therefore matters to him. Third, the writing is a mediation between reading and writing. Rousseau was reading Judges when he was compelled to flee. Writing cannot be a faithful rendering of our reading. While the reading is already engaged in the prospective writing, the writing can't quite match the reading. The effort to write writes itself into the writing. That effort shows in Rousseau's insistence on *voice*, the natural but perverted origin of language, and the way it is taken over by sight, the instrument of writing and reading. Kamuf's effort to write is mirrored in her insistence on writing.

Fourth, Rousseau's writing mediates between the two characters of the story and the role of their respective gender-positions as the motor of the narrative. I have suggested that Rousseau had reasons to identify both with the Levite and with the woman, and his sense of victimization certainly forced him into that androgynic role. For example, he makes the Levite die, too—of grief, or hatred, or desire for revenge, all the feelings he denied himself. Then—fifth mediation—there is a mediation between the two moods and modes Rousseau constantly feels involved in: the happy disposition he prides himself on, which produces the idyllic mode, and his paranoid tendencies, evoking the tragic. On the one hand, his own determination not to hate but to love his fellow humans; on the other hand, the mode of his rewriting of the story which hovers between the conventions of sweet and sour. This conflict is more than just one of literary taste; it has a bearing on his gender-politics. When he describes the second separation of the woman from her family, the political agenda of the author of *Emile* transpires clearly in the idyllic tone of the following sentence, which almost sounds like a blurb for the nuclear family:

> How happy is the family which in its purest union spends its peaceful days in the bosom of friendship and seems to have but one heart for all its members.[6]

5. Kamuf, 82, commenting on Derrida (1976:154).
6. "Heureuse famille qui dans l'union la plus pure coule au sein de l'amitié ses paisibles jours,

The idyllic tone of this encomium forecasts the emphasis on the particular kind of barbarism to come, and which is figured on the ground of the structure of the family. The particular figuration of this "ground"—"seems to have but one heart for all its members"—adopts the contrast between idyll and tragedy as a mode of writing, in that it prefigures its negative, the dismemberment of the woman's body, one heart for all its dispersed members indeed.

In relation to this, the writing mediates—six—between manner and substance. The manner inscribes a number of claims into the story. One example must suffice. In addition to the problematic conflict of modes, Rousseau begins his story with a quadruple address, and evokes the *Iliad*, that other founding text of Western civilization:

> (1) Hallowed rage of fortune, come animate my voice; I will tell of the crimes of Benjamin and the revenge of Israel; I will tell of unmatched infamy and of even more terrible punishments. (2) Mortals, respect beauty, customs, hospitality; be just without cruelty, merciful without weakness, and know how to pardon the guilty rather than punish the innocent.
> (3) O you, good-natured men, enemies of all inhumanity, you who, fearing to confront the crimes of your brothers, prefer to let them go unpunished . . . .
> (4) Blessed people, gather yourself; pronounce judgment . . .[7]

The claim against vengeance is undermined by this allusion to *the* story of vengeance, while the contradiction between the appeal to mercy in the second, and the exhortation to punish in the third address, make the writer's moral position unclear. The fourth address, a call for judgment, shifts from crime to vengeance, and turns the *prise de corps* into the crime to be judged. The allusion to the *Iliad* positions the story as an epic, a genre of male heroism and national wars. And it appeals to the muse, a feminine image of inspiration, *as* rage.[8] Where Homer begins his epic with "Sing, Goddess, the anger of

---

et semble n'avoir qu'un coeur à tous ses membres" (Rousseau, II,1212). Again, the sentence is highly ambiguous, so much so that the contradictory meanings cancel each other out in what Derrida would call a dissemination: the use of the word "membres" in a story about dimemberment, of "coeur" where the heart is subordinated to tribal interests, and the insistence on "peace" in a story about violence take all possible innocence away from the language. See Derrida, 1981.

7. Sainte colère de la vertu, viens animer ma voix; je dirai les crimes de Benjamin, et les vengeances d'Israel; je dirai les forfaits inouis, et des chatiments encore plus terribles. Mortels, respectez la beauté, les moeurs, l'hospitalité, soyez juste sans cruauté, miséricordieux sans foiblese; et sachez pardonner au coupable plustôt que de punir l'innocent.

O vous, hommes débonnaires, ennemis de toute inhumanité; vous qui, de peur d'envisager les crimes de vos frères, aimez mieux les laisser inpunis . . .

Peuple saint, rassemble-toi; prononce sur cet acte horrible . . . (Rousseau, II, 1208)

8. The allusion has a slightly stronger effect in French because of the feminine gender of the words "colère" and "vertu." The phrase "Sainte colère de la vertu" is an apostrophe addressed through the feminine nouns to the female goddess of inspiration. On apostrophe as a central device in lyric, see Jonathan Culler, "Apostrophe," in 1981: 135–154. For the political effect of apostrophe's centrality for lyric, see Barbara Johnson, 1987.

Peleus' son Achilleus and its devastation," objectifying the rage, and Virgil begins *his* rewriting with "*I* sing of arms and of a man," disposing of the rage and the muse altogether, Rousseau places the rage within the subject of inspiration, sacred as Homer's goddess, and the voice singing it—he calls his chapters *chants*, songs—in himself, as in Virgil. Hence, the story is recast as a story of revenge from the start, in a complex way writing woman into it as a subject of semiosis, but not as the damaged party.

If rage is Rousseau's muse, then, his claim that hatred and revenge are staying with his enemies is either a lie or an avowal of the cultural dispersion of his writing: he writes through them. The author dissolves into the doxa. And his story, too, is about a war about a woman, and the allusion suggests it is caused by a woman. Thus he is doing what he announced: *donner le change*, divert his enemy and his mind—by blaming the victim.

Seventh, Kamuf points out that the writing hovers between a flight from and a submission to vengeance. The Levite's act of throwing out his wife to be gang-raped in order to save himself becomes thus the founding act the writing repeats. For this act *is* a flight from vengeance *by* a submission to it, albeit that the subject of submission is split off from the subject of flight. Rousseau's double identification, with the Levite and with his wife, serves to exorcise this ambivalence.

Finally, the writing, framed by the preface which positions the author in a reality so similar to that of the story, mediates between fiction and history. Choosing a story that is both far removed from the reality of his day and, by virtue of its status in a canonical book of historiography, not disposable as "just a fiction," the writing offers allegorical relations to Rousseau's interests. This is the more effective as the Judges story itself has systematically been "redeemed" by biblical critics through the very allegorical impulse that Rousseau is acting out, and that his apologetic tendencies expose as interested. Through this allegorization it becomes difficult for us to claim a radical distinction between fictional and critical rewritings of the biblical texts, hence, to separate scholarship from this emblematic case.

One additional mediation—or is it the founding one?—cannot escape us then, because it affects the status of "truth": that between sequential narrative and still vision. The competition between these two modes of representation shows in Rousseau's third address, before the narrative proper has had a chance to begin:

> What picture am I going to set before your eyes? The body of a woman cut into pieces; her torn and throbbing members sent to the twelve Tribes; all the people, frozen with horror, raising a unanimous clamor. . . .[9]

---

9. The French is even more visually colored: quel tableau viens-je offrir à vos yeux? Le corps d'une femme coupé par pièces; ses membres déchirés et palpitants envoyés aux douze Tribus; tout le peuple, saisi d'horreur, élevant jusqu'au ciel une clameur unanime . . . (Rousseau, II, 1208).

The visual language is not just picturesque; it contributes to the rhetoric of the text in a way that involves longstanding epistemological claims. Rousseau is demonstrating here the age-old competition between language and vision that colors the positivistic truth-claim.[10] At the same time, by showing the dead flesh ("torn and throbbing members") before starting the narrative, he allows himself the reversal that follows later, *in* the narrative, where the focus will shift from the crime against the woman to the revenge set off by this sight.

A reading of Rousseau's reading leads routinely to a survey of the "mistakes" or "distortions." This gesture of comparison implies that we believe that the text of Judges can be read "wrongly," hence, by implication, also "rightly." It implies a truth, and the claim that the critic owns it. Of course, the complexities of the act of mediating between reading and writing brackets the status of this truth, but it is the search for it that I am interested in.

Peggy Kamuf claims the story is "well known." There lies the first problem. On the one hand, it is well known, as part of the biblical canon, and as such it circulates within the doxa of our culture. By virtue of its very vagueness and anonymity, the doxa is the real "owner" of the text who disowns the critic. For, on the other hand, the story is unknown. The anonymity of the victimized woman, the unbearable horror of the story, the disturbing gender aspect of the horror, and the ambiguous moral status of the Levite, make for a massive repression of this story, that most people vaguely know but few endeavor to read *against* the grain of the doxa.

Kamuf brilliantly maps ambiguities in Rousseau's position. But she also compares the two texts as "original" and "rewriting," in her allegiance to "truth-speak," in her inevitable commitment to be "right." She uses the standard procedure for the comparison: a summary of the older story. Such endeavors are compromised from the start, as summaries are already interpretations and therefore rewritings that follow the two texts to be compared. In the first sentence of her summary, she already makes a "mistake": "a Levite took as a concubine a virgin from Bethlehem." The word virginity is a mistaken doxic translation, as I have argued at length in *Death and Dissymmetry*, but even if she admittedly cannot be expected to know this, the word mistakenly replaces here another mistaken translation, "concubine." By mistakingly confusing two mistakes, Kamuf connotes the truth of these false translations: she points at a problem in words denoting the status of women by conflating two seemingly opposed, value-laden notions: virgin and concubine.[11] Equally central is another mistake. Kamuf (84) writes: "The next day,

---

"Tableau" is more insistently visual than "picture" which is more commonplace, while the order of the noun "membres" followed by strong adjectives is more "picturesque" than the English.

10. The study of the relations between visual and verbal discourse in connection to truth-claims is central for like W.T.J. Mitchell, whose *Iconology: Image, Text, Ideology* (1985) is a key-text. A brilliant "applied" study is Françoise Meltzer (1987).

11. There are more of these little "mistakes," mainly interpretations of gaps, like "exogamic

the Levite found her *dead* on the doorstep." This case demonstrates the ideological and hermeneutic problem of two tendencies central in interpretive practice: disambiguization and paraphrasis. While she is attempting to paraphrase the story, her need to make the passage unambiguously clear makes Kamuf here repeating (paraphrasing) the doxa where it sides with the Levite and ignores the crucial ambiguity of the text, which precisely refrains from stating whether the woman is dead or alive. Is the woman dead when he finds her, as she was alive enough to drag herself back to the house? Of course, this disambiguizing "lie" is of little help to the Levite.[12] Yet what matters in Kamuf's "distortion" is precisely her relying on the doxa, and her resulting blindness to the ambiguity, while her whole analysis focuses on ambiguities. Her leaning on the doxa significantly happens *à propos* of the woman's death; thus writing the woman to premature death, she becomes herself the "author of a crime."

Rousseau's major "lie" is this. He writes that the host first offers his daughter, and that the Levite cannot accept that self-sacrifice and therefore gives his wife, while in Judges the host offers both young women, an offer which is *rejected* ("but the men would not listen to him" Judges 19:25) . There is a "compulsion to repeat" in these lies that we see also in criticism, for example the "lie" is that which Rousseau and Kamuf share with the Levite himself. When he gives his report to the tribes, the Levite claims that the Benjaminites had threatened to kill him, which is a lie; they had threatened to rape him. Rousseau's Levite doubles up here, firstly on the level of the story, by adding that they had "forced" him to hand over his wife, secondly on the level of narration, by insisting that he is speaking the truth: "People of the Lord, I have spoken the truth."

This truth-speak is the painful moment where the predicament of criticism is reflected. Rousseau's interests compel him to defend the Levite while on another level of awareness he knows that the man is lying. The symptom of this contradiction is precisely the displacement of the insistence: he overdoes the lie and then, knowing that it is a lie, he insists that it is the truth.[13]

---

law" (90), not mentioned in the text and a muddled issue. Most mistakes are "lies of repetition," wherein Kamuf repeats Rousseau's lies, like "The Benjamintes refused to turn over the guilty men" (84). Elsewhere, she repeats doxic mistaken interpretations, like "the Levite found her dead on the doorstep" (84). For an extensive discussion of the Judges text in connection to these key terms referring to the institutions that regulate sexual behavior, see my study of the Book of Judges (1988).

12. If she is alive, he does the actual murdering; if she is dead, he desacralizes her body and transgresses the laws of his own status as priest by handling her body. In both cases, this man is beyond redemption. I find it significant that critics analyzing this story seem unable to face the unambiguous guilt of this unnamed individual, no more than they are willing to face guilt in cases where an Israelite hero is involved. What needs protection from the story, here, is the individual as opposed to the mass, the inhabitants of the city, the guilty tribe of Benjamin.

13. Likewise, in my analysis of Judges in *Death and Dissymmetry* I have quoted many examples in commentaries of those insistent footnotes that emphasize the problematic details of the

Kamuf displaces the Levite's founding lie by rightly insisting on the ambiguous status of his writing. Now, Kamuf is a feminist, and her analysis brings out some of the feminist issues this story raises—more acutely than any work of specialized scholarship on this tale I know of. Yet as a deconstructionist her interest is to insist on writing, and thus she passes right by the Levite's lie *in* his writing, which is precisely in his writing-as-truth-claim.

It is not my goal to criticize a wonderful literary tale or the best analysis of Judges 19 and of Rousseau's tale I know of. I am interested in what I call, with reference to Freud's concept of dream-work, the "work of truth" and its need to be spoken. Both Rousseau's and Kamuf's misses occur at the very moment they proclaim the truth. For example, Kamuf is engaged in pointing out both Rousseau's misses and those of another secular comparatist, Thomas Kavanagh,[14] whose book has the meaningful title *Writing the Truth: Authority and Desire in Rousseau*, when she herself misread Judges on, precisely, a crucial gender issue and the same narrative issue, while using the language of truth:

> In the biblical account, the "wrongness" of the attack on the Levite is signaled by the offer, *which is accepted*, to substitute for him the two women (91–2).

This analysis of moral "wrongness" is performed through a readerly "wrongness": the offer is *not* accepted, and this rejection brings forth the next and central event of the deadly gang-rape. But that entails questions about the status of the two women *as* women. The issue of the meaning and value of virginity should have been evoked *here*—with that of "concubine," whose relatedness Kamuf demonstrated in her earlier "mistake."[15] This blatant mis-

---

text they then set out to explain away. A funny case is Boling's lengthy demonstration, including visual material, that Jephthah could not know that his daughter would be the first one to meet him after his victory. Thus he shows how problematic, how unanswerable, and how compromising that very question is. See Robert G. Boling, 1975.

14. Thomas M. Kavanagh (1987).

15. To take this one step further, I must also point out my own misses: trying to argue for *my* truth: that we all inevitably miss the truth when we try the hardest to find it, I missed Kamuf's point on how Rousseau became the author of a crime, by using her piece as an example of contradiction; I overlooked Rousseau's occasional plea for gender-equity because I wanted to demonstrate his defensive male bias; and I might even be missing Judges, the story I claim you, readers of this essay, don't know well enough, thus implying that I know it better myself, that I own its truth. I misread Judges by disambiguizing the Levite's position while I know that *its* ambiguity is the only position this text can possibly take, torn as it is itself between the two sides of the social conflict it stages (I mean hereby the conflict between patrilocal nomadic marriage and virilocal residential marriage, a conflict that I have argued in *Death and Dissymmetry* to underlie these stories and to account for their horror). And *my* motivations for these misses include that I have a point to make that requires the logic that eliminates all that doesn't fit. Not to speak of my unconscious motivations, by definition outside of my reach but which I can only point at in the form of questions: what brings me time and again to Judges 19? And why must the Levite get due blame? All this leads, finally, to the flipside of this argument. If I am not going as far as pointing that out, it is because the politics of interpretation require that the unspoken be said, and that the already spoken and dominant discourse be temporarily silenced, in spite of its occasional "truth."

take compels Kamuf to ignore how Rousseau writes the apology for the Levite in precisely the gap between the rejected offer and the central event of the gang-rape. While Judges is extremely unclear here, Rousseau makes the Levite reject the host's "self-sacrifice" of his daughter.

So far, I have suggested that there is no truth in narrative and yet that we all seek it; I have claimed that in the very attempt to find it we miss it; and that both the attempt to find it and the misses are motivated by our social, cultural, and private interests. These became visible in the analysis of the complex mediations in Rousseau's case, but are equally relevant for all acts of writing and reading. Far be it from me, however, to make an anything-goes argument. The insistent issue of truth cannot be eliminated, but it must be displaced and replaced in relation to interests. Authority, the site of moral ownership that is incompatible with objective truth, is the painful site of contradiction where a scholarship committed to seeking unbiased truth sees itself in the mirror—and ineffectively breaks the mirror rather than changing itself.

Let me return to Rousseau's picture of throbbing flesh, which proclaimed the superiority of vision over narrative as a rhetorical move to allow narrative to forget vision. Vision, it turns out, is a crucial "language" in Judges 19. In order to get a different access to Judges 19 and the way it engages gender, therefore, I have looked at one of the rare visual representations of it, a "Rembrandt" drawing. It represents the moment when the Levite finds her the next morning on the threshold of the house. It is one of "Rembrandt"'s most acute representations of death, which, paradoxically, is full of movement and life, full of narrative, and it is mustering a particular device of visual narrative, speaking hands.

The drawing depicts the victim at the threshold of the house, and thus positions her literally as a liminal figure, as the embodiment of transition. In spite of the sketchiness of the representation as a whole, the steps which constitute the threshold and signify the house as real and as stone are particularly clearly drawn. I will revert to this detail, which is this drawing's mediation from truth-speak to body-language.

The moment in the biblical "pre-text" in which language and violence are intricately related is precisely the one that our drawing represents: the moment where the woman is no longer able to speak her truth of life and death, where her body is *seen*, misunderstood both by her husband and by subsequent critics, addressed, and ultimately, misused in a radical perversion of speech.

Vision is a mode of speech in this horror-story. Mis-seeing, un-seeing the woman is sketched. Her death and the story of it are narratively ambiguous. As her death begins at her exposure and ends with her dismemberment, we cannot know when exactly she dies, and we must not know it. For that incapacity to know is an important element in the biblical epistemology of gender which equates sex with knowledge in the expression "to know a woman." She dies several times, or rather, she never stops dying. It is this narrative aspect of her dying which makes this drawing so central in these reflections on death: an event that is punctual and non-narratable is turned into a slow process represented as the climax of narrative that then becomes the visual work challenging the limits of visual representation.

Whereas in Judges the event is turned from punctual into durative, the representation of this already perverted death in a allegedly static medium further explores and undermines the limits of the realm of the speakable. In Judges, moreover, the agents of the woman's death are as unclear as is its moment; the act keeps being displaced from one man to the next. This contamination by collective guilt is obviously problematic to all readers. In addition, the differentiation between discourse as the production of signs which, according to semiotics, stand in for an object, and the object of discourse, falls apart as well. Not only is this woman the object of the body-language of rape, a language that bespeaks her death; her body is also subsequently used *as* language by the very man who exposed her to the violence when he sends her flesh off as a message.[16]

The moment of this endless deferral of death visually represented is the one in which vision becomes a speech-act. The morning after the gang-rape the woman's husband opens the door to go his way, and "*behold*, there was his wife, fallen down, and her hands were on the threshold" (Judges 19:27). Two words, then, generate this drawing: "open" and "behold." The verb-form used for the act of opening is *jiphtah*, the word that rings in the name of Jephthah, the murderer of the virgin-daughter sacrificed in violence for the sake of (military) violence in Judges 11. The importance of opening as the act that allows vision while dealing death is thus emphasized by the pun on *jiphtah*/Jephthah; so is the murderous quality of opening, vision, and the body. After having opened the door the previous night for lethal sexual violence, the man opens it to contemplate its next stage, and the chilling picture he sees is here for us to see: "behold, she is fallen."

Judges is a book that problematizes language by proposing uncanny kinds of speech-acts to challenge language as purveyor of meaning. Judges is, for example, full of riddles, the speech-act of the *lacking* meaning. In addition to riddles Judges is also full of *vows*, speech-acts based on an *excess* of meaning, acts that emblematize the power of words in the most radical way. Their meaning being death, they kill. Jephthah, who first vows his daughter to death and then tricks his enemies linguistically, is the hero of this killing kind of speech. He is also, according to his name, the opener of bodies. Between the lack of meaning and an excess of meaning, speech is overruled by the force

---

16. Where the narrative seems to fail to construct history, rape becomes the sign that does; as I argue in *Death and Dissymmetry*, it becomes the generative event of Judges.

that motivates it. In the gap left by this view of language as deficient, visual representation inserts itself and becomes an alternative language; a truth-speak of its own, mistaken for body-language as the most truthful language.

This alternative language is "spoken" in the sketch of the woman who, in the Bible, is killed in and as speech. This linguistic murder occurs several times there. Before her death by the gang-rape she is surrendered linguistically, and after her death she is dispatched as language, when her body is cut into pieces and sent to the tribes of Israel, as a *letter*—a piece of writing not containing but embodying a message—and as a slaughtered piece of meat. Butchering equals writing here; and death equals vision. Rousseau *shows* this instead of *telling* it when he offers to our eyes his picture of throbbing members.

This is a case, if ever there was one, of the scandal of the speaking body.[17] Between the two moments of her murder by multiplication and publication—multiple rape and publication of her body—is the moment of vision during which the husband-opener fails to see, thus adding to, and consecrating, the murder: a semiotics of mis-seeing.

In the "Rembrandt" sketch the meaning (the woman's death) and the force (its narrativization in movement) confront each other in the paradox of representation: in order to represent the narrative of death, the drawing requires a movement that denies death precisely while pointing to its agent. That movement is *signified* (not: realistically represented) in the right hand of the woman figure. This hand is slightly blurred, while it has lines underneath it that can easily be explained away as a shadow but resist that interpretation. For the house, precisely, the safe haven denied this woman, stands between the alleged sun and its alleged shadow, so that the small lines cannot quite be a shadow and rather suggest movement.

According to Eco (1976), signs are those things which can be used in order to lie. This definition helps us understand the "lies" in the drawing: the movement of a lifeless woman, signified by the lines under her slightly blurred right hand, and the ghost-like transparency of the living man, signified by the continuous line of the stone on which he is supposed to stand. Neither sign is merely a lie; both are representational paradoxes. Just as the speech-act of the riddle in Judges undermines the narrative plot-line, so too a line here undercuts the drawing's realistic quality: the force of the speech-act of drawing crosses its own realistic meaning out. This line, too, can be easily explained away, if not overlooked altogether. But since the problems of this story have been overlooked long enough, I choose to emphasize these marginal signs.

---

17. The allusion is to Shoshana Felman's analysis of speech-act theory in *Le scandale du corps parlant* (1980), whose radicality is censored away in the English title, *Literary Speech-Acts*, (1984). Felmamn's discussion of speech-act theory is analyzed in chapter 5 of *Death and Dissymmetry*.

Alluding to Peirce's difficult concept of the sinsign, I like to think of this invisible sign of invisibility as a sign of sin.[18]

Jonathan Culler (1983) reformulates Eco's definition of the sign from the reader's perspective: a sign is everything that can be misunderstood. Misreading, then, is the key to semiosis, just as mis-seeing is the key to opening the woman's body and to representing her death. This misuse of semiosis will subsequently be literalized in the dismemberment.

How does death, here, relate to gender? The affinity, in "Rembrandt," for the Book of Judges suggests a split between two projections of women. On the one hand, there are women who are feared and therefore hated, who need to be appropriated by violence. These women are potential mates—the bride who must be violated in order to be *opened*. On the other hand, there are women who are harmless because they have already been violated. These are the victims, women as social figures of marginality with which the writing or drawing subject can identify. With the first women the subject has a relation of contiguity, which implies a continuity he fears; with the second, he has a metaphoric relationship which implies the separation that allows sympathy and hence, identification; at the same time, the danger of contiguity can be avoided by replacing the woman in metaphor. This is the rhetoric of body-language.[19]

The gesture of the woman's hand on the threshold is important in both the text and the drawing. It has often been explained symbolically. Beyond the dichotomy of literal and figurative-symbolic, the detail of the hand can be taken as a statement on the text's narrativity, which is made theatrical by the indications of visuality. The key-word here is "behold." The gesture as the drawing presents it is the self-reflexive "lie" that counteracts the grave misreading both text and drawing thematize. In Rousseau's tale, vision's overruling of voice is used as the shifter which displaces subjectivity from the woman to the husband while apologizing for the latter's culminating act of horror:

> Even the *sight* of this body, which ought to have reduced him to tears [le faire fondre en larmes], calls forth from him no more cries [ni plaintes ni pleurs]. He contemplates it with a dry and dark *look*; he *sees in it* only an object of rage and despair . . .[20]

---

18. "A *Sinsign* is an actual existent thing or event which is a sign." This quote is from an easily accessible edition of Peirce's key text in which he defines the ten categories of signs, is Charles S. Peirce, "Logic as Semiotic," in Robert E. Innis, *Semiotics: An Introductory Anthology* (1985: 7).

19. For an extensive discussion of these attitudes, see my *Reading "Rembrandt"* (1991).

20. L'aspect même de ce corps, qui devroit le faire fondre en larmes, ne lui arrache plus ni plaintes ni pleurs: Il le contemple d'un oeil sec et sombre; il n'y voit plus qu'un objet de rage et de désespoir (Rousseau, II, 1215). The word "aspect" has an emphatically visual charge, while this visuality is underlined by "contempler," "oeil," "voit."

The husband stops speaking at the moment he becomes both the subject and the victim of the violence. This transformation turns him into an agent of visuality.

The moment selected for visual representation in the drawing is well chosen because it is the painful one that produces doubt and fear in readers who, from the perspective of an utterly ideological partiality, have a stake in the moral righteousness of the character of the Levite. It is deeply confusing to see the theatricalization of this door-opener's behavior. Reading theatrically ("behold"), we see how he almost steps over the body of his wife—his first misreading of the sight—then he orders her to stand up—a second misreading, now of his position of power. When no answer comes, when her non-speech suspends the possibility of truth, we see him tie her (body) to his donkey to take her home and cut her up for semiotic misuse. Rousseau must make the man change here (*donner le change*), from speaker to seer to writer.

The drawing contradicts the Levite's visual lie by the little lines under the woman's hand, which suggest movement, hence, life. But these lines do not depict the woman as "really" alive; they only suggest that she is acting out the story of her continuous death—her death as a process that challenges the epistemological basis of our conception of death as knowable event. In order to represent her death, then, the drawing must let her move.

The question of the realistic status of the movement of the hand, then, is also an epistemological question: it raises the question of knowledge, on both the diegetic and the semiotic level. Who knows what? Does the husband know that the woman is dead? No, for if he did, he would not have ordered her to stand up. Does the reader know she is dead? I think not, for the forcefulness with which her death is argued betrays that the reader does not, cannot, know. This lack is not only a blow to the scholar whose mission is purported to be knowledge and whose rhetoric is truth-speak, but also to the reader who feels conflated with the ignorant character, the Levite. Hence the critical mistakes, accumulating when knowledge is embodied by women.

But there is more to knowledge than meets the eye. To know and to possess are both expressions for the sexual encounter from a particular ideological perspective, and are thus intimately related to each other and to gender. This equation is possible because knowledge is itself a thing one can possess: one *has* knowledge. But one cannot possess what one does not know, for how can one know whether or not one possesses it? And one cannot give what one does not possess, hence, giving the unknown is *a priori* an act of semiotic abuse. This abuse is Jephthah's crime when he vows away his daughter. To know, furthermore, is also an epistemological act whose relationship to vision is at stake, both in Judges and in "Rembrandt." Does the epistemologically failing man, in the drawing, *know* his wife, sexually and existentially, if he cannot even know if she is alive or dead? In other words, is he her husband at all at this point? It is this that his intense act of looking lets us question. From this perspective, the line that makes him transparent also makes him unreal: as the woman's husband he does not exist. This line shifts the work from realistic failure to semiotic adequacy.

My reading of this drawing is based on the refusal to endorse the separations between "literal" and "figurative," between visual and verbal, along with the acknowledgment of the impossibility of "pure" meaning—of meaning without force and of "pure" knowledge, or truth, without the metonymic contamination of its motivated pursuit. We can read this refusal of the distinctions that have dictated much of Western representational and interpretative practice in the lines moving the hand in the drawing. This hand does not "see," but it speaks about mis-seeing. More "real" because more alive than the body of the husband, the hand is about to point in accusation at her murderer. It accuses him not only of multiple and durative murder, but also of misreading, mis-seeing, and misrepresentation.[21]

The drawing insists that the husband's misreading is "wrong" epistemologically as well as morally, for in spite of Kamuf's effort to do so, the two cannot be entirely separated. It demonstrates that her gesture is phatic, body-language. The woman addresses her husband from below, in a radical re-positioning of vision. The husband, wringing his hands eloquently as in despair—speaking with his hands—cannot *see* the movement of the woman's hand, as the hand itself, exercising body-language, blocks the sight of the lines underneath it.

By interrupting the represented line of vision, hence, both emphasizing and problematizing diegetic seeing, the work does several things at once. It represents the very moment of suspension between life and death, action and inaction, thus raising the question of the husband's response and generating the following episode. It theatricalizes the visual moment, by inscribing in it the dimension of time. And it emphasizes its own status as a work of representation, willfully misreading the conventions of representational art. The husband *looks* at the woman's hand, but the *representation* of its telling movement is not for him to see.

The gift of this woman led to the public opening of her body; it led to rape, death, and dismemberment; instead of qualifying her subject-position, it destroyed it. The husband lives by this destruction: he stands over her, fails to see her, ineffectively and abusively speaks to her, and steps over her. The woman

---

21. Here is the scene of the pre-text that the drawing responds to and its narrative follow-up which, I submit, is also inscribed in the drawing:

And her lord rose up in the morning and opened [*jiphtah*] the doors of the house and went out to go his way; and behold, his patrilocal wife was fallen down at the door of the house, with her hands on the threshold. And he said to her: "up!, and let us be going" and none answered. And he took her upon the ass; and the man rose up and went to his place. And when he had come into his house he took the knife and laid hold on his patrilocal wife and divided her limb by limb into twelve pieces and sent her throughout all the borders of Israel (19:27–28).

can only speak as body. This body will be used to speak, but then it is no longer the woman who speaks. As an inevitable consequence of the scene of vision outlined by the drawing, her body is utterly robbed of its significance as herself. The man speaks, in an act which fulfills Rousseau's dream of an unmediated, direct language, as he wrote in *The Origin of Language*, but then, *over her dead body*. Begging for the merciful interpretations of his crime against women and life which will in effect be granted to him in the history of interpretation, the man's hands overshadow the speaking power of the woman's. But by opposing the lie of her hands to that of his, the drawing lets her speak against this cultural condoning of rape and murder.

Judges 19 ends with an imperative—*speak*—a masculine plural, response to the visual speech of the woman's divided flesh. The tribes address their order to speak not to the "speaker" but to the husband. The speaking body itself is misread. For Kamuf, Rousseau, and the biblical author, misguided by the Levite, the story of rape as murder becomes the story of revenge. To this scandal, the drawing opposes the prefiguration of a response. The man may be the opener of doors and bodies, but he is depicted as so weak in the drawing that his perverted speech will indeed be misread, yet in a way opposed to the misreading of the tribes. The drawing, already erasing him while enhancing the dead-living woman, will not let his lie be read at all. The line cutting through the man's substance, undermining his reality, and the lines producing the woman's movement that he cannot see becomes central.

By now, it becomes impossible to disentangle the chronological neatness of the distinction, endorsed even by Kamuf, between "original" and "rewriting." Using the "Rembrandt" as a commentary on the Rousseau, we are beginning to see the dangerous liaison between reader and writer, and the colonizing nature of mediation. When subject and object of writing, addresser and addresssee, can neither be entirely conflated nor be radically separated, it becomes urgent to revise our relationship to truth, objectivity, and knowledge. The throbbing flesh of an anonymous woman remains the solid object which resists the rhetoric of narrative Rousseau so passionately used to proclaim an impossible truth against an irrepressible hatred. If this woman had to die, it was because her body was seen, un-seen, and over-seen. Her body of writing allegorizes the danger of epistemological certainty based on abstraction and disembodied language alone. Whether the woman is blocking the husband's sight, as in the drawing, or displacing the narrative, as in the tales, or prematurely killed, as in criticism, the Judges woman allegorizes a kind of truth whose instability forces a look into the force that motivates its pursuit. Some would call it a trace—the trace which leads us back from truth-speak to body-language.

▪13▪

Lots of Writing

INTRODUCTION

Esther's dramatic second banquet, one out of many in the story, has understandably attracted painters; drama is a visually representable form of narrative.¹ Rembrandt's painting of 1660 in the Pushkin museum in Moscow is my favorite on the subject, but precisely because it does not enhance the narrativity of the scene, its dramatic tension (fig. 1). The three figures who, in the biblical story, are set in the most dramatic interaction with each other, are here represented as if enclosed by an invisible veil, absorbed in themselves, silent and isolated from each other.² Moreover, Haman, on the left, seems blind. Another painting by Rembrandt, in the Hermitage in St. Petersburg, dated 1665, represents the next episode, the downfall of the plotter. Haman is strangely represented as almost literally falling, moving forward, falling into the viewer's lap when quitting the scene; and here he is definitely blind (fig. 2).³ In this work, the scene is even more strongly drained of its narrativity; Esther is absent, Mordecai present, hence, not the narrative event but its proleptic meaning—Haman replaced by Mordecai—is represented.

Rembrandt is generally considered a narrative painter, even exceptionally so for a Dutch artist.⁴ But here, representing a lively, highly dramatic scene, movement is eliminated from the image. In this still medium, the figures are

---

1. Sandra Beth Berg, *The Book of Esther*, 31–58 for an analysis of banquets, feasts, and their relationship to Purim.
2. For an analysis of absorption in painting, as opposed to "theatricality" or the direct interaction between characters and viewer, see Michael Fried, *Absorption and Theatricality*.
3. The question whether Rembrandt intended to represent these episodes or whether the works later received their titles is as irrelevant for my perspective as the question whether "Esther" really initiated Purim or was a fictional and retrospective justification of the festival.
4. See Svetlana Alpers, *The Art of Describing*.

282 ■ ON MEANING-MAKING

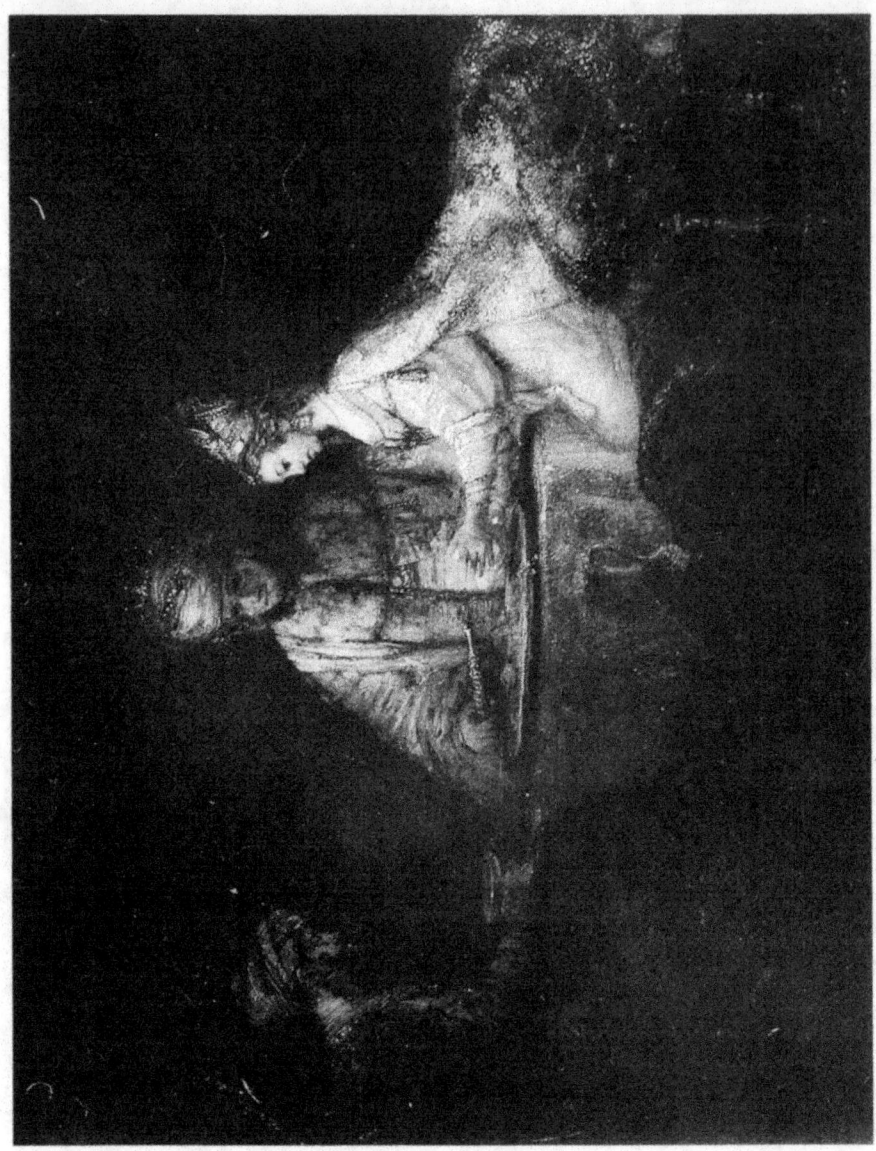

Figure 1: Rembrandt, *Esther's Banquet*, State Pushkin Museum of Fine Arts, Moscow

Figure 2: Rembrandt, detail of the Moscow *Esther*, State Pushkin Museum of Fine Arts, Moscow

emphatically arrested, as if to represent the stillness of visual art itself. And once self-reflection becomes a mode of reading these paintings, another, more complex kind of self-reflection presents itself, one which courts paradox. On the one hand, represented in a wordless medium, the scene's emphasis falls on speechlessness, the lack of communication between the figures mirroring the non-linguistic quality of the work of visual art. In contrast, the literary text uses spoken words to dramatize climactic confrontation. Both works are, in this aspect and in contrast to each other, self-reflexive, speaking the truth of their medium at the moment of diegetic truth. Neither work has any use for food, the pretext for the banquet. But there is more.

For on the other hand, the episode of Haman's downfall, following Esther's masterly plotted denunciation, offers a different, negative relationship to the respective media, a systematic opposition or counter-mirroring. In the visual text, the painting in Leningrad, blindness has a particular status that challenges the very visuality on which it is based; a status similar to the words in the New English Bible: "At that Haman was dumbfounded" (7:6).[5] Where sight fails in the visual work, words fail in the verbal one.

The failure of the two senses are combined in the remarkable phrase: "the word left his [the king's] mouth, and they covered Haman's face." (7:8)[6] The king verbalizes what he sees, and then his word causes Haman's face to be covered. Words are things that do things here, pointing out, with Austin, that words are the principal agents of this narrative. Covering Haman's face, they blind him; thus, the failure to see enters the verbal scene, just as, in the Moscow painting, the figures failed to speak. Hence, the Rembrandt only foregrounds what is already there in the text, and the neat distinction between speech and vision falls flat. The Rembrandts help us read the text by demonstrating how it has been read already.[7]

I will use these Rembrandt paintings as a gloss on "Esther," approaching the text from the perspective of these later interpretations of it. Assuming that the realm of visual representation has its own devices to support interpretive claims, I will endorse its heuristic power and accept that it has something to add that sheer verbal argumentation might well, so to speak, fail to see. What is, then, Esther's feast? I will argue that it is a feast of writing, and that its

---

5. The Hebrew has a less striking phrase: "And Haman was scared." I purposefully draw upon a modern, popularized version, because I am not so much focusing on an accurate reading of the "original" (whatever that may be) but on the cultural vitality of the text as it has grown over time.

6. Here, the Hebrew remains ambiguous: one Hebrew scholar suggested to me the translation "and Haman's face [was] clouded"; another "Haman's face fell, became bland." I allow myself to play with these possibilities, but obviously, my argument in this paper does not depend on these particular words. What matters is the power of words to defeat and kill, and the visual impotence expressed in the ambiguity of seeing as an epistemological and a perceptual act.

7. I won't go into the innumerable previous interpretations, if only through translations. Although any reconstruction of the "original" meaning is in my view doomed to failure, the attempt at getting closer requires, of course, a close analysis of the canonical Hebrew text. I wish to emphasize once more that such is not my endeavor.

Figure 3: Rembrandt, detail of the Hermitage *Esther*, State Hermitage Museum, St. Petersburg

relation to Purim is in the tension between writing and randomness, between agency and lot.

Writing is, precisely, the mediator between sight and speech. Using the representational system of language as its code, writing needs sight for its processing, for its phatic function.[8] For me, the Esther scroll is a celebration of writing, and as the climax of the story, so is Esther's banquet. Lots of writing happen in "Esther," and writing is the meeting-ground of words and images, of visual and verbal, and, specifically in "Esther," of fate and agency, of randomness and history, of providence and plotting. Writing is also the medium that produced "Esther."

In "Esther" writing partakes of, while struggling against, the lots that allegedly gave their name to Purim. For as often happens in biblical literature, the celebration is a working through of the ambivalences of what is celebrated. And there are plenty of reasons to feel ambivalent about writing. It is commonplace in cultural anthropology to consider the invention of writing the initiator and index of civilization; but it has also been acknowledged that the careful political management of literacy has contributed to the oppression of the people and the centralization of state power.[9] Writing has been a tool of the elite, a means of enforcing inequity and exploitation, of propagation of ideology through religion, and of generalizing laws; it has definitively impressed upon its practitioners a particular view of history which rendered futile collective memory and the participation of the people in oral history.[10] All these aspects can be thematized in a political reading of "Esther."

In terms of politics, the emphatic centrality of writing and of the perfection of the Persian postal system is, indeed, related to the rule of the king over many peoples, to the appropriation of power, to the abuse of power for the (attempted) destruction of a particular people and its culture. Writing is the instrument of real, historical danger (Haman's first decree). In epistemological terms, Plato warned against the destructive effects of writing on memory in the

---

8. These terms, of course, refer to Jakobson's model of communication.

9. See Lemaire, "Antropologie en schrift," 104. For the connection between religion and the economy of the state as supported by writing, see Adams, *The Evolution*. Diamond (*In Search*) provides arguments against evolutionism in this domain; Goody, *Literacy* and *The Domestication* gives a now classical critique of the repression of orality by writing. Lévi-Strauss classical text, Rousseauistic in its nostaligia, is "The Writing Lesson" in *Tristes Tropiques*. Precisely because of the romantic leftovers in the orality-literacy debate it needs pointing out that I am using the term "writing" in the limited sense of script here, not in the extended sense Derrida gave it in *Of Grammatology* but that I am, however, not claiming innocence and non-violence or, indeed, a state of culture-without-writing as the opposite of literacy. Rather, the tensions I will point out in writing as it partakes of the plot of "Esther" demonstrate the fragility of just such an opposition. I do not consider the Derridian view of writing as intrinsically incompatible with the political critique of the complicities of writing with domination.

10. Although it is widely assumed that literacy was relatively widespread in Israel from the eighth century BCE on, oral history, at one time the only form of history, has never totally disappeared from cultural life, neither in Israel nor elsewhere.

Phaedrus, and this is usually associated with the breakdown of archaic, small-scale "democracies." As it happens, in "Esther" the overruling of memory by writing also occurs, in the episode of the chronicle about Mordecai's deed, but it is embodied by Ahasuerus, the very ruler whose centralized and autocratic power ranges "from India to Ethiopia." His failing memory should not be too hastily ridiculed—a ridicule so often connected with contempt for the lack of psychological depth and of realistic plausibility that it cannot escape the charge of anachronism, if not arrogant evolutionism. Rather, it should be seen as a representation of the inevitable but ambivalent development toward the predominance of writing the text stages.[11] But if "Esther" is about writing, it is also about itself.

Given the centrality of writing in the Book of Esther, self-reflection seems a priori a relevant concept to approach the text with, and the two Rembrandt paintings provide clues for a complication of that concept. Therefore, in this paper I will reflect upon the possible uses of the concept of self-reflection and propose that it yields a perspective on "Esther" beyond the question of the historical connection between "lots" and Purim.

SELF-REFLECTION

Self-reflection is too fashionable a concept to endorse it without questioning. If the Esther scroll centers around writing, we can consider it a self-reflexive text; and if, as I will argue, it reflects on the uncertain status of writing and the ways it produces reality—the reality of the threat to, then the escape of, the Jews—we seem to have a case of postmodernism *avant la lettre*.[12] Is this pushing anachronism too far? This question can only be answered in connection with the very problematic of self-reflection, for I will argue that the attraction of the concept for contemporary criticism is not its clarity but its ambiguity which opens up the space for a view of representation

---

11. *Contra* e.g. Sasson, 1988 (337: "yet the events of barely a fortnight earlier are so hazy in his memory"; 341: "dim-witted monarchs") whose literary approach to "Esther" seems characteristic of the hidden evolutionistic ideology in much of "literary approach to the Bible" work. The view that the chronicle episode is implausible is quite general (e.g. Berg, 63). Sasson applies anachronistic criteria like psychological plausibility to present the text as a cute comical thing, typical of ancient literature. The latter is subsequently conflated with everything pre-modern: Hellenistic romance, medieval fabliaux, up to Voltaire's *contes philosophiques*. I like to think that Ahasuerus should not be judged for his intelligence, but considered an agent necessitated by the plot which is, by another turn of self-reflection, about plotting. The measuring of the story against standards of the modern psychological-realist novel is almost universal in commentaries; see e.g. Moore (LIII,LIV) who finds the characters lacking in depth and compares Haman to Oedipus, whom he fails to match. One wonders about the unstated motivation for precisely this comparison; the complicity between gender-ideology and realism also shows on LII where Mordecai is considered "the greater hero" "who supplies the brains while Esther simply followed his directions." To my mind, it is the critic who lacks in depth here.

12. Both self-reflection and ontological uncertainties are considered characteristic of postmodernism; see Hutcheon, 1988; McHale, 1987; Van Alphen, 1990.

unbound by the kind of psychological realism inherited from nineteenth-century western fiction.

Self-reflection is not only popular in literary criticism, under the influence of post-modern literature and deconstructionist writing; it has also invaded the arena of criticism of visual art. Foucault's final words of his introductory chapter of *The Order of Things*, devoted to Velazquez' *Las Meninas*, are a beautiful expression of this mode of reading:

> ... representation undertakes to represent itself here in all its elements, with its images, the eyes to which it is offered, the faces it makes visible, the gestures it calls into being ... representation, freed finally from the relation that was impeding it, can offer itself as representation in its purest form. (16)

The specific relevance of visual art for a discussion of self-reflection stems from the representational imposition of the *subject*: while literature can be about *it*self, allowing critics to forget the reader, self-reflexive art imprisons the *viewer*. This provides a relevant perspective that allows us to complicate and historicize the concept. For transposed to literature, within the framework of a reading-oriented theory of texts, self-reflection as a mode of reading entails a complication, rendered in its simplest form by the question: whose/which self is being reflected? The identity between the work and its subject—between work as labor and work as product—is not unified; it is fragmented by the intrusion of the reader whose position is inherently paradoxical: is s/he part of the self being reflected or reflected on? If so, then the self-reflective mode of reading, which subsumes the reader into the work, does not encourage the reader to reflect on self; hence, the self remains whole, while only the reflection becomes fractured; if the reader is not part of the self that is being reflected (on), then the self is disrupted from the start, and again, the reader will not be encouraged to reflect on his or her self. And I contend that the obliteration of the reader's self de-historicizes the critical endeavor, even if, or precisely when, the overt aim is historical reconstruction.

This mode of reading is made double-edged by its relationship to narcissism. As an effectively anti-realistic reading strategy, it is a reading for the work itself, the mode which makes us read, to use Linda Hutcheon's term, for the narcissism in the work.[13] Compounding the mythical, visual, and psychoanalytic connotations of narcissism, the term also illuminates the particular pictorial quality and the erotic near-gratification of self-reference. In the case of "Esther," the reader is constantly kept aware of the connection between visual beauty and power in the main character's adventures, and once the very instability of writing becomes the central theme for the self-reflexive reader, the power of beauty and the power of writing are enmeshed, and as I will argue, even the conventional gender-division falls apart.

13. See Linda Hutcheon, *Narcissistic Narrative* and her more recent *A Poetics of Postmodernism*.

The paradoxical entanglements within the concept of self-reflection are particularly visible in the heated debate that focused on Velazquez's *Las Meninas* around 1980 between philosophers and art historians, which I have analyzed elsewhere.[14] As mentioned already, Foucault, a philosopher and hence a professional discursive self-reflector, opened his study of the classical age with a thirteen-page reflection on the painting.[15] He saw inscribed into the work the invisibility of the viewer, whose place is taken by the royalties—a view which suggests to me an unexpected symmetry between the Spanish painting and the ancient text, where the royal position is taken by the outsider, Esther the Jewess. Searle, another philosopher, significantly a philosopher of language and hence of discourse, took the work as typically paradoxical, precisely because the viewer can *not* be in the same place as the royal couple, yet must be precisely there. The term paradox upset two other critics[16] and amused others, thus starting off a series of responses to both this interpretation and the painting.

The issue of these papers is the position of the viewer in relation to the mirrored image of the king and queen in the center of the work. The debate makes a good inter-text for self-reflection because, at least in the articles by

---

14. See *Reading "Rembrandt"*, ch. 7, where I develop the following typology of self-reflection through a close reading of the papers of the *Las Meninas* debate.

15. Foucault, *Order*, 3–16. The critics who took up the challenge of Foucault's self-confident *placing* of the work within his own argument made little of the specific intertextual relation between the painting and the philosophical argument, which was reversed in comparison with the subsequent critical arguments. Foucault's purpose was not to say anything special about *Las Meninas* but to make *Las Meninas* say what he, Foucault, had to say about the classical age. It seems to me that this apparent use of a "masterpiece" as a mere example is partly responsible for the emotional responses. But in Foucault's way of writing, there is no such thing as a mere example. *Las Meninas* provided the philosopher with the discourse that he needed: a visual discourse. This detour was quite functional: it enabled him to counter the charge of simplification (which, ironically, is precisely what he was charged with). Foucault relativizes this view of visuality by a strong emphasis on the irreducible difference between word and images:

> But the relation of language to painting is an infinite relation. It is not that words are imperfect, or that, confronted by the visible, they prove insuperably inadequate. Neither can be reduced to the other's terms: it is in vain that we say what we see; what we see never resides in what we say. And it is in vain that we attempt to show, by the use of images, metaphors, or similes, what we are saying; the space where they achieve their splendor is not that deployed by our eyes but that defined by the sequential elements of syntax. (9)

This attitude toward the relationship between discourse and image also holds for my heuristic use of the two Rembrandt paintings here.

16. Snyder & Cohen, "Paradox Lost." These authors' dismay seems to stem from the well-known discomfort brought forth by interdisciplinary discourse. Here is one out of many defensive reactions to the very language Searle uses:

> In the first quotation Janson seems in the Foucault-Searle line, although he does not note a "paradox" wrought by this way of seeing the painting. In the second quotation he settles for an "ambiguity," a less exotic logical crux.

Indeed, this seems to me primarily a reaction to philosophical terms. The irony is just a little too heavy handed for such a casual issue, emphasized as it is by the quotation marks which disqualify the terms they frame, the word "exotic" related to "logic," the unnecessarily ironic "wrought." The target of the irony, however, is not only the alien discourse but also, precisely, the threat emanating from "wrought by this way of seeing the painting."

Searle and Snyder & Cohen, there is a striking discrepancy between the positions the critics argue for in their discursive reflections and those they reflect—mirror—in their discourses. This discrepancy points to the argumentative "other," the connotative rhetoric of the texts. In other words, the critical texts lend themselves to the kind of specular and speculative reflexive reading that makes self-reflective reading genuinely relevant for critique.

However, such a reading strategy might also lead to a self-sufficient sense of triumph, a self-congratulatory pleasure in discovery. In other words, once self-reflection as a possibility has become commonplace reading for "narcissism" it is in danger of becoming narcissistic itself. What gets lost is a perspective on the historical position of self-reflecion, and that is, indeed, a powerful criticism against this mode of reading, to which we will have to revert.[17]

As I suggested, self-reflectivity as a mode of reading seems paradoxical; it seems that way because the self-reflexive mode leads the interpreter to submit to a position perceived to be determined by the work. As in a Hegelian master-slave dialectic, the reader is so overwhelmed by, so triumphant over, the "discovery" of self-reflexivity, that s/he tends to set his or her own position aside and submit totally to the self-reflective position seemingly proposed by the work, at the cost of self-reflection of the viewing or reading subject. But if reflection of/on the work entails reflection of/on the viewer's position, then any submissive response is paradoxically non-submissive: it refuses to obey the command of reflection. In other words, an order of non-submission can be neither obeyed nor disobeyed. This paradox mirrors the position of Esther at the moment in the narrative she receives the command to disobey (4:8–17).[18] The question of obedience as a paradox, not as a neat opposition opposing the "good" because obedient queen to her "bad" because disobedient predecessor, is thematized throughout the narrative. Bound to obey both her relative and her husband, Esther is forced to disobey both in order to obey, and thereby emancipates herself from the power of the two men over her, and of their writing. Reading "Esther" self-reflexively solicits a comparable compromise: to read anachronistically—say, post-modernistically—in order to gain a perspective on history—on "Esther" as neither realistic nor post-modern, but as the historical "other."

The paradoxes and possible confusions the concept of self-reflection proffers are produced by the ambiguity of *both* parts of the term: self and reflection.

---

17. See the introduction to Hutcheon's *Narcissistic Narratives* for a discussion of this criticism.
18. Van Alphen addresses this paradox in his book on reading attitudes and postmodernism by differentiating between the reading attitudes proposed by the text and those adopted by the reader. He distinguishes four possible attitudes in relation to the corpus he discusses: the realistic text read realistically; the post-modern text read post-modernistically; the post-modern text read realistically and the realistic text read post-modernistically. A realistic text is then a work which is not wholly realistic, but which both fits the conventions of realism and has elements that enable, or even encourage, a "post-modern," self-reflective, reading attitutde. See van Alphen *Bij wijze*, 59. In "Esther," which is neither realistic nor, of course, post-modern, the problem of obedience is thematized on the level of the narrative.

The element "self-" requires the reader to consider which self is at stake in the reflection: that of the work or/and that of the reader? I will assume that self-reflection needs to risk the reader's entanglement within the work and, thus, must endorse the reflection of/on *both* selves. This is suggested by the ambiguity of the word "reflection," meaning both (visual) mirroring and (discursive) thinking.[19] Taking self-reflection as mirroring leads one to considerations of the Lacanian mirror-stage as a first, visually based construction of the self *in* self-alienation, while discursive self-reflection leads to self-critique.

The two ambiguities of the word reflection, coupled with the two possible selves to be reflected lead to four possible positions, which together yield a useful typology of self-reflection. The mirroring and the analytical, discursive form of reflection differentiate between non-reflective, possibly unconscious doubling of the work, and a conscious position toward the work that problematizes representation. In the first case, there are two possiblities again, according to the meaning of "self" involved.

1. The fantasmatic position. If the critic responds to the self of the work only, taking it as radically other and leaving him- or herself safely out of reach— or dangerously unconscious. This is Haman's mistake when in 3:6 he fantasmatically projects his rage about Mordecai, a purely personal insult, on the insubordination of the Jews in general. Seeing Mordecai as mirroring his entire people, he fails to see the mirroring relationship between himself and Mordecai which entails the reversibility between their positions. This failure to see (himself) is Haman's *lot*, his *pur*, which will undermine his plot because it undermines his autonomy as an agent.

2. The narcissistic position. If, in contrast, the two selves are conflated in the mirroring, while the reflection remains non-reflective (i.e. non-analytical, non-discursive), the result will show symptoms of primary narcissism as described by Lacan in his paper on the mirror stage. This mode of self-reflection can be read in the self-absorptive isolation of the three figures in each of the Rembrandts. It is obviously also at stake in Haman's childish dream of grandeur when he can only imagine himself to be the object of the king's project of honoring (6:6–8). This is why Haman is blind for Rembrandt, so blind that, already curbed in the first painting, he loses his balance, falls down in the second.

The discursive mode of self-reflection, which entails that one take an explicit position on the reflexive qualities of the work and the self, can again take two distinct forms.

3. The theoretical position. If the reflection is limited to the self of the work, the work is taken as a theoretical statement about representation. The text or painting becomes a theory, *Las Meninas* a statement on classical re-

---

19. The different spellings—self-reflexion referring to mirroring, self-reflection to thinking— are not consistently differentiated, and do not hold in French, where the same word carries the same ambiguity. If we have two different words, at least they are homonyms, close enough semantically to be confused in practice.

presentation. The letters in "Esther" become statements about writing and its relationship of prevailance to reality (e.g. 1:19). The critic who states that "conveniently, Esther seems to know nothing of the irrevocability of Persian law" (Murphy, *Wisdom* 167) endorses this self-reflection without further questioning it: for him, apparently, writing produces reality, and all else is subordinated to this certainty.

4. The metacritical position. The second mode in this category, and the fourth mode of self-reflective reading, is the one in which discursive, reflective reading involves both the self of the work—the way in which it problematizes itself as representation—and the self of the critic, whose position as, say, an art historian or a philosopher is also the subject of reflection. This self-reflection requires that the splitting of the agency of writing, staged in the narrative, be taken as a representation of the position of the critic. For this mode of self-reflection we cannot take the blind Haman as a model but the seeing Esther, whom Rembrandt represents in awareness of her isolated position, yet who accepts her split subjectivity, endorses Mordecai's wish and faces death in order to save lives. Reading Haman's decree "properly," as producing reality yet leaving space for intervention in writing's feature of delay (see below), while also acknowledging the embeddedness of subject positions, she is able to produce a rewriting of the fate of the Jews (8:5). Hers is the position the critic is best off to mirror him-or herself in (table 1).

Table 1

self: reflection:	self excluded	self included
visual mirroring	1 fantasma (3:6)	2 primary narcissism (6:6–8)
discursive reflection	3 text = theory (1:19)	4 metacriticism (8:5)

One of two major problems of this mode of reading, its generality, is to be countered by specifying self-reflection according to this systematic analysis. The other, its lack of historical awareness, is harder to deal with. I would contend, however, that approaching "Esther" in this way is historical in two ways. By committing this blatant anachronism, the historical position of the critic is at least foregrounded; which is precisely lacking in less overtly anachronistic readings discussed in notes 7 and 11. Thus the unity between text and critic which is the basis of most criticism is broken up, leaving room for historical awareness, even if that awareness entails acknowledgment of the impossibility of historical reconstruction. Second, emphasizing writing as a central theme in the narrative is impossible without relating writing to power, and thus the anthropological critique of writing as the beginning of history comes within sight. In other words, an analysis of writing historicizes itself as well as historicism. Hence, the fourth category of self-reflection imposes itself: the mirroring of history in criticism, which necessitates discursive reflection, and which poses the historical position of text and reader in relation to each other.

The historical position I wish to advocate is less committed to producing a (in my view illusory) reconstruction of the past than an awareness of difference in similarity. In this line, I have argued elsewhere that the unstable beginning of patriarchy as represented in Genesis 2–3 is visible from the equally unstable ending of patriarchy we are living now.[20] Similarly, the emphasis on writing in Esther betrays the non-obviousness of writing, which becomes visible again today, in an age where writing is in the process of losing its self-evidence. The exercise of power through writing of which the (p)lot of Esther consists, can be problematized at the time of bomb-letters; the dispersal of the sender, hence, of the holder of power, in "Esther" becomes visible at the time of the information revolution; the uncertainty of the irrevocable nature of writing becomes visible at a time when computerized writing enables us to delete what was once written, to falsify copies, and to do what Esther does: to overrule in practice what was irrevocable in theory, to use similarity for difference (compare 3:12–15 with 8:9–11). In accordance with self-reflection, for the ancient author the same holds as for the modern critic: writing "Esther" produces Esther writing.

"ESTHER" WRITING ESTHER WRITING

Lots, laws, banquets, and letters: these are the gadgets used for the plot of "Esther." All these are perverted from their standard functions, and that is how they can become agents, overruling the characters that handle them. Lots are countered by plots, laws emerge out of the particular instead of regulating the general, banquets do not serve to feed but to empty, and letters are cut off from their senders. All four relate to writing: Haman's cast lot is followed up by the writing of the decree which organizes lot's randomness into plot's system; laws are emphatically written, but remain caught in the tension between the particular and the general which undermines their fixation by writing; banquets initiate the writing of decrees, and letters are, of course, the very embodiment of writing. But letters emphasize a particular aspect of writing: its problematic status as a speech act, fixing the ephemerical fluidity of speech, yet delaying its

20. See *Lethal Love*, ch. 5.

efficacy. I contend that "Esther" can be read as a reflection on just these aspects of writing.

To begin with the two central letters, then, it is obvious that the second one reverses the first, while the first was explicitly stipulated to be irrevocable (1:19). Ahasuerus/Haman's decree to exterminate the Jews is overruled, annihilated by Ahasuerus/Mordecai's decree to exterminate the enemies. At first reading, these two letters seem almost identical; they mirror each other in a beautiful symmetry. But this mirroring is possible because they are quoted indirectly; they are not written out in the canonical text. When they are written out, as in the apocryphal supplement, they are totally different, and it turns out their symmetry sacrifices their writing.[21] This is a first indication that mirroring is uncertain, that reflection needs to be reflected upon. These letters are mirroring as narrative plot elements, not mirroring as texts. And if we read the canonical text from the perspective of their difference infused by the excursus to the apocrypha, it turns out the second letter is, indeed, not just a reversal. There is a people supplemented ("and also for the Jews in their own script and language," 8:9), as well as an action ("unite and defend themselves," 8:11). And the subject of writing is increasingly diffused.

Plot and counterplot are not symmetrical on yet another score; the one is initiated by lot, the other by reading (the first letter). The lot is a random "text" read by Haman and blindly obeyed; the decree is a plotted text, and is disobeyed. The response to Haman's decree can be seen as a reflection on reading, offering an alternative to blind submission. Reading is a response, a reader-response. The letter/counter-letter confrontation offers a reader-response theory. It proposes that reading is neither fixed by, nor independent of, the text. Obedience to the text (of Haman's decree) would have been killing; disobedience in the sense of ignoring, bracketing it, would have been equally killing. This danger of binary opposition between over-estimating and under-estimating the power of writing—is represented in the narrative by the split between Haman's fall and Esther and Mordecai's elevation on the one hand, and the necessity of writing of the second decree on the other, not rendered superfluous by the victory of the two figures. What is needed to save the Jews / to make reading a historically meaningful act, is an adequate reading by a competent and committed subject who disposes of autonomous agency.[22] There cannot be exact mirroring; there is no symmetry between oppressor and oppressed, between attack and defense, between letter and answer, no more than between subject and mirror-image. With the engagement of speech in narrative, in the plot, writing can only alter what was there before.

21. See "the Rest of the chapters of the Book of Esther which are found neither in the Hebrew nor in the Syriac," *The New English Bible with the Apocrypha*, Oxford Studies Edition 1976, 3:13 insert, and 16:12 insert.
22. See Tompkins, "The Reader in History" for a relevant view of the historical importance of reading.

What, then, can the written narrative "Esther" teach us about writing, how can it make us more self-conscious about the writing we do about the writing it presents about writing—of letters as communicative action, of decrees as prescriptive behavior, of chronicles as a delayed participation in history, of writing as a mirror of the text of "Esther" ?

Writing has social functions, commented on by anthropological critique; it has a relation to narrativity, and it has semiotic functions. As it happens, writing, in "Esther," exemplifies the social functions of writing within its narrative and semiotic functions. The act of writing is emplotted in such a way as to undermine the standard social functions of writing as criticized in the orality-literacy debate. Thereby it engages reflection on the politics of writing and reading.

The primary writer is, or should be in a true autocracy, the king, who uses it to exercise his authority. But, already in his first letter condemning Vashti, the only one he even remotely writes himself, this goes awry on three levels of increasing severity. Firstly, on his own initiative Ahasuerus' authority is diluted by the agency of his "wise men" who effectively undermine the king's authentic writing by dictating its contents (1:19-20). Secondly, and as a consequence, his superiority is suspended by the generalization of his particular humiliation by the disobedient Vashti into an insult to all men ("Queen Vashti has done wrong, and not to the king alone" 1:16) that needs to be countered by a law, meant to reinforce the authority of "*all* husbands, high and low alike" (1:20).[23] And thirdly, his domination as a man, thus proclaimed to be the real issue, is undermined when Esther ends up organizing, and even doing some of the writing.[24] Hence, as if to emphasize the ambivalence of the complicity between writing and power, the state, class, and gender respectively are undermined by writing. This is the statement on the *social* function of writing that can be read in the self-reflection of writing in "Esther."

The *narrative* function of writing in the scroll further undermines the certainties writing deceptively seems to provide. The three decrees which constitute the elementary structure of the plot stage the ambivalence of writing with acuteness and detail. The first decree, banning Vashti, was meant to fix forever the obedience of wives, hence, male power over women in private and public. In its excessive ambition and fearful defensiveness, possibly parodic (Murphy 159), this intention cannot but fail, and the rest of the story will stage that failure. The submission of women cannot be fixed by writing, the story

---

23. Murphy (*Wisdom* 159) mentions this extension of event into law as one of the wisdom motifs of "Esther," recalling Prov. 31:10 ff and Sir. 9:2. For the view that "Esther" belongs to wisdom literature, see also Talmon, "'Wisdom'."

24. *Contra* many commentators who emphasize Esther's obedience, it must be stressed that she is more like Vashti than they would like. Both disobey in relation to *coming to the king*, thus taking control over their relationship with their husband. Otwell, *And Sarah Laughed*, 69, for example, only sees in Esther "the primary Old Testament example of an obedient daughter" (*sic*)

tells us. Esther's initiatives embody her agency exercized against the royal rule that stipulated the absoluteness of her powerlessness: the interdiction for her to *be*, to approach the king. Vashti's punishment, the law of the first decree, is thus overruled by Esther's symmetrical transgression.

The second decree, Haman's (p)lot, even less Ahasuerus' doing than the first, equally irrevocable but, as it happens, equally futile, is less ambitious and more cautious. It stipulates the submission—albeit absolute, in extermination—of only a portion of the population: one people instead of all wives. It is more cautious in that it is grounded not in "wisdom," human opinion that is, but in Haman's version of providence, the lot cast in his presence (3:7) in order to fix the date for the realization of the decree. Writing alone, this casting of the lot seems to say, is too shaky a ground to build on. This lot is countered by the providence Mordecai suggests to Esther in 4:14. Writing, meant to fix, does not fix well enough.

Again, the narrative mode itself, constructed as it is on temporal sequentiality, is mirrored by, and mirrors, the incidental "rests" of writing. For in the narrative writing is used to produce danger, but not defeat; and between the two lies the space of the delay inherent in writing, which undermines the fixation it aims for. This delay is a crucial feature of writing, here exploited to represent the revocability of the irrevocable. It is what makes identification between parties, writer, reader, and object, impossible, as the recent critique of anthropology has argued so well.[25] Writing's fixation entails a "not yet" which calls for a sequel, and which mirrors narrative's pursuit of an ending.[26] The narrative play of letter-writing foregrounds the unwarranted pretence of writing-as-power, as "never to be revoked."

So crucial is this feature of delay in writing that it is staged in an almost comical way in one of the episodes considered "implausible" by realistic standards and alleged against the king's intelligence by psychological standards.[27] In addition to letters, a communicative mode of writing, and decrees, the variant of the letter based on the exercise of power, the *chronicle* used in the narrative. In a "historical" narrative this is a self-reflexive genre *par excellence*, as it is incorporated in another chronicle. The events narrated by "Esther" in 2:21-23—how Mordecai saves the king—are similar to those narrated by "Esther" as a whole—how Esther and Mordecai save the Jews, thus also saving the king's integrity. Both "third-person narratives" or historical report, the chronicle and the scroll of which it is a part, represent

---

25. Fabian, *Time and the Other*, is entirely devoted to the close examination of the impossibility of what Fabian calls coevalness, the simultaneity between observation/ participation and writing. This impossibility by principle makes the very anthropological endeavor illusory.

26. See Peter Brooks, *Reading for the Plot*.

27. See Clines, *Ezra* 259, among many others for the former, Sasson for the latter criticism. As I argued above, these views based on anachronistic standards are mainly harmful in that they obscure other issues and the narrative motivations that enhance these. Thus the implicit perspective on the text does not do justice to its historical-literary specificity and is thereby implicitly complicitous with ethnocentrism or rather, as I like to call it, parontocentrism.

something outside themselves. The chronicle, in this sense, is a *mise en abyme*.²⁸ Written after the event, it is not read, not integrated into history, not acted upon, until much later. In that sense, too, it is a *mise en abyme* of this story about the delayed effect of writing.

Obviously, this chronicle-story also displays the suppression of memory by writing (Plato's warning) since Ahasuerus only thinks of rewarding Mordecai when he *reads* the event, not when it happened. But rather than interpreting this connection between writing and memory anachronistically as proof of the king's dim-wittedness, I like to see here another instance of self-reflection. For the delay of writing exemplified by this forgetfulness is utterly indispensable for the narrative plot, which in turn is indispensable for the survival of the Jews from the danger of writing, which in turn is indispensable for the instoration of Purim. Such is the lot of writing.

Ahasuerus' real power is located in this identity as the reader of the chronicle, and the adequacy of his reading; the figure had to display his failing memory in order to make his real function visible. While the written text was futile before he read it, the king is now called upon to act: that justice be done to the writing. This self-reflection addresses us: the delayed readers, called upon to see that good deeds (such as Mordecai's, which, in fact, consisted of conserving knowledge and using it to avert danger) be rewarded and no people be destroyed.

Finally, writing is also foregrounded in its *semiotic* function. If we take the Peircean typology of signs as a model, not of truth but like the Rembrandt paintings, as an approach or reading device, writing in "Esther" can be viewed as symbolic, indexical, and iconic at once, and the very fact that it fits all these categories represents its crucial place in the text. That fact is also, as I hope to show, the cement that binds the elements of the plot together.

Firstly, writing is *symbolic*, as the first, most ambitious decree demonstrates. It is used for law-making, while it embodies the law itself. This happens in three modes of expansion which turn a happening into a sign, giving it repetitive meaning: a. generalization, b. publication, and c. multiplication.

a. The generalization of Vasthi's challenge and punishment into a law turns an incident into a rule, and a random occurrence into a convention. Vasthi's crime is, precisely, the possibility for this semiotization of her act. The ambivalence of writing is immediately visible again, it is part of the package so to speak: although the event is turned into a law out of fear of spreading, the writing itself promulgates it, by spreading its meaning. Thus, out of fear of contamination a private event is turned into the sign of a generalized battle of the sexes. What is reflected (upon) here, I like to think, is the danger of generalization: it produces enemies, and turns an incident into a war.

---

28. A sign that represents the work as a whole in which it is incorporated. This term, by now quite well known, was introduced by Gide and extensively studied by Dällenbach, *Le récit spéculaire*. I have commented on, and expanded, Dällenbach's use of the term in chapter 2.

b. The writing publicizes the event, and this word must be taken as literally possible: it publicizes as a newspaper would today. The publication of the event is meant to make an impact on each and every household. Like the paper falling on the doormat, the letter about Vashti reaches the life of all men, and changes their relationships to women (1:22). Publication is the semiotic act of generalization, and makes it irrevocable.

c. The writing is multiplied, "to every province in its own script and to every people in their own language" (1:22; 3:12; 8:9). This third form of expansion by multiple translation further emphasizes the semiotic nature of the ideological act of generalization. But is also turns writing against itself. It is because of the multiplication of copies that Mordecai learns about the projected pogrom and is able to initiate counter-action, to write back.

Secondly, writing is also represented in "Esther" as *indexical*. It is emphatically material, a materiality which is signified by the king's signet-ring. This ring, meant to produce "pure" indexes—the impression of the seal into the wax—becomes the locus of the perversion of indexicality. On the one hand, the letters can be copied, but only after there has been an original, issued from the body of the king. But on the other hand, the copying proceeds via the signet taken from his finger to Haman's (3:12). It is precisely the king's mistake to take the ring off his own body, thus severing the contiguity on which indexicality is based. This is a mistake he corrects later: although he gives the retrieved signet to Mordecai, this time he seems to keep an eye on what is written in his name (8:8), and in any case, no conflict between what the king desires and what is written will arise in this later episode.

By thus emphasizing the materiality of writing, the text also establishes a continuity between writing and (other forms of) body-language. Dress becomes a form of writing when it receives semiotic status by indexical signification, such as the royal dress worn by Mordecai at his honorary tour through the city. Haman, the writer of the plot-letter, devices this indexical code himself, when adding to "royal robes" the emphatic index "which the king himself wears" (6:8). Next to the signet-ring, which gave him royal power, his identification with the king must be pushed further: Haman wants to *be* the king, and the index is the most appropriate sign to signify this impossible conflation that would render signs superfluous. Thus he stipulates that iconic signification—robes looking like royal—is not enough.

Another instance of indexical body-writing is the (conventional, hence, symbolic) sign of royal favor, expressed by touch. The index is doubly coded: the king holds the sceptre, thus extending his body into the (symbolic) sign of his power, and the sceptre touches Esther. It may be sheer luck that this tool for union of husband and wife bears an iconic relation to the tool of sexual union, also coded as power, but in any case, it also bears comparison with the material instrument of writing whose use this favorable sign will later yield to Esther.

Thirdly, writing is also *iconically* meaningful in this text. In its mode of publication the decree is displayed, a display which the demonstration of wealth as power at the first banquet foreshadowed. As a fixation of future happenings, in the decrees, and of past happenings, in the chronicle, writing also iconically signifies fate: providence as opposed to lots. In both cases, certainty is not absolute but requires additional agency as well. The writing can be undone when a subject intervenes in time—thanks to the delay inherent in writing and in narrative—just as the lots can be undone by plotting, and providence helped by courage and wit. These iconic meanings of writing, then, strengthen the connections between the different elements of the plot, already produced by the symbolic and the indexicial meanings. The semiotic functions of writing help to read "Esther" as a meaningful, relevant statement on writing as something that requires active intervention: writing requires reading; "Esther" requires us.

But if the self-reflexive text thus encourages (discursive) reflection on the act of reading, the resulting self-reflection entails reflection on the subject of that act. It seems meaningful that the subject of writing of the last letter is the one whose very existence as a subject needed to be written first: Esther, touched by the royal sceptre, ends this narrative of writing by an act of writing-as-power:

> And Queen Esther and Mordecai the Jew wrote, giving full authority and confirming this second letter about Purim. (9:29)

The narrative has accomplished its remarkable movement, from the king as subject already undermined, to the authority of the woman, commoner, foreigner, who started out as a girl without parents; a movement, also, from the hazards of the lot to the organization of Purim by writing, lot's counterpart. But it took an entire narrative to produce this full subject. For subjectivity is by no means self-evident.

THE SUBJECT OF WRITING

Foucault's remark on *Las Meninas* provoked the question: whose self is reflected in self-reflection? As it turns out, "Esther" provides this question with a new dimension, for to begin with, it stages its unanswerability. The male subject is represented as dispensable, shifting, unstable, and writing is the locus of these features. On the other hand, the female subject, most dispensable at first, is also the one which re-emerges, strengthens herself, and ultimately takes over, albeit on the very grounds of the uncertainty of subjectivity.

In order to understand the view of subjectivity that emerges from this self-reflexive text, it is necessary to eliminate the realistic and psychological readings which are so hard to avoid. I propose to bracket any attempt to see the characters in terms of psychological plausibility by foregrounding their functional status. And it then becomes obvious that as narrative agents, the characters are both unstable and exchangeable. For example, Vashti is necessary to produce Esther. In the plot, the elimination of the former produces the vacancy necessary for the latter, hence, for the unfolding of the plot. But there is more to this narrative status of the first queen. As an agent of ideological reflection she is eliminated for the sake of the ideology of male dominance. But she is eliminated only to re-emerge in Esther, who takes her place, avenging her punishment by turning disobedience into access to power. Vashti's refusal to be an object of display is in a sense a refusal to be objectivized, hence, to be robbed of her subjectivity. Esther's insistence to appear, although using the tools of display (5:1: "On the third day, Esther put on her royal robes...") is the positive version of Vashti's negative act; she appears not for show but for action, not as sheer possession but as self-possessed subject, and to drive this continuity between Esther and Vashti home, it is now she who makes the king appear at her banquet.[29]

Similarly, Haman, in all his wickedness, is necessary to produce Mordecai and his counter-plot. He seems to come out of nowhere in 3:1, but without him and his (p)lotting we would have no narrative, hence, no Purim; it is well deserved, then, that the festival is named after his initial act. Haman's introduction as newcomer and other than the established men can be seen as a narrative necessity to eliminate too close a watch on Esther's obedience by the enraged wise men of 1:16-22. Esther and Mordecai produce each other: without Esther, Mordecai would have no access to the court; without her cousin, Esther would have no access to news from the city. Both sources of information are indispensable to supplement the defects of writing. The narrative production of characters makes a psychological reading both futile and mystifying. Such a reading obscures the very issue that narrative production foregrounds: the instability of subjectivity.

With this in mind, it is easy to see that writing is the semiotic act *par excellence* where the subject is destabilized, and again, "Esther" uses that fact for its plotting. Indeed, the awareness of historical discrepancy helps us to

---

29. The sometimes alleged idea that Vashti was asked to appear naked before the king, totally ungrounded, does point to the sense of objectifying display and its gendered quality. Although Ahasuerus is criticized for his "male chauvinistic behavior" (Clines, *Ezra*, 257) Vashti's refusal, justified as it is in light of that view, is often criticized with the inconsistency typical of unreflected gender-ideology. Conflating themselves with ancient patriarchy, some critics tend to endorse, to fully underwrite, the sexism in the event rather than noticing the shakiness of male power which the episode also underscores. Zlotowitz, *The Megillah* 46-51 provides a characteristic example. Quoting ancient commentaries which deny Vashti honorable motivations, a series of negative reasons end in the judgment that she deserved death, then in the statement that she was indeed killed, and, providing a subject, the compiler ends by stating (without reference to another commentator) that Ahasuerus had her killed. Interestingly, at the very moment the critic provides this imaginary murder with a subject, he forgets to specify the subject of his own text, thus endorsing the view put forward and allowing himself to be non-reflectively reflected in ancient ideology.

reflect on the historicity of the very notion of subjectivity. As Derrida reminds us, the notion of writing as expression of the self is a modern one, emerging with the pre-romantic individualism of Rousseau, and may itself be a symptom of the loss of the self in writing. It seems to be a nicety of history that the same Rousseau used his self as a weapon against the law which decreed a *prise de corps* (!) against him. And as Peggy Kamuf recalls, it is in and through the signature, considered indexically contiguous to the body of the writer, that the illusory stability of the subject of writing is signified. The need for the signature is the need for indexicality.

But "Esther" severs the bond between the signature and the subject of writing. The coming and going of the signet-ring from body to body is the narrative representation of the subjective instability which writing promotes. Kamuf rightly emphasizes the evenemential status of the signature, its narrativity, when she writes:

> ... signature occurs in a difference from itself and an address to the other. (18)

The writings in "Esther" dramatize this mobility of the subject of writing. The chronicle of 2:23, for example, has no subject. There is neither a represented self—a chronicle is a "third-person" narrative where the thematic subject—the agent of the events—is written about, not writing; a so-called "objective" presentation—nor a signature—it was written in the presence of, hence, not by the king. The subject of the chronicle is, however, inscribed otherwise: in the structure of address, here dramatized by the delayed reading.

It is not enough, for writing to reach its destiny, that it be written in the presence of its intended reader; it must be actually read in order to accede to its full deployment *as* writing. Without the act of reading, writing remains a dead letter. In other words, the reader is the subject of writing, responsible for its consequences, for the production of reality it designs. By rewarding Mordecai, Ahasuerus shows himself a competent subject in this specific sense, and his apparently defective memory is a ploy used to drive this point home.

The description of the apparatus of royal administration and the postal system in 3:12, to give another example, whatever meaning one may give it as display of power or as circumstantial evidence of the text's historicity, can also be seen in light of the shifting subject of writing. The act of writing is broken down into its different aspects, each provided with an unclear subject: the secretaries are summoned (by whom?); the writ is issued (by whom?);[30] it is drawn up in the king's name, which means, precisely, not *by* him but *for* him by someone else; and it is sealed with the king's signet, no longer at his finger. The stamp which is designed to be proof of identity has become the index of a writing without subject.

Again, writing emblematizes a feature that the narrative also displays elsewhere. The subject is generally questioned, and the plot is built on that

---

30. By Haman, obviously, but this is not *stated*.

questioning. The irony of 6:4–6 provides one example among many. Haman must decide the honor whose destiny is Mordecai, but does so by mistaking the subject to be honored. The king mistakes Haman, assuming he is a reliable adviser; hence, naming the subject of honor is irrelevant. Haman, because he wishes to use the power to merge his subjectivity with the king's, has not revealed the name of the people to be destroyed, which would have saved his enterprise. Thus the plot is built on subjectivity by default.

As if to foreground the intimate complicity of language in this plot of mistaken identities, Haman's use of language is doubly defective when, in 6:7–9, he mistakes the identity of the man to be honored, in other words, when he misreads the king's speech: he speaks in an anacoluthon, producing "bad" language, and he misfires, producing a "bad" speech-act. Hence, the same speech-act demonstrate the failure of "writer" and "reader" due to unwarranted assumptions about the subject.

If we read the text from the perspective suggested by the Rembrandt paintings, as reflections of and on the problematic relationship between text and subject, the problematic of the subject of writing sheds light on the entire narrative: its language, its plot, and its subjects. And the reader is not spared; delayed by writing, his or her action is still on call. Haman's blindness in the St. Petersburg painting threatens to contaminate the viewer/ reader whom his body is emphatically addressing: the icon of blind eyes is dangerously indexical as body-language.

CONCLUSION

At this juncture, the critical question must be addressed: what have we gained from this willfully anchronistic mustering of a contemporary concept for this ancient text? Although it is better answered by others, I suggest a few possibilities. I have no wish to make any claim about the historical meaning of the text, let alone the authorial intention of the origin of Purim, but I do think I have been able to make a negative claim, against the nineteenth-century model of reading predominant in many readings that do claim historical validity. While the enigma of the origin of Purim and the meaning of its name is not, cannot be, solved, I have opened a space for an interpretation of the meaning of *purim* that concerns the contemporary reader while illuminating aspects of the text whose pertinence can hardly be denied.

Guided by an oddity in the two paintings by Rembrandt, I have tried to draw a few lines that break the text up while also pulling its various elements together, not in a deceptive coherence but in a problematization of unity. By looking into the various meanings of self-reflection and the ways these meanings can be seen to be dramatized in "Esther," I have developed a view on the ancient text which affects the subject of criticism. For if reading is the only way to blow life into the dead letter of the text, and if, moreover, reading is a matter of historical importance, then Esther becomes a mirror for the contemporary critic. Like her, exposing the abuse of power, the danger of writing, and the instability of subjectivity, the critic can neither escape the responsibility for her activity nor the incapsulation of that activity in historically diverse, subject-less writing.

Thus, writing criticism in the way of Esther entails that one does not obscure its predecessors nor its opponents, its complicities nor its agency. "Esther" demonstrates that writing is neither automatically a deadly bomb nor an innocent toy; closer to the time-bomb than to anything else, it can be countered by virtue of its delayed effect. Hence, when involved in the act of reading—the delayed completion of writing—any critic should be both aware of her or his implicit allegiances (reading is done in dispersal of subjectivity) and his or her inevitable contribution to action (it is an act).

In terms of allegiances, one cannot but reflect on the question of where the "rests" of one's subjectivity are: to go with Ahasuerus "wise men" and their battle or with Esther and Mordecai and their collaboration? to endorse or to reject the generalization of Vashti into "all women" yet the individualization of Esther as different from Vashti? This question of implicit allegiance to ideological positions is less obvious than it seems, precisely because obvious positions are offered as a lure. It is only too easy to disavow Haman's genocidal impulse, but the mirror also shows similarities with other generalizations from individual to a whole people, other hatreds for the other people inhabiting our land. Those other positions and their similarity to the obvious one need to be brought to awareness by a reflection that includes the critic's self. By insisting on the complicated functioning of writing and the instability of its subjects, "Esther" shows that critics are no more than other reader/writers, autonomous and stable; hence, the network of unconscious allegiances is inevitable and dangerous.

In order to draw all readers in, *purim* must be a plural form. The Rembrandt painting precisely warns the viewer not to be blind to the mirroring power of the text which stretches beyond immediate and simple historical veracity, into the realm of historical agency. Had Mordecai and Esther been as blind as Haman, they would have been inadequate readers, powerless to exploit the delay of writing. Searching for the historical origin of Purim in a forlorn past, safely out of reach, the critic forfeits her or his own *purim*. For when the lot has determined that another people is now subject to danger, the critic reading "Esther" cannot innocently submit to lots. For obedience was shown to be the wrong attitude. It is an ironic misreading of the mirror of "Esther" to see the scroll as only about the history of the Jews and one of their festivals. By reading the text as about reading-writing, one is led to reflect upon all the issues intricated with it: upon gender, power, and the state, upon genocide and otherness, submission and agency. In short, upon history.[31]

31. I thank Daniel Boyarin for having initiated the idea for this paper, and Fokkelien van Dijk Hemmes, Athalya Brenner and Ovira Shapiro for their help with the text.

Bibliography

Abicht, Ludo, "Marx, Freud, and the Writers: A New Attempt at Integration," *Style* 18 (1984): 377–86.
Alpers, Svetlana, "Interpretation without Representation," *Representations* 1, 31–42.
——, *Rembrandt's Enterprise: The Studio and the Market*. Chicago: The University of Chicago Press, 1988.
——, "Art History and Its Exclusions," in Broude and Garrard, *Feminism and Art History: Questioning the Litany*. New York: Harper and Row, 1982.
Alphen, Ernst van, "The Narrative of Perception and the Perception of Narrative," *Poetics Today* 11, 3, 483–510, 1990.
——, *Francis Bacon and the Loss of Self*. Cambridge, MA: Harvard University Press, 1993.
Althusser, Louis, *Lenin and Philosophy and Other Essays*. Translated by Ben Brewster. London: New Left Books, 1971.
——, *For Marx*. translated by Ben Brewster. London: New Left Books, 1977.
Austin, J.L., *How to do Things with Words*. Cambridge: Harvard University Press, 1975.
Bal, Mieke, *Narratology: Introduction to the Theory of Narrative*. Translated by Christine van Boheemen. Toronto: The University of Toronto Press, 1985.
——, *Death and Dissymmetry: The Politics of Coherence in the Book of Judges*. Chicago: The University of Chicago Press, 1988.
——, *Reading Rembrandt: Beyond the Word-Image Opposition*. New York: Cambridge University Press, 1991.
——, "The Politics of Citation," *Diacritics* 21, 1, 25–45.
Bakhtin, Mikhail, *Rabelais and his World*. translated by H. Iswolsky. Cambridge, Mass.: Harvard University Press, 1968.
——, *The Dialogic Imagination*, edited by Michael Holquist, translated by Caryl Emerson and Michael Holquist, Austin, Texas: University of Texas Press, 1981.
Banfield, Ann, *Unspeakable Sentences: Narration and Representation in the Language of Fiction*. London: Routledge & Kegan Paul, 1982.
Bann, Stephen, *The Clothing of Clio: A Study of the Representation of History in Nineteenth-Century Brittain and France*. Cambridge and New York: Cambridge University Press, 1984.
Barthes, Roland, *Critique et vérité*. Paris: Editions du Seuil, 1966.
——, *Elements of Semiology*. Translated by Annette Lavers and Colin Smith, New York: Hill and Wang, 1967.

———, *S/Z*. translated by Richard Miller, New York: Hill and Wang, 1975.
———, *Image - Music - Text*, essays selected and translated by Stephen Heath, New York: Hill and Wang, 1977.
———, *Camera Lucida: Reflections on Photography*. Translated by Richard Howard. New York: Hill and Wang, 1981.
———, *Empire of Signs*. translated by Richard Howard, New York: Hill and Wang, 1982.
———, *The Fashion System*. Translated by Metthew Ward and Richard Howard. New York: Hill and Wang, 1983.
———, *The Responsibility of Forms: Critical Essays on Music, Art, and Representation*. translated by Richard Howard. New York: Hill and Wang, 1985.
———, *Mythologies*. translated by Annette Lavers, New York: Hill and Wang, 1988.
Baudrillard, Jean, *Le système des objects*. Paris: Gallimard, 1968.
———, *The Mirror of Production*. translated by Mark Poster, St. Louis: Telos Press, 1975.
———, *The Evil Demon of Images*. Power Institute Publications, 3. Sydney, Australia: University of Sydney, 1988.
Baxandall, Michael, *Patterns of Intention: On the Historical Explanation of Pictures*. New Haven: Yale University Press, 1985.
Benjamin, Walter, *The Origin of German Drama*, trans. John Osborne, London: New Left Books, 1977.
Benveniste, Emile, *Problems in General Linguistics*. translated by Mary Elizabeth Meek. Coral Gables: University of Miami Press, 1971.
Berger, John, *Ways of Seeing*. New York: Pantheon Books, 1972.
Bersani, Leo, *The Freudian Body: Psychoanalysis and Art*, New York: Columbia University Press, 1986.
Bersani, Leo and Ulysse Dutoit, *The Forms of Violence: Narrative in Ancient Assyria and Modern Culture*, New York: Columbia University Press, 1985.
Betterson, Rosemary, *Looking On: Images of Femininity in the Visual Arts and Media*. New York: Columbia University Press, 1987.
Bois, Yve-Alain, "Kahnweiler's Lesson," *Representations* 18 (1987): 33–68.
Booth, Wayne C., *The Rhetoric of Fiction*, Chicago: The University of Chicago Press, 1961.
Brooks, Peter, "Narrative Desire," *Style* 18 (1984): 3: 312–27.
Broude, Norma and Mary D. Garrard, eds., *Feminism and Art History: Questioning the Litany*. New York: Harper and Row, 1982.
Bruyn, J., B. Haak, S.H. Levie et al., *A Corpus of Rembrandt Paintings*. The Hague, Boston, London: Nijhoff, 1982, 1987, 1989.
Bryson, Norman, *Word and Image: French Painting of the Anicen Regime*. New York: Cambridge University Press, 1981.
———, *Tradition and Desire: From David to Delacroix*. New York: Cambridge University Press, 1983.
———, *Tradition and Desire: From David to Delacroix*, New York: Cambridge University Press, 1984.
———, "The Gaze in the Expanded Field," 87–114 in *Vision and Visuality*, edited by Hal Foster, Seattle, Bay Press, 1988.
———, *Looking at the Overlooked: Four Essays On Still Life*, Cambridge: Reaktion Press, 1990.
———, "Art in Context," in *Studies in Historical Change*, ed. Ralph Cohen, Charlottesville: University of South Carolina Press, 1991.
Burgin, Victor et al., eds., *Formations of Fantasy*. New York: Methuen, 1986.
Carrier, David, *Artwriting*. Amherst: University of Massechusetts Press, 1987.
Carroll, Margaret Deutsch, "The Erotics of Absolutism: Rubens and the Mystification of Sexual Violence," *Representations* 25 (1989): 3–30.

Casteras, Susan, *The Substance of the Shadow: Images of Victorian Womanhood*, New Haven: Yale University Press, 1982.

Certeau, Michel de, *The Practice of Everyday Life*. translated by Steven Rendall. Berkeley: The University of California Press, 1984.

———, *Heterologies: Discourse on the Other*. translated by Brian Massumi, foreword by Wlad Godzich. Minneapolis: The University of Minnesota Press, 1986.

Chaitin, Gilbert D., "Psychoanalysis and Narrative Action: The Primal Scene of the French Novel," *Style* 18 (1984): 3: 284–301.

Chapman, H. Perry, *Rembrandt's Self-Portraits*. Princeton: Princeton University Press, 1990.

Clark, T.J., *The Painting of Modern Life: Paris in the Art of Manet and his Followers*, London: Thames and Hudson, 1985.

Culler, Jonathan, *On Deconstruction: Theory and Criticism after Structuralism*, Ithaca: Cornell University Press, 1983.

———, *Roland Barthes*. New York: Oxford University Press, 1983.

———, *Framing the Sign: Criticism and Its Institutions*, Norman and London: The University of Oklahoma Press, 1988.

———, "Textual Self-Consciousness and the Textual Unconscious," *Style* 18 (1984): 3: 369–76.

Damisch, Hubert, *L'Origine de la perspective*, Paris: Flammarion, 1987.

De Lauretis, Teresa, *Alice Doesn't: Feminism, Semiotics, Cinema*. London: McMillan, 1983.

———, *Technologies of Gender: Essays on Theory, Film, and Fiction*. Bloomington: Indiana University Press, 1987.

Derrida, Jacques, *Of Grammatology*. Translated and with an introduction by Gayatri Chakravorty Spivak. Baltimore: The Johns Hopkins University Press, 1976.

———, *La vérité en peinture*. Paris: Editions du Seuil, 1978. *The Truth in Painting*, trans. Geoff Bennington and Ian McLeod. Chicago: The University of chicago Press, 1987.

———, "Living On: Border Lines," 75–176 in *Deconstruction and Criticism*, edited by Harold Bloom et al., New york: Seabury Press, 1979.

———, *Dissemination*, translated with an Introduction and additional notes by Barbara Johnson, Chicago: The University of Chicago Press, 1982.

———, *Limited Inc*. Translated by Samuel Weber. Evanston, Ill.: Northwestern University Press, 1988.

Dreyfuss, Hubert L. and Paul Rabinow, *Michel Foucault: Beyond Structuralism and Hermeneutics*, Chicago: The University of Chicago Press, 1983.

Dijkstra, Bram, *Idols of Perversity: Fantasies of Feminine Evil in Fin-de-Siècle Culture*, New York: Rizzoli, 1986.

Eco, Umberto, *A Theory of Semiotics*. Bloomington: Indiana University Press, 1976.

———, *The Role of the Reader: Explorations in the Semiotics of Texts*, Bloomington: Indiana University Press, 1979.

———, *Semiotics and the Philosophy of Language*, Bloomington: Indiana University Press, 1984.

———, *Travels in Hyperreality*. translated by William Weaver. San Diego: Harcourt, Brace, Jovanovitch, 1986.

———, *The Limits of Interpretation*. Bloomington: Indiana University Press, 1990.

Eco, Umberto and Thomas A. Sebeok, *The Sign of Three: Dupin, Holmes, Peirce*. Bloomington: Indiana University Press, 1983.

Felman, Shoshana, "To Open the Question," *Yale French Studies* 55/56 (1977): 5–10.

———, *Jacques Lacan and the Adventure of Insight: Psychoanalysis in Contemporary Culture*. Cambridge: Harvard University Press, 1987.

Fineman, Joel, "The Structure of Allegorical Desire" in *October* 12 (1980): 47–66.

Foucault, Michel, *The Order of Things: An Archeology of the Human Sciences*, trans. Alan Sheridon, New York: Vintage Books, 1973.
———, *The Archeology of Knowledge*, trans. A.M. Sheridan Smith, New York: Vintage Books, 1975.
———, "What is an Author?," in *Language, Counter-Memory, Practice: Selected Essays and Interviews*, ed. Donald F. Bouchard, Ithaca: Cornell University Press 113-38, 1977.
———, *This is Not a Pipe*, translated and edited by James Harkness. Berkeley: University of California Press, 1983.
Frappier-Mazur, Lucienne, "Desire, Writing and Identify in the Romantic Mystical Novel: Notes for a Definition of the Feminine," *Style* 18 (1984): 3: 328-54.
Fried, Michael, *Absorption and Theatricality: Painting and Beholder in the Age of Diderot*. Berkeley: The University of California Press, 1980.
———, *Realism, Writing, Disfiguration: On Thomas Eakins and Stephen Crane*, Chicago: The University of Chicago Press, 1987.
Freud, Sigmund, *The Standard Edition of the Complete Works of Sigmund Freud*, ed. James Strachey, London: The Hogarth Press, 1953-66.
Gallop, Jane, "Lacan and Literature: a Case for Transference," *Poetics* 13 (1984): 301-8.
———, "Lacan and Literature: A Case for Transference," *Poetics* 13 (1984): 4/5: 301-8.
Garrard, Mary D., *Artemesia Gentileschi: the Image of the Female Hero in Italian Baroque Art*, Princeton: Princeton University Press, 1988.
Genette, Grard, *Narrative Discourse: An Essay in Method*. translated by Jane E. Lewin, Ithaca and London: Cornell University Press.
Gombrich, E. H., *Art and Illusion: A Study in the Psychology of Pictorial Representation*, revised edition, Princeton: Princeton University Press, 1984.
Goodman, Nelson, *Languages of Art: An Approach to a Theory of Symbols*, Indianapolis: Bobbs-Merrill, 1968.
Grimaud, Michel, "Poetics from Psychoanalysis to Cognitive Psychology," *Poetics* 13 (1984): 4/5: 325-46.
Groeben, Nrobert, "Metatheoretical Problems of the Psychoanalytical Interpretation of Literature," *Poetics* 13 (1984): 4/5: 407-20.
Habermas, Jurgen, *Knowledge and Human Interests*, trans. Jeremy Shapiro, Boston: Beacon Press, 1971.
Hasenmueller, Chrsitine, "Panofsky, Iconography, and Semiotics," *Journal of Aesthetics and Art Criticism* 36, 289.
Hershkop, Ken and David Shepard, eds., *Bakhtin and Cultural Theory*, Manchester and New York: Manchester University Press, 1989.
Heusden, Barend van, "Psychoanalysis: in Search of the Hidden Rhetoric," *Poetics* 13 (1984): 4/5: 347-60.
Hodge, Robert and Gunther Kress, *Social Semiotics*. Ithaca: Cornell University Press, 1988.
Holly, Michael Ann, *Panofsky and the Foundations of Art History*. Ithaca: Cornell University Press, 1984.
———, "Past Looking," *Critical Inquiry* 16 (1990): 371-96
Huyssen, Andreas, "Anselm Kiefer: the Terror of History, the Temptation of Myth," *October* 48 (1989): 25-46.
Innis, Robert E. (ed.), *Semiotics: An Introductory Anthology*. Bloomington: Indiana University Press, 1984.
Iverson, Margaret, "Style as Structure: Alois Riegl's Historiography," *Art History* 2,1 (1979): 62-72.
———, "Saussure versus Peirce: Models for a Semiotics of Visual Art," in A.L. Rees and frances Borzello,eds., *The New Art History*. Atlantic Highlands, NJ: Humanities Press International / London: Camden Press, 1986.

Jakobson, Roman, "Two Aspects of Language and Two Types of Aphasic Disturbances," col. 2, 239-59 in *Selected Writings of Roman Jakobson*. The Hague: Mouton, 1971.
Johnson, Barbara, *A World of Difference*. Baltimore: The Johns Hopkins University Press, 1987.
Kampen, Nathalie Boymel, *Image and Status: Working Women in Ostia*. Basel: Mann, 1981.
———, "Status and Gender in Roman Art: The Case of the Saleswoman," in Broude and Garrard,eds., 1982.
Kamuf, Peggy, *Signature pieces: On the Insititution of Authorship*. Baltimore: The Johns Hopkins University Press, 1988.
Keller, Evelyn Fox, *Reflections on Gender and Science*. New Haven: Yale University Press, 1985.
Kemp, Wolfgang, Das Anteil des Betrachters: Rezeptionsasthetische Studien zur Malerei des 19. Jahrhunderts. Munich: Maander, 1985.
———, "Death at Work: A Case Study on Constitutive Blanks in Nineteenth-Century Painting," *Representations* 10 (1983): 102-23.
Kemp, Wolfgang, ed., *Der Betrachter ist im bild: Kunstwissenschaft und Rezeptionsasthetik*. Koln: Dumont Buch Verlag, 1985.
Krauss, Rosalind, "Notes on the Index: 70s Art in America," *October* 3-4 (1976-77): 68-81.
———, "The Originality of the Avant-Garde: A Postmodern Repetition," 13-30 in *Art After Modernism: Rethinking Representation*, ed. Brian Wallis, New York, New Museum of Contemporary Art / Boston: Godine, 1984.
———, "The Master's Bedroom," *Representations* 28 (1989): 55-76.
Kristeva, Julia, *Desire in Language: A Semiotic Approach to Literature and Art*, translated by Thomas Gora, Alice Jardine, and Leon S. Roudiez, edited Leon S. Roudiez, New York: Columbia University Press, 1980.
Lacan, Jacques, *Ecrits: A Selection*, edited and translated by A. Sheridan, New York: W.W. Norton, 1977.
———, *The Four Fundamental Concepts of Psycho-analysis*, trans. Alan Sheridan, Harmonthsworth: Penguin, 1979 (or: *Le Seminaire de Jacques Lacan, Livre XI, Les quatre concepts fondamentaux de la psychanalyse*, Paris: Editions du Seuil 1973).
———, *The Seminar of Jacques Lacan*, edited by J.-A. Miller, translated by John Forrester and Sylvana Tomaselli, New York: W.W. Norton, 1988.
Laplanche, Jean, *Life and Death in Psychoanalysis*, translated by Jeffrey Mehlman, Baltimore: The Johns Hopkins University Press, 1976.
Leach, Edmund, *Claude Levi-Strauss*. Chicago: The University of Chicago Press, 1974.
———, "Michelangelo's Genesis: A Structuralist Interpretation of the Central Panels of the Sistine Chapel Ceiling," *Semiotica* 56 (1979): 1-29.
Levi-Strauss, Claude, *The Raw and the Cooked*. translated by John and Doreen Weightman. New York: Harper and Row, 1969.
Linker, Kate, *Love for Sale: The Words and Pictures of Barbara Kruger*. New York: Harry N. Abrams, Inc., Publishers, 1990.
Lyotard, Jean-François, *The Postmodern Condition: A Report on Knowledge*. Translated by Geoff Bennington and Brian Massumi, forword by Fredrick Jameson. Minneapolis: University of Minnesota Press, 1984.
MacCabe, Colin, *Theoretical Essays: Film, Linguistics, Literature*. Manchester: Manchester University press, 1985.
Man, Paul de, *Allegories of Reading: Figural Language in Rousseau, Nietzsche, Rilke, and Proust*, New Haven: Yale University Press, 1979.
———, *Blindness and Insight*, 2nd edition, ed. Wlad Godzich, Minneapolis: The University of Minnesota Press, 1983.
Marin, Louis, "The Iconic Text and the Theory of Enunciation: Luca Signorelli at Loreto (Circa 1479-84)," *New Literary History* XIV, 3 (1983): 253-96.

———, "Towards a Theory of Reading in the Visual Arts: Poussin's *The Arcadian Shepherds*" (1988): 63-90 in Norman Bryson, ed., *Calligram*.

Marshall, Brenda, *The Lacanian Body: Studies of the Unconscious in Painting and Aesthetics*, Ph.D. dissertation, University of Melbourne, 1990.

Melville, Stephen, *Philosophy Beside Itself: On Deconstruction and Modernism*, Minneapolis: The University of Minnesota Press, 1986.

Metz, Christian, *The Imaginary Signifier: Psychoanalysis and the Cinema*, translated by Celia Britton, Annwyl Williams, Ben Brewster, and Alfred Guzzetti, Bloomington: Indiana University Press, 1982.

Mitchell, W.J.T., *Iconology: Image, Text, Ideology*, Chicago: The University of Chicago Press, 1985.

Morson, Gary Saul, ed., *Bakhtin: Essays and Dialogues on his Work*. Chicago: The University of Chicago Press, 1986.

Morson, Gary Saul and Caryl Emerson, eds., *Rethinking Bakhtin: Extensions and Challenges*. Evanston: Northwestern University Press, 1989.

Moxey, Keith, "Interpreting Pieter Aertsen: the Problem of Hidden Symbolism," *Nederlands Kunsthistorisch Jaarboek* (1989): 42ff.

———, "Pieter Brueghel and Popular Culture," *The Complete Prints of Pieter Brueghel the Elder*, ed. David Freedberg, Tokyo, 1989.

———, "Semiotics and the Social History of Art," *Acts of the 27th International Congress of the History of Art*, Strassbourg (in press).

Mulvey, Laura, "Visual Pleasure and Narrative Cinema," *Screen* 16 (1975): 3-18.

Neumeyer, A., *The Search for Meaning in Modern Art*. Foreword by Sir Herbert Read. Englewood Cliffs, NJ: Prentice-Hall, 1965.

Nietzsche, Friedrich, *Werke*, ed. Karl Schlechter, Munich, 1986.

Nochlin, Linda, "The Imaginary Orient," *Art in America* May (1983): 118-26.

Orlando, Francesco, "Freud and Literature: Eleven Ways He Did It," *Poetics* 13 (1984): 4/5: 361-80.

Owens, Craig, "The Allegorical Impulse: Toward a Theory of Postmodernism," 203-35 in *Art After Modernism*, ed. Brian Wallis, New York: The New Museum of Contemporary Art, and Boston: David R. Godine, Publisher Inc., 1984.

———, "The Discourse of Others: Feminists and Postmodernism," 57-82 in Hall Foster, ed., *The Anti-Aesthetic: Essays on Postmodern Culture*. Port Townsend, Wash.: Bay Press.

Pavel, Thomas, "Origina and Articulation," *Style* 18 (1984): 3: 355-68.

Peterson, Thalia Gouma and Patricia Matthews, "The Feminist Critique of Art History," *Art Bulletin* LXIX, 3, 326-47.

Pettit, P., *The Concept of Structuralism: A Critical Analysis*. Berkeley: The University of California Press, 1975.

Podro, Michael, *The Critical Historians of Art*. New Haven: Yale University Press, 1982.

Pollock, Griselda, "Women, Art and Ideology: Questions for Feminist Art Historians," *Women's Art Journal* iv, 1983.

———, *Vision and Difference: Femininity, feminism and histories of art*. London: Routledge, 1988.

Pollock, Griselda and Rosizka Parker, *Old Mistresses: Women, Art and Ideology*. New York: Pantheon Press, 1981.

Preziozi, Donald, *Rethinking Art History: Meditations on a Coy Science*. New Haven and London: Yale University Press, 1989.

Prince, Gerald, *Narratology: The Form and Function of Narrative*. Berlin, New York, Amsterdam: Mouton de Gruyter, 1983.

Ragland Sullivan, Ellie, "The Magnetism Between Reader and Text: Prolegomena to a Lacanian Poetics," *Poetics* 13 (1984): 4/5: 381-406.

Riegl, Alois, *Das Hollandische Gruppenportrat.* ed. K.M. Swoboda, 2 volumes, Vienna: Osterreichische Staatsdruckerei, 1931.
Rose, Jacqueline, *Sexuality in the Field of Vision.* London: Verso, 1986.
Roskill, Mark, *The Interpretation of Pictures.* Amherst: University of Massachusetts Press, 1989.
Rotman, Brian, *Signifying Nothing: The Semiotics of Zero.* New York: St. Martin's Press, 1987.
Saint-Martin, Fernande, *Semiotics of Visual Language.* Bloomington: Indiana University Press, 1990.
Saunders, Gill, *The Nude: A New Perspective.* Philadelphia: Harper and Row, 1989.
Saussure, Ferdinand de, *Course in General Linguistics.* edited by Charles Bally and Albert Sechehaye, translated and annotated by Roy Harris. London: Duckworth, 1983.
Schefer, Jean-Louis, *Scénographie d'un tableau.* Paris: Galile, 1969.
Schwartz, Gary, *Rembrandt: His Life, His Paintings.* Harmondsworth: Penguin, 1985.
Searle, John, "Reiterating the Differences," *Glyph* 1 (1977): 198–208.
———, "*Las Meninas* and the Paradoxes of Pictorial Representation," *Critical Inquiry* 6 (1980): 477–88.
Shapiro, Meyer, "On Some Problems in the Semiotics of Visual Art: Field and Image-Signs," *Semiotica* 1 (1969): 223–42.
Silverman, Kaja, *The Subject of Semiotics.* New York: Oxford University Press, 1983.
———, *The Acoustic Mirror: The Female Voice in Psychoanalysis and Cinema.* Bloomington: Indiana University Press, 1988.
———, "Fassbinder and Lacan: A Reconsideration of Gaze, Look, and Image," *Camera Obscura* 19 (1989): 54–84.
Snyder, Joel and Ted Cohen, "Reflections on *Las Meninas*: Paradox Lost," *Critical Inquiry*, 7 (1980): 429–47.
Sonne, Harly, "Problems of Knowledge in Fiction," *Style* 18 (1984): 3: 302–11.
Spitz, Ellen Handler, *Art and Psyche: A Study in Psychoanalysis and Aesthetics.* New Haven: Yale University Press, 1985.
Steinberg, Leo, "Velasquez' *Las Meninas*," *October* 19 (1981): 45–54.
Steiner, Wendy, *The Colors of Rhetoric: Problems in the Relation Between Modern Literature and Art.* Chicago: The University of Chicago Press, 1982.
———, *Pictures of Romance: Form against Context in Painting and Literature.* Chicago: The University of Chicago Press, 1988.
Strozier, Robert M., *Saussure, Derrida, and the Metaphysics of Subjectivity.* Berlin: Mouton de Gruyter, 1988.
Tickner, Lisa, "Feminism, Art History, and Sexual Difference," *Genders* 3 (1988): 92–128.
Thiher, Allen, *Words in Reflection: Modern Language Theory and Postmodern Fiction.* Chicago: The University of Chicago Press, 1984.
Todorov, Tzvetan, *French Literary Theory Today: A Reader,* translated by R. Carter, New York: Cambridge University Press, 1982.
———, *Bakhtin: The Dialogic Principle.* Translated by Wlad Godzich. Minneapolis: The University of Minnesota Press, 1984.
Varga, A. Kibdi, "Stories Told by Pictures," in *Style* 22, 2 (1988): 194–208.
———, "Criteria for Describing Word & Image Relations," *Poetics Today* 10 (1989): 31–43.
———, *Discours, récit, image.* Liège and Bruxelles: Pierre Amanda, 1989.
Verhoeff, Han, "Does Oedipus Have His Complex?" *Style* 18 (1984): 3: 261–83.
Voloshinov, V.N., *Marxism and the Philosophy of Language.* translated by Ladislaw Mateijka and I.R. Titunik. New York: Seminar Press, 1973.
Westlund, Joseph, "Expanding the Method," *Poetics* 13 (1984): 4/5: 421–32.
White, Hayden, *Metahistory: The Historical Imagination in Nineteenth-Century Europe.* Baltimore: The Johns Hopkins University Press, 1973.

———, *Tropics of Discourse: Essays in Cultural Criticism.* Baltimore: The Johns Hopkins University Press, 1978.

Williams, Raymond, "Base and Spuerstructure in Marxist Cultural Theory," *New Left Review* 82, 3–16.

Wollheim, Richard, "Nelson Goodman's *Languages of Art*," 290–314 in *On Art and the Mind: Essays and Lectures*, London: Allen Lane, 1973.

Wolff, Janet, *The Social Production of Art.* New York: St. Martin's Press, 1983.

www.ingramcontent.com/pod-product-compliance
Lightning Source LLC
Chambersburg PA
CBHW070937230426
43666CB00011B/2467